CW01082143

SO DEADLY, SO PERVERSE:
50 YEARS OF ITALIAN GIALLO FILMS

VOLUME TWO

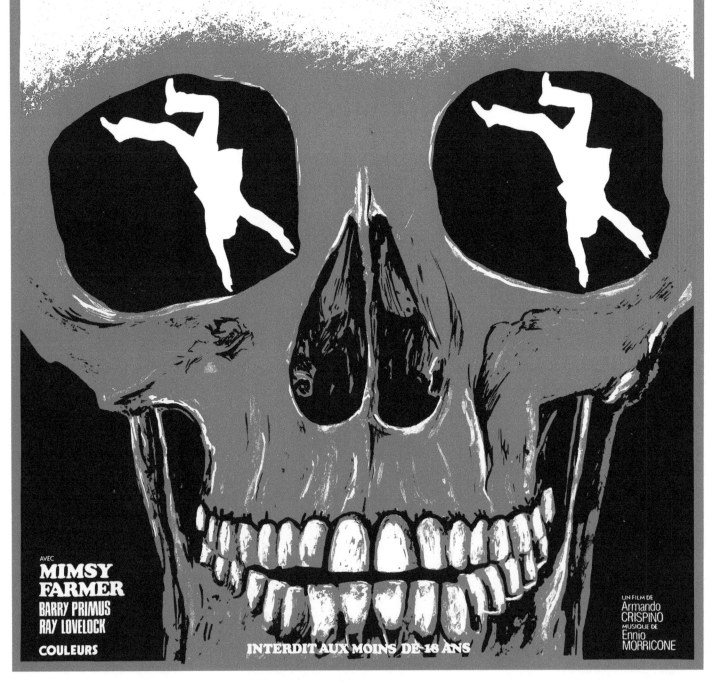

French poster for *Autopsy*; artist unknown.

SO DEADLY, SO PERVERSE:

50 YEARS OF
ITALIAN GIALLO FILMS

Volume Two

by Troy Howarth

Midnight Marquee Press, Inc.
Baltimore, Maryland, USA, London, UK

Copyright © 2015 by Troy Howarth

Cover Design: Tim Paxton
Cover artwork by Enzo Sciotti
Interior Layout: A. Susan Svehla
Copy Editor: Janet Atkinson

Midnight Marquee Press, Inc., Gary J. Svehla and A. Susan Svehla do not assume any responsibility for the accuracy, completeness, topicality or quality of the information in this book. All views expressed or material contained within are the sole responsibility of the author.

Without limiting the rights under copyright reserved above, no part of this publication may be reproduced, stored in or introduced into a retrieval system, or transmitted, in any form, or by any means (electronic, mechanical, photocopying, recording or otherwise), without the prior written permission of the copyright owner or the publishers of the book.

ISBN 978-1-936168-58-3
Library of Congress Catalog Card Number 2015912385
Manufactured in the United States of America
First Printing by Midnight Marquee Press, Inc., December 2015

For Stephanie and for the men and women
who made these films possible.

Spanish pressbook for *Deep Red*, signed in gold paint marker by Dario Argento (note smudged fingerprint!); artwork by Alberto.

contenuto (Table of Contents)

Cover for the French DVD release of *What Have They Done to Your Daughters?* from The Ecstasy of Films; artist's name illegible.

Acknowledgements

I am deeply indebted to a number of people for their contributions to this project. First and foremost, I wish to extend a special thanks to Roberto Curti. Roberto was of tremendous help in guiding me with regards to which titles I should include and omit in both volumes. He was also a great help in providing background on some of the more obscure films and the people involved in making them. Roberto has my ever-lasting gratitude for fielding many questions and for helping me whenever I hit a brick wall and was unsure of how to proceed.

Next on the list is Steve Fenton, whose expertise in the art of Photoshop made it possible for both volumes to have so many mouth-watering illustrations. I freely admit to being technologically challenged, but Steve was always able to assist in figuring out which images were suitable and in patching up those images that had some visible signs of wear and tear. Steve also volunteered to do the first pass of editing on both volumes and his sharp eye for detail picked out many little errors that I surely would have missed.

The Maltese twins, Mario and Roderick Gauci, did the more intensive second edit of both volumes and once again proved invaluable in shoring up some weak spots and making some much-appreciated recommendations and insights.

I am also indebted to Luigi Cozzi, the Italian filmmaker and fantasy film enthusiast, for contributing an afterword for this volume. Luigi is truly one of the nicest people you could hope to meet in this business and his enthusiasm for genre cinema is positively infectious. One of his first films, *The Killer Must Kill Again*, was one of the key *gialli* of the 1970s and he is also the long-time associate of Dario Argento, so it is especially apt that he should be involved in this project.

In addition, I once again need to extend a special thanks to Peter Jilmstad and Lucas Balbo, both of whom reached deep into their extensive archives and provided much of the artwork and images seen in this volume.

Tim Paxton once again donated his superb design sensibilities in devising the cover. Tim's splendid work can be seen in such publications as *Weng's Chop* and *Monster!*; he is yet another talented individual I am only too happy to have in my corner.

I am also very grateful to the immensely talented artist Enzo Sciotti, whose iconic poster artwork for Lamberto Bava's *Midnight Killer* (1986) is utilized on the front cover designed and formatted by Tim Paxton. *Maestro* Sciotti graciously agreed to allow us to utilize this artwork and he has my sincere thanks. Readers with an interest in his artwork are encouraged to check out his website at http://www.enzosciotti.com/.

I would also like to extend thanks to the following individuals, all of whom provided words of encouragement when they were needed: Mark Thompson Ashworth, Jared Burnworth, Horace Cordier, Eric Cotenas, Jonathon and Dawn Dabell, Alwin Dewaele, Michelle Gaeta, Adrian Jones, Russ Lanier, Michael Mackenzie, Eric McNaughton, Vincent Pereira, Jonny Redman, Steven Ronquillo, Ellen Vass Sanderson, Steven Smith, Tim Wickens and Chris Workman. Self-described "Festaphile" Dakota Drobnicki was of tremendous help in providing background on the late period *giallo Fatal Frames* and as well provided some good promotional images from the film. All photos and advertising materials are reproduced here in the spirit of publicity and are the property of their respective copyright holders; no rights are given or implied on our part. The various talented artists who executed the brilliantly lurid poster and advertising art for these films are credited wherever possible; special thanks are due to the people at SAC in Italy who control the copyright on these eye-catching *locandine*.

Special thanks are also owed to my parents, Gary and Diane Howarth, who have always been my number one fans and cheerleaders. I am also very grateful to my beloved Stephanie Kazamek for her boundless support and enthusiasm for my assorted writing projects.

A final thank you is reserved for my publisher Midnight Marquee Press, Inc. (Gary J. and A. Susan Svehla) that did not flinch when I revealed that this project needed to be split into two volumes (ultimately three in total). Gary and Susan's enthusiasm and passion is rare in this field, and I consider myself fortunate to be working with Midnight Marquee Press; long may our "alliance" continue …

Author's Preface

King Kong (1933) concludes with the famous (albeit oft-misquoted) line from showman extraordinaire Carl Denham (played to hyperactive perfection by Robert Armstrong), who corrects a police officer on the scene when he observes that the titular monster was felled by the intervention of some airplanes. "Oh no, it wasn't the airplanes. It was beauty killed the beast!" When we talk about the monstrous cash cow of the *giallo* film, we can substitute "beauty" with "television." It was not just the *giallo*, however. The entire Italian film industry would be brought to its knees and irrevocably altered by the behemoth of television … but more to come on that momentarily. (And just in case that opening reference seems a little too arbitrary, do not forget that *King Kong* was partly co-written by Edgar Wallace, whose influence on the genre was substantial, to say the least. Still not convinced? Deal with it.)

Like just about any popular genre, the *giallo* would be undone by revisiting the well too often. Audiences warmed to the baroque shocks of Dario Argento's *gialli* and this unleashed a flood of imitations. For many, Argento's name is synonymous with the genre. It was not just Argento who popularized the genre, however. If Argento's films were of the "killer in black slicing up young women" mold, then the so-called sexy *gialli*, popularized by such films as **The Sweet Body of Deborah** and **Orgasmo** (both 1968), proved to be influential in their own right. As the filmmakers of the late 1970s began to explore the potential of more and more graphic representations of sex and eroticism, the *giallo* became a veritable breeding ground for salacious imagery. The trend climaxed (pardon the pun) with the arrival of literal "porno *gialli*," including **Play Motel** (1979), which offered viewers a dollop of hardcore sex in addition to a thriller plot fitted out with all the trimmings. Similarly, the rising popularity of *poliziottesco* films (a form of violent crime thriller much informed by the success of such American models as *Dirty Harry*, 1971, and *Death Wish*, 1974) resulted in a number of films which sought to combine the most popular elements of those films (car chases; no-nonsense, two-fisted policeman

Italian *fotobusta* for *The New York Ripper*, hinting at the film's seedy excesses.

figures; a predisposition toward saying "to hell with the law" and enacting elaborate revenge fantasies) with the more sensational imagery of the *giallo* (graphic murder, sleazy sex acts, copious red herrings). It was bound to be too much of a good thing, though just how good it was is certainly open to discussion. Inevitably, audiences began to grow tired of such excesses. Part of this could be down to the audiences becoming more jaded, but much of it can be placed on the majority of the films themselves. Too many were hastily slapped together, with little regard for logic or construction, and sought to sell themselves on the basis of outdoing the last film's gory/seedy excesses. The genre peaked around 1971-1972, with a staggering number of thrillers emerging in that timeframe (indeed, the number goes through the roof if we include the many borderline titles which some fans enthusiastically bracket as true *gialli*); as the 1970s wore on, the numbers began to shrink. By the 1980s, things were definitely winding down as far as productivity was concerned. There is a school of thought that argues that the genre pretty much expired in 1982, after the double whammy of Argento's ***Tenebrae*** (the most self-reflexive of *gialli*) and Lucio Fulci's ***The New York Ripper*** (inarguably the most infamous of the *gialli* made by the more "respectable" end of the Italian commercial film industry). There is little doubt that *giallo* production slowed down considerably from that point on, but to suggest that the genre itself became moribund is shortsighted and arbitrary. It would be unfair to imply that this was brought about by the impact of these two key works, however. Argento's film is now regarded as a genre touchstone, but it garnered blistering reviews in the Italian press, while Fulci's film helped to seal his fate as a mean-spirited hack in the eyes of many critics. Commercially, Argento's "meta-*giallo*" was a smash hit, pulling in over 2 billion *lire* at the box-office, while Fulci's made only a fraction of that. Even so, both films certainly turned a profit and seemed to point to public desire for more *gialli*. A change was in the air, however, and it began to manifest itself in a general slowing down of output around this timeframe. The general slackness in production, however, was not limited to the *giallo*. The Italian film industry went through a crisis altogether, with many directors (including Lamberto Bava and Lucio Fulci) turning to television to make horror films and *gialli* on a smaller scale. Many of these made-for-TV *gialli* were inevitably watered down and could not compare with the lovably lurid thrillers of yore.

And what of the years since this downward spiral? The news is not altogether encouraging. Argento continues to carry the baton by virtue of his higher profile in the industry, but for all intents and purposes the Italian film industry's state of decline continues to the present day. Argento remains

French lobby card for *Tenebrae*, showing Peter Neal (Anthony Franciosa) recoiling from the corpse of the killer's latest victim.

committed to the genre (albeit with mixed results), and others have taken up his lead by continuing to explore the potential of more and more cinematic mayhem. The genre does not begin and end with Argento, however. Other filmmakers have entered the fray and have sought to make their mark, including Alex Infascelli (***Almost Blue***, 2000) and Federico Zampaglione (***Tulpa—Perdizioni mortali***, 2013), but none of these recent efforts have proven sufficiently successful to lead to a proper rebirth of the genre; instead, it continues to limp along, sometimes with interesting results but usually only managing to evoke faint memories of former glories. The more recent *gialli* of the 2000s may not be all that satisfying, but they are still *gialli* and will be reviewed accordingly. As such, the inception of this book comes at the 50th anniversary of the *giallo*; sooner than try to anticipate any new thrillers in the works from genre workhorses like Dario Argento, it seems logical enough to draw a line in the sand with 2013. It is not as if the *giallo* has been terribly prolific in recent years, anyway.

Sooner than bore the reader with an in-depth recap of what has already been covered in detail in volume one, let us keep this short and breezy. Films are listed by their best known English-language title, and chronologically by the year of their theatrical release (where applicable) and then alphabetically within the specific year. I have also attempted to make this as user-friendly as possible by highlighting the titles reviewed in bold face wherever referenced. Year of release is indicated beside the titles to better assist the reader in seeking out the title in its appropriate volume. This will hopefully help the reader to skip around and check for specific reviews as they see fit.

Giallo Reviews (1974-2013)

Note: Many of these films have been retitled over and over again, first for their theatrical exhibition and then later for their home video releases; the goal here is to assemble the best known alternate titles, with special emphasis on the countries that had a hand in producing and financing the films. The "best known" English title comes first in bold and, next to it, I have listed the country (or countries) responsible for financing the film. Titles that were predominantly financed by countries other than Italy have been omitted, but many of them are addressed in the Volume 3. I have tried to provide consistent credits information for each title, but sometimes it is impossible to supply certain credits, as many of these films do not list a producer, for example. Wherever possible, I have credited the technicians and actors by their real names, though I make note of the aliases they utilized on the film in question. Please note that these reviews are not free of spoilers, though I have tried to not reveal every surprise that the films may have in store. Home video release information is presented for the *English-friendly* DVD releases that are most readily available; those films that have not been released on DVD or Blu-ray in an English-friendly (i.e. dubbed or subtitled) edition do not have any home video information included. Bootleg (or "gray market" releases) are not included. This is not a complete or comprehensive guide to home video releases, but will hopefully enable curious fans to seek out the English-friendly releases that are available at the time of this writing.

1974

Il baco da seta (Italy)

Aka *Tejido de seda; The Silk Worm*

Directed by Mario Sequi; Produced by Antonio Gentile; Screenplay by Mino Roli; Director of Photography: Alvaro Lanzoni; Editor: Maurizio Mangosi; Music by Mario Bertolazzi

Main Players: Nadja Tiller (Smeralda Amandier); George Hilton (Didier); Riccardo Garrone (Commissioner Guarnieri); Carlos De Castro (Costas Mikaelis); Guy Madison (Robert); Evi Marandi (Yvonne)

Retired singer Smeralda Amandier becomes involved with a younger man named Costas. One night her jewelry goes missing and Costas is nowhere to be found. The police are called in to investigate and her former lover, Didier, is blamed for the theft ...

Il baco da seta (the title translates as *The Silk Worm*, suggesting another attempt at evoking the titles popular-

ized by Dario Argento) is a very weak suspense film with only a minor thriller element. It ultimately includes enough genre tropes to justify being included here, but truly only the most devoted of *giallo* buffs will want to go to the trouble of tracking down a copy.

Italian *locandina* for *Il baco da seta*; artist unknown.

Much of the plot is centered around a jewel theft, and things do not begin to heat up until the final act. Sadly, by that point it is truly too little too late. The story is dull and uninvolving, the characters are a boring lot and the material is flatly executed. There is a bit of sleaze worked in just to add a dash of spice, but here again, it does not amount to very much.

George Hilton is on hand to play one of the men implicated in the robbery, but he does not have a great deal to do and disappears for a long stretch of the movie. Nadja Tiller carries the film. She is photogenic but gives a rather hammy and affected performance as the former singing star who has fallen on hard times. Born in Vienna in 1929, she started appearing in movies in the late 1940s. She was particularly prominent in German films, but appeared in the occasional Italian or French effort as well. This was her only *giallo* credit, though she also appeared in the borderline title *The Blonde Connection* (1969). The supporting cast includes a small role for Evi Marandi, who played one of the astronauts in Mario Bava's sci-fi/horror hybrid, *Planet of the Vampires* (1965).

Nothing much really stands out as special in the film. The photography is flat. The music is unremarkable. Dialogue scenes drag on for too long. The sex scenes are a little too timid to generate the desired heat. The final twists and turns are not all that great either. Worse still, director Mario Sequi approaches the material with a complete lack of style or imagination. Apart from employing a red tint for some flashback scenes, which is hardly a gripping stylistic invention in itself, he simply locks the camera down and does not do anything interesting with the *mise-en-scène*. Sequi was born in 1913 and entered films as a production assistant in the 1930s. He began directing in 1948 and worked sporadically in that field until 1975; the film under review would mark his only foray into the *giallo* … which, given the end result, is perhaps just as well.

As a final note of trivia, shooting was originally started in 1968 and featured former American leading man Robert Taylor in the cast; the production was shut down prematurely and Taylor would die in 1969, resulting in Guy Madison being brought in to replace him when the film was subsequently bailed-out of limbo and completed.[1] It is not clear just how much time elapsed between the original footage in the can and the later reshoots, or indeed how long the film sat on the shelf once it had finally been completed. By the time the picture finally limped out to theaters, it looked very quaint indeed. This would likely explain the film's reticence with

regards to embracing more graphic sex and violence; no matter what the excuse, however, the film is a dud, pure and simple.

Notes:

1. Bruschini, Antonio and Stefano Piselli, *Giallo & Thrilling All'Italiana* (1931-1983), (Firenze: Glittering Images, 2010), p. 75.

Blackmail (Italy)
Aka *Lo Strano ricatto di una ragazza per bene*

Directed by Luigi Batzella (as Paolo Solvay); Screenplay by Paolo Savella; Director of Photography: Giorgio Montagnani; Editor: Luigi Batzella; Music by Marcello Gigante

Main Players: Brigitte Skay (Babel); Benjamin Lev (Claudio); Umberto Raho (Herman); Rosalba Neri (Stella); Claudio Giorgi (Rick); Nuccia Cardinali (Eva)

Babel is the free-spirited daughter of wealthy businessman Herman. The spoiled young woman decides that she is tired of her father's rules and persuades her no-good friends to help emancipate her by pretending to kidnap her and demand a huge ransom; they plan to use the money to buy drugs and get high. Unfortunately, things do not go as planned …

Blackmail is one of the worst *gialli* of the period; it is also one of the most laughably reactionary.

The film strains to sell a hardcore anti-marijuana message with all the po-faced sincerity of an episode of Jack Webb's popular TV show, *Dragnet*. Marijuana is seen as the gateway drug in the film's conservative *milieu*; not only is it dangerous in and of itself, but once the individual who partakes becomes immune to its charms, it will inevitably lead to harder drugs such as heroin and the like.

Italian artwork for *Blackmail*; artist unknown.

Matters are not helped by a collection of some of the most vapid and downright annoying characters imaginable. Babel is a complete trainwreck of a human being. While it is clear that her father means well, he clearly is not a very strong presence in her life. Fair enough, but this hardly justifies her being such a spoiled brat. Her main goal in life seems to be getting as wasted as possible, and she does not care who she hurts in the process. Her voracious sexual appetites also compel her to treat her long-suffering boyfriend Rick like he is less than human as he sits by and watches as she screws one random person after another, in the

less friends dancing, getting stoned, dancing some more, having sex, getting stoned again, dancing … you get the picture. One particularly ludicrous sequence starts off as a fight to the death between Babel and a woman who stumbles onto the plot, but it evolves into a Sapphic tryst; when in Rome, one supposes. The thriller angle is handled poorly and the final confrontation between the villains and the would-be heroes is marred with some of the least convincing gunplay this side of a really bad Monogram programmer from the 1940s. Worse still, the film drags by and never succeeds in creating the slightest air of mystery or excitement.

Brigitte Skay is pretty but abominable in the lead role. Her portrayal of the admittedly poorly written Babel is grating and one-note. Born in Germany in 1940, Skay started appearing in German films and television in 1963. By the end of the decade she was appearing in numerous Italian efforts, mostly those with a sexy bent, like Mario Bava's *Four Times That Night* (1969). She toplined Bruno Corbucci's *fumetto Isabella, Duchess of the Devil* (1969) and would play one of the horny teens dispatched by the killer in Bava's **Twitch of the Death Nerve** (1971). She stopped making films at the end of the 1970s. The supporting cast includes a larger-than-usual role for Umberto Raho, as Babel's father, and a less-interesting-than-usual role for Rosalba Neri. Both Neri and Skay do get to contribute to the film's considerable skin factor, however, which is an admitted compensation in a film as dire as this.

As for director Batzella, he was born in Sardinia in 1924. He entered films in 1953 and appeared in a number of pictures in minor roles, including such early *gialli* as **Night of Violence** (1965) and **Killer Without a Face** (1967). He began directing in 1966, often employing such aliases as Paul Hamus and Paolo Solvay. Batzella frequently had a hand in writing his scripts and often edited the films, as well, making him something of a bargain for producers. He directed some rather poor Spaghetti Westerns, like the irresistibly titled *Django's Cut Price Corpses* (1971), and delivered a rather atmospheric and pleasingly sexy Rosalba Neri vehicle titled *The Devil's Wedding Night* (1973). He would go on to direct *Nude for Satan* (1974), an erotic horror item sometimes erroneously credited as a *giallo*, and the infamous Nazisploitation shocker *S.S. Hell Camp* (1977). He died in 2008.

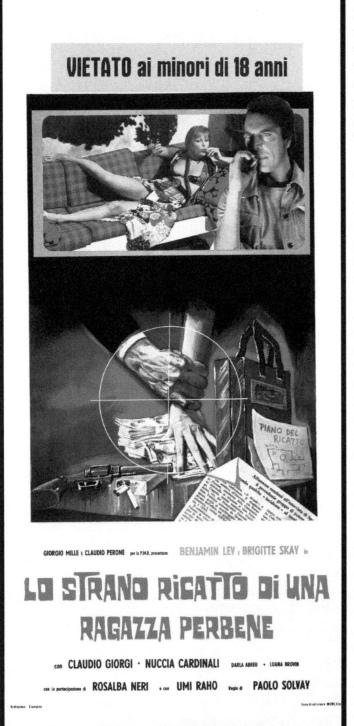

Italian *locandina* for *Blackmail*; artist unknown.

quest for the next new "experience." Herman, the father, oddly comes off as more sympathetic than the bulk of the sociopaths on display, and it is not clear if this was really the intention. Even so, the audience can hardly help feeling some pity for him as he is duped into scraping together his life's savings in an attempt to rescue his ungrateful daughter from her so-called tormentors.

Director Luigi Batzella (hiding behind the pseudonym of Paolo Solvay) stretches the film's already slim running time with seemingly endless scenes of Babel and her worth-

Clap, You're Dead (Italy)

Aka *Ciak, si muore!*

Directed by Mario Moroni; Screenplay by Roberto Mauri, Mario Moroni and Gianfranco Pagani; Director of Photography: Giovanni Raffaldi; Editor: Liliana Giboni; Music by Aldo Bonocore

Main Players: Giorgio Ardisson (Inspector Menzel); Annabella Incontrera (Lucia); Ivano Staccioli (Richard Hanson); Antonio Pierfederici (Benner); Belinda Bron (Fanny)

An actress is murdered on a film set and Inspector Menzel is called in to investigate. The list of suspects includes the

film's tyrannical and egotistical director, Benner, and the actress' spurned lover, Richard Hanson. As Menzel continues to investigate, more victims begin piling up ...

This minor thriller gets a shot in the arm from its novel concept. Unlike **The Crimes of the Black Cat** (1972), the film does not go for full-blown self-reflexiveness by having the film within the film being a *giallo*, but then again, one cannot have everything.

In fact, the film is something of a *giallo/poliziottesco* hybrid. The body count is low and the gore is kept to a minimum, but the action is well paced and it has enough humorous insights into the fragile egos and rampant narcissism of the film industry to keep the interest level up. The climax even works in a touch of the *fumetto* as the male extras in the film-within-the-film are all dressed up in *Diabolik*-style costumes; this serves a double purpose in that by making them all look alike, it is that much harder for Menzel to pick out his intended suspect.

Mario Moroni directs the film very competently; there is not much in the way of great stylistic flourishes, but he makes some good use of location work and incorporates some clever touches with theatrical lighting effects and the like. The murder scenes are generally pretty mild, but there is a shower stabbing right out of *Psycho* (1960) and the resulting nudity will also be appreciated by the skin-watchers in the audience. Production values are adequate and Aldo Bonocore's music serves its purpose without becoming too intrusive.

Characterizations are on the broad side, but this suits the somewhat satirical nature of the picture's depiction of film industry types. Benner, for example, is a wonderful caricature of a movie director. His air of self-importance is unmistakable and his many meltdowns as things go wrong and people fail to recognize his genius speak volumes. His approach seems to be to minimize the input of others as much as possible, while throwing together disparate elements and hoping that they will stick together. In short, he is the ultimate narcissistic sociopath who derives pleasure from hurting the feelings of others, and on that level he was no doubt recognized as a stand-in for many directors in the business whose egos did not quite match their actual level of talent. The long-suffering scriptwriter, on the other hand, is amusing and oddly moving as he is forced to sit idly by and watch as his script is transformed beyond recognition. Toward the end of the film, when Benner "improves" the ending, the scriptwriter asks: "What will be left of me in the final film?" to which Benner quips: "Your name in the credits!"

The peformances are generally good. Giorgio Ardisson brings a touch of sly wit and a general air of pent-up frustration to his role as Inspector Menzel. The protagonist's no-nonsense approach clashes with the egotistical film industry types he is working to protect, leading to some amusing confrontations. Beautiful Annabella Incontrera is on hand, but she is criminally underused and does not get much of a chance to register. Ivano Staccioli, previously seen as

Italian *locandina* for *Clap, You're Dead*; artist unknown.

the inspector in **The Flower with the Deadly Sting** (1973), gets to try his hand at playing a red herring that may or may not be the killer, but the show is pretty much stolen by Antonio Pierfederici's portrayal of the egotistical Benner. Pierfederici is best remembered by genre fans for his role as the priest in Mario Bava's *Black Sunday* (1960), though this film gives him much more screen time.

Not a great deal appears to be known about the director, Mario Moroni. He is presumed to have entered films in the early 1950s as a screenwriter. Among the many efforts he had a hand in writing was Mario Bava's sex comedy *Four Times That Night* (1969). He worked primarily in this capacity into the early 1980s, at which point his filmography stops cold. He directed his first picture in 1971; *Clap, You're Dead* was his second of four directorial gigs and his only *giallo*.

Death Will Have Your Eyes
(Italy/Spain)

Aka *La moglie giovane; Infamia; Triangel; Savage City*

Directed by Giovanni D'Eramo; Screenplay by Antonio Fos and Giovanni d'Eramo; Director of Photography: Francisco Sempere; Editor: Otello Colangeli; Music by Stelvio Cipriani

Main Players: Marisa Mell (Louisa); Farley Granger (Armando); Francisco Rabal (The blackmailer); Helga Liné (Yvonne); Riccardo Salvone (Stefano); Luciano Pigozzi [as Alan Collins] (Antonio)

Home Video: Mya Communication (Region 1 DVD)

Poverty-stricken Louisa meets a successful but anti-social surgeon named Armando. They are married, though

Italian *locandina* for *Death Will Have Your Eyes*; artist unknown.

Louisa soon tires of Armando's stuffy manner. She begins an affair with Stefano and decides to resort to desperate measures in order to secure her happiness. Unfortunately, she finds herself being terrorized by a blackmailer who knows her secrets ...

Death Will Have Your Eyes may be short on shocks and thrills, but it offers a very unusual slant on the typical *giallo* formula; of all the films produced within the genre during this time-frame, it comes closest to adopting what could loosely be termed a feminist perspective. While many other *gialli* and genre fare of the period were definitely viewed through a male perspective, with many of the female characters being reduced to one-dimensional window-dressing, this is a film that offers an uncommonly well-rounded female protagonist; the trials and tribulations she is subjected to merely serve to point to the problems women face in a male-dominated society.

Lest we get too carried away with this reading, it is also a brazen exploitation film that requires the statuesque Marisa Mell to disrobe on occasion. That being said, the film is fairly reticent when it comes to the seedier or more unsavory aspects of the genre. Violence is kept to a minimum and the sex scenes do not tend to drag on for as long as in so many other films of this ilk. Instead, the emphasis is shifted to characterization and suspense. The two work hand in hand, because the character of Louisa, for all her faults, is one worth rooting for.

The film also incorporates a certain amount of social commentary, being essentially a story of the "haves" versus the "have nots." Louisa is from a poor background and has such a difficult time making ends meet, that when Armando comes on the scene, she feels compelled to stay with him. He is not cruel to her, but the older man is clearly not on the same wavelength and it proves to be an unsatisfying union. Louisa has been brainwashed into thinking that having things, especially status symbols, is the key to happiness, but she soon finds out differently. Similarly, the blackmailer makes a point of damning Louisa and others of her social class for having too much at the expense of others. At one point he criticizes her bourgeois outlook, but she correctly identifies his hypocrisy by stating that he wants to get money from her in order to become bourgeois himself.

The tragic component of the story comes from the fact that Louisa has the deck stacked against her from the start. She is led astray by bad advice from her well-meaning friends, is essentially pushed into a position where she will have to sell herself in one way or another in order to survive and her attempts at emancipating herself are doomed to fail. She is by no means presented in a saintly manner, but it is possible to side with her. Indeed, even when she resorts to murder, the viewer might still be inclined to hope that she may get away with it.

Marisa Mell is excellent in the lead role. Too many of her genre appearances were content to exploit her extraordinary looks, but this is one role that gave her a chance to show what a fine actress she could be, as well. Farley Granger has very little to do as Armando, but he makes the best of the few opportunities that come his way. Granger is adept at imbuing the character with little looks and other nuanced touches that convey a mixture of vulnerability and latent violence. Francisco Rabal comes close to stealing many of his scenes as the blackmailer. The character is never given a name; his purpose, rather, is to represent that section of the populace whose desire for wealth occludes their ability to reason and rely on their more moral instincts. Born in Spain in 1926, the actor, known by his friends as Paco, made his first minor film appearances in the mid-1940s. He also established his credentials as a stage actor before making the acquaintance of the great director Luis Buñuel. The latter was impressed with Rabal's presence and took a shine to him personally and would end up casting him in three major works: *Nazarin* (1959), *Viridiana* (1961) and *Belle de Jour* (1967). Rabal would appear in films for everybody from Michelangelo Antonioni (*L'eclisse*, 1962) and Luchino Visconti (in his segment of the anthology film *The Witches*, 1967) to Enzo G. Castellari (*Eagles Over London*, 1969) and Umberto Lenzi (*Nightmare City*, 1980). Director William Friedkin would later reveal that he told his assistant to hire Rabal for the role of Charnier in *The French Connection* (1971), but he could not think of the actor's name; he simply told the assistant to get the actor who was in so many of Buñuel's films. The assistant thought he meant Fernando Rey, so Rey was flown over to New York to work on the picture; embarrassed by the mistake, Friedkin simply changed the conception of the character to better suit the urbane Rey, but he would later make it up to Rabal by casting him as one of the desperate characters in his underrated remake of *The Wages of Fear* (1953), entitled *Sorcerer* (1977). He scored a major success as Francisco Goya in Carlos Saura's *Goya in Bourdeaux* (1999). Rabal's last role was in Stuart Gordon's H.P. Lovecraft adaptation, *Dagon* (2001); he died in 2001.

Director Giovanni D'Eramo was born in Rome in 1921. He does not appear to have been very prolific. He worked primarily as a screenwriter, but also had some credits as an assistant director. Some sources indicate that he collaborated on the direction of *O.K. John* (1946), but given that this predates his other credits by several years and that he is not attributed with directing any other films until *Death Will Have Your Eyes*, this is likely a mistake. In any event, his filmography comes to a halt following this one.

The assistant director on this was none other than Claudio Fragasso, who would later become a (infamous) director in his own right, thanks to such cult favorites as *Monster Dog* (1984) and *Troll 2* (1990).

Delitto d'autore (Italy)

Directed by Mario Sabatini (as Anthony Green); Screenplay by Mario Sabatini; Director of Photography: Oberdan Troiani; Music by Franco Tamponi and Gianni Mereu

Italian *locandina* for *Delitto d'autore*; artist unknown.

Main Players: Sylva Koscina (Milena Gottardi); Pier Paolo Capponi (Marco Girardi); Luigi Pistilli (Don Lino); Krista Nell (Sonia)

A wealthy countess donates a Rubens painting to a local talent contest to be handed out as the first prize. She starts receiving calls warning her that if she does not withdraw the painting, she will live to regret it. She refuses to bend on the issue and, sure enough, she is eventually murdered. The police follow up on various leads and soon the countess' niece, Milena, finds herself in danger as well ...

Every now and again, a *giallo* emerges with a plot so garbled and needlessly convoluted that it becomes an exercise in futility. *Delitto d'autore* is one such film.

The story takes an old-fashioned staple—the desire to possess wealth—and proceeds to make it so completely incomprehensible that it never has any real chance to generate any suspense. Characters behave in a suspicious manner for the pure purpose of becoming red herrings and plot points are thrown at the viewer, which go nowhere. It is not uncommon in these films for red herrings and dead-ends to be tossed in, admittedly, but here this is done in such an out-of-control fashion that it threatens to push the movie into the realm of parody. Unfortunately, it is not approached with a sufficient awareness of its own absurdity and it pretty much just ambles from one half-baked sequence to the next.

On the plus side, the film does climax with an admittedly well-staged car chase highlighted by the (surprise?) reveal of the killer's identity. This sequence is everything the rest of the film is not. It is exciting, holds one's attention and moves at a great pace. If only the film had contained a few more scenes like it, the end result might have generated more goodwill.

Characterization is virtually non-existent and director Mario Sabatini shows no style or flair for this type of material. There is a little light nudity thrown in for good measure, but the murder scenes are flat and the mystery is simply too convoluted to be taken seriously. It all adds up to a pretty dull and listless experience.

The cast includes some welcome faces, but nobody really shines here. Sylva Koscina does what she can as the imperiled Milena, while Pier Paolo Capponi manages to hold on to his dignity as her secret husband (it is too garbled to get into here; suffice it to say, it does not make much sense on screen, either). Luigi Pistilli is on hand in an atypical role as a local priest; it is fun seeing him looking shifty in a white collar, but much like the others, he simply does not have enough to sink his teeth into.

Director Mario Sabatini was born in Tuscany in 1927. His filmography is extremely brief and it would appear that he was almost always credited under the name Anthony Green, as he is here. He directed a couple of Spaghetti Westerns, including *Sheriff of Rock Springs* (1971) and *A Gunman Called Dakota* (1972), but never established much of a reputation and only ended up helming five features between 1964 and 1981. *Delitto d'autore* was his only *giallo* credit.

Five Women for the Killer (Italy/France)

Aka *5 donne per l'assassino; Cinco mujeres para un asesinato; John Carpenter's Day-Killer*

Directed by Stelvio Massi; Produced by Carlo Maietto; Screenplay by Gianfranco Clerici, Roberto Gianviti and Vincenzo Mannino; Director of Photography: Sergio Rubini; Editor: Mauro Bonanni; Music by Giorgio Gaslini

Main Players: Francis Matthews (Giorgio Pisani); Pascale Rivault (Dr. Lydia Franzi); Giorgio Albertazzi (Professor Aldo Betti); Renato Rossini [as Howard Ross] (Police Inspector); Katia Christine (Alba Galli); Catherine Diamant (Oriana)

Journalist Giorgio Pisani is devastated when his wife dies in childbirth. He is even more shaken when he finds out that medical tests have ascertained that he is sterile, thus meaning that he cannot possibly be the father of his son. Meanwhile, a killer begins slaughtering pregnant women ...

Five Women for the Killer derives its title from Mario Bava's **Blood and Black Lace** (1964; originally titled *Sei donne per l'assassino* or *Six Women for the Murderer*), but its highly sexualized theme anticipates elements of Lucio Fulci's notorious **The New York Ripper** (1982). The latter is hardly surprising, given that the film was co-written by Gianfranco Clerici and Vincenzo Mannino, who would collaborate with Fulci on the script for that later *giallo*.

The story deals with a killer who is so frustrated by his own "inadequacies" that he feels compelled to punish women who are more fortunate. The film avoids passing moral judgment on the victims, by and large, though the generally sleazy and squalid depiction of sexual relationships may make the film appear somewhat conservative, if not downright hypocritical. The mystery is actually fairly well-handled, making the final reveal a surprising one, while the nasty murder sequences are all the more effective for being so blunt; they are only undermined by some less-than-convincing special effects work, but this is a minor quibble.

On the downside, the film is burdened with generally dull and disposable characters. Giorgio is so flatly written that he virtually disappears into the scenery, while the various victims, while sympathetically potrayed, have no real substance to them. The investigating inspector is at least given a little bit of humor, especially in his relationship with his bungling assistant, but this does not add much to the overall drama. Thrillers are typically at their most effective when the audience is emotionally involved in the action, and this is not likely to happen here, simply because nobody is really worth rooting for, one way or another. The character of the surgeon, Professor Betti, is appropriately smug and condescending to get the audience to root against him—but he lacks an opposite number, as it were.

That being said, Stelvio Massi handles the film well. The director makes excellent use of nervous, hand-held camerawork to build tension and claustrophobia, and plenty of elegant, gliding camerawork is on display. He paces the film judiciously and shows a flair for orchestrating a twist-laden narrative. With a stronger script, it may well have ended up becoming more than a relatively minor footnote in the genre; as it stands, it is by no means a forgotten classic, and it has much to recommend it for the discerning *giallo*phile. Production values are decent on the whole, though signs of low-budget haste can be spotted here and there, notably in the aforementioned special effects inserts.

British actor Francis Matthews heads the cast. This was bizarre casting in many respects, and his none-too-flattering combover hairdo merely succeeds in making him look older. The actor seems a bit adrift throughout and never succeeds in conveying the character's inner torment. It is an uncommonly wooden performance from an actor who was capable of far better work. Born in Yorkshire in 1927, Matthews started off in British television in the mid-1950s before making his film debut in 1956. Horror fans remember him best for his appearances in movies starring genre icons Boris Karloff (*Corridors of Blood*, 1958), Peter Cushing (*The Revenge of Frankenstein*, 1958) and Christopher Lee (*Dracula—Prince of Darkness*, 1965 and *Rasputin, the Mad Monk*, 1966). More apropos to the *giallo* context, he appeared in one of the instalments of the popular series of Miss Marple thrillers starring Margaret Rutherford (*Murder Ahoy*, 1964), as well as top-lining the British TV series *Paul Temple* (1969-1971), wherein he played the crime-solving murder mystery novelist. He passed away in June of 2014; *Five Women for the Killer* remains an odd foray for him into the world of Italian genre cinema. Renato Rossini gets to leave behind his usual persona as a red herring in favor of playing the inspector on the case and he seems to be having a high old time doing so. Rossini displays far more charisma and charm in his scenes than Matthews does throughout, suggesting that the film may have been better off if they had swapped roles. Incidentally, he would tackle one of the leading roles in the aforementioned **The New York Ripper**. Giorgio Albertazzi (born 1923), who plays Professor Betti, was one of Italy's foremost thespians; consequently, he is perhaps best regarded as a stage actor/director. Still, his film work includes not only Alain Resnais' arthouse masterpiece *Last Year in Marienbad* (1961, written by the equally-renowned Alain Robbe-Grillet) but the TV miniseries he starred in and directed, *Jekyll* (1969), a superlative re-imagining of Robert Louis Stevenson's horror classic in modern counter-culture terms, not to mention another *giallo*, **Fatal Frames** (1996).

Born in 1929, director Stelvio Massi entered films as a camera operator in the early 1950s. He would make the transition to director of photography in 1964 and his stylish work graced quite a few genre titles, notably Spaghetti Westerns like *The Price of Power* (1969) and *A Bullet for the Stranger* (1971), as well as the *giallo* **The Case of the Bloody Iris** (1972). He began directing in 1973 and established himself early on as one of the great masters of the *poliziottesco*, thanks to such standout entries as *Emergency Squad* (1974), *Blood, Sweat and Fear* (1975; re-uniting him with Albertazzi) and *The Iron Commissioner* (1978). He would return to the *giallo* with **Arabella, Black Angel** (1989) and retired in 1994. He died in 2004 at the age of 75.

A final bit of trivia to savor: In a bit of cheek that can hardly be believed, the film was sold in Germany for a period of time under the title *John Carpenter's Day-Killer*! Not only does the "day-killer" epithet make no sense, but given Carpenter's complete lack of involvement with this film, one

Italian *locandina* for *Five Women for the Killer*; artwork by Lucio Crovato.

can only assume that the genre icon might have been less than enthused about seeing his name attached to a relatively minor *giallo* such as this, if he had ever been made aware of the subterfuge.

The Girl in Room 2A (Italy)

Aka *La casa della paura*

Directed by William L. Rose; Produced by Dick Randall and William L. Rose; Screenplay by Gianfranco Baldanello and William L. Rose; Director of Photography: Mario Mancini; Editor: Piera Bruno and Gianfranco Simoncelli; Music by Berto Pisano

Main Players: Daniela Giordano (Margaret Bradley); Raf Vallone (Mr. Dreese); Rosalba Neri (Alicia Songbird); John Scanlon (Jack Whitman); Angelo Infanti (Frank Grant); Karin Schubert (Maria)

Home Video: Mondo Macabro (Region free DVD)

Margaret is released from prison, having been convicted of a crime that she did not commit. Looking to get back on her feet, she takes an apartment in a creepy building inhabited by strange tenants. She soon discovers that the previous occupant disappeared. Unfortunately for her, that is only the tip of the iceberg ...

The Girl in Room 2A is arguably more of a horror film than a *giallo*, but it contains enough "mystery" elements to warrant inclusion in this context.

American poster for *The Girl in Room 2A*; artist unknown.

No matter how one chooses to classify the film, chances are that most viewers will agree on this basic point: It simply is not very good. The story rambles somewhat incoherently and attempts at the mysterious are much too ham-fisted to prove successful. There is very little suspense and the horror elements are handled in a clumsy fashion. Worse still, the film crawls at a slow pace, and even the introduction of some sexy and sadistic elements does not do much to inject enough life into the proceedings.

This is one of those films where the villains are so transparently villainous that one cannot help but become exasperated with the heroine for failing to realize that she is in danger. Margaret has the makings of an interesting character, but nothing of substance is done with her. Her background as an innocent woman, who has served time for a crime she did not commit, could have yielded some thought-provoking detail, but it merely serves as a pretext; she is down-on-her-luck, so is obliged to try and make a go of it in the creepy apartment building. The assorted villains and red herrings are also sketchy in the extreme and the supernatural elements are far from convincing.

For many years, it was believed that the true culprit responsible for these cinematic atrocities was an Italian director hiding behind a pseudonym. However, leading lady Daniela Giordano has since confirmed that it really was an American director by the name of William Rose. Rose's direction is the definition of perfunctory: he flubs every opportunity for suspense and shock value and his sense of pacing and timing is way off. He was born in New York City in 1932 and got his start in films in the early 1960s. He primarily worked in the "nudie" racket, writing, directing and photographing a number of softcore sex movies, sometimes using the alias Werner Rose. An association with legendary exploitation producer Dick Randall would lead to his coming to Rome to direct this film. He would also have a hand in the writing of the indescribable *Frankenstein's Castle of Freaks* (1974), also produced by Randall. It would appear that he gave up directing following this effort, though he has continued to work sporadically as an actor; one of his most surprising credits is as dialogue director and bit-part actor on Werner Herzog's *Fitzcarraldo* (1982).

Rose was graced with an appealing cast, but he does not give them much to do. Daniela Giordano does the best she can under the circumstance as Margaret; it is not her fault that her character comes off as hopelessly dim, and she certainly does a credible job registering fear as she is put through the ringer during the last act. Giordano was born in Sicily in 1947 and she first attained recognition when she won the title of "Miss Italy" in 1966. This led to roles in such films as Don Taylor's Spaghetti Western *The Five Man Army* (1969, co-written by Dario Argento) and Mario Bava's troubled sex comedy *Four Times That Night* (1969), which would be suppressed by Italian censors (headed at the time by none other than Riccardo Freda!) until 1972. She played a small role in Sergio Martino's ***Your Vice is a Locked Room*** and only I Have the Key (1972) and would go on to appear in **Reflections in Black** (1975), as well as a supporting role in the borderline *giallo Evil Eye* (1975). She remained active until the end of the 1970s, then left films in order to pursue a career in journalism. The distinguished Raf Vallone is also on hand to play one of the creepy tenants, but compared to his heart-rending turn as the distraught father in **Death Occurred Last Night** (1970), this is truly a waste of his considerable talents. Rosalba Neri's appearance is minimal, while future hardcore star Karin Schubert plays one of the victims and gets to bare her (admittedly impressive) body in the process.

The Killer Reserved Nine Seats (Italy)

Aka *L'assassino ha riservato nove poltrone; El asesino ha reservado nueve butacas*

Directed by Giuseppe Bennati; Produced by Dario Rossini; Screenplay by Giuseppe Bennati, Paolo Levi and Biagio Proietti; Director of Photography: Giuseppe Aquari; Editor: Luciano Anconetani; Music by Carlo Savina

Main Players: Rosanna Schiaffino (Vivian); Chris Avram (Patrick Davenant); Eva Czemerys (Rebecca Davenant); Lucretia Love (Doris); Andrea Scotti (Albert); Renato Rossini [as Howard Ross] (Russell); Janet Agren (Kim); Paola Senatore (Lynn Davenant); Gaetano Russo (Duncan Foster); Eduardo Filipone (Mystery Man)

Home Video: Camera Obscura (Region 2 DVD and Region B Blu-ray)

Patrick Davenant invites various friends to take a tour of his family's long-abandoned theater. Once inside, a maniac begins picking the guests off, one by one. Attempts to leave are thwarted and it becomes apparent that they have been locked inside by somebody who is not prepared to stop until they have all been punished for past sins ...

Like **The Girl in Room 2A** (1974), this combines horror and *giallo* motifs; fortunately, in all other respects, the two films are poles apart. That said, *The Killer Reserved Nine Seats'* claim as a proper *giallo* is open to debate. Unlike earlier thrillers with a supernatural component like Mario Bava's **Hatchet for the Honeymoon** (1970), there is nothing remotely ambiguous about it. There really is a supernatural force at work here.

The basic set-up takes its cue from Agatha Christie's *Ten Little Indians*. A group of people are gathered together in an isolated locale and a maniac begins to kill them off, one after the other. The setting this time is an abandoned theater and, the use of this locale, coupled with the killer's flair for the theatrical as manifested in the use of costumes as disguises, makes it something of a precursor to Michele Soavi's **Stage Fright** (1987). The latter point is worth expanding on, as it has been somewhat overstated by some fans. Much like the influence of Bava's **Twitch of the Death Nerve** (1971)

Italian *locandina* for **The Killer Reserved Nine Seats**; artwork by Enzo Nistri.

on *Friday the 13th* (1980), one would sometimes think that Soavi's film was a blatant imitation of this comparatively obscure title, going by what some have written. The similarities are on the superficial side, however, and it is entirely possible that Soavi never even saw the film; it was by no means a major box-office hit, after all, and has slid into obscurity since its release.

The film offers plenty of suspense and some nasty murders, including one that is bound to raise a few eyebrows. One victim, a lesbian, is stabbed repeatedly and viciously in the crotch by the masked assassin; the scene does not go quite as far toward bad taste eroticism as a comparable moment in Dario Argento's *Mother of Tears* (2007), but it

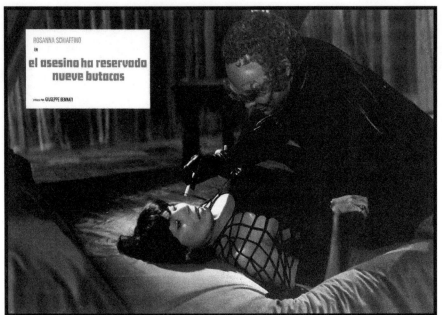

Spanish lobby card for *The Killer Reserved Nine Seats*: Vivian (Rosanna Schiaffino) is menaced by the masked killer.

stands out in relief as a particularly mean-spirited set piece. There is a general air of tawdry exploitation hanging over the proceedings, with all the female cast members (excepting "veteran" performer Rosanna Schiaffino) baring all at one point or another. That said, the film is at least honest about its exploitation leanings and it does not attempt to present itself as anything but a colorful and lurid bit of entertainment.

Director Giuseppe Bennati handles the material very well. The theater locale is effectively claustrophobic and ominous and the photography by Giuseppe Aquari lays on the shadows for ominous impact. Bennati and Aquari work soundly together, making good use of framing and camera movement to increase the suspense, and Carlo Savina contributes a decent soundtrack. The pacing is taut throughout and even the odd gratuitous sex scene does not slow down the action or detract from the overall result.

The cast includes a number of genre staples. Chris Avram has a rare leading role as the cynical Patrick. He does a good job in the role, moving from moments of unexpected sympathy to conveying an air of moral dissipation, which makes him a prime suspect from the start. Born in Romania in 1931, Avram started appearing in films in his native country in 1961. He soon migrated to Italy, where he spent the bulk of his life and career. He appeared in a few Spaghetti Westerns (*A Man Called Django*, 1971), some *poliziotteschi* (*The Iron Commissioner*, 1978) and even a few softcore items (*Emanuelle in Bangkok*, 1976), as well as such *gialli* as **Twitch of the Death Nerve** (1971) and **So Sweet, So Dead** (1972). He died in Italy in 1989 at the age of 57. Leading lady Rosanna Schiaffino is very good in the role of Patrick's ex-wife, Vivian. Of all the women in the film, she is probably the only one to have much in the way of character depth, though this could simply be a matter of Schiaffino's experience shining through. She makes Vivian into a sympathetic figure and imparts the character's fear very nicely. Schiaffi-

no was born in 1939 and was thrust into the limelight early on, winning the title of "Miss Liguria" at the age of 14. She entered films in the mid-1950s and her smoldering good looks ensured her reputation as a sex symbol. Unfortunately, her career did not really ignite as she had hoped and her name value was never as big outside of Italy as that of, say, Sophia Loren. Even so, she remained active throughout the 1970s despite cultivating a reputation for being a bit of a diva. She appeared in films for Francesco Rosi (*La sfida*, 1958), Mauro Bolognini (*The Big Night*, 1959), Vincente Minnelli (*Two Weeks in Another Town*, 1962), Edgar G. Ulmer (*The Cavern*, 1964), Damiano Damiani (*The Witch*, 1966) and others, but her popularity began to wane in the 1970s and she pretty much retired by 1977; she made a minor return with an appearance on the short-lived Italian TV series *Giorno dopo giorno* (1985), but was diagnosed with breast cancer in the early 1990s. She died at the age of 69 in 2009. The supporting cast includes an early appearance by the lovely Janet Agren; she is dispatched early on and not much is asked of her, but she does have a memorable death scene. Agren was born in Sweden in 1949 and started off as a model before making her first films in Italy in the late 1960s. Apart from minor roles in such mainstream productions as Mike Hodges' *Pulp* (1972) and Billy Wilder's *Avanti!* (1972), filmed and set in Malta and Italy respectively, she was mostly confined to low-budget exploitation fare. Horror fans best remember her for her roles in Umberto Lenzi's *Eaten Alive!* (1980) and Lucio Fulci's *City of the Living Dead* (1980). Agren retired from films in 1991 and was last rumored to be living in the United States, working as an interior decorator.

Director Giuseppe Bennati was born in Tuscany in 1929. He started working in films in the early 1950s, as a writer-director. He was not terribly prolific and only amassed 10 credits between 1951 and 1974; *The Killer Reserved Nine Seats* was his last effort and only *giallo*. He died in 2006.

Ordine firmato in bianco
(Italy)

Directed by Gianni Manera; Screenplay by Ivano Gobbo, Enrico Manera, Gianni Manera and Mario Pisu; Director of Photography: Giovanni Raffaldi; Editor: Mariano Arditi; Music by Carlo Savina

Main Players: Gianni Manera (Luca Albanese); Herb Andress (Michael Werther); Lucy Chevalier (Lucia Salvemini); Irina Maleeva (Teresa); Paola Arduini (Santina)

The Mafia orders a bank robbery to be carried out by Luca Albanese and his associates. The heist is successfully executed and the criminals take their stolen loot to a seclud-

ed locale, where they find themselves being dispatched by an unknown assailant ...

Ordine firmato in bianco begins with a long-winded onscreen proclamation that the story represents a "long-lost note from the archives of the Criminalpol." It is all a puff, of course, as the story that unfolds is simply one part *poliziottesco*, one part would-be social commentary and one-part *giallo*.

The film is thrown together in a truly haphazard fashion, with myopic camerawork and ugly art direction making the movie look much older than it really is. This effect is unwittingly reinforced by leading man/director Gianni Manera, who favors outfits which would not be out of place in a gangster film from the 1930s; it could be that he was trying to echo some of the cool of Alain Delon in Jean-Pierre Melville's classic *Le Samouraï* (1967), but Manera the actor is no Delon and Manera the director is a poor substitute for Melville.

If anything, the film is notable for its depiction of the Mafia as a sort of shadowy, vaguely supernatural presence, akin to the role of SPECTRE in the James Bond series. The big bosses are never seen, but their orders are Law and must be fulfilled to the letter; no room is allotted for error, as the protagonists soon find out. This approach is more fitting for a comic strip than to a would-be social document, and ultimately it is impossible to take the story seriously by virtue of its excessive emphasis on melodrama.

As a blend of *poliziottesco* and *giallo* motifs, the film is completely unsuccessful. It starts off as a conventional crime thriller but things take a more mysterious turn during the second act. There is even an elaborate, drawn-out dream sequence which would seem more appropriate in a horror film; this was clearly not lost on composer Carlo Savina, who scores the set piece in question with one of his cues from Jorge Grau's *The Legend of Blood Castle* (1973). Much of the film comprises long, static dialogue sequences and the few murder scenes are handled with a singular lack of flair.

Director/co-writer/leading man Gianni Manera is something of a triple threat in every sense of the word. As a director, he displays very little in the way of style or storytelling ability. As an actor, he makes for a boring and unconvincing "tough guy" protagonist. Manera was born in 1940 and worked primarily as an actor, making his debut in 1959. He appeared in a string of mostly forgotten films and TV series, including a small role in the Franco and Ciccio comedy *War Italian Style* (1965), which is most notable as one of Buster Keaton's final screen appearances. Manera made his directing debut in 1971 and would only helm three pictures altogether. *Ordine firmato in bianco* was his only *giallo* credit. He died in 2013.

Puzzle (Italy)

Aka *L'uomo senza memoria; Atormentada; L'homme sans mémoire; Der Mann ohne Gedächtnis*

Cover for the DVD release of *Ordine firmato in bianco*; artist unknown.

Directed by Duccio Tessari; Screenplay by Ernesto Gastaldi; Director of Photography: Giulio Albonico; Editor: Mario Morra; Music by Gianni Ferrio

Main Players: Luc Merenda (Edward); Senta Berger (Sara Grimaldi); Umberto Orsini (Daniel); Duilio Cruciani (Luca); Anita Strindberg (Mary Caine); Bruno Corazzari (George); Tom Felleghy (Dr. Archibald T. Wildgate)

Home Video: Another World Entertainment (Region 2 DVD)

Edward loses his memory following an accident and spends the better part of a year in England trying to remember his past life. After receiving a mysterious note, he is able to find his wife Sara, who is living in Italy. While there, a stranger who claims to be part of Edward's past terrorizes Sara and him. Will Edward be able to remember an all-important detail before their lives are completely destroyed? ...

Duccio Tessari's previous *gialli* were **Death Occurred Last Night** (1970) and **The Bloodstained Butterfly** (1971), so it is only fitting that his final contribution to the genre would prove to be similarly inventive and non-conformist.

The complex narrative reveals bits and pieces of the protagonist's complicated past, thus keeping us more or less on

Mexican lobby card for *Puzzle*; artist unknown.

it, but generally avoiding an excess of artifice. The cinematography by Giulio Albonico is slick and stylish, while Gianni Ferrio contributes another excellent soundtrack. The film is also very well paced and holds one's attention until the very end.

As mentioned above, the violence is muted, but Tessari makes an impact where it counts. Some advertising really played up the presence of a buzz saw that figures in the narrative. True, the film is not exactly loaded with dismemberment mayhem, but when the prop is introduced relatively early on there is no doubting that it will come into play at some point—and that it does, though to say more might spoil one of the film's many surprises.

the same page as him. The notion of a seemingly decent man who may have forgotten (or elected to forget, as the case may be) a violent and sordid past is an interesting one that helps to set it aside from the more run-of-the-mill *gialli* of the period. Shock effects and other sensational elements are also downplayed in favor of building a complex narrative.

The film benefits from some very compelling and interesting characters. Edward is a very engaging protagonist, one who engenders immediate audience empathy, even if we are unsure of his background. He displays intelligence and humanity and his attempts at reconnecting with his wife in an effort to reclaim his former life are oddly touching. Sara is a strong, resilient woman … not at all the usual addle-brained victim, and she is also depicted in very sympathetic terms. She has waited faithfully for her husband to come back to her, but in the meantime has struck up a friendship with Daniel, who provides her with moral support and a friendly ear. Daniel's mixed emotions over Edward's return feel very genuine, but sooner than react like a spurned lover he keeps a cool head and is sympathetic to Sara's feelings in the matter. There is also a little boy named Luca, who has become a sort of surrogate son for Sara. Luca is precocious and outspoken but never comes off as obnoxious. These are characters well worth caring about, even as the twist-laden narrative begins to reveal hidden layers.

Tessari handles the material with his usual flair and authority. The story is an intriguing one and Tessari does not rely on a lot of flashy gimmicks in order to make it work. Instead, he allows the material to speak for itself, going in for a more baroque stylistic angle when the situation calls for

The attractive cast certainly helps the film tremendously. Luc Merenda is fine as the beleaguered protagonist. He is an actor capable of conveying warmth as well as an air of menace, and this stands him in good stead in the role of Edward. He also has tremendous chemistry with his onscreen wife, thus making their complicated relationship all the more interesting and believable. Senta Berger is excellent as Sara, making her into a strong-willed but likable character who is more than capable of holding her own against the villains that are targeting Edward and her. Berger was born in Austria in 1941. She started off playing small roles (often without billing) in German films in 1950, then gradually worked her way up the ladder to becoming an international star. She was terrorized by Dr. Mabuse (*The Testament of Dr. Mabuse*, 1962), was rescued by Christopher Lee's Sherlock Holmes (*Sherlock Holmes and the Deadly Necklace*, 1962) and joined the likes of Kirk Douglas, Yul Brynner, Frank Sinatra and John Wayne for *Cast a Giant Shadow* (1966). She also has the distinction of being imposed on director Sam Peckinpah for not one, but two films: *Major Dundee* (1965) and *Cross of Iron* (1977); truth be told, it was not due to Peckinpah not liking the actress but because in both cases the producers felt the testosterone-heavy films needed a bit of romantic interest worked in. Berger co-starred with Frank Wolff in *When Women Lost Their Tails* (1972), which would prove to be the latter's final effort; he committed suicide late in the production. In recent years, she has been more active in Italian and German films. Umberto Orsini makes another genre appearance following an early role in *Interrabang* (1969), and he is exceptional as the lovelorn Daniel. Anita Strindberg puts in an appearance but does not have a lot of screen time, while the reliably seedy Bruno Corazzari is memorable as an unwelcome face from Edward's past. Corazzari was born in 1940 and made his debut in 1967, with a minor role in the superior Spaghetti Western *Death Rides a Horse*, directed by Giulio Petroni. Corazzari would become a familiar face in that genre, appearing in the likes of Sergio Corbucci's *The Great Silence*, Sergio Leone's *Once Upon a Time in the West* (both 1968), Mario Bava's *Roy Colt & Winchester Jack* (1970) and Lucio Fulci's *Four of the Apocalypse* (1975). Corazzari was also a recurring presence in the *giallo*, making apperances in **The Strange Vice of Mrs. Wardh** (1971), **Seven Blood-Stained Orchids** (1972) and **The Psychic** (1977), among others. He has not been so active in recent years, but has shown up in a few films in the new millennium.

Sadly, this would prove to be Tessari's final stab (pardon the expression) at the genre. He displayed a genuine affinity for this type of material, but his career, like so many others, would be adversely affected by the rise in popularity of Italian television in the 1980s.

Red Light Girls (Italy)

Aka *Prostituzione; Dossier rose de la prostitution; Catrice, die Nymphomanin; Die Liebesengel; Street Angels; Love Angels*

Directed by Rino Di Silvestro; Produced by Giuliano Anellucci; Screenplay by Rino Di Silvestro; Director of Photography: Salvatore Caruso; Editor: Angelo Curi; Music by Roberto Fogu

Main Players: Aldo Giuffrè (Inspector Macaluso); Maria Fiore (Primavera); Elio Zamuto (Michele Esposito); Krista Nell (Immacolata Mussomecci); Orchidea de Santis (Benedetta); Magda Konopka (Mrs. North); Andrea Scotti (Lieutenant Variale); Luciano Rossi (Faustino); Umberto Raho (Blackmail victim)

When a prostitute is murdered, Inspector Macaluso launches an investigation. As he begins to interrogate the girl's clients and associates, he discovers a sordid underworld of vice and sexual depravity. Meanwhile, the killer continues targeting the working girls ...

Truth be told, *Red Light Girls* is one of those titles that could easily have been sent to the borderline chapter [Vol. 1]. Only the overall air of sleaziness and a generally sincere (albeit flatfooted) attempt at a mystery angle manages to keep it somewhat rooted in the *giallo* proper.

On the whole, the film is something of a sensationalized social document. It purports to offer a rarified insight into Italy's prostitution racket, but all it does is trot out one cliché after the other. There is nothing insightful about its social commentary and the filmmakers make it clear that they are of the opinion that there are two kinds of hookers: those who do it because they really do need the money (these would be the "good" girls) and those who do it because they are basi-

Italian *locandina* for *Red Light Girls*; artist unknown.

cally, inherently depraved (no prize for guessing what they make of "these" girls!).

The film also works in plenty of would-be comedy, mostly at the expense of "deviant" types like homosexuals and transsexuals. This parochial attitude toward sexuality gives the movie an air of hypocrisy that makes it more unpleasant than amusing. Overall, the sense of backward thinking permeates the entire picture, making it precisely the kind of two-faced exploitation that gives the genre as a whole a bad name.

Violence is limited, but a couple of memorably squalid encounters linger in the mind. One involves a young prostitute being sodomized against her will when she informs her current client that he needs to wear protection, since she tends to get pregnant easily; when the young man's friends join in on the action, it takes an even nastier turn. What goes around comes around, however, when the young man is subsequently punished for his transgressions by some thugs employed by the local pimp, who use a beer bottle to get their own back, as it were.

All told, the film offers a very uneasy mixture of would-be docudrama, broad comedy and thriller elements, with the latter getting the short shrift in the big scheme of things. The mystery is pretty transparent and a veteran *giallo*phile should have no problem guessing the identity of the killer long before the *denouement*. The finale, incidentally, seems to quote Federico Fellini's *Nights of Cabiria* (1957), though it is doubtful that Fellini would have been much impressed by the reference.

The cast is generally bland, with genre veterans Krista Nell and Orchidea de Santis adding to the film's pictorial appeal, but being given little to do of any substance. Maria Fiore overacts abominably as the "veteran" prostitute, whose life crumbles to ruin, and Aldo Giuffrè walks through his role as the investigating inspector; the film's English track was done by a different dubbing studio than usual and European horror buffs will therefore recognize the voices of Giuffrè and his sidekick played by Andrea Scotti as belonging to the same actors who dubbed Jack Taylor and Jess Franco, respectively, in the English dub of Franco's *Female Vampire* (1973).

Director Rino Di Silvestro was born in Rome in 1932. After working in the *avant-garde* theater scene in the 1960s, he started making films in 1973. He specialized in exploitation fare with a heavy erotic content, including *Women in Cell Block 7* (1973), *Werewolf Woman* (1976) and, most infamously, *Deported Women of the S.S. Special Section* (1976). One of his last efforts was the sleazy drugs and prostitution thriller *Hanna D: The Girl from Vondel Park* (1984). He died in 2009 at the age of 77.

Spasmo (Italy)

Directed by Umberto Lenzi; Produced by Ugo Tucci; Screenplay by Pino Boller, Massimo Franciosa, Umberto Lenzi and Luisa Montagnana; Director of Photography: Guglielmo Mancori; Editor: Eugenio Alabiso; Music by Ennio Morricone

Main Players: Suzy Kendall (Barbara); Robert Hoffmann (Christian Bauman); Ivan Rassimov (Fritz Bauman); Adolfo Lastretti (Tatum); Guido Alberti (Malcolm); Monica Monet (Clorinda)

Home Video: Shriek Show Entertainment (Region 1 DVD)

Christian becomes involved in a relationship with Barbara after meeting the latter under mysterious circumstances on the beach. They retire to Barbara's apartment for some lovemaking, at which point a mysterious man named Tatum attacks Christian. Tatum is apparently killed in the ensuing struggle, but all is not what it appears ...

After a certain point, it can be argued that Umberto Lenzi's *gialli* became a lesson in the law of diminishing returns. He had helped to popularize the genre early on with such films as *Orgasmo* (1968) and *So Sweet, So Perverse* (1969), but this later entry only shows sporadic evidence of his affinity for the genre. Indeed, in a printed interview, he would dismiss the movie altogether as "a terrible film," going on to say:

> *Spasmo* had a ridiculously complicated plot, which made no sense at all. The story was a dead loss from the start; I shouldn't even have agreed to direct it.[1]

A not altogether unfair assessment, truth be told, though his feelings would later soften. In an interview included on the Shriek Show DVD release of the film, Lenzi would explain

Cover for the American DVD release of *Spasmo* from Shriek Show/Media Blasters; artist unknown.

that he stepped in at the last minute to replace Lucio Fulci, who had abandoned ship. It was in this context that he overhauled the script and transformed it into a probing psychological exercise. The earlier assessment remains closer to the mark.

The film gets off to an uneasy start when Christian falls in love (more like lust) with Barbara. He charms her with witty banter along the lines of, "You're a sweet, sweet whore," and she agrees to hop in the sack with him provided he shaves off his beard. Just a typical first date after all! From there, the story proceeds to lunge from one half-baked surprise to the next. The story truly does not make a great deal of sense and, if the final act proves to be successful at offering up a few surprises, it is largely because there is no predicting what crazy turn the story will take next.

That being said, it would be a mistake to dismiss the movie outright. It certainly is not dull. The plot may be ludicrous, but Lenzi knows it. To compensate, he piles on all the stylistic artifice he can muster. There is a recurring mannequin motif, which the director claims to have added in at the last minute, and it simply accentuates the film's quirky, offbeat appeal. It also benefits from avoiding a lot of the Argento-style clichés, which had a stranglehold on the genre during this time. The violent content is surprisingly muted and the film aims instead for an off-kilter, almost surreal vibe. Lenzi does not exactly show restraint in his approach to the material, but this would not be realistically expected of him. He zooms with abandon and generally shows the same tendency to underline every important point so that everybody in the audience will pick up on it, but while this can sometimes be a detriment, here it is all part of the film's eccentric personality. A sequence showing Christian's brother, Franz, watching home movies is especially interesting in this context. These happen to include many professional-looking set-ups and helpfully include the director's own fondness for zooming in on people's eyes.

The characterizations are also on the slim side. There is an attempt at making Christian into a complex protagonist battling inner demons, but the cod psychology and a stiff performance from Robert Hoffmann do not help matters any. Hoffmann wears two basic expressions in the film: smug and constipated. That is pretty much the high and the low of it for our "hero." Barbara is not especially well developed, either, but at least Suzy Kendall possesses an innate likability that manages to transcend any weakness in that area. Franz does not factor in until late in the narrative, but he proves to be an effectively ambiguous presence, made all the more so by a typically intense performance from Ivan Rassimov. The wonderful character actor Guido Alberti (*The Fifth Cord*, 1971) is on hand to bring a bit of gravitas to his role, but his screen time is limited and he does not get much of a chance to register.

On a technical level, the film is slick and well made. Guglielmo Mancori contributes some moody lighting in the nighttime scenes, though much of the picture unfolds in the daylight; this was another deliberate move on Lenzi's part in an attempt to avoid cliché. Ennio Morricone's score is not one of his best efforts, overall, though the main theme is memorable. The action is so chaotic and unfurls in such a frantic fashion that the film never becomes boring and on this level, at least, it has a leg up on some of the director's other efforts. Lenzi would return to the *giallo* the following year with *Eyeball* (1975), and at that point all bets were off in the Argento imitation department …

Notes:
1. Palmerini, Luca M. and Gaetano Mistretta, *Spaghetti Nightmares* (Florida: Fantasma Books, 1996), p. 69.

What Have They Done to Your Daughters? (Italy)

Aka *La polizia chiede aiuto; La lame infernale; Der Tod trägt schwarzes Leder; The Co-Ed Murders*

Directed by Massimo Dallamano; Screenplay by Massimo Dallamano and Ettore Sanzò; Director of Photography: Franco Delli Colli; Editor: Antonio Siciliano; Music by Stelvio Cipriani

Main Players: Claudio Cassinelli (Inspector Silvestri); Giovanni Ralli (Assistant District Attorney Vittoria Stori); Mario Adorf (Inspector Valentini); Farley Granger (Mr. Polvesi); Marina Berti (Mrs. Polvesi); Franco Fabrizi (Bruno Paglia); Corrado Gaipa (District Attorney)

Home Video: Shameless Screen Entertainment (Region free DVD)

When a young girl is found dead in an attic, the police initially believe it to be a suicide. The investigation reveals that it was a murder and that the girl was part of a ring of under-aged prostitutes. Soon, more girls end up being killed. Hard-nosed Inspector Silvestri and Assistant District Attorney Stori must team up to uncover who is behind of the ring before it is too late ...

Despite the title, this is not a sequel to director Massimo Dallamano's popular *What Have You Done to Solange?* (1972). It is, however, something of a loose follow-up as it delves into some of the same sordid themes.

While *Solange* was produced during the height of "Argento-mania" and offered a more classical approach to the *giallo*, this film was produced when the *poliziotteschi* was beginning to take over audience taste as the "go-to" exploitation genre. As such, the film offers a combination of the two strands. Thus, some critics consider it to be a straight *poliziotteschi*, while others lump it in with the *giallo*; truth be told, it offers a satisfying amalgamation of both and is therefore worthy of inclusion in studies of both genres.

The film offers a compelling and heartfelt examination of the way the corrupt elders of society feed off of the young. The prostitution ring is geared toward pathetic old men with a taste for young flesh, and Dallamano dwells on the details

American poster for *What Have They Done to Your Daughters?*, under an alternate title; artist unknown.

of how they abuse these children not for prurient reasons but to drive home the enormity of their actions. The plot includes some surprising developments, but is less concerned with its mystery angle than it is with exploring the more unsavory attributes of its gallery of perverts and deviants. In the film's nihilistic *milieu*, nobody is entirely to be trusted: seemingly respectable men turn out to be closet pedophiles and no one is safe from the general sense of moral decay which has taken hold of society at large.

The characters are well rounded, as usual for the director's films. Silvestri is another in a long line of radical cops inspired by Clint Eastwood's iconic titular character in Don Siegel's *Dirty Harry* (1971). He serves justice but is frustrated by the limits the law imposes on him in his work. The film addresses the unrest typified by the student riots and other social demonstrations, but the film does not castigate the younger generation for their actions. On the contrary, it is far harsher on the older generation, many of whom are presented in a vile and unflattering light. Silvestri is an ex-

perienced cop, but he is not so old and jaded that it has become just another day on the job for him. It is easy to identify with his sense of moral outrage because of the nature of the case he is investigating. By contrast, the assistant district attorney is new to this sort of investigation. Much is made of the surprise some of the older, more chauvinistic cops have toward her being a woman, but the film never stumbles into supporting or validating this kind of outmoded thinking. Stori is tough and resilient, even if she is easily shocked at the beginning by the more horrific details of the murders. At one point she is herself targeted by the murderer, but the character is not depicted as a shrieking, irrational victim; true to form, she fights back and does not roll over easily. The other cops run the gamut from typically closed-minded, vaguely comic types to more resourceful and compassionate people like Inspector Valentini. The latter seems poised to be the film's focal point early on, but Silvestri eventually supplants him when the "suicide" is discovered to be a murder. Even so, he is a character who inspires tremendous sympathy, especially when the sordid goings-on hit him a little too close to home.

Dallamano handles the material with tremendous flair, as always. The murders are remarkably nasty, but the emphasis is on the aftermath rather than on elaborately choreographed kills. One victim is literally cut into pieces and this results in some rather nauseating images as the pathologist is forced to put the body back together again for identification purposes. The matter-of-fact presentation of the more unsavory sexual details—typified when Valentini tells Stori that the first victim had sex before her death and that traces of sperm were found in the vagina, anus and stomach—helps to underline the difficult nature of the work the police are involved in, while giving a very queasy and uncomfortable dimension to the film as a whole. Dallamano's intent is not geared toward making these horrific incidents palatable or even "fun." He utilizes plenty of mobile camerawork, with a lot of expert hand-held work and good use of distorted lenses and angles. The various chase scenes are exciting and the procedural sequences are more engaging than usual. Only the final unmasking of the killer feels a little anticlimactic, though this barely has a chance to register as the film then pulls out one final, cynical twist that lays bare the corruption of the political system. Regrettably, it would prove to be one of the director's last efforts before his premature demise in a car accident in 1976; he would, however, help to develop the script for ***Rings of Fear*** (1978), another "schoolgirl in peril" thriller that would round off a loose trilogy of sorts.

Franco Delli Colli's cinematography is not quite as "pretty" as Aristide Massaccesi's work on *Solange*, but the grittier, grubbier look adds to the film's seedy ambience. Special effects work is very good, too, with a showstopper of a scene sticking in mind involving a character having a hand bisected by a nasty-looking meat cleaver. The outstanding music

Spanish newspaper ad for *What Have They Done to Your Daughters?* (from *La Vanguardia Española*, *circa* 1975); artwork by "Jano"/ Francisco Fernández Zarza.

score by Stelvio Cipriani represents arguably the composer's best work in the genre and really helps to give the film an added shot of adrenalin where needed.

The cast is also worthy of praise. Claudio Cassinelli is excellent as Silvestri. He conveys a sense of intellect, which is sometimes missing in other "rogue cop" portrayals, while his mixture of anger and disgust is also powerfully registered. The actor was born in Bologna in 1938 and began performing in Italian television in 1963, before making his film debut in 1967. This movie and Gianfranco Mingozzi's nunsploitation favorite *Flavia the Heretic* (1974) were his first really substantial screen roles, and he would go on to appear in such *gialli* as Sergio Martino's **The Suspicious Death of a Minor** (1975) and Lucio Fulci's **Murder-Rock: Dancing Death** (1984). Cassinelli also featured in such cult favorites as Sergio Martino's *Mountain of the Cannibal God* (1978) and *Island of the Fishmen* (1979) and Luigi Cozzi's *Hercules* (1983) and *The Adventures of Hercules II* (1985). Sadly, he would die in a freak helicopter accident on location in Arizona while appearing in Martino's *Hands of Steel* in 1985; he was only 46 years old. Giovanna Ralli is more than able to hold her own as Stori. She is very effective at suggesting the character's inner vulnerability while conveying a tough and resilient exterior. Born in Rome in 1935, she started appearing in films as a child, netting a role in Vittorio De Sica's neo-realist classic *The Children Are Watching Us* (1944), among others. Her career proper really took off in the 1950s, however, and she would appear in everything from Roberto Rossellini's *Il generale Della Rovere* (1959)

and *Escape by Night* (1960) to Sergio Corbucci's *The Mercenary* (1968) and Enzo G. Castellari's borderline *giallo*, *The Cold Eyes of Fear* (1971). Ralli is still sporadically active in Italian films. Mario Adorf plays Valentini beautifully. He stresses the character's decency and humanity but is also capable of showing his sense of grief and outrage later in the film. Adorf was born in Zurich in 1930. The son of an Italian father and a German mother, the multilingual actor has appeared in films in various genres and various pedigrees. He made his debut in 1954 and scored an early triumph in Robert Siodmak's *The Devil Strikes at Night* (1957), which was nominated for an Oscar for Best Foreign Film. He would go on to appear in Sam Peckinpah's *Major Dundee* (1965) but turned the director down when he was offered a role in *The Wild Bunch* (1969). He also passed on an offer from Francis Ford Coppola to appear in *The Godfather* (1972; it really was an offer he could refuse!), but would generate acclaim for his work in such arthouse hits as *The Lost Honor of Katharina Blum* (1975) and *The Tin Drum* (1979), both directed by Volker Schlöndorff. On the Italian genre side, he appeared in *poliziotteschi* like Fernando Di Leo's *The Italian Connection* (1972), Spaghetti Westerns such as Giulio Petroni's *A Sky Full of Stars for a Roof* (1968), paranoid political thrillers like Damiano Damiani's *I Am Afraid* (1977), such *gialli* as **The Bird with the Crystal Plumage** (1970) and borderline entries like *Short Night of Glass Dolls* (1971). Adorf too remains an active presence as of 2014. The supporting cast also includes appearances by two former matinee idol types. Farley Granger is cast in the throwaway role of Mr. Polvesi, the father of the initial victim. It is not a large role, but Granger gives it as much substance and heart as he can muster, indicating that he was not content to simply walk through the part for a quick payday; it is ironic that his best *giallo* would offer him one of his weaker roles, however. Similarly, Franco Fabrizi is on hand in the role of a peeping tom with a penchant for taking dirty pictures. Born in 1916, Fabrizi was a popular presence in Italian films in the 1950s. He landed major roles in Federico Fellini's *I Vitelloni* (1953) and *Il Bidone* (1955), Michelangelo Antonioni's *Le amiche* (1955) and Pietro Germi's borderline *giallo The Facts of Murder* (1959), but by the 1970s he was alternating between arthouse titles like Luchino Visconti's *Death in Venice* (1971) and genre fare like this or Aldo Lado's revenge thriller *Night Train Murders* (1975). Fellini would use him to great effect in *Ginger and Fred* (1986), which would net the actor nominations for Best Supporting Actor at the David di Donatello and Italian National Syndicate of Film Journalists awards, but this was a rare highlight among his later credits. He died in 1995.

American poster for *Autopsy*; artist unknown.

1975

Autopsy (Italy)

Aka *Macchie solari; Tensión; Frissons d'horreur; The Magician; The Victim*

Directed by Armando Crispino; Produced by Leonardo Pescarolo; Screenplay by Lucio Battistrada and Armando Crispino; Director of Photography: Carlo Carlini; Editor: Daniele Alabiso; Music by Ennio Morricone

Main Players: Mimsy Farmer (Simona Sana); Barry Primus (Father Paul Lenox); Ray Lovelock (Edgar); Massimo Serato (Gianni Sana); Carlo Cattaneo (Lello Sana); Angela Goodwin (Daniela); Ernesto Colli (Ivo)

Home Video: Blue Underground (Region 1 DVD)

During a particularly brutal summer in Italy, the suicide rate goes through the roof. Simona is working on her master's degree while employed as a pathologist. As she examines more and more of the grisly casualties due to the blistering heat, her own tentative grasp on reality begins to slip. When one of her father's mistresses turns up dead, she inadvertently becomes involved in a plot which endangers her own life ...

When approached as a standard *giallo*, à la Argento, *Autopsy* can seem a major disappointment. This deliberately-paced character study is part psychological study, part mood piece and part *giallo*, but the latter element may seem muted if one approaches it with expectations of killers dressed in black slicing up nubile young victims.

According to co-writer/director Armano Crispino, the idea for the film arose out of the news:

> The sunspot idea came from a newspaper article [...] It was all about an increase in apparently inexplicable suicides which all happened together during the summer, but which in reality were caused by a strange solar phenomenon that produced paratoxic reactions in psychologically vulnerable individuals.[1]

The sunspot motif is laced throughout the film and provides a very interesting narrative hook, which helps to distinguish the film from others of its ilk, but ultimately the true motivator of the mystery proves to be far more banal: greed.

The protagonist is a character that proves difficult to empathize with, but this is clearly a deliberate move. Simona is bright and studious but hopelessly backward in her social graces. She is attractive but cultivates a vaguely androgynous look thanks to a somewhat "masculine" hairdo. Even so, she triggers all manner of unwelcome advances on the part of the macho men in her workplace, a factor no doubt also inspired by the stifling heat which puts the characters on edge. Worse still, she is involved with a boyfriend, Edgar, who is unbelievably crass and sexist. At one point, Simona's co-worker Ivo attempts to force himself on her and ends up suffering at her hands as a result. Sensitive Edgar's reply is to quip, "Well, you can't blame the poor bastard for trying." Simona's uptight attitude about sex prompts Edgar to refer to her as "Ice cube" and she also finds herself being drawn to the complicated Father Paul, who proves to be a fascinating character in his own right. It is gradually revealed that Father Paul is suffering from guilt due to a past accident, where the former champion racing-car driver plowed into a group of spectators during a race. This has all the makings of bad soap opera, but it is presented with such conviction that it ends up working remarkably well. Simona's attraction to Father Paul comes to a head (pardon the expression) when he takes confession from her and she admits that she is in love with him. Simona's conflicted attitude toward sex, coupled with her awkard social skills and obvious intelligence, make her an uncommonly complex heroine for a *giallo*. She initially comes off as cold and neurotic, but as the story unfolds, the audience begins to sympathize with her more; by the end, we are fully on her side.

Crispino begins the film with a shocking montage sequence, removed from some prints, depicting the chain-reaction of suicides. The deliberately random images, set to an atonal score by Ennio Morricone, announces right off the bat that this is not going to be a typical Italian thriller. The outbursts of violence are shocking when they do occur, but much of the running time is devoted to character development and generating and sustaining a palpably oppressive atmosphere. If the film is reminiscent of anything, it calls to mind elements of Roman Polanski's *Repulsion* (1965), which also dealt with a sexually repressed female protagonist. However, while Polanski's movie charted his character's gradual mental deterioration in an almost clinical fashion, Crispino's offers a more hopeful point of view. Simona may have her issues, but she is not beyond redemption.

Crispino and cinematographer Carlo Carlini create some striking images, especially during a stalking scene set inside a crime museum. Crispino later admitted that he invented this musem out of whole cloth:

> I constructed the exhibition of photographs by developing and enlarging the best photographs from a text on criminology. [...] We invented some very effective settings.[2]

Even more alarming than the admittedly gruesome photographs, however, are the truly bizarre-looking manequins used to recreate various suicide scenarios. The mannequins are clearly portrayed by actors in heavy make-up, but the illusion is artfully achieved and generates some genuine *frissons*.

Mimsy Farmer gives an outstanding performance as Simona. Farmer was not above wandering through some of her genre films with an air of disinterest, but she clearly responded to the complexities of this character and ended up giving one of her best performances. The leading lady's vaguely neurotic screen persona is ideally suited to the role, but most crucially she is able to reveal the vulnerability and humanity

Spanish poster for *Autopsy*; artist unknown.

of the character, making her into a figure worth investing in. Ray Lovelock is also very good as her loutish boyfriend, Edgar. Lovelock's baby-faced countenance is bearded here (as it was in the superior Spanish-Italian zombie film, *Let Sleeping Corpses Lie*, 1974, directed by Jorge Grau) and this gives him a gruffer look. He and Farmer do not have great chemistry, but this is a plus. They really do not belong together. American actor Barry Primus plays the other main character, Father Paul. Primus was born in New York City in 1938 and came to acting in 1962. He played one of the lead roles in Martin Scorsese's *Boxcar Bertha* (1972) and was cast again by Scorsese as Robert De Niro's pal in *New York, New York* (1977). He has worked largely in television and *Autopsy* appears to have been an atypical foray for him into the world of European cinema. He was recently seen in David O. Russell's Oscar-nominated *American Hustle* (2013). The supporting cast includes good roles for reliable character actors like Massimo Serato (excellent as Simona's playboy father) and Ernesto Colli (memorably creepy as the lab assistant who tries to molest Simona).

Notes:
1. Palmerini, Luca M. and Gaetano Mistretta, *Spaghetti Nightmares* (Florida: Fantasma Books, 1996), p. 39.
2. *Ibid.*

FEMI BENUSSI · GIACOMO R. STUART · KRISTA NELL in

VIETATO ai minori di 18 anni

LA SANGUISUGA CONDUCE LA DANZA

con ALAN COLLINS · MARZIA DAMONY
BARBARA MARZANO · MARIO DE ROSA · LEO VALERIANO · RITA SYLVA · HALINA KIM
un film di ALFREDO RIZZO | una produzione TO.RO. Cinematografica - Roma | TECHNICOLOR

Italian *locandina* for The Bloodsucker Leads the Dance; artwork by Ezio Tarantelli.

The Bloodsucker Leads the Dance (Italy)

Aka *La sanguisuga conduce la danza; Danza macabra; L'insatiable Samantha; La marque de Satan; The Passion of Evelyn*

Directed by Alfredo Rizzo; Screenplay by Alfredo Rizzo; Director of Photography: Aldo Greci; Editor: Piera Bruni; Music by Marcello Giombini

Main Players: Femi Benussi (Sybil); Giacomo Rossi-Stuart (Count Richard Marnack); Krista Nell (Cora); Patrizia Webley (Evelyn); Luciano Pigozzi [as Alan Collins] (Gregory); Mario De Rosa (Jeffrey)

Home Video: Image Entertainment/Redemption (Region free DVD)

Count Richard Marnack is taken with the actress Evelyn, who bears an uncanny resemblance to his late wife,

and he invites her and her friends to come stay with him in his castle for the weekend. They take him up on the offer, but soon come to regret this. A family curse begins to come into play as a murderer starts killing off the guests, chopping their heads off for good measure ...

There is a special place reserved in hell for the worst *gialli*, and as such, *The Bloodsucker Leads the Dance* is in good company with the likes of *La Bambola di Satana* (1969), *Blackmail* (1974) and many more "gems" yet to come.

The setting is Ireland, but it is plainly really Italy and everybody on the English-language dub speaks with a posh British accent. The timeframe is 1902, but a modern-looking car can be glimpsed in one of the opening shots. There is an attempt at delivering a properly suspenseful thriller with some salacious elements, but it all reeks of sheer desperation. Suffice it to say, it is just one, sad, shoddy affair.

Production values are virtually non-existent. The lighting is flat and harsh throughout, generating zero atmosphere or mood. Director Alfredo Rizzo is fond of playing out long, tedious dialogue scenes in static master shots, zooming in and out on occasion just to break the tedium; it does not work, however. The gore effects are laughably achieved and the sex scenes mostly consist of the actors listlessly and awkwardly pawing at each other with no sense of genuine passion.

Even so, compared to some of Rizzo's other *giallo*-flavored films of the period, such as *Naked and Lustful* (1974), this one does ultimately make a game effort of delivering up a legitimate murder mystery. The title and Gothic trappings may lead one to expect a supernatural menace, but the final (albeit garbled) explanation roots the film very firmly in the real world. Unfortunately, the *Ten Little Indians*-style formula of a group of people being picked-off by a maniac works best when the characters generate some level of interest, and this most definitely does not apply here. The English dubbing certainly does not help any, and the dialogue includes such unintentional howlers as, "The world is a stage, but sometimes not," but none of the actors approach the material with much conviction anyway; truly, it is hard to blame them. Rizzo interrupts the action with fairly regularly timed doses of sexploitation (including the *de rigeur* lesbian coupling sequence), but for all the skin on display, the film never overcomes a general feeling of being quaint and old hat. Indeed, were it not for some contemporary-looking hairstyles (again, the period detail is not one of the movie's strong suits), one would be forgiven for mistaking it for an older effort than it really is.

The cast includes a number of welcome faces for genre buffs, but nobody really gets much of a chance to register. Femi Benussi is the nominal lead, but her role as the mysterious housekeeper is a stock one, and she seems to be aware of that. Giacomo Rossi-Stuart sleepwalks as the charming but mysterious count, while Krista Nell is stuck playing the token bimbo-numbskull of the group, an act that wears out its welcome early in the film. Luciano Pigozzi is on hand to play yet another mysterious servant, while Mario De Rosa overacts abominably as the religiously preoccupied butler.

Director Alfredo Rizzo was born in Nice in 1902. He worked principally as an actor, making his debut in the late 1930s. He was something of an all-purpose minor league character actor, appearing in small roles in the likes of *Quo Vadis?* (1951), *Roman Holiday* (1953) and *La Dolce Vita* (1960). A more telling example of what his later career would shape-up to become came with his role as the leering theater manager in *The Playgirls and the Vampire* (1960). He began directing in 1971, but his output was not very prolific, directing only eight features and ending with the borderline *giallo Alessia ... Un Vulcano Sotto la Pelle* (1978). He would continue appearing in films sporadically after that and died in 1991 at the age of 89.

Calling All Police Cars
(Italy)

Aka ...*a tutte le auto della polizia; The Maniac Responsible; Without Trace*

Directed by Mario Caiano; Produced by Roberto Angiolini; Screenplay by Massimo Felisatti and Fabio Pittorru; Director of Photography: Pier Luigi Santi; Editor: Romeo Ciatti; Music by Coriolano Gori [as Lallo Gori]

Main Players: Antonio Sabàto (Commissioner Fernando Solmi); Luciana Paluzzi (Inspector Giovanna Nunziante); Enrico Maria Salerno (Police Chief Carraro); Gabriele Ferzetti (Professor Andrea Icardi); Elio Zamuto (Professor Giacometti); Ettore Manni (Enrico Tummoli)

Home Video: Mya Communication (Region 1 DVD, under the title *Without Trace*)

A young girl goes missing and her father, Professor Icardi, pulls strings to ensure that the case is made a top priority. Police Chief Carraro assigns Commissario Solmi and Ispettrice Nunziante to investigate and the former resents that the case is being handled as a special favor because of her father's political clout. Eventually the girl is found dead and it is revealed that she was involved in an underage prostitution ring ...

Calling All Police Cars bears all the signs of being influenced by Massimo Dallamano's schoolgirl-in-peril *gialli*. The film incorporates the same seedy backroom abortion subplot found in *What Have You Done to Solange?* (1972) and offers up a similar mix of *giallo* and *poliziottsechi* tropes found in *What Have They Done To Your Daughters?* (1974). It also fails to bring much originality to the table.

The bulk of the film is something of a straightforward police procedural, with a little terse social commentary worked in for good measure. Working-class police officers square off against elite members of high society, recalling

Luigi Comencini's *The Sunday Woman* (1975), but the commentary feels arbitrary and a touch insincere. Toward the end of the film, things switch into proper *giallo* mode, with plenty of subjective camerawork, black-gloved hands and arterial spray as the killer begins picking off the characters who know too much. The two strands never come together as coherently as they did in Dallamano's model, but the film is by no means a total wash.

On the plus side, the story is interesting even if it fails to break any new ground. Greater attention to characterization would have been appreciated, but the set-up is good and the overarching theme of the corruption of innocence remains a potent one. Screenwriters Massimo Felisatti and Fabio Pittorru adapted the script from their story "*A scopo di libidine*," which had been published in 1974. Felisatti (born in 1932) and Pittorru (born in 1928) were no strangers to the *giallo*; they had collaborated on the screenplays for *The Weekend Murders* (1970) and *The Night Evelyn Came Out of the Grave* (1971), while Pittorru also had a hand in *The*

Italian *locandina* for *Calling All Police Cars*; artist unknown.

Red Queen Kills Seven Times (1972) and Felisatti helped to pen *Strip Nude for Your Killer* (1975). They also wrote the miniseries *Albert e l'uomo nero* (1976), which contains some mild *giallo* elements. Not surprisingly, the two were also active in the *poliziotteschi*, notably collaborating on the script for Sergio Martino's *Silent Action* (1975). They would also contribute to the popular Italian TV series *Qui squadra mobile* (1973-1976), which included some of the same characters that would crop up in this film, though they would not be played by the same actors.[1]

The film would have benefitted from a more inspired director, however. Reliable hack Mario Caiano delivers a few nasty murder scenes—notably a bathtub assault which turns very bloody because of the combination of the victim's feet being wet and the blood spraying on the floor make it difficult for the poor girl to get any kind of traction—but he seems a bit lost with dialogue scenes. The pacing is much too slow and production values betray the film's low-budget origins. Lallo Gori's score again shows him to be one of the least-inspired composers of *giallo* soundtracks, though the funkier cues suit the film's police thriller leanings.

The cast certainly promises much, but few of the actors are given a chance to register. Antonio Sabàto is a bland and unmemorable lead. The role of Solmi calls for an actor with the fire and intensity of Franco Nero; Sabàto simply coasts through the film looking mildly annoyed, whereas somebody like Nero or even Claudio Cassinelli would have better tapped into the character's rage and frustration. Luciana Paluzzi (replacing the less bankable Stefanella Giovannini from the TV show) plays the role of Solmi's distaff associate, Nunziante. Sadly, the character is paper-thin in this particular incarnation, causing Paluzzi to literally disappear into the scenery. Enrico Maria Salerno is very good as the testy police chief who has to straddle the line between seeing that justice is served and at the same time please his "masters" in the political arena, while Gabriele Ferzetti brings gravitas to his role as the clueless father who cannot come to grips with the reality that he was never really there for his daughter. Ferzetti was born in Rome in 1925. He made his film debut in 1942 and graduated to leading man status in the 1950s. In Michelangelo Antonioni's *L'Avventura* (1960), he played his most celebrated role as the *ennui*-ridden bachelor whose lover (Lea Massari) suddenly goes missing. He would go on to appear in such international co-productions as John Huston's *The Bible... In the Beginning* (1966), Peter Hunt's *On Her Majesty's Secret Service* (1969) and Ennio De Concini's *Hitler: The Last Ten Days* (1973), as well as appearing in the likes of Sergio Leone's *Once Upon a Time in the West* (1968)[2] and Liliana Cavani's *The Night Porter* (1974). He was recently seen in Luca Guadagnino's *I Am Love* (2009), which netted a Golden Globe nomination for Best Foreign Film, Ferzetti died at the venerable age of 90 in December, 2015. More emphasis on the characters played by Salerno and Ferzetti may have helped to give the film greater dramatic weight, but sadly this would not prove to be the case.

Among the supporting cast are familiar character actors like Ettore Manni, Franco Ressel and Fulvio Mingozzi, while Hungarian-born Ilona Staller shows up as one of the prostitutes; Staller would later change her name to Cicciolina and become one of Italy's most popular stars of the hardcore sex film scene, after which she improbably pursued a political career.

Notes:
1. Curti, Roberto, *Italian Crime Filmography: 1968-1980* (Jefferson: McFarland & Company, Inc., 2013), p. 129.
2. The actor Leone originally had in mind to play the crippled railroad tycoon, Mr. Morten, was none other than Enrico Maria Salerno. French actor Robert Hossein was also penciled-in for a period before Ferzetti nabbed the memorable role.

Deep Red (Italy)

Aka *Profondo rosso; Rosso—Farbe des Todes; Rojo oscuro; Les frissons de l'angoisse; Dripping Deep Red; The Hatchet Murders; The Deep Red Hatchet Murders*

Directed by Dario Argento; Produced by Salvatore Argento; Screenplay by Dario Argento and Bernardino Zapponi; Director of Photography: Luigi Kuveiller; Editor: Franco Fraticelli; Music by Giorgio Gaslini and Goblin

Main Players: David Hemmings (Marcus Daly); Daria Nicolodi (Gianna Brezzi); Gabriele Lavia (Carlo); Glauco Mauri (Professor Giordani); Macha Méril (Helga Ulmann); Clara Calamai (Carlo's mother); Eros Pagni (Superintendant Calcabrini); Giuliana Calandra (Amanda Righetti); Nicoletta Elmi (Olga)

Home Video: Blue Underground (Region free DVD and All region Blu-ray); Arrow Video (Region free DVD and All region Blu-ray)

During a conference on parapsychology, psychic Helga Ulmann senses the presence of a twisted mind in the audience. The experience rattles her badly and the very person she was on the verge of unmasking later kills her. English pianist Marcus Daly witnesses the murder and is bugged by the feeling that he saw some vital clue that he is not able to remember. As he begins to investigate with the aid of journalist Gianna Brezzi, he finds himself being stalked by the killer ...

Dario Argento had become something of a celebrity in Italy by the time he came to make *Deep Red*. He had made an ill-fated attempt at abandoning the *giallo* with *Le cinque giornate* (1973), but that film was a costly flop and it did little to further his reputation abroad. However, the success of the TV series *Door into Darkness* did much to increase his popularity, and, knowing where his bread was buttered, he decided to revisit the *giallo*. He did so with a vengeance.

Argento wrote the screenplay for *Deep Red* in collaboration with Bernardino Zapponi. Zapponi, born in Rome in 1927, was best known for his collaborations with Federico Fellini on such gems as the "Toby Dammit" segment of *Spir-*

its of the Dead (1968) and *Fellini's Casanova* (1976). He proved invaluable in making *Deep Red* into one of Argento's best-plotted pictures. As Zapponi explained:

> He [Argento] phoned me and said that he loved the idea of a mediumistic séance in which a member of the circle picks up the thoughts of a murderer. There was still no real plot at that point, so I endeavored to blend his ideas with mine and restrain his urge to insert "splatter" scenes.[1]

The film would therefore have the benefit of a (mostly) logical script with a solid structure, though the violence would by no means be muted; indeed, compared to his first three *gialli*, *Deep Red* is notable for its savagery. Zapponi further explained:

> It's more difficult for the average person to identify with someone who gets murdered, perhaps, by a shot from a revolver, while everyone can "comprehend" the impact of a more everyday traumatic event.[2]

Thus, the killings in *Deep Red* have an especially skin-crawling quality because they are rooted in fears and sensations that one can readily identify with. This is especially evident in the scene where one character has their teeth repeatedly smashed against the sharp edge of a mantelpiece or the bathtub scalding of another victim. There is a savagery and precision to these scenes and this elevates them to something only hinted at in the director's previous films; it truly becomes a matter of murder as performance art.

The film begins with the standard credits—white lettering against a black background—but they are interrupted by an ambiguous fragment of story which hints at what is to come. A child's lullaby plays, a scream echoes out, a bloodied knife is rudely projected into frame and a pair of child's feet enter from screen right; the scene then fades to black and the credits resume. It is almost as if Argento cannot wait to get the movie started. This sense of dynamic forward momentum is evident throughout the film. The original Italian edit runs 126 minutes[3], making it one of the longest films covered in this book, but it is distinguished by a rapid, almost nervous sense of pacing. Argento indulges his propensity for elaborate tracking shots, sometimes stopping the narrative dead in its tracks as his camera glides in a fetishistic manner over the assorted odds and ends and mementos of the killer's twisted mind. Style and narrative work hand in hand, however, resulting in a film of sharp focus and terrific impact. Unlike many *gialli*, this one actually plays fair with the viewer. Early on, Marcus enters Helga's apartment after the latter has been murdered; as he makes his way down the corridor, we in the audience are shown his point of view through a gliding subjective camera movement. The camera glides past the Expressionist artwork lining the hallway, and

Italian *locandina* for *Deep Red*; artist unknown.

the more attentive viewers will notice something ever so odd on screen left. It goes by quickly, but it is most definitely there. Nowadays, in the age of DVD and Blu-ray, it is possible to freeze-frame and see the all-important clue that will nag at Marcus for the next two hours: the murderer's face reflected in a mirror. It is a bold touch, and one that pays off in dividends; if many other *gialli* (including Argento's own) have been known to cheat, the same cannot be said of this one.

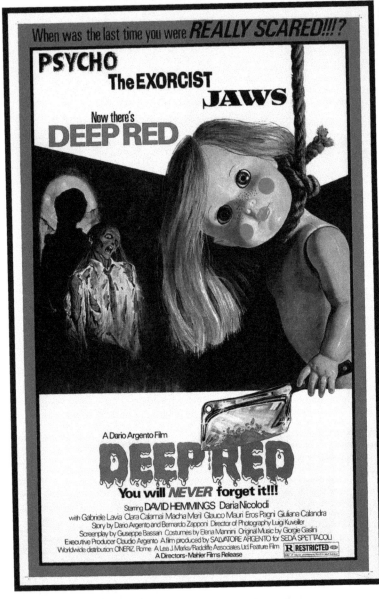

American poster for *Deep Red*; artist unknown.

Argento's direction is a marvel throughout. He utilizes plenty of mobile camerawork, but the film is not quite as overtly baroque as some of his subsequent work, such as *Opera* (1987). The camera roams and takes on an eerie life of its own when the mood strikes, but there is a solid, grounded approach to characterization and plot development. The compositions are eye-catching, with some Cubist formations and use of deep focus standing out in relief. Luigi Kuveiller's elegant lighting coupled with the sensuous camerawork by Ubaldo Terzano (the long-time camera operator for Mario Bava) results in one of the best-looking films of its genre. The sets and art direction are ravishing throughout, though some of the special effects work by Carlo Rambaldi (including an unconvincing burning building effect) does date the picture somewhat. Even so, the film looks remarkably rich and stylish, belying the fact that it was not nearly so lavishly budgeted as Argento's subsequent works.

In addition to a properly ingenious mystery plot, the script offers some well-developed characterizations. Marcus

is one of Argento's most interesting protagonists. He is an artist and an out-and-out neurotic, but he is also an unabashed sexist and chauvinist. He stumbles his way through the narrative in a bit of a haze, trying to come to grips with a vital clue but generally failing to make much headway on his own. If anything, Marcus does not so much act as react to the stimuli around him; he sets out to accomplish goals, but is stymied at every turn. His pride and his preconceived notions about the superiority of the male is put to the test and gradually destroyed as the film unfolds. This allows Argento to dispense with the oft-trotted-out argument that his works are basically misogynistic in tone; he does not side with Marcus' antiquated beliefs, but has a great deal of fun puncturing them and reducing them to rubble by the end of the film. Marcus meets his match (and then some) in the figure of Gianna Brezzi. Gianna is a brash reporter who lands the pianist in hot water when she splashes his picture across the front page of the paper and exaggerates his role in witnessing the crime by claiming that he saw the murderer's face; well, truth be told, he did at that—but it will take much soul-searching before he finally comes to that realization himself. Gianna is outspoken, funny and comparatively "masculine." When she speaks of women's rights at one point, Marcus testily cuts her off, stating that men are stronger and more resourceful than women. Gianna shows this up in a variety of ways, whether it be by initiating their romantic relationship, beating Marcus at arm wrestling or literally pulling his ass out of the fire when he is in danger. There can be no doubt that Gianna is the true "hero" of the film, even if we see the proceedings through Marcus' admittedly faulty eyes.

The director's flair for creating suspense and atmosphere is in full force here, but the thing that makes *Deep Red* so special, above all else, is the sheer coherence and strength of its screenplay. Without wanting to deprive Argento of due credit, much of this seems attributable to Zapponi, whose contribution to the film has seldom been properly appreciated. Zapponi's ability to take wild ideas and give them logic had already put him in good stead with Fellini, and he performed a similar miracle of sorts here. Argento clearly approached *Deep Red* with the intention of validating his status as "the Italian Hitchcock." The plethora of cash-ins and rip-offs that greeted his initial successes had begun to die down by this period in time, thus leaving Argento in a good position to come back and reclaim his chosen terrain. *Giallo* productivity was already on the decline by this period, the genre having effectively peaked in the years of 1971 and 1972; there was less competition, in essence, and Argento was not about to revisit this landscape without being sure that he had a potential winner on his hands. Zapponi would recall working on the film with great affection, but his hopes of continuing to work with Argento as he had done with Fellini would not be realized. Zapponi would go on to write **Plot of Fear** (1976) for Paolo Cavara (who had delivered one of the best Argento imitations with **The Black Belly of the Tarantula**, 1971), but Argento was not keen on repeating their collaboration. When asked if he would have liked to work with the director again, the screenwriter replied:

> Yes, I'd be pleased to, even though Dario, like Fellini, attaches great importance to being the "author" of his films and doesn't want scriptwriters who have a definite personality working with him for fear of being stifled.[4]

Was it truly ego on Argento's part that prevented him from continuing to work with Zapponi? The answer to that is not so easy to pin down, but there is little doubt that his guidance and attention to detail would have been most welcome on some of the director's later, more chaotically plotted efforts.

For Argento, the film would mark an important development toward the macabre. *Deep Red* is more overtly horrific and ghoulish than his first three *gialli*; the murders are more intense, the violence is more traumatic, the blood is several shades redder … deep red, indeed. The movie's tremendous box-office performance enabled Argento to pursue a different type of story for his next two projects. *Suspiria* (1977) and *Inferno* (1980) would explore the world of black magic, witchcraft and fever dreams, though both would feature the requisite killer with black gloves and both have elements linking them with the *giallo*. Their explicit reliance on the supernatural, however, would remove them from the field of the thriller and helped to fuel a renewed interest in horror in the popular Italian cinema culture.

Special note must also be made of the extraordinary music score. Long stretches of the film almost function as macabre music videos, with the imagery and music melding together to create a terrifying sense of rhythm. The various murder scenes explode with dynamic music which make it evident that something very unpleasant is about to happen, but it is not melodramatic suspense music of the old school. This is progressive rock at its most outré and aggressive. In his splendid book on the director, *Dario Argento: The Man, The Myths & The Magic*, Alan Jones quotes Argento:

> Giorgio Gaslini started composing the *Deep Red* music […] Gaslini didn't seem to understand the new spirit of the film and the soundtrack he presented to me was awful. I had three months to come up with an alternative and after flying to London to see if Pink Floyd were interested—they weren't—started asking Roman musician friends of mine for ideas.[5]

Argento was pointed in the direction of a new band known as Cherry Five, and he was impressed with their work. They then re-orchestrated some of the themes Gaslini had already recorded and came up with some new ones of their own,

including the film's signature title track, which was inspired by Mike Oldfield's memorably creepy "Tubular Bells," the music used to such tremendous effect by William Friedkin in *The Exorcist* (1973). Their music would make a deep impression on viewers across the globe, including director-composer John Carpenter, whose theme music for *Halloween* (1978) would owe more than a little to Oldfield and Goblin. Realizing that the name Cherry Five might sound a little incongruous on such a scary horror-thriller, the band was re-christened Goblin and the rest, as they say, is history. The group underwent some changes from their initial members, but the following musicians were involved in the creation of the soundtrack for *Deep Red*: Massimo Morante (guitars), Claudio Simonetti (keyboards), Fabio Pignatelli (bass) and Walter Martino (drums and percussion). The group would continue to evolve and eventually succumbed to in-fighting and other assorted dramas, but they would go on to score *Suspiria*, as well as the Argento co-produced *Dawn of the Dead* (1978), written and directed by independent horror king George A. Romero. The group would not be credited with scoring *Tenebrae*, due to a dispute that led to drummer Agostino Marangolo being replaced by a drum machine, but they would be credited on the soundtracks for **Phenomena** (1985) and the Argento production of *The Church* (1989), directed by Michele Soavi. They would reunite for Argento's later *giallo* **Sleepless** (2001) before falling out yet again. They have since mended fences once more and have been touring the globe to great success in recent years. The impact their music had on *Deep Red* and on the horror and suspense genres in general cannot be overstated. Their throbbing, insistent music helped to introduce a new style of scoring for a new generation of composers and filmmakers. In addition, their music for *Deep Red* proved so popular that the original soundtrack release sold over one million copies; the *giallo* had gone platinum! The group's popularity would become firmly associated with Argento, who despite not being a musician himself would be only too happy to take credit for assisting in their soundtracks on *Suspiria* and *Dawn of the Dead*. No matter how one slices it, however, the director gave the group a major opportunity and they seized it with a vengeance; it would become a mutually beneficial relationship all around.

The cast is headed by British actor David Hemmings, who is splendid as the slightly bewildered Marcus Daly. He brings all manner of neurotic tics to the part but ensures that he retains audience sympathy by highlighting his mixture of fear and curiosity, along with a strain of bemused humor. Hemmings' casting was a deliberate reference on Argento's part to his iconic role in Michelangelo Antonioni's anti-*giallo*, *Blow Up* (1966). In that film, Hemmings played a photographer who believes he has photographed a murder and drives himself to the brink of insanity trying to prove it to himself and others. *Blow Up*'s success made Hemmings into a major international star. The actor was born in 1941 and began acting as a child on the stage and in films. Fol-

Spanish lobby card for *Deep Red*: Marcus makes a gruesome discovery in the old villa.

lowing the success of *Blow Up*, he was cast in a number of thrillers, notably Richard C. Sarafian's Italian-set *Fragment of Fear* (1970), wherein he plays a reformed junkie who travels to Rome to find out who murdered his beloved aunt. Hemmings ended up making a number of pictures in Italy during the 1970s, including Enzo G. Castellari's *The Heroin Busters* (1977), which was also scored by Goblin. In the late 1970s and '80s, he channeled his energies to the production side of the business, forming the company Hemdale with his business partner John Daly and directing numerous films and TV shows, many of them in the U.S., including episodes of *The A Team* and *Airwolf*. His old friend, director Ken Russell, lured him back in front of the camera with a choice supporting role in *The Rainbow* (1989), and he would gradually begin appearing in such major productions as Ridley Scott's Oscar-winning *Gladiator* (2000) and Martin Scorsese's Oscar-nominated *Gangs of New York* (2002). By this stage in the game, Hemmings' striking good looks (which bordered on the pretty when he was a young man) had evolved into a very craggy, portly and almost unrecognizable visage better suited to character roles. He scored a late period triumph with his role as the loutish Lenny in Fred Schepisi's critically acclaimed *Last Orders* (2001), but he died of a heart attack while filming the horror film *Blessed* in Romania in

2003; the movie was released posthumously the following year. Hemmings has tremendous chemistry with leading lady Daria Nicolodi, making them perhaps the most appealing and believable couple in all of Argento's filmography. Nicolodi is terrific as the vivacious and outspoken Gianna. It would prove to be a significant moment in her career. Born in Florence in 1950, she established her credentials as a theater actress before making her screen debut in Francesco Rosi's *Many Wars Ago* (1970). She then nabbed a major role in Elio Petri's *Property is No Longer a Theft* (1973), which is where she caught Argento's eye. Nicolodi and Argento embarked on a lengthy, tumultuous relationship during the filming, and, at one point, as a bit of trivia, she is seen throwing the photograph of one of Marcus' old girlfriends into the trash. The picture is of actress Marilù Tolo, who had been involved with Argento prior to his relationship with Nicolodi. She and Argento would collaborate on the script for *Suspiria*, in which she was scheduled to play a major role; she sustained an injury prior to filming, however, and Stefania Casini played her role instead. She also collaborated on the script for the film's eagerly anticipated follow-up, *Inferno*, but Argento denied her screen credit, thus adding even more strain on an already complicated relationship. They remained together until 1985 but were never married;

their union produced a daughter, Asia, who would go on to become another major fixture in Argento's cinema. Nicolodi would enjoy a more harmonious (albeit platonic) relationship with Mario Bava, whom she regarded as something of a father figure; he directed her to great effect in his final works, *Shock* (1977) and *La Venere d'Ille* (1978), two films, which, along with *Property Is No Longer a Theft* and *Deep Red*, represent her best screen work. Nicolodi would also appear in films by Luigi Cozzi (*Paganini Horror*, 1989), Lamberto Bava (the *giallo* **Delirium: Photos of Gioia**, 1987) and even one by her daughter, the semi-autobiographical *Scarlet Diva* (2000). The same year as *Deep Red*, Nicolodi also top-lined a popular miniseries for Italian TV titled *Ritratto di donna velata*; some references list it as a *giallo*, but it is more of a paranormal suspense melodrama with plenty of Gothic overtones and therefore falls outside of the scope of this study. She has been only sporadically active in films in recent years. The supporting cast includes excellent performances by Gabriele Lavia (who would go on to direct a borderline *giallo* of his own, *Evil Senses*, 1986, in addition to appearing in Argento's *Inferno* and **Sleepless**) as the sexually-tormented Carlo, Clara Calamai (Luchino Visconti's *Ossessione*, 1942) as Carlo's sweetly senile mother, Macha Méril (Luis Buñuel's *Belle de Jour*, 1967) as the ill-fated psychic, Glauco Mauri (Liliana Cavani's *The Guest*, 1971) as Marcus' ally, Professor Giordani and redheaded child actress Nicoletta Elmi (**Twitch of the Death Nerve**, 1971), who makes an unforgettable impression as a sadistic child who loves to torture lizards.

Deep Red remains a classic of its kind, a fantastic fusion of style and substance, which many have imitated and none (including arguably Argento himself) have quite matched; it is undoubtedly one of the key *gialli* and a cornerstone of Italian genre cinema.

Notes:
1. Palmerini, Luca M. and Gaetano Mistretta, *Spaghetti Nightmares* (Florida: Fantasma Books, 1996), p. 158.
2 *Ibid*, p. 159.
3. The full-length Italian cut was never dubbed entirely into English; thus scenes never dubbed play in Italian with English subtitles in the home video releases. Argento prepared a shorter version, cut to 106 minutes, for release in other European markets, including the U.K. This version was completely dubbed into English. Some sources indicate that Argento prefers this shorter edit, but the man himself has yet to make such a claim "officially" in any interview. When the film was released in the U.S., it was cut even further, to 98 minutes. With almost a half-hour of material scrapped, this edit emphasized the gore and scares but much of the plot was lost; not surprisingly, American critics who had no idea that the film had been so thoroughly eviscerated criticized the film for being "incoherent."
4. Palmerini, Luca M. and Gaetano Mistretta, *Spaghetti Nightmares* (Florida: Fantasma Books, 1996), p. 159.

5. Jones, Alan, *Dario Argento: The Man, The Myths & The Magic* (Godalming: FAB Press, 2012), p. 65.

Eyeball (Italy/Spain)

Aka *Gatti rossi in un labirinto di vetro; El ojo en la oscuridad; Labyrinth des Schreckens*

Directed by Umberto Lenzi; Produced by Joseph Brenner and José María Cunillés; Screenplay by Umberto Lenzi and Felix Tusell; Director of Photography: Antonio Millán; Editor: Amedeo Moriani; Music by Bruno Nicolai

Main Players: Martine Brochard (Paulette Stone); John Richardson (Mark Burton); Ines Pellegrini (Naiba Campbell); Andrés Mejuto (Inspector Tudela); Jorge Rigaud (Reverend Bronson); Daniele Vargas (Robby Alvarado); Mirta Miller (Lisa Sanders)

Home Video: Marketing Film (Region 2 DVD, under the title *Labyrinth des Schreckens*)

A group of tourists on vacation in Barcelona find themselves targeted by a crazed killer with a fixation on gouging out one of the eyes of his (or her) victim. Mark Burton falls under suspicion as the killings appear to be connected to a scandal in his past, but there is no shortage of red herrings to choose from. The killings continue before a clue is unearthed which exposes the murderer's identity ...

Eyeball would prove to be Umberto Lenzi's last filmic *giallo*; sadly, it would also prove to be his worst effort in the genre.

The Italian title awkwardly attempts to shoehorn the film into the already-passé trend toward "animal-themed" *gialli* popularized by Dario Argento's early thrillers. The title translates as *Red Cats in a Maze of Glass*, and is explained (albeit clumsily) when an eyewitness to one of the crimes describes the red raincoat-garbed assassin as looking like a red cat; talk about colorful metaphors! In any event, the over-reliance on clichés pretty much kills the film dead in its tracks early on, and only a few scenes hint at the flair Lenzi displayed for this type of subject matter in earlier efforts.

In an interview, Lenzi would recall the movie with mixed emotions:

[It] was shot in several poorly equipped locations around Barcelona, with mediocre actors. [...] The film itself is not bad, but its low budget shows.[1]

Given the director's less-than-enthusiastic opinion of **Spasmo** (1974), it is a little surprising to see that he did not view this project with the same attitude. Just going by what is onscreen, it seems that his interest in the project was minimal at best. He overdoes the zoom shots, revels in cultural stereotypes (John Bartha in the role of an American tourist is seldom seen without his cowboy hat and cigar clenched between his teeth), works in a gratuitous lesbian love angle (thus allowing for some salacious imagery) and generally allows the film to unfold in a slack and unimaginative fash-

Italian *locandina* for *Eyeball*; artwork by Renato Casaro.

elogue views of the city, thus padding the running time to no discernible effect. The pacing is also rather slow and there is plenty of unintended humor to boot.

Bruno Nicolai's soundtrack is one of the few truly inspired elements on display. Nicolai's score works hard to build suspense where none exists and his catchy themes certainly detract from some of the tedium. The cinematography by Antonio Millán is unremarkable and fails to capitalize on any of the potential for mood and atmosphere, while the production values do indeed betray the haste with which the production was assembled, as Lenzi correctly indicated.

John Richardson and Martine Brochard head the cast. The latter is saddled with an unflattering hairstyle and a godawful pair of oversized sunglasses, but at least she gives a decent performance in the pivotal role of Paulette. The role is more extensive than the usual damsel-in-distress routine and she acquits herself very well under the circumstances. The same cannot be said for Richardson, who nevertheless delivers exactly the type of performance one would expect from him: dull and wooden. The supporting cast includes such familiar faces as Jorge Rigaud, Fulvio Mingozzi and Tom Felleghy, while Andrés Mejuto plays the role of the crotchety inspector who is looking forward to retirement. Spanish horror buffs will be pleased to note the presence of the beautiful Mirta Miller, who appeared in several of Paul Naschy's most popular vehicles, including *Dr. Jekyll vs. the Werewolf* (1972) and *Count Dracula's Great Love* (1973). Miller participates in the film's lesbian subplot and gets a gratuitous nude scene or two into the mix. Here again, at the risk of sounding sexist, it is moments like these that help to make the film bearable.

Lenzi would later direct the American-made *Hitcher in the Dark* (1989), which is often erroneously listed as a *giallo*; instead, it is a fairly generic horror flick with very little of the director's dynamic craftsmanship in evidence. He would however ultimately stumble upon a successful career as a *giallo* novelist after retiring from the movies.

Notes:
1. Palmerini, Luca M. and Gaetano Mistretta, Spaghetti Nightmares (Florida: Fantasma Books, 1996), p. 69.

Giochi erotici di una famiglia per bene (Italy)

Aka *Juegos eroticos amorales*

Directed by Francesco Degli Espinosa; Screenplay by Renato Polselli; Director of Photography: Angelo Baistrocchi; Editor: Roberto Colangeli; Music by Felice Di Stefano and Gianfranco Di Stefano

Main Players: Donald O'Brien (Professor Riccardo Rossi); Erika Blanc (Eva); Malisa Longo (Elisa Rossi); Maria D'Incoronato (Barbara)

ion. There is a memorable murder scene set inside a carnival funhouse, but beyond that the images are generally flat and functional with none of the nervous energy one can expect to find in his better pictures, notably the many rip-roaring *poliziotteschi* he was making around this same time.

The final reveal of the killer's identity makes for an agreeable twist, though the perpetrator's rationale for plucking out an eye from each victim is on the laughable side. Sadly, it proves to be one of the few real surprises in the film. The shocks are telegraphed throughout and, in lieu of interesting characters, there is not much of an opportunity to generate a lot of suspense. Lenzi indulges in plenty of trav-

Professor Riccardo Rossi is an upstanding member of the community. He is deeply conservative and is morally opposed to everything from divorce to sexual promiscuity, and has established a reputation based on the courage of his convictions. However, when he discovers that his wife, Elisa, is having an affair, all bets are off and he kills her sooner than go through a divorce and sully his reputation. He then starts receiving threatening phone calls and begins seeing strange things, pushing him ever closer to the brink of madness ...

While watching *Giochi erotici di una famiglia per bene*, one would be forgiven for thinking it was an unusually low-key Renato Polselli movie. After all, Italy's premiere master of the odd and outré was responsible for providing the story and the screenplay for this mixture of sex, horror and *giallo* elements. In the hands of another director, however, it does not play out in quite so bizarre a fashion as it may have done with Polselli at the helm.

The story offers up a critique of the hypocrisy of the bourgeois class, with its pompous protagonist serving as a moral crusader who decries the sorry state of the society in which he lives. He finds divorce to be a horrible concept, and when one person suggests that not all marriages are created equal and some simply do not withstand the test of time, his reply is a curt but revealing, "Well, that doesn't concern me." Fair enough, but due to the fact that this prig is in a position of influence and authority which enables him to support a bill which is seeking to outlaw divorce, it is plain to see that his petty prejudices are not simply a matter of personal taste but a means to an end which can affect others as well. Very little sympathy is generated for the character, however, making it clear that Polselli and director Francesco Degli Espinosa are using him as an opportunity to poke fun at the moral crusader types which inflict themselves on every culture and society.

The mystery angle is coherently plotted by Polselli's standards, but the end result does not really offer up enough surprises to make it worthwhile. There is not much in the way of violence, though the filmmakers do not skimp on the sleaze, which is consistent with Polselli's M.O. Director Degli Espinosa handles the movie in a rather flat but brisk fashion. The pacing is good and the film certainly cannot be accused of being overlong, only clocking in at around 80 minutes, but there is not much in the way of aesthetic value. Polselli himself would have indulged in more elaborate and over-the-top imagery, but on the other hand there is always a chance that the story would have become more muddled, and the dialogue more prone to pretentious pseudo-intellectual gibberish.

Production values are very slim indeed, with much of the film confined to the same unimaginatively dressed set standing in for Rossi's home. Special effects work is virtually non-existent and the music score neither propels nor damages the picture; it is simply there. On the whole, the movie looks cheap and impoverished, which it most certainly was.

The small ensemble performs capably enough. Donald O'Brien is Professor Rossi, and he is rather good at playing the character's stiff-necked, unduly proud aspects but overacts a little when it comes to conveying his deteriorating mental state. Born in France in 1930, he was the son of Irish parents who had settled in that country. O'Brien, whose real first name was Donal but who later had it changed to Donald since it was often misspelled as such, began appearing in films and television in the 1950s. Early on, he landed roles in

Italian *locandina* for *Giochi erotici di un famiglia per bene*; artist unknown.

major films by the likes of Robert Bresson (*The Trial of Joan of Arc*, 1962) and John Frankenheimer (*The Train*, 1964), but by the end of the 1960s he would become a staple in Italian genre cinema. He was featured in such Spaghetti Westerns as Sergio Sollima's *Run, Man, Run* (1968) and Lucio Fulci's *Four of the Apocalypse* (1975), as well as war films like Enzo G. Castellari's *The Inglorious Bastards* (1977) and the borderline *giallo*, *Sex of the Witch* (1973). O'Brien also appeared in the notorious *Zombie Holocaust* (1980), which was later sold in America under the irresistible moniker of *Dr. Butcher, M.D.*, with O'Brien's character name of Dr. Obrero being adjusted accordingly. He suffered a devastating setback that year when he was involved in a nasty car crash which left him paralyzed for a period of time, but he rallied and went back to work, albeit in less strenuous roles. He stopped acting in the mid-1990s, and reportedly died in 2003, though some sources indicate that he is still among the living. Erika Blanc is on hand to play the prostitute that Rossi engages after he "liberates" himself from his wife. Blanc looks terrific and smolders with raw sexuality, but the character does not have a lot of meat to her (pardon the pun) and she is mostly consigned to modeling eye-catching outfits and go-go boots when not completely naked. Malisa Longo does not engender a tremendous amount of sympathy as Rossi's unfaithful wife, but performs her role efficiently and makes for a striking presence regardless. Longo made her debut in Antonio Margheriti's **Naked You Die** (1968) and would later appear in the dismal *The Red Monks* (1988), footage of which would be reworked into Lucio Fulci's *A Cat in the Brain* (1990).

Director Francesco Degli Espinosa was born in Rome in 1933. He began working in films in the 1950s as a production assistant, and then he rose through the ranks to become a writer and director as well. He was not terribly prolific and extant filmographies only credit him with two efforts as a director, the other being a not-terribly-well-remembered Spaghetti Western boldly titled *Once Upon a Time in the Wild, Wild West* (1973), which he signed as Enzo Matassi.

The Killer Must Kill Again
(Italy)

Aka *L'assassino è costretto ad uccidere ancora; Il ragno; The Dark is Death's Friend*

Directed by Luigi Cozzi; Produced by Sergio Gobbi and Umberto Lenzi [as Umberto Linzi]; Screenplay by Luigi Cozzi and Daniele Del Giudice; Director of Photography: Riccardo Pallottini; Editor: Alberto Moro; Music by Nando De Luca

Main Players: George Hilton (Giorgio); Antoine Saint-John [as Michel Antoine] (Killer); Femi Benussi (Blonde); Cristina Galbó (Laura); Eduardo Fajardo (Inspector); Alessio Orano (Luca)

Home Video: Mondo Macabro (Region free DVD)

Giorgio witnesses a killer disposing of his victim's corpse. Sensing an opportunity to indulge in some blackmail, he compels the killer to murder his wife and get rid of the body, while Giorgio plays it off as a kidnapping to the police and his wealthy father-in-law. Things become complicated when Luca and his naïve girlfriend Laura steal the killer's car, complete with the body in the trunk ...

Before he became associated with pulpy fantasy films with a juvenile streak, Luigi Cozzi directed one of the great, often unsung, *gialli* of the 1970s. *The Killer Must Kill Again* embroiders on the terrain popularized by his "mentor," Dario Argento, and in so doing he creates a unique thriller that stands apart from the pack.

The film is distinguished by a nasty edge and a streak of mordant black humor. The characters are an unsavory lot. Nobody really comes close to being truly sympathetic, with the possible exception of the put-upon killer, who is, let us face it, nobody's idea of a true role model. The world the characters inhabit is cold and self-involved, prefiguring the tone of Argento's much later **Opera** (1987). Everybody is on the make in one way or another, and justice is a relative concept. The humorous edge is typified in the chain reaction nature of the narrative, which seems indebted to Mario Bava's **Twitch of the Death Nerve** (1971). One bad act leads to another, which in turns leads to another and then another. The killer's initial crime, which is never really clarified, results in his being blackmailed by Giorgio; he agrees to comply with his requests, but things spiral out of control through a series of extraordinary bad luck. If ever there were a killer in the history of the *giallo* with an unerring ability to be in the wrong place at the right time, it would be the one in this film.

The humorous touches are many and range from the blatant to the subtle. Giorgio and his wife live in an apartment with an overwhelming yellow color-scheme—how very appropriate in the world of the *giallo*! When Giorgio takes the killer to discuss his plan to murder his wife, he picks a cinema that happens to be showing Cozzi's first film, the barely-released sci-fi fantasy *The Tunnel Under the World* (1969), with Cozzi himself in attendance as the projectionist, anxiously peering out from his office to see how the film is going over. Ther fact that they discuss these delicate plans in a public but essentially deserted and innocuous locale could be seen as a little in-joke on the film's inability to find a large audience. Then there is the killer himself, deprived of a name and wearing a hangdog expression that speaks volumes as to his down-trodden place in the world. He is ruthless and efficient, but his timing is awful. After killing Giorgio's wife, he stuffs her corpse in the trunk, then goes back inside the house to remove all traces of his having been there; when he comes back outside to dispose of the body, he finds that the car has been stolen. Later, he catches up with the thieves and doles out a little retribution, but things are complicated yet again by the arrival of a ditzy hitchhiker. And so it goes.

The film is not shy about playing things in a mean and nasty key, however. The generally unsympathetic characters stabbing each other in the back is nothing new to the *giallo*, but Cozzi arguably takes things a step further. The nameless killer is almost presented in a pitiable fashion, and yet he has elements to him that are truly skincrawling. When we first meet him, he is seen putting the body of his first victim into a car. He takes his time arranging the body, touching the girl's lifeless thighs and breasts in a way that suggests a queasy necrophiliac undercurrent. Later, he and Giorgio are seen talking shop at an ice-skating rink and he leers in a sleazy manner at a young girl practicing on the ice. His implied perversion finally comes to the fore when he tracks Luca and Laura, the would-be juvenile delinquents who steal the car, to their seaside get-away. Cozzi indulges in some very effective cross-cutting, as he contrasts two similar yet very different actions. The killer rapes the terrified Laura while Luca indulges in some backseat screwing with the hitchhiker he picks up while supposedly getting Laura something to eat. Luca's sleazy, sex-obsessed persona comes off as unfavorably as the killer's, in his own way, and reaches an apex of poor taste when he brings the blonde back to the house hoping to get a little *ménage à trois* action going. Given the implication that Laura is still a virgin and has been seen fighting off Luca's clumsy advances, his grossly inappropriate behavior comes off as calculated compared to the killer's more vengeance-minded actions. Ultimately, the contrast between these two scenes is very effective and tends to linger in the mind on a more emotionally resonant level than your typical *giallo*.

Cozzi handles the movie with precision. The narrative is interesting and loaded with twists and turns, but it never sacrifices logic in favor of shock effect. The pacing is smooth and steady throughout. Cozzi does not go in for the kind of overtly stylized visuals one expects from Bava or Argento, but the film is well photographed by Riccardo Pallotini. According to Cozzi's commentary on the Mondo Macabro DVD release, the project was cash-strapped, but this is never evident in the finished product. The expert editing and an appropriately stark soundtrack by Nando De Luca add to its ultimate appeal.

The director was able to assemble an impressive cast for the picture. Top-billed George Hilton is really more of a guest star here. He is nevertheless excellent as the cold, calculating, money-hungry Giorgio. Hilton's ability to move from playing sympathetic characters to ones less so made him among the genre's most valuable staple players, and he certainly pulls out all the stops by reveling in the character's devious nature. Antoine Saint-John (billed as Michel Antoine) plays the real lead in the role of the killer. Saint-John's naturally distinctive features, with hollow cheeks, high cheek bones and expressive eyes, made him an inspired piece of casting for the role, and it is surprising that other filmmakers did not follow suit; he really should have become more of a genre icon in the long run. Born in France in 1940, Saint-John be-

Italian *locandina* for *The Killer Must Kill Again*; artist unknown.

gan appearing in films in 1971. One of his first roles was as the Mexican General in Sergio Leone's *Duck You Sucker* (1971), which is the instance where he caught Cozzi's eye. Saint-John would adopt several different names for his movie credits, including Domingo Antoine and Antoine St. John, but his distinctive features ensured that he stood out in all of them, even in minor roles. He was featured in big-budget fare like John Milius' *The Wind and the Lion* (1975), starring Sean Connery, but is best remembered by genre fans for his appearance as the ill-fated painter who unlocks the gates of hell in Lucio Fulci's *The Beyond* (1981). He seems to have stopped making films in the 1980s, but according to Cozzi's commentary on the Mondo Macabro DVD release of the title under review, he was always more of a theater actor. Eduardo Fajardo (**Knife of Ice**, 1972) is very good as the wily Inspector who knows that Giorgio is not to be trusted, while Femi Benussi brings an unexpectedly touching *naïveté* to her role as the hitchhiker who gets mixed up in the mayhem. The two youths who steal the car and may or may not live to regret it are played by Cristina Galbó and Alessio Orano, both of whom put in good performances. Galbó was born in Spain in 1950 and began appearing in films while yet a child. In the late 1960s and 1970s, she performed in a number of popular genre entries, including Narcisco Ibáñez Serrador's stylish borderline *giallo The House That Screamed* (1969), Jorge Grau's brilliant *Let Sleeping Corpses Lie* (1974) and Massimo Dallamano's **What Have You Done to Solange?** (1972). One of her last roles was in the Eugenio Martín horror thriller *Supernatural* (1983), which is also sometimes lumped in with the *giallo* genre. She stopped making films in the 1980s and, according to some sources, has since gone into flamenco dancing. Alessio Orano was born in 1945 and made his big-screen debut in Damiano Damiani's *The Most Beautiful Wife* (1970), where he met actress Ornella Muti, whom he would marry in 1975; they divorced in 1981. Orano's striking looks made him well-suited to ambiguous characters, typified by his role in Mario Bava's *Lisa and the Devil* (1973); initially presented in a sympathetic light, he is ultimately revealed to be a necrophile and a murderer. His career seemed to lose steam in the late 1970s, but he returned to the *giallo* in 1990 with an appearance in Lamberto Bava's TV film **Eyewitness** (1990). He has been retired since the 1990s.

Director Luigi Cozzi was born in Busto Arsizio in 1947. He became interested in films as a child and parlayed this passion into a full-time career. He made his directing debut with *The Tunnel Under the World*, then turned his attention to writing about the cinema, praising and interviewing marginalized filmmakers like Mario Bava and Antonio Margheriti long before it became fashionable to do so. Cozzi's friendship with Dario Argento turned into a life-long business partnership, beginning with his collaborating on the screenplay for **Four Flies on Grey Velvet** (1971) and serving as assistant director and bit-part actor in the film as well. They would continue to collaborate on everything from **Door into Darkness** (1973) and *Le cinque giornate* (1973) to **Phenomena** (1985) and **The Stendhal Syndrome** (1996) and would become partners in a successful Rome-based cinema shop, "Profondo Rosso," which was named after one of Argento's most popular films. Cozzi would continue to make movies on his own, as well, often under the name of Lewis Coates; but while Argento favored more serious fare, Cozzi's love for fantasy, science fiction and trash cinema nudged him in a different, more light-hearted direction. Among his more popular works are the sci-fi adventure *Starcrash* (1978), the *Alien* (1979) cash-in *Contamination* (1980) and the Lou

Ferrigno vehicles *Hercules* (1983) and *The Adventures of Hercules II* (1985). Cozzi's last directing credits to date are the Dario Argento documentaries *Dario Argento: Master of Horror* (1991) and *Il mondo di Dario Argento 3: Il museo degli orrori di Dario Argento* (1997), but there have been rumblings of more projects being in store. His final foray in the *giallo* field was in the Argento-produced TV series **Turno di notte** (1987).

The Police Are Blundering in the Dark (Italy)

Aka *La polizia brancola nel buio*

Directed by Pasquale Elio Palumbo (as Helio Colombo); Screenplay by Elio Palumbo; Director of Photography: Giancarlo Pancaldi; Editor: Francesco Bertuccioli; Music by Aldo Saitto

Main Players: Joseph Arkim (Giorgio D'Amato); Gabriella Giorgelli (Lucia); Elena Veronese (Sara); Francisco Cortéz

A paralyzed photographer-cum-inventor invites some models to his villa for a shoot. When the girls start turning up dead, reporter Giorgio D'Amato begins to investigate ...

The Police Are Blundering in the Dark starts off with a scene that can almost be taken as a parody of the genre's excesses. A woman asks a passerby to help her with her flat tire, and the director cuts to some clunky subjective, handheld camerawork, cueing the viewer that a killing is about to take place. During the clumsily staged attack, the killer tears at the woman's shirt, tearing it open and revealing her breasts (good thing she does not appear to believe in wearing a bra!). This results in some footage of the woman running for her life, her breasts bouncing up and down, as the killer follows suit. A poorly staged murder scene then follows, with some unconvincing stage blood working overtime to sell the illusion of a throat slicing. The problem is, it is not meant to be funny ... and the film has only just begun.

It would be nice to say that the film improves after this point, but that would be dishonest. What unfolds is a truly bizarre mishmash of *giallo*, erotic and sci-fi elements that comes close to defying description. In some respects, it manages to outdo the likes of **La bambola di Satana** (1969), **Blackmail** (1974), **Ordine firmato in bianco** (1974) and **The Bloodsucker Leads the Dance** (1975), making it arguably the worst of the *gialli* from the genre's "golden age." It is not a badge that anybody associated with the film should wear with pride, but it does make it stick out from the rest of the pack!

The title would seem to suggest a *poliziottesco*, which is all the more surprising given that the police play only a very minor role in the proceedings. The film clocks in at less than 80 minutes, and yet it feels much longer. Even at such a short duration, it is loaded with filler: lengthy shots of characters

Italian *locandina* for *The Police Are Blundering in the Dark*; artist unknown.

looks like a grade Z 1970s porn film, albeit withtout the "action." As if that is not bad enough, director Helio Colombo saps the interest of virtually every scene by showing a complete lack of insight into the cinematographic process. The pacing is not just slow … it crawls. The final unveiling is a spectacular cheat too, as it relies on the ludicrous notion that one of the characters has developed a machine which can photograph people's thoughts! Well, if you open the door to that kind of plotting, then all bets are truly off and writer Ernesto Gastaldi's oft-vocalized complaint that too many *gialli* cheat the audience sounds more on the money than ever.

Sources differ on the film's original production date, with Antonio Bruschini and Stefano Piselli indicating 1972 in their book *Giallo & Thrilling All'Italiana (1931-1983)* and the website *Nocturno* specifying 1973. Regardless, the film, which had been shot under the bizarre title of *Il giardino delle lattughe* (which literally translates as *The Lettuce Garden*!)[1], would sit on the shelf for several years before seeing the light of day; perhaps it would have been better for everybody if it had stayed buried. Director Helio Colombo (birth name: Pasquale Elio Palumbo) was a producer in the music field. He made this film hoping to break into the movie industry as well, but clearly learned a valuable lesson in the process; he never had anything to do with any further film endeavors.

Notes:
1. http://www.nocturno.it/news/i-gialli-di-confine

Reflections in Black (Italy)

Aka *Il vizio ha le calze nere; El vicio tiene medias negras; Vice Wears Black Hose*

Directed by Tano Cimarosa; Produced by Giovanni Carrino; Screenplay by Adriano Bolzoni and Luigi Latini de Marchi; Director of Photography: Marcello Masciocchi; Editor: Romeo Ciatti; Music by Carlo Savina

Main Players: John Richardson (Inspector Lavina); Dagmar Lassander (Leonora Anselmi); Ninetto Davoli (Marco); Magda Konopka (Contessa Orselmo); Giacomo Rossi-Stuart (Anselmi); Daniela Giordano (Concetta); Tano Cimarosa (Detective)

A woman is slashed to death when she opens her door in the middle of the night. Inspector Lavina begins to investigate the crime, but before he can uncover many clues, another woman is killed in a similar fashion. It is soon determined that the women have a link in common and that the killer likely is planning to target some other victims as well...

Reflections in Black wallows in sleaze to no genuine effect, but this at least gives it a certain seedy appeal, which is absent in the worst *gialli* of the period. It may be trash, but at least it is honest trash.

The screenplay is a muddle of clichés with very little in the way of invention. The final twist reaches back to *Psycho*

sitting around doing nothing in particular. One is reminded of the less-inspired works of director Jess Franco, who will sometimes dwell on insignificant sequences to a maddening degree when his films do not have enough plot to fill the running time.

Production values are non-existent, make-up effects fail to convince, the photography is atrocious, the acting is insulting and the dialogue is downright laughable. It basically

45

(1960) for some inspiration, and this admittedly provides the film with one of its few genuine surprises.

On the whole, the film is barely competent in its execution. The pace is slow and the main thrust of the narrative is sidelined by plenty of Sapphic loving, but perhaps this is just as well; the only time the film really perks up at all is when it gets down and dirty on this front. The production values are slim and none of the technical credits stand out as being more than average.

The cast includes a number of familiar faces, none of whom are given a chance to shine here. Beautiful Daniela Giordano has just a few minutes of screentime, while genre stalwart Giacomo Rossi-Stuart is on hand to act officious and suspicious. Leading man John Richardson is as lifeless as ever and Dagmar Lassander is lost with a characterization that makes very little sense in the long run; she does appear to enter into the sleazier side of things with some gusto, however.

Director Tano Cimarosa displays little affinity for the genre or for filmmaking altogether. Indeed, it is worth noting that it has since been revealed that he did not actually direct the film at all. Born in Messina in 1922, he entered movies as an actor in 1963. His first standout role was as a member of Lee J. Cobb's Mafia "family" in Damiano Damiani's *Day of the Owl* (1968). He appeared in a number of films, some of them classy (*Cinema Paradiso*, 1988) and some of them far from it (Renato Polselli's *giallo* **Delirium**, 1972). He graduated to directing with this effort, but according to an interview with his assistant on the film, Gianni Siragusa, he did not take to it like a fish to water. He initially planned to shoot in Sicily, but that was vetoed in favor of the more cost-effective San Benedetto del Tronto, a fishing port toward the southern end of Italy. According to Siragusa, Cimarosa was soon overwhelmed by scheduling woes and called upon him to assist; Siragusa ended up handling the technical side of things while Cimarosa focused more on the actors, with Cimarosa cast in a major role as Richardson's goofy but

Italian *fotobusta* card for *Reflections in Black*.

efficient assistant. Cimarosa would go on to direct two more films, at least in name only; rumors abound that he needed bailing-out on those occasions as well, leading him to focus exclusively on acting for the remainder of his career. He passed away in 2008, at the age of 86.

Snapshot of a Crime (Italy)
Aka *Istantanea per un delitto*

Note: This film was never released theatrically and was first seen on home video in 1987.

Directed by Mario Imperoli and Ezio Alovisi (as Arthur Saxon); Screenplay by Mario Brenta, Vito Bruschini and Mario Imperoli; Director of Photography: Luciano Tovoli; Editor: Otello Colangeli; Music by Franco Bixio

Main Players: Erna Schürer (Mirna); Monica Strebel (Claudia); Luis La Torre (Luca); Lorenza Guerrieri (Stefania)

Luca is involved in a relationship with Mirna, when the latter suddenly becomes dissatisfied and dumps him. Looking to ease his pain, Luca begins seeing a model named Stefania. One day, Stefania suggests spicing-up their sex life by setting up a camera to take some snapshots of them indulging in a little S/M. When Stefania goes missing, her friend Claudia believes that Luca has done something terrible. Things become complicated further when Mirna starts sending Luca copies of the rough-sex pictures ...

Snapshot of a Crime has all the ingredients for a twisty and sleazy thriller, but the elements never come together and the end result is an exercise in tedium.

The slowly paced narrative is much too muddled for its own good. The characters and their relationships make very little sense. Luca is a total sleaze who generates no sympathy, while the various women in his life function as little more than window dressing. There is very little suspense to be found and, despite a fair amount of nudity, it is never terribly titillating either.

The film is closer in tone to the sexy *gialli* inspired by *Les Diaboliques* (1955) than it is to the more popular Argento-style thrillers, making it seem like something of a throwback. One of the major problems with the film is its reticence. It is much too timid where it counts, with some very lethargic and unenthusiastic sex scenes and very little in the way of violence. One could overlook these things if the narrative were more engaging, but as it stands it simply limps from one half-hearted set piece to the next.

It is easy to imagine a more enthusiastic filmmaker like Umberto Lenzi or Massimo Dallamano making something interesting out of such material, but director Mario Imperoli is not up to the task. The settings and scenery help to provide some interest, as does the elegant cinematography by Luciano Tovoli. Tovoli was on the rise as one of the country's major cinematographers when this film was made, and he would go from it to collaborating with Michelangelo Antonioni on *The Passenger* (1975). He would then work with Dario Argento

Italian locandina for *Snapshot of a Crime*; artwork by P. Franco.

blank and wooden performance as the mysterious Mirna, while Luis La Torre is equal parts boring and unsympathetic as Luca. With such dull and listless performers (and performances) at its core, the film is obviously handicapped even further, though it was likely a lost cause from the get-go.

Director Mario Imperoli was born in Rome in 1931. He appears to have been active for only a brief window of time, from 1970 until his death in 1977 at the age of 46. He was also responsible for the borderline *giallo Mia moglie un corpo per l'amore* (1973), as well as the *poliziottesco Come Cani Arrabbiati* (1976).

Unfortunately, the film would sit on the shelf for years, never attaining any kind of theatrical release and only being released in Italy on VHS in 1987. This was not due to its quality, however. As weak as it is, the result is certainly better than some of the other ones that did get a theatrical release. No doubt it was simply down to financial woes on the part of the production company. When the time finally came to complete the picture, it was entrusted to Ezio Alovisi. Born in Rome in 1933, Alovisi has worked primarily in the theater and in television. His function was basically that of post-production supervisor, though the final assemblage and presentation of the material is his; as such, the credits list it as an "Arthur Saxon" film "realized" by Mario Imperoli.

Strip Nude for Your Killer (Italy)

Aka *Nude per l'assassino; Desnuda ante el asesino; Nue pour l'assassin; Der geheimnisvolle Killer*

Directed by Andrea Bianchi; Screenplay by Andrea Bianchi and Massimo Felisatti; Director of Photography: Franco Delli Colli; Editor: Francesco Bertuccioli; Music by Berto Pisano

Main Players: Edwige Fenech (Magda Cortis); Nino Castelnuovo (Carlo Bianchi); Femi Benussi (Lucia Cerrazini); Solvi Stubing (Patrizia); Franco Diogene (Maurizio Montani); Erna Schürer (Doris)

Home Video: Blue Underground (All region Blu-ray); Shameless Screen Entertainment (Region free DVD)

A fashion model dies during a botched abortion and it is covered up and made to look like a death from natural causes. Later on, a maniac begings targeting the models and employees of the agency with whom she was employed ...

The title says it all: *Strip Nude for Your Killer* does not aspire to be great art, but it can be seen as fun, kitschy entertainment. How many *gialli* include the sight of an obese male victim being killed off in his tightie-whities, let alone end on a tasteless gag about anal sex? Add in plenty of J&B Whisky plugs and you have yourself a rip-roaring good time.

Genre specialist Massimo Felisatti devised the cheerfully lurid scenario. Born in 1932, Felisatti entered films as a writer in 1969; his other *giallo* credits include *The Weekend*

on *Suspiria* (1977), helping the director to create a searing palette of primary colors that literally popped off the screen, in addition to revisiting the *giallo* with Luigi Comencini's *The Sunday Woman* (1975) and Argento's *Tenebrae* (1982). How he came to be involved in a minor B film such as this is open to speculation, but no doubt he was in between jobs at the time; it is to the film's benefit that he was available, regardless, as his lighting gives the picture an atmosphere and sense of class that it otherwise would not have had in its favor. There is also a decent music score from Franco Bixio. Bixio would also collaborate on a number of soundtracks with Vince Tempera and Fabio Frizzi, including the Lucio Fulci films *Four of the Apocalypse* (1975) and the *giallo The Psychic* (1977); the main theme heard over the credits is, in fact, a variation on one of the songs heard in *Four of the Apocalypse*.

The cast is as uninspiring as the material, unfortunately. Erna Schürer (*La bambola di Satana*, 1969) gives her usual

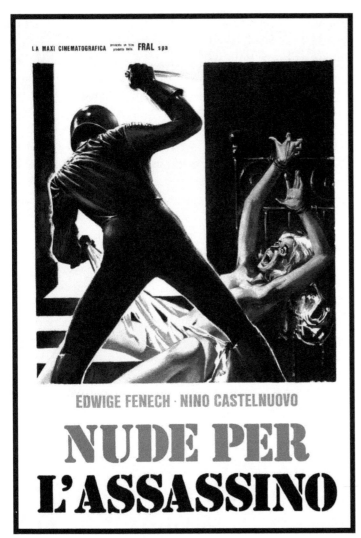

Italian *locandina* for *Strip Nude for Your Killer*; artwork by "Symeoni"/Sandro Simeoni.

Murders (1970), *The Night Evelyn Came Out of the Grave* (1971) and *Calling All Police Cars* (1975). In an interview included on the Blue Underground Blu-ray release of the film, Felisatti notes that the loosening standards in censorship resulted in a glut of films with salacious content. This is especially evident in the thriller genre, which presented ample opportunity for sensational imagery, especially where sexually twisted maniacs and sexually promiscuous victims were concerned. *Strip Nude for Your Killer* was therefore part of a trend which would later climax (pardon the pun) with even more graphically sexual entries, some of which would even cross the line into hardcore, including the infamous *Giallo a Venezia* (1979), directed by Mario Landi. As Felisatti explains in the interview, however, the titles were amended to reflect the input of director Andrea Bianchi when it became clear that the sexualized component of the violence far exceeded the scripter's original intentions. In essence, the film would become too lurid even for the tastes of its original screenwriter!

The story incorporates an anti-abortion theme but, fortunately, does not dwell too much on parochial attitudes toward sex and sexuality. Given that so much of the running time is devoted to various trysts and leering images of the

various actresses removing their clothes, it would have been hypocritical for Felisatti and Bianchi to push too much in the way of a conservative message. As it stands, the film is less interesting as a mystery than as a brazen slice of sexploitation. Original ideas are few and far between; the killer's get-up even copies that seen in Massimo Dallamano's *What Have They Done To Your Daughters?* (1974). That said, the film's shameless lack of taste and tact is truly remarkable. Nothing is remotely subtle about the sexploitation angle, and the violence has a truly seedy dimension that makes it one of the more memorably unpleasant examples of its genre. Breasts and penises are sliced and amputated, one victim is violated anally by a knife and so on. It may be tacky and sordid, but truly, what do you expect from a film with such a title as this?

On the upside, it is definitely one of the more polished and professional examples of the sleazy *giallo* subgenre. Franco Delli Colli's cinematography is crisp and clear throughout and, if it does not offer up any stunning images *per se*, it at least gives the film the semblance of class. Production values are quite decent and the make-up effects by Marcello Di Paolo are convincing. Berto Pisano contributes a catchy soundtrack, which effectively underlines the seedier aspects of the story.

The cast includes *giallo* queen Edwige Fenech in her last thriller appearance of the decade. By this stage in her career, Fenech had proven to be a capable comedienne and was quite busy with lighter, frothier fare like Nando Cicero's *The Sexy Schoolteacher* (1975). Fenech is in good form as the photographer/aspiring model who helps investigate the murders. She looks absolutely ravishing, appears unembarrassed in her many nude and sexy scenes and does her best to add a bit of depth to a character that is pretty much all surface. Nino Castelnuovo does what he can as the so-called hero, but he is such an irritating sex-hound that he does not stand much of a chance with regards to winning over audience sympathy early on. He had already appeared in *Psychout for Murder* (1969), but this would mark his final foray into the *giallo*. The supporting cast includes Femi Benussi and Erna Schürer, both of whom had already had ample exposure in the genre; they continue the trend here, with Benussi making for a likable presence who does not have nearly enough to do and Schürer giving her usual blank slate of a performance.

Director Andrea Bianchi was born in Rome in 1925. He began writing and directing films in 1971, initially taking credit on Italian co-productions directed by foreign directors for quota purposes (including *Treasure Island*, directed by John Hough and starring Orson Welles and *What the Peeper Saw*, directed by James Kelley and starring Mark Lester, Britt Ekland and Hardy Krüger). His first "proper" directing gig came with the infamous *poliziottesco Cry of a Prostitute* (1974), starring Henry Silva and Barbara Bouchet; Bianchi's propensity for politically incorrect violence and a generally sexist disposition came through loud and clear his first time out the gate. His work would almost always have a sexploitation angle, including his bizarre blend of sex and zombies, *Burial Ground: Nights of Terror* (1981), which is almost certainly his most "beloved" film. He has been inactive since the mid-1990s.

The Sunday Woman
(Italy/France)

Aka *La donna della domenica; La mujer del domingo; La femme du dimanche; Die Sonntagsfrau*

Directed by Luigi Comencini; Produced by Marcello D'Amico; Screenplay by Agenori Incrocci (as Age) and Furio Scarpelli (as Scarpelli), based on the novel by Carlo Fruttero and Franco Lucentini; Director of Photography: Luciano Tovoli; Editor: Antonio Siciliano; Music by Ennio Morricone

Main Players: Marcello Mastroianni (Commissioner Salvatore Santamaria); Jacqueline Bisset (Anna Carla Dosio); Jean-Louis Trintignant (Massimo Campi); Aldo Reggiani (Lello Riviera); Maria Teresa Albani (Virginia Tabusso); Claudio Gora (Garrone)

When architect Garrone is murdered, Police Commissioner Santamaria is assigned to investigate. His inquiry takes him into the upper echelons of Turin society. At the top of the list of suspects are Anna Carla Dosio and her homosexual friend Massimo Campi. When Santamaria begins to close in on the truth, the killer strikes again ...

A few entries in this book could have easily gone into the borderline chapter. *The Sunday Woman* is one such film. It has the elements one associates with the *giallo*, but its treatment is far from orthodox and the end result is more comic than thrilling or suspenseful.

The story was adapted from the novel of the same name, written by Carlo Fruttero and Franco Lucentini, by the distinguished screenwriting duo of Age and Scarpelli. The two writers had a hand in the scenarios for such hits as Mario Monicelli's Oscar-nominated *Big Deal on Madonna Street* (1958), Alberto Lattuada's *Mafioso* (1962) and Sergio Leone's epic Spaghetti Western *The Good, The Bad and The Ugly* (1966), but this was the closest they ever came to penning a proper *giallo*.[1] As one might expect from their other credits, they latched onto the more comic and idiosyncratic elements, resisting the urge to go in for typical *giallo* tropes, though the nature of the murder which sets the plot into motion is lurid enough on its own. To be blunt, the victim, a man known for his insatiable sexual appetites, is bludgeoned to death with a large stone phallus. This leads to an amusing scene wherein the bemused Santamaria has to pay a visit to the eccentric sculptor responsible for crafting the offending member (so to speak), who in turn treats the policeman to a tour of his workshop, which is littered with similar statues of various sizes and colors.

The bulk of the film is dedicated to exposing the more unsavory side of its posh, upper-class characters. The setting of the narrative is specified as Turin, but one could argue that the critique of the idle rich could just as easily be applied to other cities and cultures as well. The various members of the pampered elite complain about the heat, bemoan the lack of competent and trustworthy servants and generally stab each other in the back at the drop of a hat. They pose as moral and upright, but they engage in all manner of illicit activities by way of recreation and generally come off as a hypocritical group of self-absorbed bastards. The intrusion of the working-class police inspector bothers them partly because it puts a cramp on their style and partly because he is obviously not "one of them." Anna Carla likens the police to the Mafia, a comparison that the good-natured Santamaria is quick to laugh off, but there is a clear implication that he is seen as a member of the middle-class and, as such, is automatically inferior; indeed, he is warned by his superiors to tread lightly for this very reason. The police have their place, after all, and it is not amid the "polite" ranks of the upper crust. The commentary is kept light and flippant, however, ensuring that the film does not become a stale polemical piece.

The story basically plays fair by the rules of the genre, however. There is a string of clues for Santamaria to investigate and red herrings are abundant. One of the major clues involves a clever bit of word play that goes over Santamaria's head as it involves a colloquial expression which he is not familiar with. It is likely to go over the head of most viewers, too, if it comes to that, but it is still fair play and is preferable to some of the more unlikely plot twists that burden many lesser *gialli*. The violence quota is minimal, but the lurid nature of the initial killing, coupled with a memorable stalking scene that culminates in another burst of off-screen violence later in the film, helps to keep it rooted in the genre. The final reveal of the killer's identity is surprising but logically developed, while the finale implies quite strongly that none of this has had much of an effect when it comes to changing the petty, backstabbing and superficial ways of the privileged elite.

Director Luigi Comencini displays a deftness of touch throughout. The comedy of (bad) manners is just light enough, while the seedier elements of the scenario are dealt with in a matter-of-fact fashion. The film therefore avoids the more leering, sensationalized approach of other *gialli* while also working as an engaging character piece with a comedic bent. Technically, the film is polished throughout. Luciano Tovoli's expert cinematography yields some impressive views of Turin, while Ennio Morricone contributes a jaunty soundtrack that underlines both the obsessive and comic undertones of the piece.

The characterizations are rich and well delineated and the movie benefits immensely from an excellent cast. Commissioner Santamaria is sharper and more refined than the usual *giallo* flatfoot; he wears nicely tailored suits and presents himself with an air of elegance. This aspect makes him an ideal candidate to infiltrate the world of the rich and jaded, but his working-class background still manifests itself

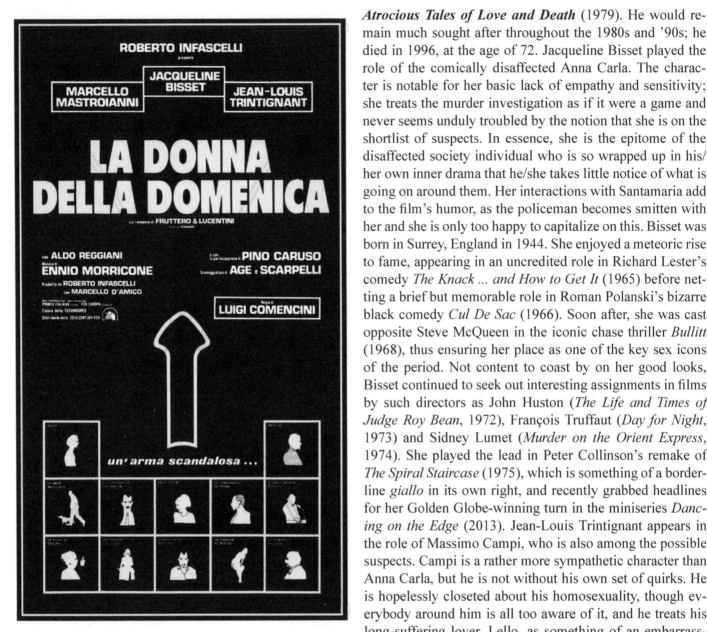

ROBERTO INFASCELLI
presenta

MARCELLO MASTROIANNI   JACQUELINE BISSET   JEAN-LOUIS TRINTIGNANT

LA DONNA DELLA DOMENICA

dal romanzo di FRUTTERO & LUCENTINI

con ALDO REGGIANI   e con la partecipazione di PINO CARUSO
Musica di ENNIO MORRICONE   Sceneggiatura di AGE e SCARPELLI

Prodotto da ROBERTO INFASCELLI
con MARCELLO D'AMICO

PRIMEX ITALIANA   FOX EUROPA
Colore della TECHNOSPES
Distribuito dalla 20th CENTURY FOX

Regia di LUIGI COMENCINI

un' arma scandalosa ...

Italian *locandina* for *The Sunday Woman*; artist unknown.

too much for their comfort. Marcello Mastroianni is excellent in the role, though unfortunately his distinctive voice is missing from the film's English-language dub. Mastroianni was born in Lazio, Italy, in 1924. He made his film debut with an uncredited bit part in *Marionette* (1939) and went on to make another unbilled appearance in Vittorio De Sica's neo-realist classic *The Children Are Watching Us* (1944). His star began to rise in the 1950s, culminating when director Luchino Visconti cast him in the lead role of his beautiful *Le Notti Bianche* (1957). He would go on to appear in Visconti's *The Stranger* (1967) and De Sica's *Yesterday, Today and Tomorrow* (1963), but he found his most fruitful collaboration with Federico Fellini, who would cast him in such films as *La Dolce Vita* (1960), *8½* (1963) and *City of Women* (1980). He would be Oscar-nominated for *Divorce Italian Style* (1961), *A Special Day* (1977) and *Dark Eyes* (1987), and would go on to appear in another, similarly impish *giallo*

Atrocious Tales of Love and Death (1979). He would remain much sought after throughout the 1980s and '90s; he died in 1996, at the age of 72. Jacqueline Bisset played the role of the comically disaffected Anna Carla. The character is notable for her basic lack of empathy and sensitivity; she treats the murder investigation as if it were a game and never seems unduly troubled by the notion that she is on the shortlist of suspects. In essence, she is the epitome of the disaffected society individual who is so wrapped up in his/her own inner drama that he/she takes little notice of what is going on around them. Her interactions with Santamaria add to the film's humor, as the policeman becomes smitten with her and she is only too happy to capitalize on this. Bisset was born in Surrey, England in 1944. She enjoyed a meteoric rise to fame, appearing in an uncredited role in Richard Lester's comedy *The Knack ... and How to Get It* (1965) before netting a brief but memorable role in Roman Polanski's bizarre black comedy *Cul De Sac* (1966). Soon after, she was cast opposite Steve McQueen in the iconic chase thriller *Bullitt* (1968), thus ensuring her place as one of the key sex icons of the period. Not content to coast by on her good looks, Bisset continued to seek out interesting assignments in films by such directors as John Huston (*The Life and Times of Judge Roy Bean*, 1972), François Truffaut (*Day for Night*, 1973) and Sidney Lumet (*Murder on the Orient Express*, 1974). She played the lead in Peter Collinson's remake of *The Spiral Staircase* (1975), which is something of a borderline *giallo* in its own right, and recently grabbed headlines for her Golden Globe-winning turn in the miniseries *Dancing on the Edge* (2013). Jean-Louis Trintignant appears in the role of Massimo Campi, who is also among the possible suspects. Campi is a rather more sympathetic character than Anna Carla, but he is not without his own set of quirks. He is hopelessly closeted about his homosexuality, though everybody around him is all too aware of it, and he treats his long-suffering lover, Lello, as something of an embarrassment as a result. Campi is quick to quip and make light of the violence erupting around him, but he is basically shown in a positive light, at least compared to the other members of his class, and Trintignant's winning performance ensures that he steals his scenes with ease. Prolific character actor Claudio Gora plays the murder victim Garrone. Garrone is a cheerfully despicable pervert. He leers and makes lecherous advances to every woman in sight and it truly surprises no one that he comes to a bad end; even so, he is such a colorful character that one hates to see him make an exit so early on. Gora is marvelous in the role, which breaks from his usual run of stuffy authority figures. Born in Genoa in 1913, he began appearing in films in the late 1930s. He featured in Pietro Germi's early borderline *giallo The Facts of Murder* (1959), as well as Umberto Lenzi's ***Seven Bloodstained Orchids*** (1972), in addition to such diverse films as Dino Risi's *Il Sorpasso* (1962, which co-starred Trintignant), Camillo Mastrocinque's *An Angel for Satan* (1966), Mario Bava's *Danger: Diabolik* (1968) and Damiano Damiani's *Confes-*

sions of a Police Captain (1971). He even played the role of the arch-criminal in *The Death Ray of Dr. Mabuse* (1964). Gora also directed a handful of films, including *Eager to Live* (1953), which netted him a Silver Ribbon prize from the Italian National Syndicate of Film Journalists. Among the actors in the cast of that film was none other than Marcello Mastroianni. Gora died in 1998 at the age of 84.

As for director Comencini, he was born in 1916. He started off making documentaries in the late 1930s, then moved into features in the late 1940s. Comencini enjoyed much success and critical acclaim and was nominated for three Palme d'Or awards at the Cannes Film Festival (for *Misunderstood*, 1967, *Delitto d'Amore*, 1974 and *Traffic Jam*, 1979), among other honors. He was a prolific filmmaker and remained active until the 1990s. He died in 2007 at the age of 90. *The Sunday Woman* would remain his only brush with the *giallo*.

Notes:

1. That being said, they also wrote the screenplay for *Double Murder* (1977). Directed by Steno and starring Marcello Mastroianni, Agostina Belli, Peter Ustinov and Ursula Andress, it dealt with a Police Commissioner (Mastroianni) investigating a bizarre double murder in an apartment complex. The tone is comic and the mystery angle is downplayed and of the old-fashioned "whodunit" school, so it does not quite make the cut as a true *giallo*.

The Suspicious Death of a Minor (Italy)

Aka *Morte sospetta di una minorenne; Extraña muerte de una menor*

Directed by Sergio Martino; Produced by Luciano Martino; Screenplay by Ernesto Gastaldi and Sergio Martino; Director of Photography: Giancarlo Ferrando; Editor: Raimondo Crociani; Music by Luciano Michelini

Main Players: Claudio Cassinelli (Paolo Germi); Mel Ferrer (Police Superintendant); Lia Tanzi (Carmela); Adolfo Caruso (Giannino); Gianfranco Barra (Teti); Jenny Tamburi (Gloria); Massimo Girotti (Gaudenzio Pesce); Barbara Magnolfi (Floriana)

A young girl is killed and it transpires that she was connected with an underground racket dedicated to underage prostitutes and drug trafficking. Undercover police officer Paolo Germi teams up with juvenile delinquent Giannino to uncover the mastermind behind the operation, but a hired killer ensures that prospective leads will be unable to talk ...

The Suspicious Death of a Minor is Sergio Martino's oddest *giallo* of the 1970s. Compared to his earlier entries, it bears plenty of signs of hedging its bets. The *giallo*'s popularity was beginning to wane by this time, despite the continued popularity of Dario Argento's works, and this film would therefore straddle the line between two other more overtly bankable genres: comedy and *poliziotteschi*. To say it is an uneasy mixture would be an understatement, but for all its defects the film has plenty to recommend it.

Argento's **Deep Red** (1975) explicitly influenced the movie in several respects. Given that Argento's film hit Italian theaters in March of 1975 and this one was released in August of the same year, this would imply that Martino's film was rushed through pretty quickly. This is hardly unusual in this period of rapid productivity in the Italian movie industry. Argento enjoyed the luxury of being allowed time to prepare and execute his films, while Martino and his peers in the lower end of the Italian popular cinema were accustomed

Italian *locandina* for *The Suspicious Death of a Minor*; artwork by Averardo Ciriello.

Milano: a sprawling metropolis in Northern Italy. Paul Chianese, a tough cop, is fighting single-handed against the city's underworld to solve the murder of a teenage girl. This cop would rather die than admit defeat.

CLAUDIO CASSINELLI   MEL FERRER

and with JENNY TAMBURI   Directed by SERGIO MARTINO

TOO YOUNG TO DIE

Anglo export tradepaper ad for *The Suspicious Death of a Minor*; artist unknown.

to working more quickly. Two of the kill scenes incorporate imagery found in Argento's picture, notably a woman's head being smashed through a pane of glass and the use of boiling water in another scene. The two films even share a running gag involving a rickety old car: in this one, it belongs to the protagonist, while in the Argento classic it belonged to intrepid reporter Gianna Brezzi; the fact that it is a similar make and model in both films, and both are equipped with a faulty door which refuses to open, puts this firmly in the realm of "homage." Similarly, the score by Luciano Michelini betrays a definite Goblin influence. The tremendous popular success of their score for ***Deep Red*** would result in a number of Goblin-esque soundtracks, truth be told, and Michelini's was arguably one of the first to follow their example. Overall, the score would not be out of place in an Italian comedy, but the main title theme, with its use of an obsessively repeated melody and an organ, cannot help but evoke memories of the main theme for Argento's film. In any event, the similarities between the two are generally on the superficial side. ***Deep Red*** took the *giallo* a step closer to the horror genre, while Martino's thriller seems rather mild in comparison.

The screenplay by Martino and *giallo* veteran Ernesto Gastaldi is an interesting grab bag of ideas. The first half of the film could be mistaken for a comic *poliziottesco*, while the bulk of the second half delves more deeply into the sordid and twisty waters of the thriller. The motivation is sexual in nature, but not in the usual way one typically sees in these films. The teenage prostitution racket angle is actually downplayed somewhat compared to the drug trafficking ring. Martino and Gastaldi therefore avoid the more sordid aspects of the story, making it seem particularly restrained compared to the likes of Massimo Dallamano's ***What Have They Done To Your Daughters?*** (1974). The mystery angle is less concerned with who did it (the killer is revealed early on, even if we do not know who he is by name) than with who is orchestrating it. The final reveal puts the film firmly on the same terrain as Dallamano's *giallo/poliziottesco* hybrid, among other *gialli*, by launching an attack on the pampered upper class, who literally profit from the exploitation of the lower class youth. The commentary lacks the sting found in the Dallamano film or in Luigi Comencini's ***The Sunday Woman*** (1975), however, suggesting that Martino and Gastaldi were not as passionate in pursuing their socio-political message.

One of the more pleasing gags involves Giannino taking one of the girls associated with the prostitution ring to a movie theater to meet with Paolo. The film being shown is ***Your Vice is a Locked Room and Only I Have the Key*** (1972). Martino also works in some amusing slapstick, notably during an extended car chase, and the running gag with Paolo breaking his glasses every time he gets a new pair is nicely integrated as well.

As usual, the director does a fine job of keeping the action moving at a good pace. The story proves engaging, if a little too light and insubstantial for its own good, and the occasional bursts of violence are all the more shocking because of the generally amiable tone of the piece. Giancarlo Ferrando's cinematography is slick and professional, while Michelini's score sets the right tone.

The cast is also quite good. Claudio Cassinelli is splendid as the undercover agent with a rebellious streak. The character is similar to the one he played in ***What Have They Done To Your Daughters?*** (1974), but his anger and frustration are comparatively muted here. Even so, he finds himself bucking against the system and his rage over being reined in by his politically connected superiors is much the same as in that earlier effort. Cassinelli displays a flair for light comedy on this occasion that was seldom exploited in other films and he handles the schizophrenic nature of the material with great agility. Second-billed Mel Ferrer does not show up until about the halfway point and is basically stuck in a glorified cameo appearance. He brings his customary presence and authority to the part of Paolo's superior, but it is a dull role and there is not much he can do to enliven it. Ferrer was born in New Jersey in 1917. The son of an affluent family, he attended college at Princeton and tried his hand at everything from writing to dancing on Broadway before making his film debut with an uncredited appearance in *The Fugitive* (1947), directed by John Ford. Ferrer graduated to lead roles in no time, including Fritz Lang's stylish western *Rancho Notorious* (1952) and the popular swashbuckler *Scaramouche* (1952). He appeared in the ill fated Michael Powell and Emeric Pressberger musical *Oh ... Rosalinda!!* (1955) before co-starring with his then-wife Audrey Hepburn in King Vidor's sluggish version of *War and Peace* (1956). Ferrer began gravitating toward European genre films in 1960, when he appeared in the French-Italian production of *Blood and Roses*, directed by Roger Vadim, and the French-British version of *The Hands of Orlac*, co-starring Christopher Lee.[1] Ferrer also enjoyed some success as a director and a producer, notably producing the hit thriller *Wait Until Dark* (1967) as a vehicle for Audrey Hepburn, while his acting appearances began to become more and more confined to the Italian exploitation scene in the 1970s. He would go on to feature in the *giallo* **The Pyjama Girl Case** (1977) and would work again with Martino on *The Great Aligator River* (1979).[2] He has the distinction of appearing in two very different films with basically the same name: in Tobe Hooper's *Eaten Alive* (1977) he added a touch of class as one of the visitors to a strange hotel run by the truly bizarre Neville Brand, while in Umberto Lenzi's *Eaten Alive!* (1980) he added name value to a grisly tale of cannibalism in South America. Ferrer remained active through the 1980s, mostly guest-starring on TV series like *The Love Boat* and popping up in the odd movie of the week, but he worked only sporadically in the 1990s; he died in 2008 at the age of 90. The supporting cast includes roles for Aldo Massasso and Barbara Magnolfi, both of whom would go on to appear in other *gialli*; he would appear in Dario Argento's **Sleepless** (2001), while she would top-line the sleazy **The Sister of Ursula** (1978). Massimo Girotti, who plays the role of a wealthy businessman who seems to be connected to the murders, also puts in a strong performance. Born in 1918, he started out in films in 1940. His first really notable film was Luchino Visconti's *Ossessione* (1943), wherein he played the drifter who is seduced by Clara Calamai into helping dispose of her husband. His good looks and athletic physique made him ideal casting for heroes and villains alike; he would go on to appear in numerous *pepla* (Riccardo Freda's *Sins of Rome*, 1953) in addition to "arty" fare like Visconti's *Senso* (1954) and Bernardo Bertolucci's *Last Tango in Paris* (1972). One of his best roles was as the patriarch in Pier Paolo Passolini's ambiguous parable *Teorema* (1968). He would remain active until his death in 2003 at the age of 84.

Notes:

1. Legend has it that Christopher Lee was the actor Vadim originally had in mind to play the role of Leopoldo De Karstein in *Blood and Roses*.

2. Another Ferrer/Martino connection worth noting: when Roger Corman acquired the rights to Martino's horror-fantasy *Island of the Fishmen* (1979), he decided to cut the film down and hired director Joe Dante (who got his start cutting trailers for Corman) to film a new prologue. Ferrer was hired to play a role in this prologue and the new edit would be released in the U.S. under the title of *Screamers*.

1976

Blazing Magnum
(Italy/Canada)

Aka *Una Magnum Special per Tony Saitta; Spécial magnum; Escándalo en la residencia; Feuerstoß; Strange Shadows in an Empty Room*

Directed by Alberto De Martino [as Martin Herbert]; Produced by Edmondo Amati and Maurizio Amati; Screenplay by Vincenzo Mannino [as Vincent Mann] and Gianfranco Clerici [as Frank Clark]; Director of Photography: Aristide Massaccesi (as Anthony Ford); Editor: Vincenzo Tomassi (as Vincent P. Thomas); Music by Armando Trovajoli

Main Players: Stuart Whitman (Captain Tony Saitta); John Saxon (Sergeant Ned Matthews); Martin Landau (Dr. George Tracer); Tisa Farrow (Julie Foster); Carole Laure (Louise Saitta); Gayle Hunnicutt (Margie Cohn)

When Louise Saitta dies in Montreal, her brother Tony, a hard-nosed Ottawa Police captain, comes to pay his respects. Tony soon discovers that his sister was murdered and sets out to find who was responsible. In so doing, he discovers some things about his sister that he was not expecting ...

This Italian-Canadian co-production offers another variation on the *poliziotteschi/giallo* hybrid. The title and the emphasis on spectacular action set pieces make it an ideal candidate for the *poliziottesco* genre, but the structure of the film is very much rooted in the realm of the "whodunit" and some memorably brutal murder sequences will surely appeal to genre aficionados.

As one may well expect from a film directed by Alberto De Martino, this one does its best to camoflauge its Italian origins. Much of it was filmed on location in Montreal, Quebec, the cast is well stocked with familiar American character actors and it was even shot with direct sound. Only the presence of Armando Trovajoli's cheerfully funky music score and some memorably outré elements indicate that a more "European" sensibility is at work. The end result is notable for its sheer energy and enthusiasm and surely stands among the director's more notable pictures.

The character of Captain Tony Saitta is straight out of a typical *poliziottesco*. He is ruthless, tunnel-visioned and

STUART WHITMAN · JOHN SAXON · MARTIN LANDAU

Special Magnum

TISA FARROW · CAROLE LAURE · JEAN LECLERC
GAYLE HUNNICUTT
Musique de ARMANDO TROVAIOLI · Mise en scène de MARTIN HERBERT · EASTMANCOLOR

Belgian poster for *Blazing Magnum*; artist unknown (artwork modeled after the original Italian poster design).

two-fisted as they come. Unlike the morally righteous characters played in so many of those films by the likes of Franco Nero or Maurizio Merli, however, Saitta is driven by one thing: bull-headed vengeance. Saitta does not care who he hurts or what sort of impact his actions have, he is simply determined to see that he finds the person (or people) responsible for his sister's death. That the script by Vincenzo Mannino and Gianfranco Clerici (who would later work on Lucio Fulci's **The New York Ripper**, 1982) allows this aspect of the film to deepen as the story unfolds is part of its appeal. In Saitta's eyes, Louise is something of a saint and he clings to this idea until the evidence begins to reveal a different side to her that he never knew. As chief suspect Dr. Tracer says at one point, "The people we're closest to are the ones we know the least."

Characterization is not really the film's strong suit, however. Truth be told, much of the kudos for the film's success belong not to De Martino, but to second unit director Rémy Julienne. Born in France in 1930, Julienne entered movies in the mid-1960s as a stunt performer and co-ordinator. He became renowned for his flair for staging and executing high-speed chase sequences, a function he performed in such films as Peter Collinson's *The Italian Job* (1968), Henri Verneuil's *The Burglars* (1971), Stuart Rosenberg's *Love and Bullets* (1979), John Glen's *For Your Eyes Only* (1981) and many

others. He last worked on Ron Howard's *The Da Vinci Code* (2006). Julienne's skills help to make the film's big action set piece, with Saitta chasing a suspect through the streets (among other locales!) of Montreal, into a jaw-dropping *tour-de-force*. The sequence can hold its own compared to more celebrated chase sequences in the likes of Peter Yates' *Bullitt* (1968) and William Friedkin's *The French Connection* (1971) and it really helps to amp up the film's excitement factor. In fairness to De Martino, however, he paces the material very well and stages some memorable sequences on his own. One such moment, with a woman being murdered in front of her blind friend, is particularly powerful.

From a technical perspective, the film has much to recommend. Aristide Massaccesi's cinematography is stylish without being unduly fussy, while Vincenzo Tomassi's editing is crisp and efficient throughout. Trovajoli's score really heightens the thrill aspect of the movie, as well.

American actor Stuart Whitman heads the cast. Whitman has been criticized in some circles for being too old and out-of-shape for the role, but this seems more than a little unfair. Granted, Whitman was not a young man when he made the film, but he still comes off as appropriately intimidating in his fight scenes and has a tremendous presence to boot. Whitman is also a fine actor and is able to convey the character's inner turmoil over his sister's chequered past without resorting to hand-wringing melodramatics. Born in San Francisco in 1928, Whitman earned his rugged persona early on with a stint in the Army, during which he excelled as a lightweight boxer. He started acting on stage and soon caught the eye of casting directors in Hollywood, making his film debut in 1951 with unbilled bit roles in two of the seminal sci-fi films of the period: Rudolph Maté's *When Worlds Collide* and Robert Wise's *The Day the Earth Stood Still*. Whitman's tough guy image made him ideal casting for war films and Westerns, but he impressed critics with his role as a child molester trying to overcome his illness in Guy Green's *The Mark* (1961); he would be nominated for his only Oscar for the film. By the 1970s, he began showing up in various low-budget horror and action films, including Curtis Harrington's *The Cat Creature* (1973), Monte Hellman's *Shatter* (1974), Laurence Harvey's *Welcome to Arrow Beach* (1974) and Tobe Hooper's *Eaten Alive* (1977). He remained active until the year 2000, then retired to a quiet life on his ranch. John Saxon is good as Saitta's friend, Ned Matthews, who works with the Montreal police. It is not a terribly deep role, but Saxon brings his customary presence and charisma to it and he and Whitman have good chemistry in their scenes together. Martin Landau plays principal suspect Dr. Tracer. Landau is very good in the role, though his presence is greatly diminished in the second half of the picture, once the action quota begins to ramp up. Born in Brooklyn in 1928, Landau started off as a cartoonist but developed the acting bug and began appearing in stage productions in the 1950s. He started acting on television in 1953 and made his first film in 1959. One of his earliest roles was as James Mason's gay henchman, Leonard, in Alfred Hitchcock's *North By Northwest* (1959). He alternated between film and TV throughout the 1960s, achieving his greatest visibility as one of the leads on the hit program *Mission: Impossible* (1966-1969). By the 1970s, apart from another cult series *Space: 1999* (1975-1977), he was often appearing in B-grade movies, including a tacky made-for-TV version of *The Fall of the House of Usher* (1979). Stints in cheap horror films both good (*Without Warning*, 1980) and bad (*The Being*, 1983) helped to pay the bills, but he achieved a major comeback when he was cast by Francis Ford Coppola in *Tucker: The Man and His Dream* (1988) and Woody Allen in *Crimes and Misdemeanors* (1989); he would be Oscar-nominated for both roles. He finally won a well-deserved Oscar with his funny but poignant portrayal of the drug-ravaged Bela Lugosi in Tim Burton's fanciful biopic *Ed Wood* (1994). He remains an active presence in films and television. Gayle Hunnicut puts in good performance as the coquettish Margie. Hunnicut was born in Texas in 1943 and started acting in 1966. She married English actor David Hemmings (*Deep Red*, 1975) in 1968 and they were married until 1975. She appeared in a number of films with Hemmings, including the thriller *Fragment of Fear* (1970), and also starred in Peter Collinson's remake of *The Spiral Staircase* (1975). Horror buffs will likely remember her best for her role in John Hough's *The Legend of Hell House* (1973). Tisa Farrow is better than usual as the blind Julie, who helps to unlock the mystery. Farrow was born in Los Angeles in 1951. The daughter of director John Farrow and actress Maureen O'Sullivan, and the younger sister of actress Mia Farrow, she started appearing in films in 1970. Unlike her sister, Tisa's career never really took off and she was mostly restricted to minor roles, including one in Woody Allen's *Manhattan* (1979). She scored her best role in James Toback's *Fingers* (1978), opposite Harvey Keitel, but after appearing in three low-budget Italian genre films (Lucio Fulci's *Zombie*, 1979; Antonio Margheriti's *The Last Hunter*, 1980; Aristide Massaccesi's *Anthropophagus*, 1980) she basically dropped out of sight; rumors abound about what happened to her, ranging from issues with drug addiction to taking up work as a taxicab driver in New York City.

The House with Laughing Windows (Italy)

Aka *La casa dalle finestre che ridono; Das Haus der lachenden Fenster; La maison aux fenêtres qui rient; La porte de l'enfer; The House of the Laughing Windows*

Directed by Pupi Avati; Produced by Antonio Avati and Gianni Minervini; Screenplay by Antonio Avati, Pupi Avati, Gianni Cavina and Maurizio Costanzo; Director of Photography: Pasquale Rachini; Editor: Giuseppe Baghdighian; Music by Amedeo Tommasi

Main Players: Lino Capolicchio (Stefano); Francesca Marciano (Francesca); Gianni Cavina (Coppola); Giulio Pizzirani (Antonio Mazza); Bob Tonelli (Mayor Solmi); Eugene Walter (Priest)

Home Video: Image Entertainment (Region 1 DVD); Shameless Screen Entertainment (Region free DVD)

Stefano journeys to a small village to execute a commission: he is to restore a fresco depicting the martyrdom of Saint Sebastian in the local church. Stefano finds that the painting exudes a strange fascination and, as he investigates the troubled history of its late creator, he realizes that he is digging into some secrets that somebody does not want uncovered...

Many *gialli* are sleazy. Quite a few are absurd. A number are over-the-top. A handful are memorable for their sadism. But only a very precious few dig beneath the surface and succeed in crawling under the skin of the viewer, affecting them on a deep-rooted subconscious level and offering up genuine *frissons* in place of facile shock effects. *The House with Laughing Windows* is one such film.

In an interview included on the Shameless DVD release of the film, co-writer/director Pupi Avati explains that the idea originated from a scary story that used to be told to him and his brother at bedtime. The impact of this childhood tale left a lingering impression, and when he decided he wanted to try his hand at a genre subject, he was able to incorporate elements of it into his scenario. Indeed, as Avati explains in the same interview, the project was born out of sheer desperation following the disappointment of having his film *Bordella* (1976) confiscated by the censors in Italy, who suppressed it for a period of time after deeming it obscene. Looking to come up with a film that could be made quickly and economically in the hopes of salvaging his career, Avati plunged into this movie with a mixture of humility and professional unease. The end result would become the most popular effort of his career.

The film mixes elements of the horror genre with the *giallo*, and for this reason its status as a *giallo* is sometimes contested. It is certainly an unusual example of the Italian thriller, but this is part of its appeal. At its heart, it offers up a puzzle that the protagonist must spend much of the narrative trying to piece together, while an unknown killer (or killers) stalks the sidelines and silences those who may be able to help him in this task. Therefore, it is very much a *giallo* and a very satisfying one at that, though it is also part of a trend toward a more unorthodox approach to the genre which arose, in part, out of a sheer need to take the thriller in different directions as it threatened to become stagnant and repetitive.

Avati's emphasis on the rural aspect of the setting ties the film in with Lucio Fulci's *Don't Torture a Duckling* (1972). These were not the only *gialli* to avoid urban settings, but they were probably the ones that made the best use of the rural landscape. Avati plays up the contrast between the "outsider" figure (the protagonist) and the superstitious

...oggi ho ritratto quella svergognata mentre crepava...

EURO INTERNATIONAL FILMS presenta

LINO CAPOLICCHIO
FRANCESCA MARCIANO
GIANNI CAVINA in

LA CASA DALLE FINESTRE CHE RIDONO

un film di **PUPI AVATI**

con GIULIO PIZZIRANI · VANNA BUSONI · ANDREA MATTEUZZI · BOB TONELLI
PIETRO BRAMBILLA · FERDINANDO ORLANDI

prodotto da **GIANNI MINERVINI** · **ANTONIO AVATI** per la A.M.A. film s.r.l.

colore della TECHNOSPES

GRAFITALIA Editoriale · ROMA ·

Anno di edizione MCMLXVI

Italian *locandina* for *The House with Laughing Windows*; art-work by Piero Iaia.

young people stay there because it is so stagnant and lifeless. There is only one restaurant and nightlife is virtually non-existent. The sense is of a place where time stands still. It also has a definite air of death and decay, which certainly makes sense by the end of the picture.

The mystery angle of the plot is very well plotted and the payoff is truly chilling. Some plot holes become evident on reflection, but chances are that most first-time viewers will not even have much occasion to think about them. On the whole, the story is engrossing and holds together very well; whatever problems it may have are no doubt due to the haste with which the film was put together. Indeed, the fact that it looks as polished and classy as it does is a testimony to the skill of Avati and his collaborators. Only a few overt shock effects are on display, but numerous subtle touches prove to be unnerving; in one scene, Stefano enters an abandoned room and switches on the light, only to see a bag of grain swaying back and forth in the distance—is it swinging due to the wind or has somebody been in there? Similarly, the tape recording Stefano finds of the mysterious painter's paranoid rantings and ravings offer an eerie mixture of the poetic and the profane, with the man's creepy voice creating a definite sense of dread and unease. Avati dispenses with some of the most shocking imagery under the opening titles. A fantasy scene (or is it?) depicting a man being stabbed repeatedly in the style of the fresco of Saint Sebastian announces right off the bat that this is a horror film as well as a thriller, but for the bulk of the picture Avati focuses more on mood and build-up. The revelation at the end lingers, however, as much for what it leaves unanswered as for the unforgettable imagery of what it does show.

Avati paces the action beautifully. He opts for a slow-burn approach, which may seem a little sedate for some viewers, but it works perfectly for this film. Given his almost anthropological approach to detailing the village and its environs, it makes sense that he takes his time establishing the proper mood in order to better understand the actions and attitudes of his characters. Avati filmed the movie with a sparse crew, but everybody rose to the challenge and gave their best. Cinematographer Pasquale Rachini makes excellent use of light and shadow, contrasting the sunny atmosphere of the bucolic countryside with the oppressive nature of the dank, decaying interiors. The mural itself is an alarming sight, notable for its latent sadism, as it seems to bask in the pain and suffering of Saint Sebastian. It is an image that is not easily forgotten. Amedeo Tommasi's score is exceptionally effective, as well.

Lino Capolicchio is excellent as Stefano. He makes the character very sympathetic throughout, even as his growing fixation on the mystery threatens to push him toward insanity. Capolicchio had already appeared in ***Dirty Angels*** (1969) and would go on to star in the far more conventional *giallo* ***The Bloodstained Shadow*** (1978). The supporting cast is small and does not include many familiar faces (though actor/co-writer Gianni Cavina was a regular collaborator of

locals, who regard him with a suspicious eye. The film is by no means a love letter to the rural communities that the village represents; it is implied that incest is a typical way of life in such communities and that people cling to their intolerant and bigoted attitudes. By contrast, Stefano is presented as quiet and studious. He is there to perform a job and is focused on this, though he takes a little time to avail himself of a little romance along the way. Avati does a tremendous job of detailing the atmosphere of the village, which is wrapped-up in a sense of ritual and tradition. It is explained that few

the director's), but one that stands out is Eugene Walter, who plays the small but pivotal role of the village priest, who disapproves of the fresco. Walter is not even billed in the credits, but he certainly deserves mention. Born in Alabama in 1921, he did a stint in the service before immigrating to France in the 1950s; he then relocated to Rome in the 1960s. He made his film debut with an uncredited role in Vincente Minnelli's *Two Weeks in Another Town* (1962). He struck up a friendship with Federico Fellini, which led to roles in *8½* (1963) and *Juliet of the Spirits* (1965), but he was seldom more than a bit-part player. He can also be seen in the *gialli* **The Black Belly of the Tarantula** (1971) and **The Pyjama Girl Case** (1977). He died in 1998 at the age of 76. It should also be noted that rotund co-writer Maurizio Costanzo would turn himself into Italy's foremost talk-show host in a self-titled program which ran for over 25 years.

Director Pupi Avati was born in Emilia-Romagna, in Bologna, in 1938. His childhood was scarred by the bombings and devastation of World War II, but he found solace in movie theaters watching melodramas and genre films, which helped to take his mind away from grim reality. A viewing of Fellini's *8½* (1963) made him determined to become a filmmaker himself, and he entered the industry in the late 1960s as an assistant director. He made his directing debut in 1970 and soon established himself as a highly cultured *auteur* capable of going back and forth from genre to genre, always stamping each project with a deeply personal touch. Horror fans do not quite know what to make of his work; movies like this or his idiosyncratic zombie film *Zeder* (1983) do not exactly hew to the standard conventions and his emphasis on mood and atmosphere over shock effects puts him in a different category from other Italian genre filmmakers. It is this aspect which makes his work so very unique, however, and it can be argued that the review of this movie in *The Encyclopedia of Horror Films* was right on the money when it was suggested that it was he, rather than Argento, who represented Mario Bava's true "spiritual successor" in the field of Italian horror. Avati has always bristled at being pegged down to any one genre, however, and insists that he is no great student of the genre; indeed, it seems likely that it is his lack of interest in following trends that makes his work so fresh. In any event, Avati's canon has attracted critical acclaim and has ranged from comedies and musicals to documentaries and *gialli*; in the latter category he would also direct **Tutti defunti ... tranne i morti** (1977) and write **The Room Next Door** (1994). He has been nominated for many prestigious awards, notably several times as both director and writer for the David Di Donatello Awards (Italy's version of the Oscars), winning for *The Story of Boys & Girls* (1989) and *Incantato* (2003), as well as netting the honorary Luchino Visconti Award in 1995. Avati remains an active presence in the Italian movie industry and is one of the "veteran" players who is able to go back and forth between working in films and television.

Plot of Fear (Italy)

Aka ... *e tanta paura; Terror infinito; Bloody Peanuts*

Directed by Paolo Cavara; Produced by Ermanno Curti, Guy Luongo and Rodolfo Puttignani; Screenplay by Paolo Cavara, Enrico Oldoini and Bernardino Zapponi; Director of Photography: Franco Di Giacomo; Editor: Sergio Montanari; Music by Daniele Patucchi

Main Players: Michele Placido (Inspector Gaspare Lomenzo); Corinne Cléry (Jeanne); Eli Wallach (Pietro Riccio); Quinto Parmeggiani (Angelo Scanavini); John Steiner (Hoffmann); Jacques Herlin (Pandolfi); Tom Skerritt (Chief Inspector); Enrico Oldoini (Lomenzo's assistant)

Home Video: Raro Video (Region free DVD)

When two people with no apparent connection turn up murdered, Inspector Lomenzo is assigned to investigate. At the scene of both crimes, the killer leaves behind an illustration from the children's book "Shockheaded Peter." Eventually it transpires that both victims were connected to a bizarre club with a bent toward sexual fetishes and that both were witness to an unfortunate prank that went horribly awry ...

Plot of Fear is one of the more unusual thrillers of its period. It adopts a gently sardonic approach but it does not pull any punches when it comes to the seedier aspects of its convoluted narrative. The end result is striking and original, to say the least.

According to an interview with co-writer Enrico Oldoini, included on the Raro Video DVD release of the film, the story originated with director Paolo Cavara but was heavily reworked by himself and Bernardino Zapponi. The latter had just collaborated with Dario Argento on **Deep Red** (1975), but anybody viewing this film expecting something along the same lines will be in for a disappointment. The film reworks a similar narrative trope—that is, a book ends up playing a major role in unraveling the mystery—but beyond that, this is a very different type of thriller. Cavara had already delivered one of the best out-and-out Argento imitations with **The Black Belly of the Tarantula** (1971), but here he was clearly motivated to try for something different. In place of the usual "killer-in-black" routine, this one goes for a darkly ironic, deeply paranoid examination of the corrupting influence of power.

In a way, the movie builds on the *poliziotteschi/gialli* hybrids, which had been proliferating since around 1974. Yet while efforts like **What Have They Done To Your Daughters?** (1974) and **Blazing Magnum** (1976) sought to mix the tough, two-fisted nature of the police film with the gory and seedy side of the thriller, this one goes for something a little more off-key. The narrative divides its attention between the "regular" police force, as represented by Inspector Lomenzo, and the private security firms which are in the pocket of the corrupt ruling class. The latter is represented by the cheerfully despicable Pietro Riccio, who lords over his operation like a smiling, benevolent father figure; beneath this cheery exterior, however, is a black heart and bile in the place of blood. Cavara does not focus much on elaborate action scenes or artfully choreographed massacres; instead, the violence erupts suddenly, in a deliberately clumsy fashion. The police are presented as a well-meaning but hopelessly compromised organization and justice is, at best, an idealized concept that has no real place in the film's squalid landscape.

The plotting is chaotic but holds one's attention. The various clues are hidden in the open, as they had been in **Deep Red**, but things do not resolve themselves as neatly as they had in Argento's film. The evil force here is not a lone maniac acting out a neurotic fantasy; rather, it is an entire group of people who infect the society around them because of their power and their inherent lack of empathy and humanity. If anything, the film seems especially indebted to Pier Paolo Pasolini's scandalous *Salò, or the 120 Days of Sodom* (1975) in that it depicts an upper crust segment of society who literally get off on controlling and humiliating their "lesser" peers/subjects. This is a segment of society for whom greed is a way of life. They already have everything

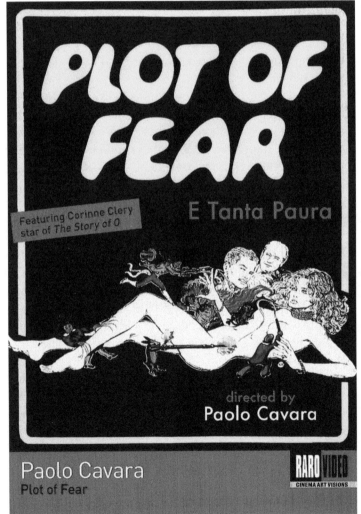

Cover for the DVD release of *Plot of Fear* from Raro Video; artwork by French comics illustrator Guido Crepax.

they could possibly want, but there is always room for a bit more. In place of intimacy and love, they thrive on indulging every perverse whim that comes to mind. It is a dark, despairing world they inhabit, but by the same token the film avoids becoming unduly depressing by virture of its strain of impish dark humor.

Much of the humor is concentrated in the character of Inspector Lomenzo. Lomenzo is the proverbial "fish out of water" type floundering amid the callous indifference of the people he is attempting to protect. Like Inspector Tellini in **The Black Belly of the Tarantula**, he is distinguished by his basic humanity. Cavara again goes to pains to show him enjoying something of a normal life outside of his work. Yet while Tellini was unsure of himself and given to brooding introspection, Lomenzo is much more outgoing and aggressive. He has a temper and a decidedly "Latin" disposition, but he also has intelligence and a capacity for compassion. He makes for a likable lead and his nonplussed reactions to some of the more bizarre characters he encounters is key to the film's comic tone.

Cavara again displays an innate flair for this type of material. If his first *giallo* was one of the best "traditional" examples of the genre, then this remains one of the most engaging of the more "offbeat" *gialli*. It is therefore to be regretted that he would not return to the genre in future, as he surely could have continued to deliver the goods. There is plenty of nudity and implied debauchery, while the various murder scenes are effectively handled. He also shows genuine concern for characterization, allowing his actors an opportunity to add a bit of color to their roles. The cinematography by Franco Di Giacomo is stylish, while the art direction is loaded with interesting details making every scene stimulating to observe. The appealingly funky music is by Daniele Patucchi.

Michele Placido gives a good account of himself as Inspector Lomenzo. Placido brings out the quirks of the character while also conveying his more grounded attributes. Born in 1946, Placido got his start on the Italian stage before making his film debut in 1972. His early credits included Gianfranco De Bosio's *Moses the Lawgiver* (1974), Giuseppe Patroni Griffi's *The Divine Nymph* (1975) and Marco Bellocchio's *Victory March* (1976), as well as the borderline *giallo Mia moglie un corpo per l'amore* (1973). He would go on to appear in **The Pyjama Girl Case** (1977) before playing his most iconic role, "Commissario" Corrado Cattani, in Damiano Damiani's acclaimed TV serial *La Piovra* (1984); the series was so popular that it spawned eight further seasons, as well as a stand-alone TV movie in 2010, but Placido bailed after season four in 1989. He would also play a memorably nasty villain in Michele Soavi's superior crime thriller, *The Goodbye Kiss* (2006). Placido began working as a writer/director in 1990, though he also continues to act. The beautiful Corinne Cléry plays his love interest. Cléry's role as Jeanne is an interesting one, though not enough time is spent on exploring what makes her tick; her relationship with Lomenzo works well because she and Placido have excellent chemistry. Cléry was born in Paris in 1950 and made her film debut in 1967. She first attracted international recognition with her role in Just Jaeckin's popular slice of erotica *The Story of O* (1975) and she would go on to provide ample sex appeal to everything from the gritty borderline *giallo Hitch Hike* (1977) to the James Bond adventure *Moonraker* (1979) to Lucio Fulci's memorably steamy S/M melodrama *The Devil's Honey* (1986). Her later *giallo* credits would include an episode of **Giallo: la tua impronta del venerdi** (1987) and the obscure **28° Minuto** (1991). She has been inactive in films since 2010. The supporting cast includes a couple of surprising faces from the American movie scene. Eli Wallach, of course, was no stranger to Italian films and he gives his usual excellent performance as the seedy Pietro Riccio. Riccio is a small role but a crucial one, and Wallach is expert at conveying copious amounts of detail in his limited screen time. He was born in Brooklyn in 1915 and began acting on Broadway in 1945. As a member of the Actor's Studio, he was well versed in Method acting but displayed a willingness to appear in all manner of films and different roles. He appeared in quite a few TV plays in the early 1950s before making his film debut with a Golden Globe-nominated turn in Elia Kazan's lurid *Baby Doll* (1956), which was written by Tennessee Williams and also featured *giallo* veterans Carroll Baker (in her own cinematic debut) and Karl Malden. Wallach would go on to appear in John Sturges' *The Magnificent Seven* (1960), John Huston's *The Misfits* (1961) and Richard Brooks' *Lord Jim* (1965) before being cast by Sergio Leone in *The Good, The Bad and The Ugly* (1966). Wallach's wonderfully vivid characterization allowed him to steal the show from star Clint Eastwood and it arguably remains his most popular film credit. He would go on to feature in a few other Italian productions, including Carlo Lizzani's *Crazy Joe* (1974) and Sergio Corbucci's *The White, The Yellow and the Black* (1975), in addition to appearing in numerous films back in the United States. Wallach remained active on screen into his 90s, and was recently seen in the likes of Clint Eastwood's *Mystic River* (2003), Roman Polanski's *The Ghost Writer* (2010) and Oliver Stone's *Wall Street: Money Never Sleeps* (2010). He died, a venerable 98 year old, in June 2014. More surprising is the presence of Tom Skerritt, who is cast in a role so minor that any day player could easily have filled it. Skerritt does fine with what he has to do, but it is a nothing part and no amount of wild gesticulating can improve it. Born in Detroit in 1933, he began appearing in films in the early 1960s. Following guest roles on numerous TV series, he scored a success as part of the ensemble of Robert Altman's *M*A*S*H* (1970). He made a few films in Italy in the mid-'70s, including Giuseppe Colizzi's *Run, Joe, Run!* (1974), but he never became a staple of the European exploitation scene. He would go on to claim top billing

in Ridley Scott's *Alien* (1979) and appeared in the likes of David Cronenberg's *The Dead Zone* (1983), Tony Scott's *Top Gun* (1986), Gary Sherman's *Poltergeist III* (1988), Clint Eastwood's *The Rookie* (1990), Seth MacFarlane's *Ted* (2012) and many others. He remains active in films and television.

1977

Crazy Desires of a Murderer
(Italy)

Aka *I vizi morbosi di una governante*

Directed by Filippo Walter Ratti (as Peter Rush); Screenplay by Ambrogio Molteni; Director of Photography: Gino Santini; Editor: Sergio Muzzi; Music by Piero Piccioni

Main Players: Corrado Gaipa (Inspector); Roberto Zattini; Isabelle Marchall (Ileana De Chablais); Annie Carol Edel (Berta); Giuseppe Colombo [as Beppe Colombo] (Frank Hoffman); Patrizia Gori (Elsa Leiter)

Ileana De Chablais invites a group of friends to accompany her to her grandfather's castle in the country. A deranged killer begins to pick the guests off, while a wily police inspector attempts to get to the bottom of the mystery ...

Crazy Desires of a Murderer seems like an old-fashioned bit of hokum … and for good reason. It was actually made in 1973 and sat on the shelf due to financial hardships for the production company.

The film is something of a throwback to the *gialli* of the late '60s and early '70s, with its gloomy castle setting and cast of characters hopping into bed with one another. Indeed, the emphasis on sexual shenanigans borders on the softcore, and in this respect it anticipates the trend toward more graphically sexual thrillers in the coming years.

The ridiculous story offers little in the way of surprises, though it is always a pleasure having a police inspector on the case who has a bit of charm and intellect besides. Beyond that, however, the film moves from one over-extended sex scene to the next, with the odd murder tossed in for good measure. The killer's *modus operandi* extends to plucking the eyes out of the victims' heads and this results in a few gruesome images. The crude prosthetic work is betrayed by flabby editing, however, but still it is a relief to actually see some *giallo* elements at all following an opening act that seems to drag on for an eternity.

Production values are nothing to write home about. It was a cheaply produced film, and looks it. The lighting by Gino Santini is lacking in atmosphere and even the normally reliable Piero Piccioni stumbles rather badly with a completely unremarkable soundtrack. Director Filippo Walter

Italian *locandina* for *Crazy Desires of a Murderer*; artwork by Lucio Crovato.

Ratti seems most concerned with getting his actresses to disrobe more than anything else, and the end result plays like a Renato Polselli film without the bizarre flourishes.

Overall the characters are as forgettable as the actors playing them. The only real standout is Corrado Gaipa as the inspector. Gaipa was a prolific actor and dubbing artist (he reportedly provided the Italian voices of Alec Guinness in the *Star Wars* films and Burt Lancaster in Luchino Visconti's *The Leopard*, 1963[1]), but this appears to have been the only time he claimed top billing in a film. It is a shame that it had to be such a shoddy one as this, but to his credit he plays his role with style. He was born in Palermo in 1924 and made his film debut in 1960. Gaipa was featured in several *gialli*, including *The Fifth Cord* (1971) and *My Dear Killer* (1972), in addition to *poliziotteschi* like Fernando Di Leo's *The Boss* (1973) and sexy comedies like Lucio Fulci's *The Eroticist* (1972). He also turned up as Don Tommasino in Francis Ford Coppola's *The Godfather* (1972). He died in 1989, at the age of 65. The supporting cast also includes an appearance by Giuseppe Colombo, who would later switch gears and become a producer; among his credits in that area are the Dario Argento films *The Stendhal Syndrome* (1996) and *The Phantom of the Opera* (1998). Colombo also had a minor, unbilled role in *The Police Are Blundering in the Dark* (1975), thus according him the unenviable distinction of having appeared in two of the worst *gialli* of their period.

Director Filippo Walter Ratti was born in Rome in 1914. He entered movies as an assistant director in the late 1930s, but by the end of the 1940s was directing. He was sometimes credited as Filippo Maria Ratti or under the pseudonym Peter Rush, as he is credited here. *Crazy Desires of a Murderer* is his only *giallo* credit; it would also prove to be his last effort. His filmography stops cold in 1977.

Notes:
1. http://www.imdb.com/name/nm0301403/bio?ref_=nm_ov_bio_sm

Death Steps in the Dark
(Italy/Greece)

Aka *Passi di morte perduti nel buio*

Directed by Maurizio Pradeaux; Produced by Aldo Ricci and Dimitri Dimitriadis; Screenplay by Arpad De Riso and Maurizio Pradeaux; Director of Photography: Aldo Ricci; Editor: Eugenio Alabiso; Music by Riz Ortolani

Main Players: Leonard Mann (Luciano Morelli); Robert Webber (Inspector); Vera Krouska (Ingrid Stelmosson); Antonio Maimone (Omar Effendi)

A woman is murdered aboard a train heading to Athens. Fashion photographer Luciano Morelli is among the suspects detained by the Greek police. Teaming up with his dim-witted model girlfriend, Ingrid, Luciano sets out to clear his name and unmask the real killer ...

Maurizio Pradeaux's second *giallo*, following *Death Carries a Cane* (1973), is an old-fashioned affair burdened with plenty of unfunny comedy relief.

The Greek locales would seem to promise some "exotic" scenery, but the truth is the film may as well have been set in one of the usual Italian locations. Nothing interesting is done with the setting and there is very little of aesthetic interest on display in the film as a whole.

The screenplay by Pradeaux and Arpad De Riso is something of a throwback to the Agatha Christie School of murder mysteries. Things get off on the appropriately old-school note with a murder aboard the Istanbul-Athens Express and the finale involves assembling the various suspects in a single locale and using a bit of trickery to force the murderer to show his hand. Unfortunately, there are not many surprises and the reveal of the killer's identity fails to generate much interest.

Pradeaux apes his successors in the genre with some derivative imagery. The close-ups of the killer's wildly expressive eye is a quotation from Dario Argento's ***The Cat O'Nine Tails*** (1971), while one slaying reuses the blood clouding the water effect that was used so memorably in Mario Bava's ***Blood and Black Lace*** (1964). There is plenty of hand-held subjective camerawork and a bit of comic safecracking also recalls ***The Cat O'Nine Tails***. The use of the fashion *milieu* also recalls a number of thrillers, ranging from Bava's ***Blood and Black Lace*** and ***Hatchet for the Honeymoon*** (1970) to Andrea Bianchi's ***Strip Nude for Your Killer*** (1975). There is also plenty of softcore lesbian groping which would not have been out of place in Bianchi's cheerfully sordid thriller.

The abundance of comedy puts the film closer in tone to entries like Bava's ***The Girl Who Knew Too Much*** (1963) or Sergio Corbucci's ***Atrocious Tales of Love and Death*** (1979), but the humor falls flat and is not nearly so smoothly integrated into the proceedings. There is some pleasure to be had in the investigating inspector's recurring issues with indigestion or his exasperated responses to the stupidity of some of the people he encounters, but the running gag involving Ingrid's air-headed misunderstanding of virtually ever situation in which she finds herself wears thin very quickly. The film literally ends on a "cute" comic freeze-frame, but they really need not have bothered.

Pradeaux's direction is flat and functional as usual. He shows no real flair for the genre and, despite indulging in a bit of graphic bloodshed and T&A (though the extreme, clinical close-ups of tongues flicking at each other during one love scene borders on the gross), the film could easily be mistaken for a late '60s entry. Riz Ortolani contributes an atypically listless soundtrack, while the cinematography by Aldo Ricci fails to bring out the natural beauty of the landscape. The flick also moves at a sluggish pace and never generates any real suspense or thrills.

Leonard Mann, who gives a rather grating performance as Luciano, heads the cast. Mann plays the role much too lightly and never convinces as a man desperately trying to clear his reputation. He is also a dull protagonist, though in fairness to the actor there really is not much for him to do with such a role. Mann was born in New York in 1947 and made his way to Italy in the late 1960s to break into films. He appeared in a few Spaghetti Westerns, including Ferdinando Baldi's *The Forgotten Pistolero* (1969), then began appearing in *poliziotteschi* like *The Left Hand of the Law* (1975). He appeared in the borderline *giallo The Body* (1974) and would go on to appear in such thrillers as ***The Perfect Crime*** (1978) and ***The Monster of Florence*** (1986). In the 1980s, he began alternating between European assignments and more American pictures, including the slasher movie *Night School* (1981). One of his final acting roles was in Monte Hellman's straight-to-video horror film *Silent Night, Deadly Night III: Better Watch Out!* (1989). As movie work began to dry up, Mann reportedly turned to schoolteaching in Los Angeles; more recently, he has tried his hand at directing with the documentary *Syuxtun* (2012). Veteran American actor Robert Webber plays the inspector. He shows a flair for

Anglo poster art for *Death Steps in the Dark*; artist unknown.

comedy but is generally constrained by the purely functional nature of his scenes. His voice is also not present on the English-language dub. Born in California in 1924, he did a stint in the Marine Corps during World War II before catching the acting bug. He started off as a stage actor before making his film debut in 1950. Webber's career was something of an oddity: a steadily working actor who was trapped somewhere between being a character player and a leading man. He gave strong performances in Sidney Lumet's *12 Angry Men* (1957), Jack Smight's *Harper* (1966) and Robert Aldrich's *The Dirty Dozen* (1967) and had a rare lead role in Freddie Francis' *Hysteria* (1965) for Hammer Film Productions. In addition to guest starring on dozens of popular TV shows, he appeared as a camp hitman in Sam Peckinpah's *Bring Me the Head of Alfredo Garcia* (1974) and sent up his tough guy image in Blake Edwards' *The Revenge of the Pink Panther* (1978) and *S.O.B.* (1981). *Death Steps in the Dark* was part of a brief foray he made into the world of European cult cinema starting from the mid-1960s. Webber remained much in demand until his death from Lou Gehrig's disease in 1989.

RIZZOLI FILM presenta un film di **LUIGI ZAMPA**
JOHNNY DORELLI / **SYDNE ROME**

IL MOSTRO

RIZZOLI FILM presenta un film di **LUIGI ZAMPA** · **JOHNNY DORELLI** · **SYDNE ROME** in "IL MOSTRO" · con **RENZO PALMER** · **YVES BENEYTON** · **ENZO SANTANIELLO** **GIANRICO TEDESCHI** · **ORAZIO ORLANDO** nel ruolo di Pisani · **ANGELICA IPPOLITO** musiche di **ENNIO MORRICONE** | **SERGIO DONATI** | **UGO TUCCI** · **CLAUDIO MANCINI** produttore associato **GIUSEPPE GIOVANNINI** · fotografia **MARIO VULPIANI** · COLORE TECHNOSPES

Italian *locandina* for *Il Mostro*; artwork by Studio Casaro.

Il Mostro (Italy)

Aka *Criminalia; The Fiend*

Directed by Luigi Zampa; Produced by Claudio Mancini; Screenplay by Sergio Donati; Director of Photography: Mario Vulpiani; Editor: Franco Fraticelli; Music by Ennio Morricone

Main Players: Johnny Dorelli (Valerio Barigozzi); Sydne Rome (Dina); Orazio Orlando (Commissioner Pisani); Renzo Palmer (Baruffi); Yves Beneyton (Giorgio Mesca)

Down on his luck Valerio Barigozzi has an ex-wife who loathes him and a son who adores him. His professional life is a mess, however, and his dreams of becoming a star journalist are quickly fading away. One day he receives a note in the mail stating that a well-known TV personality is to be killed; it is signed "Il Mostro." Barigozzi's superiors think he is just trying to grab a quick headline and laugh the note off, but when the man turns up dead, Barigozzi becomes a suspect. When a second note arrives, he sees it as his opportunity to launch himself into the public eye ...

Il Mostro was sold as something of a comic thriller, thanks to the presence of lead actor Johnny Dorelli, but it is in fact far from a comedy, though it does have its amusing moments.

According to screenwriter Sergio Donati, the project had a complicated birth:

> It's a script I really loved, but it was made three or four years after it was written and, when it came out, it was a bit out of time. At first it was to be produced by Franco Committeri, who gave the script to Volontè. Then it was the period of *committed* films, such as *Investigation of a Citizen Above Suspicion* and *Lulu the Tool*. "Yes, I like it very much, I like the setting in the world of journalism, but it's too commercial a story ..." "Well, we can change it a bit, take inspiration from the Valpreda case ..." [...] so, in 15 days I wrote *Slap The Monster on Page One* and put *Il Mostro* aside. [...] Then Zampa read the original script for *Il Mostro* and loved it. He remained absolutely faithful to the page. The protagonist was Dorelli, who perhaps was not the most suited for the role; what is more, the story was a bit old by now.[1]

The film opens with some images that may seem familiar, and for good reason. They are actually taken from Luciano Ercoli's **Death Walks on High Heels** (1971). Following a nasty slashing, the film pulls back and reveals Valerio sitting in the audience with his young son. Valerio is unimpressed by the spectacle of blood and violence held together by a flimsy plot, while the son Luca is very impressed indeed. Donati's criticism of the genre and its excesses are made evident early on, but he does not succumb to hypocrisy. His *giallo* will be well plotted, highly logical, emotionally resonant and not reliant on flashy *grand guignol*.

The film deals with a number of weighty themes, notably the problems between parents and their children and the responsibility of the press. Valerio loves his son Luca but is an absent parent. His ex-wife is more concerned with her latest lover. As such, Luca is left to a world of imagination, which does not prove the best place for him to be. Luca idolizes his father, who inadvertently fills the boy's head with ridiculous notions thanks to his macho posturing and temperamental outbursts. As a reporter, Valerio comes to symbolize the worst of the worst. He succeeds in making his name but in the process he also turns the killer into an even bigger celebrity; the two become mutually dependent upon each other, and this is a relationship that is doomed to end badly. Valerio is merely part of a bigger problem, however. The paper's senior director clings to moral ideals, but his money-hungry son has no such scruples; when the series on the killings becomes a hit with the public, the son uses this as a reason to discredit his father's "outdated" ideology. Sensationalistic headlines become the order of the day and Valerio is trapped in the middle, even as he begins to realize what a farce the whole thing has become. Valerio's reputation, such as it is, is a flash in the pan. He is the big thing of the moment—but only for the moment. When he comes to realize this, he tries to do the right thing, but it is too late; he is beholden to the mythology he has created and it becomes necessary to keep the circus rolling for as long as possible. Donati's satirical approach manifests itself as a popular singer, Dina, is hired to do a song in tribute to the killer and his crimes. Donati's impatience with the callous manner in which tragic events are commercialized is writ large in this context and links into other socially conscious films of the era, including Paddy Chayevsky's *Network*, memorably brought to the screen by Sidney Lumet in 1976.

Social commentary is at the forefront, but Donati and director Luigi Zampa also pay lip service to *giallo* conventions. The mysterious letters and the killer's habit of "branding" his victims are all elements one would expect to find in a typical thriller. Donati may have a wry sense of humor about the genre's conventions, but happily he is not stuffy about it. The film manages to lampoon the more ridiculous excesses while also working as a thriller in its own right. The final reveal of the killer's identity—to say nothing of the motivation that triggered it all—is not only logically worked through but genuinely surprising. The end result is a film that lingers in the mind long after it is over.

Zampi directs the film with great precision. He does not go in for extravagant visual devices, but neither is his approach in the least pedestrian. The focus is on the very strong story and characterizations, but he paces the material very well and builds suspense very solidly indeed. The shifts in tone between comedy, drama and suspense are beautifully handled and the finale, as indicated, is uncommonly powerful. Ennio Morricone's splendid score is another major asset.

Lead actor Johnny Dorelli was best known in Italy for his comedy roles. As such, his presence may have worked against the film's reception. There are certainly some laugh-out-loud moments along the way, but the movie asks much more out of him than to indulge in mugging and pratfalls. Valerio is a complex, multi-layered character—egotistical, insensitive and bigoted—but also emotionally vulnerable. He truly loves his son, but his fixation on his career has blinded him to being there for him on a consistent basis. Dorelli makes the character sympathetic but not mawkishly so; he is a difficult character to warm to in some respects. Born in Milan in 1937, Dorelli entered films in 1956. He also achieved some measure of success as a songwriter and

singer. He was married to actresses Catherine Spaak and Gloria Guida. Dorelli's films were popular with Italian audiences, but few of them made much of a ripple outside of Italy. One such vehicle—*Arrriva Dorellik* aka *How to Kill 400 Duponts* (1967)—actually lampooned the "Diabolik" comics before the cult Mario Bava adaptation had even hit the screens! He has been inactive in movies since the mid-2000s. Second-billed Sydne Rome is effective as the singer who gets mixed up in the murders. Her billing is something of a cheat, however, since she is actually in the film for about 10 minutes and does not show up until nearly an hour in. She does get a nude scene, however. She was born in Akron, Ohio in 1951 and entered films with a role in the Richard Johnson spy pastiche *Some Girls Do* (1969), and became a staple in the Italian movie scene thereafter. She landed the lead role in Roman Polanski's bizarre sex comedy *What?* (1972), wherein she spent much of her screen time in the nude; most of her film work was similarly reliant on her good looks and willingness to show off her physique, but she also displayed genuine flair as a comedienne.

Director Luigi Zampa was born in Rome in 1905. He studied to be an architect but decided to pursue movie work, entering the industry in the 1930s as a screenwriter and assistant director. He made the transition to directing in the 1940s and helmed nearly 40 films until he retired in 1979. One of his last credits was the borderline *giallo The Flower in His Mouth* (1975), with Jennifer O'Neill, Franco Nero and James Mason. He died in 1991 at the age of 86.

Notes:
1. Pergolari, Andrea, *La fabbrica del riso – 32 sceneggiatori raccontano la storia del cinema italiano* (Rome: unmondoaparte, 2004), p. 117-118.

Nine Guests for a Crime
(Italy)

Aka *Nove ospiti per un delitto*

Directed by Ferdinando Baldi; Produced by Mario Di Nardo; Screenplay by Fabio Pittorru; Director of Photography: Sergio Rubini; Editor: Enzo Micarelli; Music by Carlo Savina

Main Players: John Richardson (Lorenzo); Arthur Kennedy (Ubaldo); Massimo Foschi (Michele); Caroline Laurence (Giulia); Rita Silva (Greta); Loretta Persichetti (Patrizia); Venantino Venantini (Walter); Sofia Dionisio (Carla)

Home Video: Camera Obscura (Region 2 DVD)

An aging patriarch, Ubaldo, assembles his children and their spouses at his island getaway. Before long, a killer begins picking them off. It is revealed that the family has been harboring a secret which has come back to haunt them ...

Before he made the transition to producing, Mario Di Nardo worked as a screenwriter. One of his key credits as a writer was Mario Bava's **Five Dolls for an August Moon** (1970). Bava was so displeased with his script that he threw it aside and improvised feverishly in the hopes of improving the end product. What Di Nardo thought about all of this is open to speculation, but he clearly believed in the basic concept because *Nine Guests for a Crime*, which he produced, follows the same basic template.

The screenplay by *giallo* veteran Fabio Pittorru offers yet another variation on the *Ten Little Indians* story, as a group of characters assemble in a secluded locale and are picked off by a killer. The film is part of the subgenre of "desert island *gialli*," typified by the likes of **Five Dolls for an August Moon** or **Top Sensation** (1969), but it also taps into the Gothic horror genre in some respects as well. The horror elements do not manifest themselves by way of shadowy atmosphere, however, but in the concept of a family united by a shameful secret that is threatening to destroy them. In this respect, the film evokes such works as Mario Bava's *The Whip and the Body* (1963), though the stylistic treatment of the material is very different.

In common with other *gialli* of the period, the film also revels in the bad manners of its characters. Many Italian thrillers focus on symbolic family units, but this one is literally a family—and a singularly dysfunctional one at that. They are also representative of the idle rich, thus linking-in with the sociological commentary, which runs throughout a number of these movies. The "commentary," as such, is not terribly deep or meaningful, but it is evident that the general notion of the upper class as indolent and corrupt is part of the fabric of the narrative. Nobody is really worth a damn in this story: the patriarch is petty and cruel, while the assorted siblings and their significant others stab each other in the back at every turn and are almost all involved in some kind of an illicit affair. This provides the ideal hothouse atmosphere for a story of death and retribution, and the film does not waste much time in getting down to the nitty-gritty.

The murders are not staged with a tremendous amount of creativity, it must be admitted, but note should be made of one memorably nasty sequence wherein one character is trapped in some netting, shot several times and then set on fire. More emphasis is placed on the sexual shenanigans, though the various trysts are not drawn out to the same graphic extent as in other, sleazier *gialli* of the period.

Ferdinando Baldi directs the film with some style and a good sense of pacing. It is by no means his best work as a director, indicating that his true strengths were in other genres (notably Spaghetti Westerns), but he does a good, workmanlike job with the material. On the whole, the picture probably best serves as an example of what a movie like **Five Dolls for an August Moon** would have been like in the hands of a less imaginative filmmaker. While Bava's effort, for all its narrative issues, is loaded with directorial touches of an inspired nature, Baldi's is never more than adequate. He makes good use of framing and keeps things humming at

Italian *locandina* for *Nine Guests for a Crime*; artwork by Piovano / Studio Paradiso.

a good pace, but it is a relatively impersonal project that does not really bring anything new to the table.

Technical credits are uneven. Sergio Rubini's deliberately bleached, overexposed cinematography has some eye-catching moments. Much of the action unfolds in harsh sunlight, making it something of a precursor to Dario Argento's *Tenebrae* (1982), but the occasional shadowy night time scene shows a flair for atmosphere as well. Special make-up effects are sadly lacking. Characters hit point blank by shotgun fire fall to the ground and writhe, but there is hardly any blood visible; there is also a spear through the neck gag that is undone by some slack editing. Carlo Savina again displays very little affinity for the genre. He composed some memorable scores for the likes of Jorge Grau's *Bloody Ceremony* (1973) and Mario Bava's *Lisa and the Devil* (1973), but his *giallo* scores always tend to be a little bland, and this one is no exception. Savina recycles some music from *Lisa and the Devil*, which merely serves to remind one of how unremarkable his new compositions are.

Arthur Kennedy puts in a decent performance as the embittered patriarch, Ubaldo. His screen time is not all that extensive, but he conveys the character's dark, twisted undercurrent in a convincing manner. Kennedy was born in Massachusets in 1914 and started off as a stage actor. He would bounce back and forth between films and theater for many years. He won acclaim in the role of Biff in the original Broadway run of Arthur Miller's *Death of a Salesman* in 1949; he won a Tony for his performance, but when Laslo Benedek brought the play to the screen in 1951, Kennedy was replaced by Kevin McCarthy. Kennedy's movie career got underway in 1940, and he would become a popular presence in many major films, amassing an impressive 5 Academy Award nominations along the way (4 of them under Mark Robson's direction). Among his career highlights were Raoul Walsh's *High Sierra* (1941), Fritz Lang's *Rancho Notorious* (1952), Nicholas Ray's *The Lusty Men* (1952), Anthony Mann's *The Man from Laramie*, Edgar G. Ulmer's *The Naked Dawn*, William Wyler's *The Desperate Hours* (all 1955), Vincente Minnelli's *Some Came Running* (1958; his other Oscar nod), Richard Brooks' *Elmer Gantry* (1960), David Lean's *Lawrence of Arabia* (1962) and Richard Fleischer's *Fantastic Voyage* (1966). By the 1970s, Kennedy was doing a lot of "bread and butter" work in the commercial end of the Italian film industry; he was splendid as the hot-headed, bigoted policeman who torments hero Ray Lovelock in Jorge Grau's superb *The Living Dead at Manchester Morgue* (1974), but he failed to make a significant impression in the likes of Alberto De Martino's *The Antichrist* (1974) or Aldo Lado's *The Humanoid* (1979). He did not appear in many films or TV shows in his final years, but did cram in a few minor credits before his death in 1990. John Richardson and Massimo Foschi played Kennedy's sons. Richardson gives his usual flat and listless performance, while Foschi at least shows some signs of life in the admittedly flashier role of the sexually voracious Michele. The standout among the supporting cast, however, is Venantino Venantini. Venantini has a field day as Walter, the sleazy husband of one of Kennedy's sexually promiscuous daughters. He was born in 1930 and made his film debut in the mid-1950s. Venantini would appear in everything from "prestige" pictures like Carol Reed's *The Agony and the Ecstasy* (1965) to softcore erotica like *Emanuelle II* (1975). He was also a familiar presence in Italian horror (*City of the Living Dead*, 1980), *poliziotteschi* (*Contraband*, 1980) and *gialli*, including **The Red-Headed Corpse** (1972) and **Seven Deaths in the Cat's Eyes** (1973). He remains active in Italian films to this day.

Director Ferdinando Baldi is one of many gifted craftsmen in the Italian movie industry who has failed to attract much in the way of serious critical attention. *Nine Guests for a Crime* may not show him working at the top of his game, but he does not embarrass himself here either. He was born in 1917 and began working in films in the early 1950s as a writer and a director. He is also rumored to have worked on the aforementioned *The Whip and the Body* as a production assistant, but he was already well established as a director by this time, so this may be a bit of misinformation that has been accepted as fact in some circles. In any event, Baldi's career really flourished in the 1960s when he started working in the Spaghetti Western genre. Among his many credits are *Texas, Adios* (1966), *Django, Prepare a Coffin* (1968), *The Forgotten Pistolero* (1969) and *Blindman* (1971). He also directed two films in 3D, including the wonderfully bizarre Western *Comin' at Ya!* (1981) and the *Raiders of the Lost Ark* knockoff *The Treasure of the Four Crowns* (1983). He died in 2007, at the age of 90.

The Psychic (Italy)

Aka *Sette note in nero; Siete notas en negro; L'emmurée vivante; Murder to the Tune of Seven Black Notes*

Directed by Lucio Fulci; Produced by Franco Cuccu; Screenplay by Lucio Fulci, Roberto Gianviti and Dardano Sacchetti; Director of Photography: Sergio Salvati; Editor: Ornella Micheli; Music by Franco Bixio (as Bixio), Fabio Frizzi (as Frizzi) and Vince Tempera (as Tempera)

Main Players: Jennifer O'Neill (Virginia Ducci); Gianni Garko (Francesco Ducci); Marc Porel (Luca Fattori); Gabriele Ferzetti (Emilio Rospini); Ida Galli [as Evelyn Stewart] (Gloria Ducci); Jenny Tamburi (Bruna); Fabrizio Jovene (Commissioner D'Elia); Bruno Corazzari (Canevari); Luigi Diberti (Judge)

Home Video: Severin (Region free DVD)

Virginia Ducci has the gift of extrasensory perception. One day, she is assailed with the vision of a woman being walled-up alive. She believes it to be the memory of a crime that has already occurred and tries to convince her skeptical husband, Francesco, but he refuses to believe her. It transpires that the vision is connected to the disappearance of a young woman who used to be Francesco's lover, and when the woman's corpse is found walled-up in his cottage, he comes under suspicion of murder. Virginia tries desperately to clear his name, but it soon becomes apparent that the vision also entails another crime which has yet to occur...

The Psychic marked another step for director Lucio Fulci toward the horror genre. It is definitely a *giallo*, no question about it, but it contains elements of the paranormal, which would become a hallmark of his later macabre works. For Fulci, it was a movie that inspired strong feelings:

> It's one of my most beautiful, and at the same time, unsuccessful films and it cost me a lot of grief for personal reasons ... As a film, it's extremely mechanical and I'd gladly do it again tomorrow; I just adore mechanical scripts.[1]

The picture marked the first of several important collaborations between Fulci and screenwriter Dardano Sacchetti. Sacchetti was born in 1944 and established himself as a major force in genre filmmaking in the 1970s. He collaborated with Dario Argento on the screenplay for **The Cat O'Nine Tails** (1971), but a later association on *Inferno* (1980) proved to be more contentious, with Sacchetti not receiving any credit on the final release print. After his initial alliance with Argento, he went on to co-write the screenplay of Mario Bava's **Twitch of the Death Nerve** (1971), which proved to be a more fulfilling experience; he would work with Bava again on the director's final film, the ghost story *Shock* (1977). Sacchetti's credits encompass collaborations with some of the most significant directors in the field of Italian horror, suspense and fantasy, including Lamberto Bava (*Demons*, 1985), Sergio Martino (*Hands of Steel*, 1986), Damiano Damiani (*Amityville II: The Possession*, 1982), Antonio Margheriti (*Cannibal Apocalypse*, 1980), Enzo G. Castellari (*1990: The Bronx Warriors*, 1982), Michele Soavi (*The Church*, 1989) and Umberto Lenzi (*Ironmaster*, 1983). Sacchetti continued working with Fulci on some of the director's most popular films, including *Zombie* (1979), *City of the Living Dead* (1980), *The Beyond* (1981) and the controversial **The New York Ripper** (1982). The collaboration between the two men was sometimes complicated, as Sacchetti explained in an interview:

> Fulci has always suffered from the knowledge that I was the one who wrote the stories, which has made him extremely jealous of me, and this has led him to systematically disparage my work in order to give himself importance.[2]

That said, Sacchetti, in his intro to *The Beyond* screened during the "Italian Kings of the Bs" retrospective at the 61st Venice Film Festival in September 2004, described the way producers used to hand him a plotline on Friday evening and he would be expected to come up with a complete script by Monday morning ... which meant locking himself in for the weekend with only whisky and cigarettes for company. Even so, Fulci and Sacchetti's relationship began on a positive note with *The Psychic*. Sacchetti put it thus:

That was a period of great harmony, a creative time, which was extremely valid and enjoyable. We began with [*The Psychic*], a film I love dearly but which was not really understood.[3]

The story deals with the concept of fate. Virginia is blessed (or cursed) with the gift of second sight, which enables her to see fractured glimpses of events which have either occurred in the distant past or have not yet transpired. In trying to avert a potential tragedy, Virginia merely fights against the inevitable. No matter how hard she struggles, the fact remains that these glimpses must be played out in reality. The paranormal component of the narrative points toward the gradual shift of the *giallo* into the horror genre; indeed, the *giallo*'s significance in Italian pop culture would gradually diminish in large part due to films made by two of its most significant practitioners: Dario Argento's *Suspiria* (1977) and Fulci's *Zombie. Zombie,* inspired by the tremendous box-office success of George A. Romero's *Dawn of the Dead* (1978), would open the floodgates of horror and gore in the Italian popular movie scene.

Despite Fulci's criticism that it suffers from a mechanical narrative, the story and structure of the film is immensely satisfying. The use of fragmented visions assailing the heroine harkens back to the traumatic event that haunts the deranged killer in Bava's **Hatchet for the Honeymoon** (1970), and Fulci's stylistic use of sharp zoom-ins to her eyes conveys a sense of entering into the character's frame of mind. Fulci would soon find himself staging scenes of spectacular gore and sadism, thus earning himself the appellation of "Godfather of Gore" among adoring horror fans, but this film is notable for its restraint. The violence is quick and sudden and the overall approach is stately and measured. Fulci seems to take great pleasure in putting his heroine through the paces as she attempts to solve a puzzle that is almost certain to end in tragedy.

The Psychic compares well to Fulci's previous *gialli*, but sadly it proved to be a box-office disappointment. The producers invested a sizable sum in the movie, which certainly shows on screen, but for whatever reason, it failed to connect with audiences. Fulci always bristled at being compared with Argento, but it seems obvious **Deep Red** (1975) inspired him to some extent. The sequence of Virginia hacking into the wall, uncovering a body, recalls a similar scene involving David Hemmings in the Argento movie, while elements of the score seem to be directly impacted by the success of Goblin's prog-rock soundtrack. That a commercially successful model inspired the film is hardly surprising. Indeed, this is the basic backbone of the Italian film industry. Fulci takes a leaf out of Argento's hit, but in so doing, he delivers his own unique take on the material. Fulci's approach is far more logical and plot-driven, in its own way, versus the more baroque and fanciful method of Argento. The irony in all this is that Fulci would soon eclipse Argento as Italy's most cheerfully over-the-top director of horror films, many of which were truly unconcerned with plot or narrative. For the time being, however, the movie's failure cost Fulci dearly and put him in an awkward position for the next couple of years. His fortunes would only revive when he found himself at the helm of *Zombie*, a project he was not originally attached to direct.[4] From that moment on, Fulci's own destiny as a filmmaker would undergo a radical change. The former director of comedies, Spaghetti Westerns and thrillers would be reborn as a "Master of Horror."

As indicated above, the production was granted a generous budget, and this is obvious onscreen. The cinematography by Sergio Salvati is elegant and loaded with memorable images. Salvati had already worked with Fulci on the superior Spaghetti Western *Four of the Apocalypse* (1975) and the horror spoof *Young Dracula* (1975), and he would become one of the director's most loyal and reliable collaborators. His work on films like *Zombie*, *The Beyond* and *The Black Cat* (1981) provided Fulci with some of the most memorable images of his career. The settings and costumes are appropriately classy, as befits the upper crust environs in which the story is set, and special make-up effects are generally very good; the opening flashback scene even quotes a memorable demise from **Don't Torture a Duckling** (1972). The music score by the trio of Fabio Frizzi, Vince Tempera and Franco Bixio also deserves a nod. The three had already scored *Young Dracula* and *Four of the Apocalypse* and would go on to do the same on his final Western, *Silver Saddle* (1978). Frizzi, however, would become another major player in Fulci's subsequent horror career, composing haunting soundtracks for the likes of *Zombie*, *City of the Living Dead* and *The Beyond*. Their music for *The Psychic* ranges from sub-Goblin compositions during some of the more hysterical sequences to a haunting title theme that seems indebted to Ennio Morricone's "pocket-watch chime" theme from *For a Few Dollars More* (1965). The use of a saccharine song over the opening titles may well draw sneers from some viewers, but the lyrics have a certain thematic weight and the song makes for a nice contrast to the generally grim goings-on.

Unfortunately, the film is burdened with a rather wooden central performance from Jennifer O'Neill. O'Neill's one-note interpretation of Virginia grates early on and does not improve much as the story unfolds. She was born in Brazil in 1948 but was raised in New York. She started off as a model and began appearing in films in the late 1960s. After featuring in Howard Hawks' *Rio Lobo* (1970), she scored her most iconic role in Robert Mulligan's sweetly romantic *Summer of '42* (1971), but her subsequent film work has been spotty at best. She first came to Italy to star in Luigi Zampa's borderline *giallo The Flower in His Mouth* (1975), opposite Franco Nero and James Mason, and subsequently played a memorable supporting role in Luchino Visconti's swansong *The Innocent* (1976), on which she met actor Marc Porel, with whom she had a tumultuous relationship. O'Neill's ca-

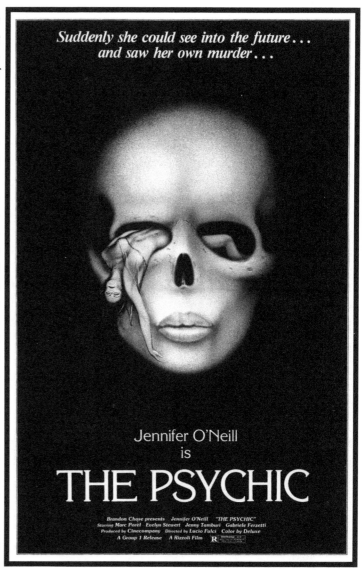

Suddenly she could see into the future... and saw her own murder...

Jennifer O'Neill is

THE PSYCHIC

American poster for *The Psychic*; artist unknown.

reer was rumored to have been compromised by issues with substance abuse, and allegations also abound that she introduced Porel to narcotics as well. In any event, she would continue appearing in films, including David Cronenberg's *Scanners* (1981), but much of her subsequent work would be on the small screen. O'Neill's performance is the film's Achilles heel, but she is supported by a number of fine actors, including her off-screen lover of the time, Marc Porel. Porel is marvelous as the slyly humorous parapsychologist, Luca. It is a very different character from the one he had played in **Don't Torture a Duckling**, and he appears relaxed and engaged throughout. Gianni Garko is in fine form as Virginia's husband, Francesco. Garko is required to convey an air of moral ambiguity, and he does this with great skill. The distinguished Gabriele Ferzetti is also on hand to play Emilio Rospini, a chief suspect in the mystery. Ferzetti does not have a lot of screen time, but his charismatic presence adds some gravitas to the proceedings.

Fulci would revisit the *giallo* with his most controversial film, **The New York Ripper** (1982), but by that stage in the game his reputation as a purveyor of gory thrills preceded him. His earlier thrillers like this, however, show a very different side of the man and his work. Viewers who can appreciate an interesting story, well told, should find much to love here.

Notes:
1. Palmerini, Luca M. and Gaetano Mistretta, *Spaghetti Nightmares* (Florida: Fantasma Books, 1996), p. 59.
2. *Ibid*, p. 59.
3. *Ibid*, p. 125.
4. *Zombie* was originally offered to Enzo G. Castellari, who did not feel an affinity for the subject matter and suggested Fulci in his place. The film was titled *Zombi 2* in Italy because *Dawn of the Dead* had been issued there, to great success, as *Zombi*. The European version of Romero's splatter watershed was overseen by co-producer Dario Argento, who made changes to the editing and scoring of the picture.

The Pyjama Girl Case
(Italy/Spain)

Aka *La ragazza dal pigiama giallo; La chica del pijama Amarillo; Blutiger Zahltag; Die Frau aus zweiter Hand*

Directed by Flavio Mogherini; Produced by Giorgio Salvoni; Screenplay by Flavio Mogherini and Rafael Sánchez Campoy; Director of Photography: Carlo Carlini; Editor: Adriano Tagliavia; Music by Riz Ortolani

Main Players: Ray Milland (Inspector Thompson); Dalila Di Lazzaro (Glenda Blythe); Mel Ferrer (Professor Henry Douglas); Michele Placido (Antonio Attolini); Renato Rossini [as Howard Ross] (Roy Conner); Ramiro Oliveros (Inspector Ramsey)

Home Video: Blue Underground (Region free DVD)

The horribly mutilated body of a young woman is found on a beach in Australia. The police are investigating, and the case catches the interest of the retired Inspector Thompson. The latter gets special permission to conduct his own "unofficial" investigation and he discovers a link to Italian immigrant Antonio Attolini and his friend, German immigrant Roy Conner ...

The Pyjama Girl Case belongs to a relatively rare subgenre, the fact-based *giallo*. The story was inspired by a real-life mystery that unfolded in 1934 in the village of Aubrey, New South Wales in Australia. A farmer discovers the charred body of a young woman in a sewage drain; the autopsy revealed that she had been shot in the throat and then brutally beaten to death before an attempt was made to destroy all the evidence by setting the corpse on fire. Attempts at identifying the victim were stymied; nobody appeared to have any idea who she was, which was a surprise for all involved given that Aubrey was the type of small town where everybody knew everybody. The only clue of note was a pair of silk pyjamas found among the girl's remains. The

body was put on display in an attempt to figure out the girl's identity, but the combination of the warm weather and the advancing state of decomposition made the authorities take an unprecedented step. They had the remains preserved and sealed in a special see-through container, thus allowing people to get a look at the body from all angles. Different theories were bandied about over the next 10 years before a break in the case revealed the girl's identity. She was Linda Agostini, a British girl who came to Australia and married another migrant, an Italian by the name of Antonio Agostini. An investigation revealed that Linda had run away from her husband in 1934 and that she had not been seen since. Antonio was arrested, interrogated and confessed to accidentally killing his wife. The confession was viewed with skepticism, as forceful techniques were used in the interrogation, but ultimately he was charged with the murder and incarcerated on charges of manslaughter and was sentenced to jail for six years. The public fascination with the case continued to grow over the years as different theories began to emerge. Australian author Hugh Geddes wrote a study of the case, published in 1978, under the title of *The Pyjama Girl Case*. A more recent study by another Australian writer, Richard Evans, titled *The Pyjama Girl Mystery*, casts doubt on the accepted theory that Linda Agostini was the real victim; according to his research, too many physical discrepancies exist between the remains of the victim and the descriptions of Agostini's build and body structure. Much like the infamous Black Dahlia case, the Pyjama Girl Case continues to inspire debate and interest among crime scholars.

The story was first dramatized on film in the Australian documentary short subject *The Pyjama Girl Murder Case* (1939). This *giallo* by Flavio Mogherini seeks to update the case but retains many of the basic facts in telling the story. Mogherini's approach avoids crass sensationalism and displays a surprising sensitivity. In the film, the character of Glenda Blythe substitutes for Linda Agostini. She is Dutch, not English, and in some respects the character is developed in a more sympathetic fashion. Whereas Linda Agostini was an alcoholic and a party girl, Glenda is exploited because of her good looks and naïve disposition. Glenda is not a total babe in the woods; she is free and open in her sexuality, but is motivated by a desire to find love and happiness in the long run. Her relationships all end in disappointment. Her husband, Antonio, is a loser and a dullard, her old flame Roy is only interested in sex and Professor Douglas, the older man she pins her hopes on, turns out to be a superficial poseur. The scene where she realizes that she has been duped by Douglas is one of the most affecting in the film; her subsequent decision to strike out at the men who are leering at her by charging them for a sexual dalliance is not presented in a titillating fashion, as it represents the last desperate act of a woman trying to break free of her oppressive environs.

Mogherini handles the film with tremendous style and attention to detail. The structure of the story is ingenious, alternating between police procedural and domestic drama.

The police scenes work well because the character of Inspector Thompson is so humorous and engaging. He has a bawdy sense of humor and clearly is bored out of his skull as a retiree, so finding himself in the middle of an investigation such as this re-energizes him and gives him a sense of purpose. He is deliberately contrasted with the dull Inspector Ramsey, who is officially in charge of the investigation. Ramsey represents the cold, bureaucratic side of the modern police force, while Thompson evokes the more colorful, intuitive and deductive old school approach.

Mogherini also highlights the racist underpinnings in the case. The closed-minded attitude of the locals toward "outsiders" puts Glenda, Antonio and their friend Roy at an obvious disadvantage. They are all three from other countries, and as such they are viewed with an air of distrust by the xenophobic culture at large. This aspect certainly has its origins in the real-life investigation. The notion of pinning the crime on an Italian was desirable at the time, as it suggested that only somebody "different" could perpetrate such heinous acts. Mogherini's emphasis on this backward-thinking mentality helps to give the film a real emotional punch, though the finale is far less ambiguous than it might have been if it had been made later, when the identity of the victim once again became a point of contention.

The film moves at a very good pace and remains gripping throughout, partly because of the jigsaw structure and partly because the characters and their relationships are so genuinely interesting and carefully worked out. Carlo Carlini's cinematography is gorgeous to look at. He and Mogherini do great work together, keeping the camera moving in an unobtrusive way and using color and décor to create a sense of mood and atmosphere. The overall impact is greatly aided by a terrific disco-infused soundtrack by Riz Ortolani. The use of a couple of songs, performed by singer Amanda Lear, may well make the film seem a little dated, but they serve as a pleasant chorus-like commentary on the action and are well integrated into the soundtrack.

The casting is top-notch. The beautiful Dalila Di Lazzaro gives a sensitive and moving performance as Glenda. She is a character truly worth rooting for, and Di Lazzaro makes her immensely sympathetic; her transformation from a sensual, free-spirited woman to a disappointed and crushed shadow of her former self is most convincing. Di Lazzaro was born in 1953. She began appearing in films in 1972, with an uncredited bit part in Sergio Martino's *Your Vice is a Locked Room and Only I Have the Key*. She soon graduated to leading lady status thanks to her appearance in Mario Mancini's inept *Frankenstein '80* (1972); she would revisit the Frankenstein story to far greater effect in Paul Morrisey's tongue-in-cheek 3-D splatterfest *Flesh for Frankenstein* (1973), in which she played one of mad scientist Udo Kier's beautiful "zombies." She would go on to appear in Dario Argento's *Phenomena* (1985), but has been relatively inactive since the late 1990s. Ray Milland is splendid as the cantankerous but charming Inspector Thompson. Milland

Italian *locandina* for *The Pyjama Girl Case*; designer unknown.

spent the latter part of his career playing cranky old men, but this role allows him to add in some welcome humor, and he seems to respond well to the challenge. He was born in Wales in 1905 and spent much of his youth pursuing athletic disciplines like boxing and horseback riding, but eventually began appearing in roles on the London stage. He made his film debut in 1929 and gradually worked his way to Hollywood, where he initially specialized in callow youth characterizations. By the 1940s he had become a bankable leading man, top-lining the likes of Lewis Allen's *The Uninvited*

(1944) and Fritz Lang's *Ministry of Fear* (1944). In 1945, Billy Wilder cast him as the alcoholic, down-on-his-luck writer Don Birnam in his powerful drama about addiction, *The Lost Weekend* (1945); the role was unlike anything Milland had ever played and he won an Oscar for his efforts. Milland continued to appear in meaty roles in films throughout the years, including memorable turns as a modern-day Mephistopheles to Thomas Mitchell's Faustian counterpart in John Farrow's political fantasy *Alias Nick Beal* (1949), as the suave murderer in Alfred Hitchcock's 3-D showcase *Dial M For Murder* (1954) and the titular character in Roger Corman's *X: The Man with the X-Ray Eyes* (1963). In the mid-1950s, he also turned to direction and scored a notable cult success wih 1962's apocalyptic parable *Panic in Year Zero*; concurrently, he would begin exploring the medium of television, where he even had his own program, *The Ray Milland Show*, which ran from 1953 to 1955. Like so many aging stars, he started appearing in European ventures and low-budget horror films in the 1970s: he was in *Frogs*, *The Thing with Two Heads* (both 1972, where he memorably appears as a bigot who has his head sewn onto the body of hulking black actor "Rosey" Grier), *The House in Nightmare Park* (1973), the borderline *giallo The Student Connection* (1974) and others; he was also nominated for an Emmy for his role in the acclaimed miniseries *Rich Man, Poor Man* (1976). He remained active until his death from cancer in 1986. The supporting cast includes a number of familiar *giallo* veterans, including Mel Ferrer as Professor Douglas, Michele Placido as Antonio and Howard Ross as Roy; all three give strong performances, with Placido in particular impressing as the sad-sack husband who is unable to cope with his failure in life.

Director Flavio Mogherini was born in Tuscany in 1922. He started off as a production and costume designer, working on such films as Pietro Francisci's *Hercules* (1958), Pier Paolo Pasolini's *Accattone* (1961), Henry Levin and Mario Bava's *The Wonders of Aladdin* (1961) and Giuliano Montaldo's *Machine Gun McCain* (1969). He began directing in 1972 and would helm 14 features before his death in 1994; his final film was his second *giallo*, **Crime of Passion** (1994).

Tutti defunti... tranne i morti (Italy)

Aka *Neun Leichen hat die Woche*

Directed by Pupi Avati; Produced by Antonio Avati and Gianni Minervini; Screenplay by Antonio Avati, Pupi Avati, Gianni Cavina and Maurizio Costanzo; Director of Photography: Pasquale Rachini; Editor: Maurizio Tedesco; Music by Amedeo Tommasi

Main Players: Gianni Cavina (Martini); Francesca Marciano (Ilaria); Carlo Delle Piane (Dante); Greta Vayan (Hilde); Michele Mirabella (Buster); Bob Tonelli (Ariano); Giulio Pizzirani (Giulio)

Dante arrives at a creepy castle and offers to sell the residents a book that is reputed to contain a prophecy pertaining to their future. The strange family offers to put Dante up for the night and he accepts their offer, though he soon wishes he had not. In time, a killer in black begins bumping off the family and servants ...

Following the success of **The House with Laughing Windows** (1976), writer/director Pupi Avati and his brother, writer/producer Antonio Avati, decided to revisit the genre. Sooner than deliver more of the same, however, they concocted a comic send-up, which would stand in stark contrast to their very serious hit thriller.

The title translates to *Everybody is Deceased ... Except for the Dead*, and this should provide a clue as to how the story will unfold. Inspired by Agatha Christie's *Ten Little Indians* (most effectively adapted for the screen by René Clair as *And Then There Were None* in 1945) and John Willard's stage play *The Cat and the Canary* (most famously filmed by Paul Leni in 1927), Avati's *giallo* spoof is played strictly for laughs. Avati introduces some wonderfully imaginative kill sequences—one victim has dynamite stuffed in her mouth, another turns up covered in ice in the freezer, one more is done in by a hairdryer that has been rigged to deliver a nasty surprise, still another is electrocuted—but they are also played for chuckles rather than shock value. Gore is kept to a minimum, but Avati does a skillful job of building a sense of Gothic atmosphere in the claustrophobic confines of the castle. Indeed, the careful attention to detail and atmosphere results in a few legitimately eerie moments as the killer stalks his victims in the dimly lit corridors.

The story is resolved via a very ingenious gimmick involving the grave markers for the various victims, but to say too much about this would be to give the game away. Suffice it to say, the story works as both a suspense piece and as a comedy. *Giallo* buffs may find it a little too whimsical and restrained, but taken on its own terms it is a charming and well-paced offering. What is most striking about it, however, is just how different it is from **The House with Laughing Windows**, even if the two films share a similar interest in the rural landscape of Italy. Avati displays his immense talent by jumping from genre to genre. Never content to be tied down to one particular style, he would continue to go from one type of film to another, always displaying a flair for the material but seldom repeating himself in the long run. This ability to switch from one extreme to another sets the director apart from many of his contemporaries, most of whom excelled in one genre but floundered when they ventured outside of their comfort zone.

The characters are a memorably eccentric lot. The family comprises various oddballs, including a chronic masturbator who has to undergo shock treatment to control his compulsions, an eccentric who believes he is an American cowboy and a demented matriarch who tries to keep her dignity even as she reveals herself to be as crazy as the rest. The servants include a lunatic with a lazy eye and a dwarf maid, who is

Italian *locandina* for *Tutti defunti … tranne i morti*; artist unknown.

killer is presented in the usual attire of a black cloak and an oversized fedora, and the eerie chuckling and raspy voice evoke the sexless, threatening voices of the killers in Dario Argento's films.

The director reassembled much of the same team from **The House with Laughing Windows** for this film. Pasquale Rachini's moody lighting is in a different style from his sun-drenched approach to the earlier effort; it suits the Gothic flavor of the movie very well and results in some beautiful, mist-laden images. Amedeo Tommasi's bouncy score has something of a 1920s jazz quality to it and is also very effective in this context. As for Avati, he does a wonderful job keeping the material moving at a good pace. The 1940s setting is meticulously detailed throughout and helps to give the film a different ambience from other *gialli* of the period. The gags are funny, the plot holds one's attention and the final reveal is genuinely effective.

The cast includes several holdovers from Avati's first *giallo*: Gianni Cavina is very good as the intrepid but basically inept Martini, while beautiful Francesca Marciano is effective as Ilaria, who fulfills the function of damsel-in-distress. Diminuitive Bob Tonelli is also on hand again, this time playing one of the shiftier relatives who may or may not be behind the series of murders. The main new face in the ensemble is that of Carlo Delle Piane, who gives a wonderful performance as the faint-hearted salesman, Dante. Delle Piane (born in 1936) had been in films since the late 1940s, but he became a favorite of Avati while working on this picture; they would reunite on such diverse projects as the TV miniseries *Jazz Band* (1978), another miniseries titled *Dancing Paradise* (1982) and the critically acclaimed *Regalo di Natale* (1986).

Watch Me When I Kill (Italy)

Aka *Il gatto dagli occhi di Giada; Die Stimme des Todes; The Cat's Victims*

Directed by Antonio Bido; Produced by Gabriella Nardi; Screenplay by Antonio Bido, Roberto Natale, Vittorio Schiraldi and Aldo Serio; Director of Photography: Mario Vulpiani; Editor: Maurizio Tedesco; Music by Trans Europa Express

Main Players: Corrado Pani (Lukas); Paola Tedesco (Mara); Franco Citti (Pasquale Ferrante); Fernando Cerulli (Giovanni Bozzi); Giuseppe Addobbati (Judge); Paolo Malco (Carlo)

Home Video: VCI Entertainment (Region free DVD); Shameless Screen Entertainment (Region free DVD)

A pharmacist is murdered and Mara catches sight of the killer as he flees from the scene. Mara turns to her boyfriend, Lukas, for assistance. As Lukas begins to investigate, more people fall victim to the killer. In time, Lukas uncovers a surprising motivation for the string of killings ...

The original Italian title, which translates to *The Cat with the Jade Eyes*, makes it clear that this is looking to evoke the

actually played by an actor in drag. The bumbling Dante and an equally inept private investigator, Martini, represent the "heroes."

Avati indulges in some marvelous bits of slapstick, notably in the various murder sequences: a man is stabbed but reacts nonchalantly as if irritated that somebody could possibly be so rude, while another victim is so oblivious to her surroundings that she fails to notice that the killer is throwing daggers at her and just narrowly missing the intended target. The highlight is undoubtedly a scene wherein a victim watches in amazement as an inept attempt is made to put poison in her drink; it is a marvelous, off-kilter moment that is all the more effective for not being overdone. The

LA **P.A.C.** PRODUZIONI ATLAS CONSORZIATE PRESENTA

CORRADO PANI · PAOLA TEDESCO ■

IL GATTO DAGLI OCCHI DI GIADA

CON **FRANCO CITTI** · **FERNANDO CERULLI** · **GIANFRANCO BULLO** CON **PAOLO MALCO**
CON LA PARTECIPAZIONE DI **BIANCA TOCCAFONDI** REGIA DI **ANTONIO BIDO**
COLORE DELLA TECHNOSPES S.P.A. NEGATIVO GEVACOLOR MUSICHE TRANS EUROPA EXPRESS s.l. EDIZIONI **RCA**

Italian *locandina* for *Watch Me When I Kill*; artist unknown.

gialli of the early 1970s. More to the point, it is an out-and-out homage to Dario Argento.

The routine scenario was co-written by veteran Roberto Natale, whose earlier credits included Mario Bava's *Kill, Baby ... Kill!* (1966) and two films for director Massimo Pupillo: *Terror-Creatures from the Grave* (1965) and *Bloody Pit of Horror* (1965). He also had a hand in bringing Ernesto Gastaldi's play ***A... come assassino*** to the screen in 1966. Unfortunately, the script (which was also co-authored by director Antonio Bido and several other collaborators) is undu-

ly derivative and offers very few surprises. The final reveal of the killer's motivation in committing the crimes is one of the few flourishes of imagination to be found in the picture, but by then it is a matter of "too little, too late."

Characterization is another sore spot. Simply put, there is nobody in this film worthy of our investing any emotion. It is not that they are too unsympathetic or morally reprehensible; after all, the genre flourishes on such shoddy excuses for human beings. Instead, they are simply too thinly drawn and dull to sustain much interest.

In lieu of any real inspiration, director Antonio Bido falls back on aping the films of Dario Argento. The original title evokes the so-called "animal trilogy" of ***The Bird with the Crystal Plumage*** (1970), ***The Cat O'Nine Tails*** (1971) and ***Four Flies on Grey Velvet*** (1971). There is a garotting that recalls ***The Cat O'Nine Tails***. Another victim is scalded to death, recalling ***Deep Red*** (1975). The latter is also evident in the creepy old house that the amateur detective goes to investigate at one point. A series of threatening phone calls with the killer speaking in hushed, ambiguous tones is another Argento standard, as is the clue overheard in the background of one of the calls. And lastly, the score by music group Trans Europa Express seems intent on evoking the music of Goblin in ***Deep Red*** at all costs.

All of this is not to say that *Watch Me When I Kill* is a lousy example of the genre. It may lack much in the way of originality, but it is competently made and does not overstay its welcome. Bido's enthusiasm for the genre manifests here and there; some of the killings are unexpectedly effective, notably the bathtub demise of one of the key supporting players. Mario Vulpiani's cinematography is professional if unremarkable, while the Goblin-esque score is effective.

Corrado Pani, who gives a decent performance as Lukas, heads the cast. The character is not particularly interesting and Pani resorts to mannerisms, like chomping on a cheroot as if he has wandered in from a Sergio Leone Western, as a means of compensating. Pani had previously appeared in ***Interrabang*** (1969) as well as the borderline *giallo Testa giù gambe in aria* (1972), but this would prove to be his final brush with the genre. Paola Tedesco plays Mara, who fails to make much of an impression, while Franco Citti easily steals a number of scenes as Pasquale. His role in the murders is left ambiguous for a while, and Citti is one of the few actors in the cast who seems able to convey much in the way of an inner life to his character. Citti was born in Rome in 1935. He was "discovered" by filmmaker Pier Paolo Pasolini, who cast him in major roles in such movies as *Accatone* (1961), *Mamma Roma* (1962), *Oedipus Rex* (1967) and *The Decameron* (1971). Citti also worked for the likes of Francis Ford Coppola (*The Godfather*, 1972), Elio Petri (*Todo Modo*, 1976) and Valerio Zurlini (*Black Jesus*, 1968), in addition to popping up in more "populist" fare like the Spaghetti Western *Kill Them All and Come Back Alone* (1968) and the *poliziottesco Live Like a Cop, Die Like a Man* (1976).

Director Antonio Bido was born in 1949. He broke into films in the mid-'70s as an assistant director before making his debut with this movie. It proved successful enough to enable him to follow up with another *giallo*, *The Bloodstained Shadow* (1978). Bido would continue working sporadically until the year 2000, but his output was never very prolific and his career was almost certainly compromised by the general collapse of the Italian film industry in the 1980s.

1978

The Bloodstained Shadow
(Italy)

Aka *Solamente nero; Terreur sur la lagune; Blutige Schatten*

Directed by Antonio Bido; Produced by Teodoro Corrà [as Teodoro Agrimi]; Screenplay by Marisa Andalò, Antonio Bido and Domenico Malan; Director of Photography: Mario Vulpiani; Editor: Amedeo Giomini; Music by Stelvio Cipriani (Note: the score was performed, without credit, by Goblin)

Main Players: Lino Capolicchio (Stefano D'Arcangelo); Stefania Casini (Sandra Sellani); Craig Hill (Don Paolo); Massimo Serato (Count Pedrazzi); Juliette Mayniel (Signora Nardi); Sergio Mioni (Dr. Aloisi); Alina De Simone (Medium)

Home Video: Blue Underground (Region 1 DVD)

Stefano returns to Venice to visit his brother, the priest Don Paolo. The latter complains that the community has fallen into degradation and alludes to some strange goings-on involving a local medium and some seemingly upstanding but actually corrupt individuals. One night, Don Paolo witnesses the medium being strangled by a killer in black, and he soon finds himself being threatened if he reveals what he has seen. Stefano starts to investigate, hoping to spare his brother further grief...

Following the success of *Watch Me When I Kill* (1977), Antonio Bido was asked to direct his second *giallo*. As Bido explains in an interview included on the Blue Underground DVD release of *The Bloodstained Shadow*, this unexpected offer came out of the blue and caught him off-guard, as he did not have any scenarios lying around which would fit what the producers at Produzioni Atlas Consorziate had in mind. Fortunately, a friend of the director's wife had a short story gathering dust that fit the bill, thus allowing the young filmmaker to direct his second *giallo* in rapid succession.

The film embraces the "regional" aspect found in such *gialli* as Lucio Fulci's *Don't Torture a Duckling* (1972) and Pupi Avati's *The House with Laughing Windows* (1976); not surprisingly, Bido is an admitted fan of Avati's works in particular. The notion of a closed-off society lorded over by a corrupt aristocracy gives the film something of a so-

cio-political edge, but the commentary is muted compared to the fiery intensity found in Fulci's work for example. Even so, Bido does a nice job of evoking the atmosphere of the community. It is nominally set in Venice, but Bido explains in the interview on the Blue Underground DVD that much of the film was shot on location in Murano, with the goal of creating a stylized representation of Venice. Bido's aim, as such, is to create a generic representation of a "backwards" community; it is not meant to be Venice, specifically, as the story could easily be transposed to other, similar regions throughout Italy.

Italian *locandina* for *The Bloodstained Shadow*; artwork by Lucio Crovato.

Where the film stumbles rather badly is in the pacing, which is all over the map. At nearly two hours, it is one of the longest *gialli* of the period, but the material does not justify such a running time; with tighter editing, it may have emerged as a stronger, more suspenseful film. As it stands, the result is sporadically effective, with some memorable set pieces spread throughout, but much of it is slack and the movie suffers accordingly.

Greater attention to characterization would also have been appreciated. The characters suffer from the same generic quality that dogged the ones in **Watch Me When I Kill**, suggesting that Bido was in need of a stronger writing collaborator to give more depth and feeling to the people populating his stories. One of the more potentially interesting figures is the corrupt aristocrat, Count Pedrazzi, who lords over the village from his opulently appointed castle. Pedrazzi is callous and cruel, and if Bido succumbs to negative stereotyping by making him both a homosexual and a pedophile, it at least makes the character properly despicable in context. Sadly, he does not play a very large role in the proceedings. Bido would have done well to have expanded that role and

Italian poster for *The Bloodstained Shadow*.

paid less attention to his less interesting co-conspirators in the unsavory goings-on in the village.

The story also explores the theme of Catholic guilt, which makes the film part of a subgenre of sorts among Italian thrillers. The community is unified by their faith, but there is a jaundiced aspect to this. The sense of fear and hypocrisy that permeates the setting suggests that their "faith" is tenuous at best, while Don Paolo's complex backstory ("I wasn't always a priest," he tells his brother) suggests early on that his place in the community may be tainted at best. Religious icons become weapons (Don Paolo is nearly brained when a heavy stone crucifix comes crashing down) or clues to the mystery (a painting with a religious theme holds the key to a past trauma, though Stefano fails to recognize this until it is almost too late), and the role of the Church is reduced to keeping people's secrets by virtue of the oath of the confessional.

For all its missteps, the film represents a significant improvement over Bido's first thriller. His direction is smoother and more confident and the various murder scenes are staged for maximum nasty impact: one character is pushed face-first into a fireplace, another is stalked through an armory before being speared to death, another is crushed when a speedboat charges at him in the Venetian canals, etc. The imagery is somewhat undone by Mario Vulpiani's unnecessarily harsh lighting, but some nice compositions and camera movements are in evidence nevertheless. The film also benefits from an excellent music score. As Bido explains on the Blue Underground DVD interview, he originally commissioned Goblin to score the picture, but the producers balked at their asking price. Stelvio Cipriani was hired to do it instead, but when the time came to arrange and record the music, Bido was allowed to have his cake and eat it too: Goblin would add extra pizzazz by arranging and recording the score themselves, though only Cipriani was credited for contractual purposes.

The cast is uneven. Lino Capolicchio was cast because of his role in **The House with Laughing Windows**, but he is not nearly as effective here. In fairness, Stefano is something of a blank slate, and too much effort is expended toward making him a red herring as well, but Capolicchio's bland, disinterested performance is a disappointment just the same. Craig Hill is very good as the tormented Don Paolo. Hill had appeared in quite a few Spaghetti Westerns—including the Western/*giallo* hybrid **The Masked Thief** (1973)—so this role marked a nice change of pace for the actor. In the Blue Underground DVD interview, Bido recalls having to coax the actor into giving a more relaxed performance, but the end result was worth the effort. Stefano's love interest, Sandra, is well played by the gorgeous Stefania Casini. Sandra is not a tremendously well-developed character, but Casini's sensitive acting makes her tremendously likable. Not surprisingly, the film is at its most tense when she is in danger. Casini was born in 1948 and began her film and television career in 1970. Following an early success with her role in Pietro Germi's *A Pocketful of Chestnuts* (1970), she appeared in several movies that endeared her to European Cult Cinema enthusiasts. For Paul Morrissey, she was one of Vittorio De Sica's sexually voracious daughters in *Blood for Dracula* (1974); for Stelvio Massi, she played Gastone Moschin's sexy but dimwitted girlfriend in *Emergency Squad* (1974); and for Dario Argento, she played the dancing student who befriends Jessica Harper's heroine in *Suspiria* (1977). Casini also appeared as a prostitute in Bernardo Bertolucci's *1900* (1976), where she (in)famously pleasured Robert De Niro and Gerard Depardieu manually on camera during a graphic threesome. In more recent years, Casini has focused on the production end, producing and directing a number of films and documentaries, mostly for the national RAI TV network.

Sadly, *The Bloodstained Shadow* would remain Bido's last encounter with the *giallo*. His subsequent career would prove to be very spotty and attempts at revisiting the genre with a new thriller have thus far failed to come off the ground. Given that *The Bloodstained Shadow* displayed a marked improvement over his first effort, it is entirely possible that he would have continued to improve over time, if only the opportunities had been presented to him.

Pensione Paura (Italy)

Aka *La violación de la señorita Julia*

Directed by Francesco Barilli; Produced by Tommaso Dazzi and Paolo Fornasier; Screenplay by Barbara Alberti, Francesco Barilli and Amedeo Pagani; Director of Photography: Gualtiero Manozzi; Editor: Amedeo Salfa; Music by Adolfo Waitzman

Main Players: Luc Merenda (Rodolfo); Leonora Fani (Rosa); Francisco Rabal (Marta's lover); Lidia Biondi (Marta); Jole Fierro (Rodolfo's lover)

During World War II, Marta and her daughter Rosa are left to attend to the family business, while the father is engaged in combat. Unsavory types populate the hotel they run, but business being what it is, they cannot afford to send any of the people away. When Marta dies, Rosa is left in charge. One of the guests, Rodolfo, has his lecherous sights set on deflowering the young girl. Meanwhile, a killer begins picking off the guests ...

Anybody who has ever seen Francesco Barilli's bizarre psychological horror film *The Perfume of the Lady in Black* (1974), which is often erroneously listed as a *giallo*, will not be surprised to find that his one "true" *giallo, Pensione Paura*, is an unorthodox example of the genre. For this reason, it tends to disappoint more traditional genre fans, but its pleasures are many and varied.

The film is unusual for its setting, among other things. While Pupi Avati's satirical ***Tutti defunti ... tranne i morti*** (1977) was set in the late 1940s, it did not make explicit reference to World War II; Barilli's picture, on the other hand,

Italian *locandina* for *Pensione paura*; artwork by Ermanno Iaia.

is inextricably linked to the horror and chaos wrought by the war. The hotel is situated in the countryside, far from the major action seen in the big cities, but the shadow of the war looms large over the narrative. Food supplies are limited, the number of men and women serving in the military curtails the influx of potential guests and the sounds of overhead planes serve as a sporadic reminder of what is transpiring in the world at large.

Barilli also explores the theme of Fascism, as Rodolfo is revealed to be in cahoots with the Blackshirts. Rodolfo is a particularly vile and despicable character. He uses his lover for her jewelry and proposes to ditch her once he has succeeded in selling the diamonds to a couple of Fascist operatives in exchange for a wad of cash and a forged passport. His leering interest in Rosa also explodes in the film's most horrific set piece, as he uses his aging lover to lure the young girl to their bedroom, where he proceeds to rape her while the older woman strokes his naked backside. It is a grim and powerful scene that mercifully avoids bad taste eroticism; the viewer is firmly on the side of Rosa as she is traumatized into "becoming a woman." Rodolfo is therefore indicative of a particularly loathsome section of society that had no qualms about selling out the people around them in exchange for a bit of comfort and luxury.

Admittedly, this is one of the more borderline *gialli* that made the cut in this context. The thriller elements are rather subdued and Barilli's emphasis on mood, atmosphere and characterization over lurid shock effects will not necessarily sit well with some viewers. That said, the whodunit aspect of the plot is worked out in a satisfactory manner and the assorted twists and turns the narrative takes in its final section are genuinely surprising. Violence erupts quickly and clumsily, but the director does not dwell on it for the sake of sensationalism. The rape scene is far more upsetting than any of the kill sequences, and this is arguably as it should be.

Barilli directs with great care and precision. The visuals are artfully composed and Gualtiero Manozzi's expert cinematography wallows in sensual textures: the mud used to cover up two of the victims, the sweat glistening on Rodolfo's back as he violates Rosa, the pool of blood Rosa steps in with bare feet, the colored light playing off the contours of the art direction, etc. The period detail is immaculate without being too fussy, and production values are solid throughout. The music score by Adolfo Waitzman moves effectively from the understated to the frenetic; the Argentinian composer also worked on such European horror films as León Klimovsky's *Dr. Jekyll vs. the Werewolf* (1972), Jess Franco's *The Other Side of the Mirror* and Claudio Guerin Hill's borderline *giallo A Bell from Hell* (both 1973), but this was his only foray into the *giallo* proper.

Luc Merenda is splendid as the repugnant Rodolfo. Merenda subverts his normally heroic screen image, wearing a sleazy looking mustache and greasing his hair back; it is not just a physical transformation, however, but a case of real acting on his part as he transforms into the most loathsome character of his career. Francisco Rabal gives a good performance as Marta's lover, who spends the film isolated from the rest of the characters as he lives in fear for his life; the character is a deserter and he fears that he will be discovered and executed for his cowardice. Rabal manages to make the character somewhat sympathetic, though he is not entirely what he may initially appear. The film is completely owned, however, by Leonora Fani. She is brilliant as the multi-layered Rosa. She starts the film as a naïve dreamer, but the horrors that are inflicted on her cause her to grow up in a

hurry; the character proves to be resilient, strong-willed and able to hold her own against the sundry unpleasant characters she is forced to deal with. Fani was born in Cornuda, Veneto, Italy in 1954 and started appearing in films in the early 1970s. One of her earliest credits was the bizarre *Dog Lay Afternoon* (1976), which contrary to its title was not a softcore spoof of Sidney Lumet's riveting *Dog Day Afternoon* (1975); instead, it told the story of a young girl who is traumatized when she witnesses her mother having sex with the family dog! Fani appeared in the borderline *giallo Perché si uccidono* (1976) and in Stelvio Massi's *poliziottesco The Last Round* (1976) and went on to appear in one of the sleaziest of all *gialli*, **Giallo a Venezia** (1979). She stopped appearing in films in the 1980s and presumably retired to a domestic life.

Francesco Barilli was born in Parma in 1943. He entered movies in the 1960s as an assistant director, working with the likes of Pier Paolo Pasolini on *Hawks and Sparrows* (1966). Barilli was also an actor in such films as Bernardo Bertolucci's *Before the Revolution* (1964); he would continue making sporadic screen appearances, more recently turning up in Carlo Vanzina's **Sotto il vestito niente – L'ultima sfilata** (2011). He began working as a screenwriter in the 1970s and his first brush with the *giallo* came when he collaborated on the script for Aldo Lado's **Who Saw Her Die?** (1972). He made his feature directing debut with *The Perfume of the Lady in Black*, which can best be described as a horror film in the style of Roman Polanski. *Pensione Paura* was his follow-up, and it seemed to announce great things, but his career never really took off; his films failed to rake in the same kind of money as those of Dario Argento. His deliberately off-kilter approach has not endeared him to many fans of the Italian horror scene. He most recently contributed to the horror movie *The House in the Wind of the Dead* (2012), both as an actor and as a "special guest director," though what that means is open to speculation.

The Perfect Crime (Italy)

Aka *Indagine su un delitto perfetto; Eine mörderische Karriere; Mord in Perfektion*

Directed by Giuseppe Rosati and Giuseppe Pulieri (as Aaron Leviathan); Screenplay by Giuseppe Rosati; Director of Photography: Jerry Delaware; Editor: Franco Fraticelli (as Frank Robertson); Music by Carlo Savina

Main Players: Gloria Guida (Polly); Leonard Mann (Paul De Revere); Joseph Cotten (Sir Arthur Dundee); Anthony Steel (Superintendant Jeff Hawkins); Adolfo Celi (Sir Harold Boyd); Alida Valli (Lady Clementine De Revere); Janet Agren (Lady Gloria Boyd); Paul Muller (Gibson)

When the chairman of a major corporation in England is killed, his board members are thrown into a tizzy. The elections for the new chairman are several days off and it would seem that somebody is trying to inch his/her way up the ladder by killing off the competition. Detective Super-

intendant Hawkins attempts to get to the bottom of things before everybody turns up dead ...

The Perfect Crime is pretty much a perfect bore, but it deserves note as being arguably the most utterly predictable *giallo* of them all.

The routine screenplay by director Giuseppe Rosati piles on clichés with a trowel, but surprises are nowhere to be found. The characters range from the dull to the disagreeable, and only a very capable cast succeeds in injecting the slightest bit of interest into the proceedings. The final twist is so transparent that it can be seen coming within the first half-hour, and attempts at dark humor fall flat.

Director Giuseppe Rosati shows no particular flair for this type of subject matter. The pacing is slow, the coverage is as basic as it gets and very few memorable sequences can be recommended. In the way of spoilers, one particularly nasty death scene involves Sir Arthur performing an emergency surgery on himself to deal with his wonky pacemaker (the killer used an electrical frequency to make it go haywire), but this is the closest the film comes to really developing a pulse. It is worth noting that Rosati was replaced late in the filming by Giuseppe Pulieri; given how flat and listless the majority of the material is, one cannot help but wonder if the odd (and very infrequent) sequence such as this was filmed by Pulieri as a means of salvaging the material.

As a piece of filmmaking, *The Perfect Crime* is perfectly adequate, but nothing more. The cinematography and editing are very basic and the movie does not offer up the kind of stylized imagery one can find in the more inspired Italian thrillers of the period. Gore is kept to a minimum and even the sex angle is downplayed, with only a little nudity on display courtesy of leading lady Gloria Guida. The music score by Carlo Savina is bland, as well.

On the plus side, the film offers up an impressive cast. Gloria Guida is a marvelously photogenic presence, but her role as the *femme fatale* is poorly developed. Guida does the best she can under the circumstances, but her naturally likable screen persona clashes with the needs of the role and helps to keep her function in the film somewhat obtuse, if not completely unbelievable. Guida was born in 1955 and entered movies in 1974. Her stunning looks and willingness to disrobe for the camera made her a natural "blonde bombshell," and she appeared in quite a few sexy comedies and dramas with an erotic bent. She appeared in the borderline *giallo So Young, So Lovely, So Vicious* (1975) for Silvio Amadio, but made her most memorable impression as one of the leads in Fernando Di Leo's extraordinary *To Be Twenty* (1978). She has been more or less inactive in films since the 1980s, following her marriage to singer/comedian Johnny Dorelli of *Il Mostro* (1977) fame. Second-billed Leonard Mann is not actually in the film very much and he fails to make much of an impression while he is on screen. British actor Anthony Steel and *giallo* veteran Franco Ressel capably play the plodding policemen, while

Cover for VidAmerica's 1980s U.S. VHS release of *The Perfect Crime*; artist unknown.

familiar faces like Alida Valli, Paul Müller and Tom Felleghy stop by to collect a paycheck. Joseph Cotten and Adolfo Celi play the senior members of the board, while the beautiful Janet Agren is on hand as Celi's unfaithful wife. Cotten and Celi easily steal the film from their co-stars, even if both of them coast by on their natural charisma. Celi was already a familiar presence in *gialli* thanks to such films as *Who Saw Her Die?* (1972) and *Eye in the Labyrinth* (1972), but *The Perfect Crime* would provide Hollywood legend Cotten with his only genre credit. Cotten was born in Petersburg, Virginia in 1905. He started off working in advertising before trying his hand at being a theater critic. He caught the acting bug and began appearing on stage, eventually becoming one of the members of Orson Welles' famed Mercury Theatre Players. He made his film debut with a plum supporting role in Welles' masterpiece *Citizen Kane* (1941) and would go on to appear in other films for the director, sometimes in an uncredited cameo capacity, including *The Magnificent Ambersons* (1942) and *Touch of Evil* (1958). While Welles' star floundered due to ego problems, Cotten's quickly ascended. He became a popular leading man and character star, impressing as the psychotic Uncle Charley in Alfred Hitchcock's *Shadow of a Doubt* (1943), as the lovelorn artist in William Dieterle's *Portrait of Jennie* (1948) and as the disillusioned hero of Carol Reed's classic *noir The Third Man* (1949), opposite Welles and Alida Valli. He remained popular and in demand throughout the 1950s and '60s, but gradually began accepting supporting roles and doing more and more television, including memorable episodes of *Alfred Hitchcock Presents*. In the 1960s, he began appearing in some Italian productions, including Sergio Corbucci's Spaghetti Western *The Hellbenders* (1967). By the 1970s, he started appearing in such horror films as Robert Fuest's *The Abominable Dr. Phibes* (1971) and Mario Bava's *Baron Blood* (1972). His last major credit was a small role in Michael Cimino's infamous flop *Heaven's Gate* (1980). Cotten suffered a debilitating stroke in 1981, which left him paralyzed and unable to speak; he underwent intensive physical therapy and regained his ability to walk and speak, but he opted not to return to the screen for fear of disappointing on set. He died in 1994, at the age of 88.

The movie had a complicated production history. Filming commenced in 1976 and close to an hour's worth of material was already in the can when the producer went bankrupt; the plug was pulled on the project, and it seemed destined to disappear for good. However, assistant director Giuseppe Pulieri believed in the project and searched for investors to raise enough capital to complete the film. He finally managed to get the money together in 1978, and, with the aid of doubles to replace the actors (who had naturally moved on to other projects), was able to finish the picture. Pulieri supervised the final assembly, cobbling scenes together by reusing insert shots and close-ups as a means of making up for material which had never been filmed, as Rosati was no longer involved in the project.[1] Rosati and Pulieri, incidentally, had worked together on a number of projects, including the *poliziotteschi Silence the Witness* (1974), *The Left Hand of the Law* (1975) and *Hot Stuff* (1976). *The Perfect Crime* was one of Rosati's final films; his last credit was contributing to the screenplay for the salacious comedy *With Aunt It's Not a Sin* (1980), starring Italy's first hardcore sex star Marina Frajese, which marked the only "official" directing credit of Giuseppe Pulieri.

Notes:

1. Grattarolla, Franco, *È arrivato il risolutore. Intervista a Giuseppe Pulieri*, "Cine 70 e dintorni" #7, 2006, p. 25.

Rings of Fear
(Italy/West Germany/Spain)

Aka *Enigma rosso; Red Rings of Fear; Tráfico de menores; Das Phantom im Mädchenpensionat; Trauma; Virgin Killer*

Directed by Alberto Negrin; Produced by Leonardo Pesarolo, Antonio Tagliaferri and Artur Brauner; Screenplay by Peter Berling, Marcello Coscia, Massimo Dallamano, Franco Ferrini, Alberto Negrin and Stefano Ubezio; Director of Photography: Eduardo Noé; Editor: Paolo Boccio; Music by Riz Ortolani

Main Players: Fabio Testi (Inspector Gianni Di Salvo); Christine Kaufmann (Christina); Ivan Desny (Chief Inspector Louis Roccaglio); Jack Taylor (Michael Parravicini); Helga Liné (Mrs. Russo)

Home Video: Full Moon/Wizard Entertainment (Region 1 DVD)

A young girl is brutally raped and murdered. When her body is discovered wrapped in plastic in the river, Inspector Di Salvo is assigned to investigate. He soon uncovers a hotbed of corruption and underage prostitution linked to a posh girls' college, but when he comes close to uncovering a lead, the murderer strikes again ...

Rings of Fear originated with writer/director Massimo Dallamano and was intended to form the final part of his so-called "schoolgirls in peril" trilogy. Sadly, Dallamano's life was cut short when he died in a car crash in 1976, and the script he had helped to prepare would undergo some changes before reaching the screen in 1978. The film endured a tortuous production, with original director Piero Schivazappa (*The Frightened Woman*, 1969) being replaced early on by Alberto Negrin, according to a review of the film by Steve Fenton in *European Trash Cinema*. Co-star Jack Taylor would later recall in an interview with Fenton:

> That was a film that was never finished, actually. I know that it's out on video, but it was never finished. The film started was never finished, and so they just took bits and pieces of it and ... it was a dreadful experience.[1]

One of the things that is most readily apparent in watching this film is how invaluable Dallamano was to the previous instalments in the trilogy. He was a gifted craftsman who knew how to deliver the goods on a purely exploitative level without allowing his films to become prurient or hypocritical in the process. The same cannot be said for director Alberto Negrin, whose blunt handling of the material in this movie results in a seedy, grimy thriller that lacks the strong social conscience of the previous efforts. He does manage at least one memorable sequence—Di Salvo's rough interrogation of a suspect on a moving rollercoaster—but beyond that his approach is at best functional.

The characters are thinly drawn and the pacing is much too slack. Apart from a few well-timed shocks and some memorably overripe dialogue ("Somebody with a cock this big raped Angela Russo and threw her in the river!" barks Di Salvo at one point), the film never really catches fire. Suspense is virtually non-existent, but it has to be admitted that the final reveal of the killer's identity comes as a genuine surprise. Sadly, very little invention is on display beyond that, and one can only guess at how much of the strictly routine scenario bears Dallamano's original imprint.

The film also lacks the classy production values of *What Have You Done to Solange?* (1972), as well as the sheer kinetic force of *What Have They Done to Your Daughters?* (1974). Negrin's flat-footed direction fails to make much of the various would-be suspense sequences, while the production appears to have been hastily mounted and executed. A motorcycle chase scene seems primed to evoke memories of the thrilling chase set piece in *What Have They Done to Your Daughters?*, but it is all a tease: the scene is over before it even gets started. Make-up effects are crude, and Negrin wallows in shower-room nudity and back-street abortions in a manner that seems genuinely distasteful. Riz Ortolani's score is comprised of cues composed for other films, with his main theme for Dallamano's quirky *poliziottesco Superbitch* (1973) getting a particular workout.

Fabio Testi gives an enjoyable performance as the hot-headed Di Salvo. On the face of it, he is something of a continuation of Claudio Cassinelli's morally outraged police inspector in *What Have They Done to Your Daughters?*, but the shading and nuance present in that earlier characterization is nowhere to be found here. Di Salvo's one peculiar attribute is an obvious preference for the companionship of cats over people; given what he sees in his line of work, however, one can hardly blame him! Testi's natural charisma and presence goes a long way toward making the character interesting, and he does a decent job of carrying the film on his broad shoulders. Christine Kaufmann plays his on-again/off-again love interest, Christina. The character is so poorly developed that she fails to make much of an impression; she is a kleptomaniac of sorts, which could have been an interesting character trait, but here again nothing much is made of that and she drops out of the story early on. Austrian actress Kaufmann (born 1945) does what she can, but apart from showing a bit of skin she is not asked to do much; Kaufmann fared much better in films like Mario Bonnard and Sergio Leone's *The Last Days of Pompeii* (1959), Gottfried Reinhardt's *Town Without Pity* (1961) and Gordon Hessler's *Murders in the Rue Morgue* (1971); she was briefly married to Tony Curtis, whom she met on the set of *Taras Bulba* (1962). Spanish horror veterans Jack Taylor and Helga Liné show up in supporting roles; Taylor is appropriately sleazy as one of the

Italian newspaper ad for *Rings of Fear*; artist unknown.

chief suspects, while Liné (whose role in Spanish genre cinema can be seen as roughly analogous to that of Barbara Steele in the Italian strain) has a few nice moments as the grieving mother of one of the victims. Born in Oregon in 1936, Taylor got his start appearing on American TV shows, then migrated to Mexico, where he appeared in a number of films, including *The Curse of Nostradamus* (1960). Taylor eventually made his way to Europe, where he found some popularity appearing in genre fare for the likes of Jess Franco and Amando De Ossorio, including *Succubus* (1967), *Count Dracula* (1970) and *The Ghost Galleon* (1974). Apart from *Rings of Fear*, Taylor would feature in the infamous Spanish splatter film *Pieces* (1982), which is often viewed by fans as something of an honorary *giallo* in its own right. He previously co-starred with Testi in the borderline *giallo Due occhi per uccidere* (1968).[2] Taylor snagged a notable late career role as a rare book collector in Roman Polanski's Euro-horror homage *The Ninth Gate* (1999) and remains busy in the European film scene to this day.

Alberto Negrin was born in Casablanca in 1940. He started off writing and directing for Italian television. *Rings of Fear* marked his debut as a feature film director. It would also remain his only effort for the big screen, but he remains active (and prolific) as a director for the small screen.

Notes:
1. Fenton, Steve, "Taylor-Made in Europe: Cleo, Franco, Arnie & The Blind Dead!" *Tame* fanzine, 1992.
2. Long believed to be a lost film, *Due occhi per uccidere* resurfaced in 2013 when a private collector was able to purchase a 35mm print in an auction. It was subsequently transferred to DVD and shared among fellow collectors; far from being a proper *giallo*, it ultimately emerged as a rather indifferent crime thriller with slight sci-fi undertones.

The Sister of Ursula (Italy)
Aka *La sorella di Ursula*

Directed by Enzo Milioni; Produced by Armando Bertuccioli; Screenplay by Enzo Milioni; Director of Photog-

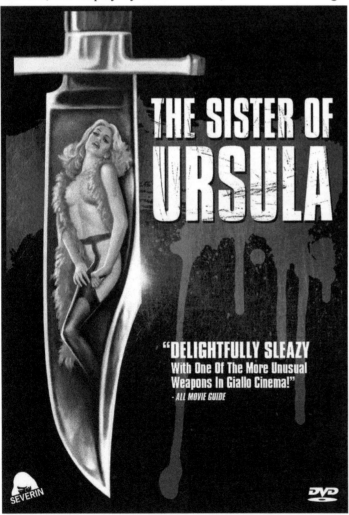

"DELIGHTFULLY SLEAZY
With One Of The More Unusual
Weapons In Giallo Cinema!"
- ALL MOVIE GUIDE

Cover for the American DVD release of *The Sister of Ursula* from Severin; artist unknown.

raphy: Vittorio Bernini; Editor: Francesco Bertuccioli and Franco Di Pietro; Music by Mimi Uva

Main Players: Barbara Magnolfi (Ursula Beyne); Stefania D'Amario (Dagmar Beyne); Anna Zinnemann (Vanessa); Marc Porel (Filippo Andrei / Gianni Nardi); Antiniska Nemour (Jenny)

Home Video: Severin (Region free DVD)

Ursula and Dagmar are left a sizeable inheritance when their father dies. They set out to find their estranged mother and cut her in on the inheritance and stop at a luxurious hotel by the sea along the way. While there, a maniac begins killing off some of the guests. Ursula, who possesses psychic abilities, is convinced that she is going to be the next victim ...

The *giallo* was in pretty dire straits by 1978. The popularity of the *poliziotteschi* was giving way to a renewed interest in horror, while sexy comedies continued to pack in audiences on a regular basis. Relaxing censorship standards also allowed for an increase in graphic sexual content. *The Sister of Ursula* therefore delivers a mixture of horror and thriller elements, while explicitly demonstrating a gradual slide into the world of pornography.

In an interview included on the Severin DVD release of the film, writer/director Enzo Milioni indicates that the film was made on a bet with producer Armando Bertuccioli. Milioni had apparently written an ambitious screenplay which attracted the interest of heavy-hitters like Dirk Bogarde, Valentina Cortese and Gabriele Ferzetti; however, the three of them also came equipped with a hefty price tag and Bertuccioli was unable to raise the necessary financing right away, so he suggested to Milioni that they hedge their bets by making a quick thriller on the cheap before aiming for the stars and making the bigger budgeted film. The latter never transpired, and in some respects it would have been better if *The Sister of Ursula* had never happened.

Much of the film's problem lies in its inability to do well by its disaparate components. The thriller elements are predictable, the horror ones are hokey and the sex ends up becoming the main focal point, but very little of it is actually erotic. Milioni focuses on one protracted sex scene after the other while the point and purpose of the narrative tends to be forgotten; it would not be such an unforgivable move if the scenes in question actually generated some heat, but they do not. The sex pushes the boundaries about as far as can be imagined for the period, with simulated oral action and thrusting and moaning aplenty, and it is not much of an exaggeration to say that they probably take up a good third of the running time.

As noted above, the thriller aspect of the plot is less than gripping. The killer targets the various female cast members and basically ravages them to death with a large phallus. It is a novel concept on the one hand but also inherently distasteful and absurd, and the attempt at concealing the murderer's identity is undone by the fact that the various close-ups of his eyes reveal them to be green—and green eyes are in short

Another woman falls victim to the killer in *The Sister of Ursula.*

supply among the cast. The final revelation is therefore not much of a surprise and the garbled explanation for the killer's perverse M.O. is about as absurd as one might expect.

Characterizations are completely unremarkable, production values are slim and the too bright cinematography by Vittorio Bernini ruins any potential for mood and atmosphere. Gore effects are kept to a minimum—sensibly, the murders are implied rather than graphically shown—while Mimi Uva's synth-laden soundtrack feels like it would be more at home in a hardcore sex film than a thriller.

The beautiful Barbara Magnolfi heads the cast. She proved herself to be a very capable actress in other films, but the deck is stacked against her here. Magnolfi is the most disagreeable heroine imaginable, engendering absolutely zero audience sympathy, and she is saddled with one idiotic line of dialogue after the other. The best that can be said for her, ultimately, is that she looks absolutely ravishing. The daughter of a French mother and an Italian father, Magnolfi was born in France in 1955. She started off as a model then began working in films in 1969. One of her earliest appearances was a small role in Sergio Martino's **The Suspicious Death of a Minor** (1975), but she found her greatest success in the role of the catty Olga in Dario Argento's *Suspiria* (1977). Magnolfi fell in love with actor Marc Porel, whom she married in 1977; their marriage would end in tragedy when Porel died of an apparent overdose in 1983. Magnolfi took time away from the business after suffering this loss, but she started acting again from the mid-1980s until the early 1990s. She seemed to have abandoned the business altogether, but returned to the screen once again in 2013. Stefania D'Amario played her sister Dagmar. She never displayed the talent that Magnolfi did on a good day, and sadly the script does not do her any favors either; the actress walks through the film with an air of confusion written on her face and fails to make much of an impression. D'Amario was active in Italian exploitation films beginning with 1976's *Deported Women of the SS Special Section* and she would appear in Lucio Fulci's *Zombie* (1979) and Umberto Lenzi's *Nightmare City* (1980) before scoring minor roles in "classier" fare like Michelangelo Antonioni's *Identification of a Woman* (1982). She has been inactive since the early

'80s. The cast also includes the aforementioned Marc Porel, who is uncomfortably cast as a junkie somehow mixed up in the mystery; given the rumors surrounding his death, it is not very pleasant seeing him shooting up on screen, but he brings his usual charisma to a role that simply is not worthy of his talents.

Director Enzo Milioni was born in Rome in 1934. He entered films as a screenwriter in 1971. *The Sister of Ursula* marked his debut as a director, but he would not have a very prolific career. He directed only four features between 1978 and 1989.

1979

Atrocious Tales of Love and Death (Italy)

Aka *Giallo napoletano; Días de amor y venganza; Mélodie meurtrière; Leichen muß man feiern, wie sie fallen; Neapolitan Mystery*

Directed by Sergio Corbucci; Produced by Achille Manzotti; Screenplay by Giuseppe Catalano, Sabatino Ciuffini and Elvio Porta; Director of Photography: Luigi Kuveiller; Editor: Amedeo Salfa; Music by Riz Ortolani

Main Players: Marcello Mastroianni (Raffaele Capece); Ornella Muti (Lucia Navarro); Michel Piccoli (Victor Navarro); Renato Pozzetto (Commissioner Voghera); Zeudi Araya Cristaldi (Elizabeth); Capucine (Sister Angela); Tomas Arana (Walter Navarro)

Mandolin player Raffaele Capece is hired to serenade a stranger in the middle of the night; while doing so, the stranger jumps to his death and knocks Capece unconscious in the process. The musician is held as a possible suspect, but Commissario Voghera believes that he is innocent. When Capece finds himself in the vicinity when another similar death occurs, he goes undercover to find out who is responsible and to clear his own name ...

Sergio Corbucci's sole foray into the *giallo* begins with a telling visual: a close-up of black-and-white, side-by-side images of director Alfred Hitchcock and comic actor Totò. The contrast is fitting, as *Atrocious Tales of Love and Death* is very much a mixture of thriller and comedy elements.

The story was devised by the director and plays out in a pleasingly oddball fashion. There are plenty of viable red herrings as well as enough mayhem to confirm that Corbucci was not being elitist about venturing into the *giallo* genre. The film does not really tread the seedy or brutal areas of the genre, but it nevertheless works as a satisfying whodunit while sending-up some of the conventions in a good-humored fashion.

The strong characterizations add to the film's appeal. Raffaele Capece is a likable protagonist. A down-on-his-

ACHILLE MANZOTTI presenta

MARCELLO MASTROIANNI · ORNELLA MUTI
e RENATO POZZETTO
in un film di SERGIO CORBUCCI

GIALLO NAPOLETANO

con ZEUDI ARAYA · CAPUCINE
e con MICHEL PICCOLI partecipazione PEPPINO DE FILIPPO
musica composta e diretta da RIZ ORTOLANI NAZIONALMUSIC EDIZIONI MUSICALI MILANO · prodotto dalla IRRIGAZIONE CINEMATOGRAFICA
regia di SERGIO CORBUCCI colore della TELECOLOR

Italian *locandina* **for** *Atrocious Tales of Love and Death*; **artist unknown.**

ty-stricken background contrasted with the much more affluent Victor. Lucia Navarro enters the story as the ultimate beautiful woman of mystery, and it is revealed that she is actually the wife of Victor's drug-addled son, Walter. Lucia is a nurse, and her status as a member of the working-class immediately separates her from the aesthete Victor and his generally indolent (and misguided) offspring. She proves to be a woman of tremendous will and ingenuity and, as such, gives Victor an unexpected run for his money. By contrast, *Commissario* Voghera is a sharp parody of the officious bureaucrat with a knack for bluff and bluster but little genuine common sense. Voghera's interactions with the wily Raffaele are a joy to watch, as the small-time musician manages to outwit him at every turn while also showing himself to be far more astute in the art of detection.

Unlike a number of comic thrillers of the period—including Steno's *Double Murder* (1977), which also starred Marcello Mastroianni—*Atrocious Tales of Love and Death* fits into the genre by virture of its cheerfully morbid disposition. The violence quotient is quite low, especially when one considers the sadistic streak exhibited by Corbucci in his Spaghetti Westerns (just think of the horrors that befell *Django*, 1966, for example), but the string of murders coupled with the final revelation of the killer's motivation root the film firmly in the realm of the *giallo*. Corbucci admittedly plays much of the movie for laughs, but suspense is still generated by virtue of the audience's sympathy for Raffaele and the desire to see him clear his name.

Corbucci directs the film with an eye toward pacing and comic timing. Fortunately, the jokes are legitimately funny and are well integrated into the material; Italian comedy does not always translate very well to a foreign audience, but the snappy dialogue and expert performances help to make this a welcome exception. The elegant cinematography by Luigi Kuveiller yields some impressive imagery, while Riz Ortolani's catchy music score is a welcome bonus; he even quotes his most popular hit, with the Oscar-nominated "More" from *Mondo Cane* (1962) being heard on the radio at one point.

Marcello Mastroianni, who gives a splendid performance as Raffaele Capece, heads the outstanding cast. Mastroianni had a special knack for playing charming characters, and this is certainly the case here. The actor was never content to coast on his good looks and indeed was openly uncomfortable with the press' insistence on depicting him as a "Latin Lover," so a character role such as this must have been particularly welcome to him. He is funny and sympathetic throughout and also has some oddly touching moments as his character's desire for wealth and success comes to the foreground. The gorgeous Ornella Muti is very good as Lucia Navarro. The character is enigmatic at first but deepens and becomes more interesting as the story unfolds. Muti conveys the character's inner strength and resentment toward her snobbish in-laws very effectively and also displays a good sense of comic timing in her scenes with Mastroianni. Victor Navarro

luck musician, he survives by virtue of his quick wit. He is pushed into the mayhem by some shady business associates to whom he owes a favor, and only pursues his own investigation in the interest of saving his own skin; unlike the typical Argento protagonist, who is driven by a morbid compulsion, his motivation is therefore of a purely practical variety. He worships the distinguished conductor Victor Navarro and is taken aback when the maestro ends up being involved in the mystery. The two men share a similar love of music and a comparable physical defect, namely a lame leg, but the way in which they acquired their handicap is contrasted in a meaningful fashion: Raffaele suffered from polio as a child, whereas Victor damaged his leg while playing polo; the symbolism is obvious, with Raffaele's pover-

is well played by the distinguished Michel Piccoli. His flair for expressing an intellectual but decadent character is put to very good use here as his character looks down his nose at Raffaele and the other "inferior" Neaopolitans. Piccoli was born in Paris in 1925. He started acting on stage, before making his movie debut in 1945; Piccoli's early career was none too impressive, but he began a long and fruitful collaboration with the great surrealist filmmaker Luis Buñuel with *Death in the Garden* (1956), which would go on to encompass such classics as *Diary of a Chambermaid* (1964), *Belle de Jour* (1967) and *The Discreet Charm of the Bourgeoisie* (1972). Piccoli's real film breakthrough happened in 1963, when Jean-Luc Godard cast him as the indecisive screenwriter in *Contempt*. Piccoli would vacillate between commercial assignments and more "arthouse" fare, appearing in the likes of Basil Dearden's *Masquerade* (1965), Mario Bava's *Danger: Diabolik* (1968), Alfred Hitchcock's *Topaz* (1969), Marco Ferreri's *La Grande Bouffe* (1973) and Elio Petri's *Todo Modo* (1976)—the last two co-starring Mastroianni among many others. Piccoli remains active to this day and recently appeared in the sleeper hit *Holy Motors* (2012).

Director Sergio Corbucci was born in Rome in 1926. He parlayed his interest in movies into a career, first by working as a film critic, then making the jump to filmmaker in his own right. He made his directing debut in 1951 and soon established himself as a capable journeyman at home in diverse genres like *pepla* (*The Slave*, 1962) and comedies (*Totò, Peppino e... la dolce vita*, 1961). He directed his first Western, *Grand Canyon Massacre* (1964), under the pseudonym of Stanley Corbett. However, he signed *Django* (1966) under his own name, and in the process established himself as "the other Sergio" to a legion of devoted Spaghetti Western fans; if Sergio Leone was the undisputed King of the genre, then Corbucci was its Crown Prince. His style mixed the poetic with the chaotic, the artful with the jagged; savage violence and a nihilistic streak would often be contrasted with grotesque flourishes of comedy. Over the next decade, Corbucci delivered a number of standout titles in the genre, including *The Great Silence*, *The Mercenary* (both 1968), *The Specialist* (1969), *Compañeros!* (1970) and *Sonny and Jed* (1972). As the Western started to fall out of favor in Italy, Corbucci moved toward other genres with less success. *Atrocious Tales of Love and Death* was the only *giallo* he ever directed, though he had a hand in the first of the "real" cinematic *gialli* as a co-writer on Mario Bava's **The Girl Who Knew Too Much** (1963). Corbucci died in 1990 at the age of 63.

Giallo a Venezia (Italy)

Aka *Thrilling in Venice*

Directed by Mario Landi; Produced by Gabriele Crisanti; Screenplay by Aldo Serio; Director of Photography: Franco Villa; Editor: Mario Salvatori; Music by Berto Pisano

Main Players: Leonora Fani (Flavia); Jeff Blynn (Inspector Angelo De Paul); Gianni Dei (Fabio); Mariangela Giordano (Marzia); Eolo Capritti (Maestrini)

The bodies of Flavia and Fabio are found near a canal in Venice; Flavia has been drowned and Fabio stabbed to death. Inspector De Paul begins to investigate and soon has even more murders on his hands as various suspects are killed in horrible ways. The dogged policeman is bugged by the feeling that the initial killings do not make sense, but still more people will die before everything falls into place ...

Gialli do not come much grubbier than *Giallo a Venezia*. The film has acquired something of an infamous reputation due to its rampant misogyny, and for once the reputation is actually deserved.

The film builds on the sleazy excesses of **Play Motel** (1979), but is paradoxically not quite so graphic when it comes to the sexual content. The earlier film indulged in some graphic depictions of sex, right down to some penetration shots, while this one does not go quite that far. Even so, there is still plenty of sleazy action going on, and the thriller

Inspector De Paul (Jeff Blynn) interrogates Marzia (Mariangela Giordano) in *Giallo a Venezia*; note the hardboiled egg!

elements are far more pronounced. That is not to say that the film is actually suspenseful or even engaging—it certainly is not.

Play Motel's main focal point was kinky perversion, while Mario Landi's focus here seems to be on cringe-worthy sadism. The various murder scenes are done with a nasty edge that is hard to shake, and the mostly convincing special make-up effects were clearly prominent in the film's budget. The movie begins with Fabio being stabbed repeatedly in the crotch. Another murder scene sees a victim shot, doused in gasoline and set ablaze. Yet another features a prostitute being stabbed over and over again in the vagina with a pair of shears. And probably the most infamous sequence sees a woman being tied to a kitchen table and gruesomely dismembered; the killer even takes the time to awaken her at one point when she passes out, just to ensure that she does not miss out on any of the "fun." The seedy, grimy production values and the almost perverse pleasure the filmmakers seem to derive out of staging these mean vignettes gives the picture a definite charge, yet it is still difficult to warm to the finished product for a variety of reasons. Just focusing on the violence for the time being, it is certainly not unusual for one of these films to be accused of displaying an outright hostility toward women. The explicitly sexualized manner in which much of the mayhem plays out gives the film an especially unsavory edge which does seem to validate some of these criticisms. That being said, it is not likely that any particular thought was put into this aspect; it is simply a by-product of the genre's excesses, with each director looking to make his mark by going overboard in one area or another in an attempt to stand out from the rest of the crowd. *Play Motel* did it by virtue of its graphic sleaze; *Giallo a Venezia* does it by way of its hard-to-shake images of graphic dismemberment.

From a technical perspective, there is very little to appreciate here. Mario Landi is very much of the "if it's in focus, let's move on" school of filmmaking. There is very little creativity in his staging, apart from the odd shot of the victims' writhing reflected in the dark glasses favored by the killer, and his pacing is leaden in the extreme. The film drags on and on, and even the regular insertion (pardon the pun) of another sexual encounter does not do anything to give the film any zest. Franco Villa's cinematography is nothing but functional and the music score by Berto Pisano is recycled from other scores, notably his soundtrack for *Interrabang*. The only real standout is the make-up effects from Mauro Gavazzi, which are noteworthy for their splashy realism.

The cast is generally on par with the rest of the production. Jeff Blynn plays Inspector De Paul. With his moptop of hair, porno mustache and penchant for eating hardboiled eggs (a peculiar character trait which soon becomes rather nauseating), Blynn is one of the most unlikely and unengaging *giallo* protagonists imaginable. Bearing in mind that the script really does not give him much to do beyond obsessing over the illogical opening murders and eating lots of eggs, it still has to be noted that the actor has all the charisma of a wet dishtowel. Blynn was born in New York City in 1954 and got his start on screen acting in some German films before making his way to Rome. He appeared in several *poliziotteschi*, including Mario Caiano's *Weapons of Death* (1977) and Alfonso Brescia's *Napoli ... la camorra sfida, la città risponde* (1979), but *Giallo a Venezia* would remain his only *giallo* credit … which is just as well. He stopped making films in the 1990s and is rumored to have left the cinema in favor of running his own restaurant in Rome. The pretty Leonora Fani is Flavia, while Gianni Dei plays her sexually deviant husband Fabio. Fani had impressed with her performance in *Pensione paura* (1977), but she has little to do here beyond engaging in various sexual acts ranging from masturbation to public screwing. Dei is similarly functional but unimpressive and fails to make more of an impression. Born in 1940, he made his film debut with an uncredited role in Lucio Fulci's *The Jukebox Kids* (1959) and went on to be a prolific presence in everything from horror films (*The Seventh Grave*, 1965) and Spaghetti Westerns (*The Sheriff Won't Shoot*, 1965) to *gialli* (*Spirits of Death*, 1972) and borderline *gialli* (*The Killers Are Our Guests*, 1974). His most prominent role was as the bedridden psychopath who uses ESP to wreak havoc in *Patrick Lives Again* (1980), which was also directed by Mario Landi. The best performer in the movie, though she does not get much of a chance to prove it, is Mariangela Giordano. Born in 1937, she entered films in the 1950s, appearing in quite a few *pepla* (*Ursus*, 1961; *Romulus and the Sabines*, 1962) and Spaghetti Westerns, including Antonio Margheriti's *Vengeance* (1968). She made her *giallo* debut with *La stirpe di Caino* (1971) and was also featured in such horror films as Michele Soavi's *The Sect* (1991) and Jess Franco's *Killer Barbys* (1996). She would reunite with Dei and Landi on *Patrick Lives Again* but is undoubtedly best remembered for her role in Andrea Bianchi's bizarre *Burial Ground: The Nights of Terror* (1981), in which she has a vaguely incestuous relationship with her young son ... played by adult "little person" Peter Bark.

Director Landi was born in Sicily in 1920. He helmed his first film in 1950 but was mostly active in television. *Giallo a Venezia* was part of a series of sleazy exploitation efforts he made toward the end of his career and would remain his only brush with the genre. He died in 1992 at age 71.

Killer Nun (Italy)

Aka *Suor Omicidi; La monja homicida; La petite soeur du diable; Geständnis einer Nonne*

Directed by Giulio Berruti; Produced by Enzo Gallo; Screenplay by Giulio Berruti and Alberto Tarallo; Director of Photography: Antonio Maccoppi; Editor: Mario Giacco; Music by Alessandro Alessandroni

Main Players: Anita Ekberg (Sister Gertrude); Paola Morra (Sister Mathieu); Joe Dallesandro (Dr. Patrick Roland); Lou Castel (Peter); Massimo Serato (Dr. Poirret); Alida Valli (Mother Superior); Daniele Dublino (Director)

Home Video: Blue Underground (Region free DVD and All region Blu-ray)

Sister Gertrude, a nun at a church-controlled insane asylum in Belgium, is experiencing a crisis of faith brought on by a belief that she is riddled with cancer. She begs Dr. Poirret to run further tests on her, but he is insistent that there is nothing physically wrong with her and refuses to help. Sister Gertrude has the doctor removed from the staff and replaced by the young, good-looking Dr. Roland. As Sister Gertrude descends further and further into sexual obsession and mania, a killer begins offing the elderly and infirm patients ...

The opening titles proudly announce that *Killer Nun* is "based on true events that took place in a Central European country not many years ago." Do not fall for it, however, as this over-heated exploitation item was pretty much invented out of whole cloth.

As noted by Steve Fentone in his definitive study of the "nunsploitation" genre, *AntiCristo—The Bible of Nasty Nun Sinema & Culture*, the notion of the "wayward nun" can be traced back to the middle ages. Numerous historical cases are on file regarding nuns who found themselves at the center of a scandal by becoming pregnant and succumbing to other "earthly" pleasures, while literary antecedents include the likes of Giovanni Boccaccio's *The Decameron*.[1] In terms of film, however, the genre exploded with a vengeance with the release of Ken Russell's *The Devils* (1971). This incendiary exploration of religious hypocrisy and hysteria was greeted with media frenzy; many critics lambasted the film as an exercise in bad taste, while others saw past the surface and appreciated the movie's artistry and exceptional performances. Controversy equals big bucks, however, and it is no surprise that the film made a particularly strong impact in Catholic countries like Spain and Italy. A *filone* of similar pictures would include the likes of Jess Franco's *The Demons* (1972),

Domenica Paolella's *The Nun and the Devil* (1973) and Giuseppe Vari's *Sister Emanuelle* (1977). As the *giallo* began to flounder in the excesses of the late 1970s, it was probably only a matter of time before it became "acquainted" with the nunsploitation film. *Killer Nun* would mark the only hybridization of the two strands, which is somewhat surprising given the commercial potential of such a marriage.

According to an interview with director Giulio Berruti, which is included on the Blue Underground DVD and Blu-ray release of *Killer Nun*, the film began life when producer Enzo Gallo saw the title "Killer Nun" used as a headline in a newspaper. He did not think much of the accompanying story, but he loved the title and promptly put it under copyright. Berruti and Alberto Tarallo were then entrusted with developing an appropriately salacious narrative. Interestingly, according to Steve Fentone, Gallo was later sued for plagiarism, though he would emerge victorious in the case.[2] In any event, their combined efforts managed to cram in plenty of sleaze and properly "scandalous" elements, even if it is much too transparent to work effectively as a thriller.

Cover for the British DVD release of *Killer Nun* from Shameless Screen Entertainment; artist unknown.

Italian *locandina* for *Killer Nun*; artist unknown.

The film tips its hand much too early on, thus making it easy to guess who is really responsible for the killings. Sister Gertrude has all the signs of a classic red herring, and behaves accordingly. She is subject to blackouts, flies off the handle into terrifying fits of rage, leaves the hospital at one point to dress up in black pantyhose and seduce a man in a local restaurant and generally behaves in so over-the-top a fashion that the experienced *giallo*-phile will not believe for one second that she could possibly be the killer. Gertrude also displays a contempt toward men, though she is quick to note at one point that she prefers them in sexual matters; even so, she also displays an interest in female flesh, and this

results in a lesbian interlude with her adoring roommate, Sister Mathieu. In a cynical move typical of the "having your cake and eat it too" mentality which underlines so much exploitation cinema, the firmly lesbian Mathieu also succumbs to male temptation when she and Dr. Roland engage in a little oral hanky-panky on the operating table in the asylum's infirmary.

Berruti handles the film competently. The pacing is a little on the slow side, but his coverage of scenes occasionally shows flashes of inspiration and the various murder scenes have a mean edge to them; one memorably nasty sequence sees a woman bound and gagged with surgical bandages as the killer gleefully goes to town on her with pins and a scalpel. The final reveal of the killer's identity is hardly surprising and the film's denunciation of the restrictions the church places on sexuality is undercut by the leering presentation of scenes it is supposedly depicting in a condemning fashion.

Anita Ekberg tries hard, but is generally over-the-top and unconvincing as Sister Gertrude. Ekberg's glamorous persona simply does not lend itself to the character's profession, though she clearly is doing her very best to explore the character's neuroses with commitment. Ekberg was born in Sweden in 1931. Her beautiful looks and statuesque physique made her something of a natural sex symbol, and she rose to prominence when she won the title of Miss Sweden in 1950. She came to the U.S. as part of a modeling contract and was put under contract for film work to Howard Hughes, but the eccentric producer failed to make use of her services and she found herself making B-movies for Universal, notably *Abbott and Costello Go To Mars* (1953). She caught the attention of Federico Fellini, who cast her in her most iconic role, as the bombshell movie star Sylvia in *La Dolce Vita* (1960). The image of her splashing around in the Trevi Fountain and locking lips with a smitten Marcello Mastroianni is truly one of the most iconic of '60s cinema, and she would renuite with Fellini again on his segment of *Boccaccio '70* (1962), as well as playing a version of herself in *Fellini's Intervista* (1987), where she was reunited with Mastroianni. In terms of the *giallo*, she was in the first version of *Screaming Mimi* (1958), which would later be unofficially redone by Dario Argento as **The Bird with the Crystal Plumage** (1970), and also appeared in Ferdinando Merighi's **The French Sex Murders** (1972). She more-or-less retired from films in the 1990s and died in January of 2015. The gorgeous Paola Morra plays Sister Mathieu. She is not necessarily very convincing in the role, but her willingness to disrobe is exploited often and she certainly makes a memorable impression in that sense. Morra (born in Rome in 1960) only had a very brief film career, but she also featured in Walerian Borowczyk's contribution to the nunsploitation cycle, *Behind Convent Walls* (1978); she disappeared from the screen in the early '80s. Joe Dallesandro, who can charitably be described as badly miscast, played Dr. Roland. Dallesandro's expressions range from the blank to the bug-eyed, and he almost appears to have been under the influence in some scenes; in any event, he fulfills the function of the Adonis-like male for the sexually frustrated nuns, but is never remotely credible in the role of a doctor. Dallesandro was born in Pensacola, Florida in 1948. He became something of a gay icon in the 1960s thanks to his work with Andy Warhol and Paul Morrissey at "The Factory," where he was photographed in a number of portraits, often unclothed. He was a natural presence for films but his acting range, especially early on, was rather limited. Even so, he impressed as the small-time hustler in Morrissey's *Flesh* (1968) and would go on to star in a number of the director's films, including *Trash* (1970) and *Heat* (1972). Morrissey and Dallesandro went to Italy in 1973 to make a pair of back-to-back horror parodies for producer Carlo Ponti. *Flesh for Frankenstein* (1973) cast Dallesandro as a laborer who becomes mixed up in Baron Frankenstein (Udo Kier)'s plans to create a monster, while in *Blood for Dracula* (1974), he was the Communist-leaning antagonist to the sickly Count Dracula (Kier, again), deflowering every virgin in sight in a plan to prevent the Count from securing some much-needed virgin blood. Dallesandro stuck around Italy for a period of time and appeared in the likes of Vittorio Salerno's *The Savage Three* (1975) and Fernando Di Leo's *Madness* (1980). Dallesandro's personal life included brushes with addiction and problems with the law, but he kept plugging away and was able to secure roles for directors like Francis Ford Coppola (*The Cotton Club*, 1984, where he appeared as "Lucky" Luciano) and Steven Soderbergh (*The Limey*, 1999). He remains an active presence to this day and has improved dramatically as an actor since the days of *Killer Nun*. The supporting cast includes roles for such *giallo* veterans as Lou Castel, Alida Valli and Massimo Serato, with the latter arguably giving the best performance as the dignified Dr. Poirret.

Director Giulio Berruti has worked extensively as a screenwriter (he co-wrote Corrado Farrina's unusual vampire film *They Have Changed Their Faces*, 1971) and editor, but his directing output is limited to two films. *Killer Nun* marked the end of his brief directorial career.

Notes:
1. Fentone, Steve, *AntiCristo—The Bible of Nasty Nun Sinema & Culture*, (Godalming: FAB Press, 2000), p. 9
2. *Ibid*, p. 163.

Play Motel (Italy)

Directed by Mario Gariazzo (as Roy Garrett); Produced by Armando Novelli; Screenplay by Mario Gariazzo; Director of Photography: Aldo Greci; Editor: Vincenzo Tomassi; Music by Ubaldo Continello

Main Players: Ray Lovelock (Roberto Vinci); Anna Maria Rizzoli (Patrizia); Antonio De Teffè [as Anthony Steffen] (Inspector De Sanctis); Mario Cutini (Willy); Antonella Antinori (Anna De Marchis); Enzo Fischella (Rinaldo Cortesi); Marina Hedman [as Marina Frajese] (Loredana Salvi)

When the seemingly upright but actually degenerate Rinaldo Cortesi takes a prostitute named Loredana Salvi to the "Play Motel" for a little fun, their kinky sex games are captured on film. Cortesi goes into a panic when an anonymous blackmailer begins extorting money from him, but as he is fearful for his reputation he does not go to the police. When Loredana turns up murdered, Cortesi becomes a prime suspect of Inspector De Sanctis. The cop hires an aspiring actor, Roberto Vinci, to go undercover and flush out who is in charge of the ring of blackmail and murder ...

Films like **Strip Nude for Your Killer** (1975) and **The Sister of Ursula** (1978) may have pushed the *giallo* into the realm of sexploitation, but they showed some measure of restraint and could not accurately be described as pornography. *Play Motel*, on the other hand, takes the next big step and brings the *giallo* firmly (as it were) into the world of hardcore sex. It would not, however, be the last such fusion of the thriller and the openly pornographic.

Censored poster for *Play Motel*.

Censored Italian newspaper ad (from *Il Corriere della Sera*, 9/79) for *Play Motel*.

Writer/director Mario Gariazzo seems far more interested in the sex angle than the thriller one; the body count is relatively low and the final revelation of the killer's identity seems blazingly obvious from the get-go. It is almost as if the director could not have been bothered to really try as he figured the film's true *raison d'être* would be in its protracted sex scenes; he may well have been right in a sense, but it makes the movie rather heavy going since the sex is not terribly "hot," anyway.

Gariazzo's direction is generally limp (no pun intended) and uninspired, though the occasional overhead angle shows he was trying, at least sporadically, to give the film a little bit of style. The production values befit a '70s-era porno, which is highly appropriate, and the disco-infused soundtrack by Ubaldo Continello seems especially apt in this context as well. Gore is kept to a bare minimum and the various stalk-and-kill sequences are so unimaginatively handled that the film barely registers as a thriller at all.

The emphasis on kinky sex gives way to some dark humor. The assorted high-class perverts all get off on dressing up and doing naughty things to one another. One coupling involves a man outfitted as the Devil and a woman decked-out in a nun's habit, another involves a man donning a cardinal's garments and yet another has a man done up as an animal tamer while his partner is made up like a lion. In one scene, a man even uses a champagne bottle as a phallus and inserts it into a hooker's anus, which seems to provide her with a certain amount of pleasure and certainly seems to bring a smile to his face. It is all far too ridiculous to be taken seriously, and there is some half-hearted social commentary in the hypocritical nature of many of the victims who pass themselves off as pillars of the community while indulging in such absurd sexual shenanigans behind the backs of their wives and husbands.

Unfortunately, the film never catches fire. The sex scenes drag on and on interminably, the characters are completely forgettable and the cheap look of the production denies it even the allure of any aesthetic value. Gariazzo also paces the film horribly, making it seem much longer than it really is. The only thing more drawn out than the sex scenes are the various police procedural sequences; the combination of the two proves to be deadly.

The cast appears to be appropriately unimpressed by their material. Ray Lovelock walks through his role with an air of smug disinterest. Lovelock had done fine work in his earlier *gialli* like **Oasis of Fear** (1971) and **Autopsy** (1975), but here he is saddled with a dull role that requires him to stand on the sidelines for much of the picture. His wife and cohort in the undercover game is played by Anna Maria Rizzoli, a pretty actress who brings a little much needed charm and enthusiasm to her scenes. Rizzoli does not get to enter in on the "action," either, but true to exploitation cinema double standards, she is still asked to strip nude during one of her undercover missions. Anthony Steffen, who is so wooden here that one is half-tempted to check for signs of *rigor mortis*, plays the plodding Inspector De Sanctis. The supporting cast includes some familiar genre faces like an unbilled Fulvio Mingozzi (collecting a paycheck for an afternoon's work as he walks in and out of one scene), as well as some talent from the porno side of the Italian film industry. Among these, Swedish-born Marina Hedman (billed as Marina Frajese) makes the most significant impression during the aforementioned "naughty nun" vignette.

Mario Gariazzo was born in Biella in 1930. He made his directing debut in 1962 and soon found himself at the helm of a series of very cheap Spaghetti Westerns, including *God Will Forgive My Pistol* (1969) and *Day of Judgement* (1971). He also worked in the *poliziottesco* genre, notably directing Philippe Leroy and Klaus Kinski in *The Bloody Hands of the Law* (1973). Horror fans will know him best for directing one of the sleazier Italian rip-offs of William Friedkin's *The Exorcist* (1973), titled *The Eerie Midnight Horror Show* (1974). One of his more popular titles, however, was the tearjerker *The Balloon Vendor* (1974), featuring Hollywood veterans Lee J. Cobb and James Whitmore. By the late 1970s he was working extensively in the sexploitation field. Gariazzo's first brush with the *giallo* came when he contributed the story to the Spaghetti Western-*giallo* hybrid **The Masked Thief** (1973), but *Play Motel* would remain his final entry in the genre. He died in 2002 at the age of 71.

1980

Murder Obsession
(Italy/France)

Aka *Murder Obsession (Follia Omicida); Delirium; Fear; The Wailing*

Directed by Riccardo Freda; Produced by Enzo Boetani, Giuseppe Collura and Simon Mizrahi; Screenplay by Antonio Cesare Corti, Riccardo Freda and Fabio Piccioni; Director of Photography: Cristiano Pogány; Editor: Riccardo Freda; Music by Franco Mannino

Main Players: Stefano Patrizi (Michael Stanford); Anita Strindberg (Glenda); Silvia Dionisio (Deborah); John Richardson (Oliver); Laura Gemser (Beryl); Henri Garcin (Hans Schwartz); Martine Brochard (Shirley)

Home Video: Raro Video (Region free DVD and All region Blu-ray)

Michael Stanford is a well-known actor. While filming a thriller, he becomes obsessed with the idea of revisiting his family home. He invites some of his friends to accompany him. Michael reconnects with his mother, Glenda, whom he has not seen in 15 years and discovers that she is not in good health. It is soon revealed that Michael suffered a breakdown as a child, during which time he murdered his father, who was a renowned musician. As Michael begins to sift through his past, his friends start getting killed off ...

Murder Obsession offers up a grab-bag of disparate elements: diabolism, Gothic horror, *giallo* and gore. The end result is undeniably schizophrenric, but this is part of its charm.

The film marked Riccardo Freda's return to directing following an absence of nearly 10 years. The back-to-back disappointments of **The Iguana with the Tongue of Fire** (1971) and *Tragic Ceremony* (1972), both of which he disowned, no doubt cooled his enthusiasm for filmmaking. Perhaps he felt somewhat out of place among the raucous excesses of the 1970s, but with his flair for staging action scenes, it is to be regretted that he never explored the potential of the *poliziottesco*. In any event, *Murder Obsession* marked something of a homecoming for the director, as it allowed him to explore familiar terrain while spicing things up with more contemporary traits.

In a sense, the film is part of a small trend among Italian horror movies: the modern-day Gothic. An early example can be found in Antonio Margheriti's *The Virgin of Nuremberg* (1963), where the modern world is contrasted with the stately elegance of its castle setting. Mario Bava explored similar terrain in *Baron Blood* (1972), giving the film a vein of dark humor thanks to nice touches like its ancient castle equipped with Coca Cola machines. *Murder Obsession* is cut from much the same cloth. The gloomy, oppressive vil-

la with its unreliable electrical supply would not be out of place in one of Freda's classic chillers like *The Terror of Dr. Hichcock* (1962) or *The Ghost* (1963), but the styles of its modern protagonists and the sometimes shocking nature of its violence are enough to remind the viewer that this is not a typical Italian Gothic. Freda piles on the quaint strokes, regardless, and anybody familiar with his back catalogue of films will get a comfortable feeling of déjà vu when they see characters wandering around drafty corridors with lighted candelabra or the inevitable shot through a window pane streaked with rain. There is even a good old-fashioned thun-

Italian *locandina* for *Murder Obsession*; artwork by Ezio Tarantelli.

derstorm and a wonderfully over-the-top dream sequence straight out of a Roger Corman Edgar Allan Poe movie. The effect of the latter is compromised by its laughable oversized spider effect, but overall it is a genuine *tour-de-force* scene that shows that Freda had lost none of his flair for baroque imagery.

The story is intriguing, both as mystery and as a psychosexual case study. The conflict is purely Oedipal in nature, as Michael murders his father and comes home to face up to the consequences. This being a *giallo*, however, things are not as they appear. There is a queasy implication of incestuous longing between the young man and his still-elegantly beautiful mother, Glenda. The latter reacts with palpable jealousy to the presence of Michael's pretty girlfriend, Deborah, while the relationship between Glenda and her long-suffering servant, Oliver, is loaded with weighty inferences as well. Similarly, Michael is clearly drawn to his glamorous co-star, Beryl, who is lusted after by their director Hans. With all these mixed signals and pent-up jealousies, it is only a matter of time before violence erupts. Adding to the bizarre undercurrent of melodrama is the fact that Michael is the spitting image of his late father. This is all the stuff of high Gothic melodrama and Freda treats it as such, but the unsettling allusions help to give the film a kinky edge.

The supernatural also comes into play, though this aspect sits somewhat uneasily in the bigger picture. The revelation of a character with extrasensorial powers suggests that Freda and company were looking to capitalize on the suc-

Cover for the American Blu-ray release of *Murder Obsession* from Raro; artist unknown.

cess of Brian De Palma's *Carrie* (1976), though this aspect is rather muted and does not play a huge role in the film's overall story arc. Similarly, the devil-worshipping element comes out of left field and takes the story in an unexpected direction. Again, the "everything but the kitchen sink" approach is typical of Italian genre fare, but Freda is to be congratulated for assembling these ideas together in a way that is even remotely coherent.

The film is also noteworthy for its bloodthirsty murder sequences. One character is gutted like a deer, another loses gray matter to an axe blow, still another is decapitated by a chainsaw and so forth. Freda began embracing graphic bloodshed in **The Iguana with the Tongue of Fire**, so this is not necessarily surprising. However, that film was a crude, somewhat seedy work; its excesses therefore came across as more cynical than anything else. Here, the contrast between the elegant *mise-en-scène* and the contemporary excesses seems a bit jarring, though this is clearly a calculated move on the director's part. In its own way, the film seems to be Freda's way of bidding adieu to the stately charm of the old days; he could not have known it when he was making it, but the film also represented a final farewell to his days as a filmmaker.

Unfortunately, the picture was greatly compromised for its eventual U.S. release. Freda had Franco Mannino score the movie with classical piano pieces by Bach and Liszt, among others, but the American version suffered from the imposition of a synth soundtrack. The cheesy strings and repetitive doodlings merely serve to undercut the film's eerie ambience, and the awkward English dubbing does not help matters either. Fortunately, the original Italian version is now available on Blu-ray thanks to Raro Video, thus making it easier to better appreciate Freda's original intentions.

Freda's direction is much more stylish and assured than it had been on **The Iguana with the Tongue of Fire**. Apart from a few minor missteps—mostly along the lines of lingering for too long on some unconvincing special effects work—the film is beautifully crafted and moves at a slow but steady pace. Freda takes the time to build mood and atmosphere, reminding one of the core values embraced by Gothic filmmakers of the 1960s, but he does not stint on the more exploitive elements. He again tries a little too hard to pile on the red herrings—one character's explanation for wearing black gloves in the bathroom really needs to be heard to be believed—but the overall effect is closer to the quality of **Double Face** (1969) than his shoddy and disappointing '70s efforts. Cristiano Pogány's cinematography is quite beautiful, and the use of classical music offers a nice contrast to the gory goings-on.

Stefano Patrizi heads the cast playing the dual roles of Michael and his late father, who is glimpsed via flashbacks. Patrizi is not the most expressive actor in the world, but he does a capable job and is good at conveying the character's inner turmoil. Patrizi was born in 1950 and made his film debut in 1973. He scored a nice supporting role in Luchino Visconti's *Conversation Piece* (1974) and was featured in the all-star disaster thriller *The Cassandra Crossing* (1976), along with such luminaries as Sophia Loren, Richard Harris and Burt Lancaster. Patrizi stopped acting not long after *Murder Obsession* and went into business as an advertising executive, but he has started making infrequent film appearances in more recent years. Silvia Dionisio plays Michael's girlfriend Deborah. She is very good in the role, even if the part is somewhat reactionary in nature. Dionisio was born in Rome in 1951 and started appearing in films as a child actress in the mid-1960s, making her debut with an uncredited bit part in John Schlesigner's *Darling* (1965). She married director Ruggero Deodato in 1971; they divorced in 1979. Her most significant "cult" credits include Paul Morrissey's *Blood for Dracula* (1974) and Deodato's *Waves of Lust* (1975) and *Live Like a Cop, Die Like a Man* (1976). She stopped acting in the early 1980s. Laura Gemser plays Michael's other love interest, Beryl. Gemser is strikingly beautiful but gives a decidedly wooden, one-note performance. She was born in Java in 1950 and first came to attention as a nude model in various men's magazines in Europe. Gemser made her movie debut in 1974 and the following year she attained stardom thanks to her starring role in Bitto Albertini's *Black Emmanuelle* (1975). She went on to play the role of Emanuelle in a series of erotic films, including Giuseppe Vari's *Sister Emanuelle* (1976) and Artistide Massaccesi's *Emanuelle and the Last Cannibals* (1977). She remained active in exploitation flicks until retiring in the early 1990s and was married to actor Gabriele Tinti (whose *giallo* credentials include **Death Occurred Last Night**, 1970) from 1976 until his death in 1991. The real standout, however, is Anita Strindberg in the role of Glenda. Strindberg is very powerful in the role, shifting from frail to aggressive without missing a beat. Sadly, she did not often have a chance to show her acting chops, as so many of her roles traded on her good looks and impressive physique, but this film leaves one in no doubt as to her talent. John Richardson makes his final *giallo* appearance as Oliver. Richardson was drawing to the close of his acting career by the time he made this film; he would act only sporadically from this point on, including a very brief role as the architect responsible for *The Church* (1989), directed by Michele Soavi and produced by Dario Argento. Perhaps fittingly, this stands as one of his more persuasive performances; his stiffness actually adds to the character's off-kilter persona and he has a few nice moments along the way.

After this, Riccardo Freda would never be able to get another film off the ground. He turned his attention to advising younger filmmakers, including Bertrand Tavernier, with whom he collaborated on *The Revenge of the Musketeers* (1994); Freda started directing the picture but fell out of favor with the producers and was fired, so Tavernier took over and claimed sole credit. Freda remained an outspoken *raconteur* until his death in 1999.

Norewegian VHS sleeve for *The Secret of Seagull Island*.

The Secret of Seagull Island
(Italy/U.K.)

Aka *L'isola del gabbiano; Les tigres sont laches; Killermöven greifen an; La isla de la gaviota; Seagull Island*

Directed by Nestore Ungaro; Produced by Nestore Ungaro and Bob Kellett; Screenplay by Jeremy Burnham, Augusto Caminito and Nestore Ungaro; Director of Photography: Armando Nannuzzi; Editor: Angelo Curi and Tony Lenny; Music by Tony Hatch

Main Players: Prunella Ransome (Barbara Carey); Nicky Henson (Martin Foster); Jeremy Brett (David Malcolm); Vassili Karis (Giulio); Pamela Salem (Carol); Gabriele Tinti (Enzo Lombardi); Fabrizio Jovene (Inspector Casati); Sherry Buchanan (Mary Ann); Umberto Raho (Doctor)

Barbara Carey ventures to Italy to meet up with her sister, Mary Ann. When she arrives she discovers that Mary Ann has gone missing. Barbara turns to Martin Foster, with the British Embassy, for assistance and they discover a link between her and reclusive millionaire David Malcolm. Bar-

bara goes undercover and attracts Malcolm's attention; he becomes infatuated with her and invites her to visit his private abode on Seagull Island ...

The Secret of Seagull Island is a co-production between Italy and England, which was originally produced as a five-part miniseries[1] for broadcast in the U.K. It was then whittled down to a manageable feature-film length and released theatrically elsewhere—including Italy—to theaters. Not surprisingly, the cutting made nonsense of the story, but the theatrical version remains the only edition that is easy to get hold of today.

The film's status as a *giallo* is somewhat debatable. The thriller elements are so mild that it cannot hope to compare with the other, more aggressively violent thrillers of the period. It helps to remember that the film was originally made for television, but even in that context it seems awfully tame and talky. A number of excellent TV miniseries would be condensed into effective theatrical release editions—Tobe Hooper's genuinely frightening version of *Salem's Lot* (1979) comes to mind—but *The Secret of Seagull Island* surely is not among them.

David (Jeremy Brett) charms Barbara (Prunella Ransome) in *The Secret of Seagull Island.*

Producer/director/co-writer Nestore Ungaro appears to be the main culprit in this context. He succeeds in coming up with a scenario that had some potential for surprise and suspense, but his lax direction only succeeds in sapping it of any real impact. The film plays rather like a quaint episode of the PBS *Mystery!* series, which is not necessarily a bad thing in itself; with the benefit of some good writing and acting, such programs are certainly appealing in their own right. Sadly, this does not prove to be the case here. The story drags, the actors are generally hamstrung by the boring characters they are playing and the production does not even manage to take proper advantage of the scenic locales. In short, it is a bit of a dud, and a dull dud at that.

In essence, the problem with the film is this: the British and Italian approach to making thrillers is simply not compatible. When Michelangelo Antonioni went to England to make *Blow-Up* (1966), he had the full support of his producers and did not need to worry much about making compromises. Nestore Ungaro is no Antonioni, even if comparing these two very different projects is a little unfair. Arguably, a closer match can be found in the likes of Lucio Fulci's *A Lizard in a Woman's Skin* (1971), which offers a decidedly Italian spin on an Agatha Christie-style murder mystery; it is even set in England for good measure. Yet Fulci made no attempt to restrain his style or downplay the more macabre elements of the material. Ungaro, on the other hand, seems beholden to delivering a conventional mystery, and the Italian settings are merely there to create a touch of the exotic or the picturesque. The end result is closer to the weaker efforts of Alberto De Martino in its overall air of blandly conventional efficiency.

The dull characters do not help any. Barbara is very much of the "plucky heroine" variety, but she is flatly drawn and does not engender much audience sympathy. The love story between her and Martin develops much too quickly and fails to convince, but this is likely a by-product of the cutting to get the film to manageable length. As for Martin, he is an agreeable sort but does not have much substance to him. David Malcolm is slightly more interesting, but he is a noteworthy exception in the overall scheme of the picture.

Ungaro's direction is professional but uninspired. He does not succeed in generating much suspense and the various action scenes seem a little clumsy and half-hearted as well. The editing of the feature version is a disaster, with characters appearing and reappearing randomly, but the production values are slick and look doubly so in light of the some of the less savory *gialli* of this particular period.

Prunella Ransome puts in a decent performance as Barbara, but she is unable to overcome the deficiencies in the writing. She was born in Croydon in 1943 and began appearing in films in 1967, with a Golden Globe-nominated supporting role in John Schlesinger's *Far from the Madding Crowd*. She would go on to such films as Clive Donner's *Alfred the Great* (1969) and Richard C. Sarafian's *Man in the Wilderness* (1971), in addition to guest-starring on such popular British TV series as *Man at the Top* and *The Persuaders*. She scored her most noteworthy "Euro-Cult" credit with her role as the pregnant and imperiled heroine of Narciso Ibáñez Serrador's disturbing *Who Can Kill a Child?* (1976). Ransome died in 2002 at the age of 59. Jeremy Brett, whose performance ranges from the pleasantly understated to the not-so-pleasantly over-the-top, played David Malcolm. Brett was born in Warwickshire in 1933 and began appearing on screen in the mid-1950s. He alternated between stage, screen and TV work, featuring as Audrey Hepburn's suitor in *My Fair Lady* (1964) and as a memorably twitchy serial rapist in *The Very Edge* (1963), but his real claim to fame would not occur until after his appearance in this film. In 1984, he was cast on Granada TV's series *The Adventures of Sherlock Holmes*, where he played the great detective. Brett's performance was praised by many but was also scolded in some quarters as being too over-the-top and removed from Sir Arthur Conan Doyle's cool and logical detective. Even so, the series was a hit and Brett would continue to play the role off and on in various series and TV films for the remainder of his career. Brett's issues with bipolar disease and heart problems would dog him in his later years and he died at the age of 61 in 1995. Nicky Henson plays the heroic Martin, who gives an engaging performance. Henson was born in London in 1945. He started appearing in films in the mid-1960s, often in comedies, but horror buffs will remember him for his roles in Michael Reeves' *Witchfinder General* (1968), where he played Ian Ogilvy's sidekick, and Don Sharp's *Psychomania* (1972), where he heads a motorcycle gang whose pact with the Devil allows them to return from the grave and wreak havoc on polite society. He remains active in British films and television. Genre stalwarts like Gabriele Tinti, Fabrizio Jovene and Umberto Raho represent the Italian end of the production.

Nestore Ungaro is something of a mystery. He does not appear to have had much of a career as a director and seems to have specialized more in underwater second unit material, notably in the Italian *Jaws* knock-off *Tentacles* (1977). *The Secret of Seagull Island* is one of only two directing credits to his name; both, incidentally, were in the TV miniseries field.

Notes:
1. A number of Italian miniseries—or *sceneggiati*—were produced which contain elements of the *giallo*, but only a handful embrace the more pulpy or generally sensationalized elements which typify a *giallo* proper. Thus, *sceneggiati* such as *L'amaro caso della baronessa di Carini* (1975), *Ritratto di donna velata* (1975), *Albert e l'uomo nero* (1976), *Dov'è Anna?* (1976, directed by the gifted Piero Schivazappa, whose *The Frightened Woman*, 1969 is sometimes classified as a *giallo*), *L'ultimo aero per Venezia* (1977) and *La dama dei veleni* (1979, based on John Dickson Carr's famous "locked room mystery," *The Burning Court*, published in 1937) may have ample atmosphere but they remain watered-down and overly talky whodunits. By contrast Sergio Martino's **The Scorpion with Two Tails** (1982, which originated as a seven-part miniseries and was then cut down to one feature length film) and **Private Crimes** (1993) are a little more geared toward the lurid and have a stronger affinity with the cinematic strain of *gialli*.

Cover for the Spanish VHS release of *Trhauma*; artwork by Reyes.

Trhauma (Italy)

Aka *Démence*

Directed by Gianni Martucci (as John Martucc); Produced by Alberto Marras; Screenplay by Alessandro Capone and Gaetano Russo; Director of Photography: Angelo Bevilacqua; Music by Ubaldo Continiello

Main Players: Gaetano Russo [as Ronald Russo] (Andrea); Domitilla Cavazza [as Dafne Price] (Lilly); Roberto Posse (Carlo); Timothy Wood (Paul); Franco Diogene (Bitto)

Andrea and Lilly invite some of their friends to spend the weekend at their secluded villa in the country. What starts off as an idyllic break from reality turns into a nightmare when a murderer starts picking everybody off one by one ...

Trhauma—no explanation is provided for the odd spelling—offers a routine and rather boring variation on the

RIUSCIRAI PIÙ A SPEGNERE LA LUCE PRIMA DI ADDORMENTARTI?

TRHAUMA

con
RONNY RUSS   DAFNE PRICE
TIMOTHY WOOD
Regia: Gianni Martucci
Colore della STACO FILM S.p.A.
Produzione: JOINT WORKING GROUP s.a.s.

Italian *locandina* for *Trhauma*; artist unknown.

"body count" *giallo*. In some respects it is more akin to the slasher films of the period, but given the fact that *gialli* like Mario Bava's **Twitch of the Death Nerve** (1971) and Sergio Martino's **Torso** (1973) had helped to pave the way for that genre, it is perhaps only fitting that the circle should close with Italian filmmakers looking to copy the formula themselves.

The movie was clearly made hastily and on a very low budget. The murder sequences do not even have any oppor-tunity to become particularly graphic since there presumably were no funds for complicated special make-up effects; in-stead, we tend the see the messy aftermath, which is gener-ally accomplished via the liberal application of stage blood on the actors' bodies. An early scene of the killer indulging in a bit of necrophilia with a nude, buxom victim seems to promise that the film will hew close to the sleazy excesses of other thrillers of the period, but this does not materialize; on the whole, it is a rather tame affair.

The story is certainly nothing original, but the presenta-tion of the killer is somewhat unusual. The hulking murderer is shown openly from the very beginning; his propensity for playing with Legos clearly marks him as deranged in the film's psychological visual shorthand. As such, the movie is not so much a whodunit as a '*why*-done-it,' with the reason for the killings being withheld until the end of the picture. This approach is hardly without precedent in the *giallo*, but it does offer a nice twist on the usual formula. Sadly, the motivation is pretty easy to guess and attempts at making the character come off as something of an awkward, overgrown child are not particularly successful.

The hackneyed screenplay is loaded with moments that only serve to insult the viewers' intelligence. Characters do exactly the opposite that common sense would seem to dic-tate and are so thinly drawn that they disappear from mind once they have been off screen for any length of time. There really is nobody in the film worth rooting for, truth be told, and this certainly works against any potential for suspense.

Gianni Martucci's sluggish, unimaginative direction adds to the air of *ennui*. He shows absolutely no flair for building suspense or atmosphere, resulting in a thriller with-out thrills and a horror film without any real sense of men-ace. The ugly cinematography by Angelo Bevilacqua and a generally hideous soundtrack by Ubaldo Continiello are the proverbial final nails in the coffin. A *giallo* without any in-teresting imagery, a memorable score, a pleasantly demented narrative or any memorable murder set pieces is a very curi-ous beast indeed.

The cast is as bland as the characters they play. The only really familiar face for *giallo* fans is rotund Franco Diogene, who repeats his over-the-top obese perv routine from **Strip Nude for Your Killer** (1975). Diogene was born in Sicily in 1947 and began appearing in films in the mid-1960s. His credits include everything from mainstream vehicles like Alan Parker's *Midnight Express* (1978) to low-budget Ital-ian horrors like Lucio Fulci's *The Sweet House of Horrors* (1989); his *giallo* credits also include small roles in Sergio Martino's **The Suspicious Death of a Minor** (1975) and Dario Argento's **The Stendhal Syndrome** (1996). He died in 2005 at the age of 57. Domitilla Cavazza is an attractive presence, but her performance as Lilly, the film's nominal heroine, is lackluster. Cavazza's film career did not extend much beyond *Trhauma*, though it is hard to imagine that the picture did much to further anybody's career.

Director Gianni Martucci was born in Milan in 1946. He started working in movies as a screenwriter in the early 1970s and his first credits include such minor *gialli* as **Naked Girl Killed in the Park ...** (1972) and **The Flower with the Deadly Sting** (1973). He began directing in 1975, but his sparse filmography has nothing of any real value: he helmed the mediocre *poliziottesco Blazing Flowers* (1978) and a poor horror film "presented" by Lucio Fulci, titled *The Red Monks* (1988). The latter would prove to be his last-ever credit.

1981

Il Ficcanaso (Italy)

Directed by Bruno Corbucci; Produced by Giovanni Di Clemente; Screenplay by Alessandro Continenza, Bruno Corbucci, Pippo Franco and Raimondo Vianello, from a story by Aldo Florio and Ernesto Gastaldi; Director of Photography: Giovanni Ciarlo; Editor: Daniele Alabiso; Music by Franco Micalizzi

Main Players: Pippo Franco (Luciano Persichetti); Edwige Fenech (Susanna Luisetti); Sergio Leonardi (Lino); Luc Merenda (Paolo); Pino Caruso

Luciano is a deliveryman who suffers from bizarre dreams. He begins to believe that his dreams might be premonitions, and he turns to Susanna, a beautiful friend with whom he is in love, for guidance. Susanna is very interested in parapsychology and believes that Luciano might have the gift of extrasensory perception. As if all of this is not enough, Luciano gets mixed up in a series of murders and begins receiving strange phone calls from a caller who identifies himself as Luciano's "guardian angel" ...

The waning popularity of the *giallo* did not stop filmmakers from looking to parody its excesses. Send-ups of the genre had begun in the early 1960s, of course, but by this stage in the game the emergence of spoofs such as this merely served to remind viewers of how mired in cliché the genre had become.

Il Ficcanaso (the title translates as "The Nosy One," an illusion to the inquisitive nature of the protagonist and a reference to actor Pippo Franco's rather large proboscis!) begins with an amusing sequence as the beleaguered protagonist Luciano Persichetti is trying desperately to get some sleep. The pulsing colored light from the discotheque next door serves to bathe the scene in alternating red and green lighting, making it look like something out of Dario Argento's *Suspiria* (1977). Admitting defeat, Luciano gets up and tries to calm his frazzled nerves by finding something to watch on television. Every channel appears to be running a late-night horror film and Luciano's delicate sensibilities do not respond favorably to such stimuli; making the joke even more amusing is that every clip shown on TV, from station to station, is from Lucio Fulci's *City of the Living Dead* (1980)!

Director Bruno Corbucci also sends up the genre's fetish for stylized dream sequences, as Luciano is assailed with bizarre nightmares that may or may not indicate a proclivity toward premonitions. Corbucci trots out all the usual elements, such as slow motion and deliberately off-kilter imagery, and does a good job of parodying the genre's use of such sequences. Similarly, Luciano is dogged by a series of phone calls from a breathless, androgynous-sounding individual who passes himself (or herself) off as a "guardian angel." The phone calls are, of course, a long-standing *giallo* trope and are therefore ripe for parody; not one to miss a beat, Corbucci also works in the image of the killer's gloved hands and some subjective camerawork for good measure.

Violence is downplayed in favor of laughs, but the experienced hand of writers like Ernesto Gastaldi and Alessandro Continenza can be detected in the film's skilful use of the *giallo* format. The mystery is actually fairly well worked out and it builds to an effective climax, which manages to spoof the (admittedly non-genre-related) famed sequence in *Goldfinger* (1964) where James Bond (Sean Connery) is threatened by a strategically placed laser beam. There is also much humor to be had in the form of the harried Police Commissioner: he pops pills regularly to stay awake, still

Cover for the Italian DVD release of *Il Ficcanaso*; artist unknown.

Italian *locandina* for *il Ficcanaso*; artist unknown.

nium. Edwige Fenech is on hand to play the buxom Susanna, with whom Luciano is understandably infatuated, while her parapsychologist boyfriend is played by Luc Merenda; it is nice seeing these genre veterans sending up their images (two-fisted *poliziottesco* hero Merenda proves useless in a gunfight, while Fenech spends one scene with her breasts hanging out for no particular reason) and appearing to have a good time doing so.

Director Corbucci is the younger brother of director Sergio Corbucci. He was born in Rome in 1931 and followed his brother into the movie business in the 1950s. He worked largely as a screenwriter, contributing to such films as Alberto De Martino's *Horror* (1963), the *giallo* spoof **Whatever Happened to Baby Totò?** (1964) and his brother's Spaghetti Western classics *Django* (1966) and *The Great Silence* (1968). He began directing in the mid-1960s and specialized in pictures with a comedic bent, such as the spy spoof *James Tont Operation U.N.O.* (1965); he would later direct Tomas Milian in the Nico Giraldi series of *poliziotteschi*, including *The Cop in Blue Jeans* (1976) and *Swindle* (1977). He died in 1996 at the age of 64.

Madhouse (Italy)

Aka *There Was a Little Girl; And Then She Was Bad; Scared to Death; Flesh and the Beast; Party des Schreckens*

Directed by Ovidio G. Assonitis (as Oliver Hellman); Produced by Ovidio G. Assonitis and Peter Shepherd; Screenplay by Ovidio G. Assonitis, Stephen Blakely, Roberto Gandus and Peter Shepherd; Director of Photography: Roberto D'Ettorre Piazzoli; Editor: Angelo Curi; Music by Riz Ortolani

Main Players: Trish Everly (Julia Sullivan); Michael MacRae (Sam Edwards); Dennis Robertson (Father James); Morgan Hart (Helen); Edith Ivey (Amantha Beauregard); Allison Biggers (Mary Sullivan); Jerry Fujikawa (Mr. Kimura)

Home Video: Dark Sky Films (Region 1 DVD)

Julia and Mary are twin sisters who share an unusual bond; Mary's cruelty toward Julia prompts the latter to run away and start her own life far from her sibling's influence. Years later, in the days leading up to the twins' 25th birthday, their uncle Father James attempts to arrange a reconciliation. Mary is in the hospital suffering from a terrible illness and Julia goes to visit, but she soon wishes she had not. When Mary escapes from the hospital, Julia's friends start getting killed off...

Madhouse is something unusual—a *giallo* filmed in America, with direct sound, by an Italian crew—which failed to secure any kind of a theatrical release in Italy. As such, the fact that it tends to be overlooked in studies on the genre is hardly surprising; put into proper context, however, it actually has much to offer.

The story is much influenced by the slasher films of the period, notably J. Lee Thompson's slick *Happy Birthday to*

PIPPO FRANCO · EDWIGE FENECH

il

FICCANASO

un film di **BRUNO CORBUCCI**

con SERGIO LEONARDI | con la straordinaria partecipazione di **LUC MERENDA**

con LAURA TROSCHEL | e la partecipazione straordinaria di **PINO CARUSO**

UNA PRODUZIONE CLEMINTERNATIONAL CIN.CA s.r.l. | COLORE della TELECOLOR | ttf

lives at home with his mother and is always being detained by his men, who fail to recognize him at key moments. The end result does not wholly embrace the genre's excesses, to be sure, but it still works as a narrative as well as a series of skillfully portrayed sight gags.

In many respects, the film belongs to its star, comic actor Pippo Franco (real name Francesco Pippo). He co-authored the screenplay and pretty much carries the movie single-handedly, though some welcome genre personalities are on hand to offer solid support. His performance as the cowardly Luciano is essential to the film's success, and happily he does not let it down. Franco's exaggerated, fearful reactions may seem a little over-the-top, but they suit the pantomime nature of the material. Franco was born in Rome in 1940. He began appearing in films in the 1960s and his credits include everything from Billy Wilder's *Avanti!* (1972) to Sergio Martino's anthology comedy *Don't Play with Tigers* (1982). Franco worked almost exclusively in comedies and his work did not tend to travel outside of Italy. He would go on to write, direct and score *A Tough Nut to Crack* (1981), but this would be his only effort as a director and composer; the film, incidentally, contains elements of the *giallo*, but not enough to warrant inclusion in this context. He has worked only sporadically since the start of the new millen-

Me (1981), which premiered mere months before this one. In common with the two films is the theme of a protagonist being terrorized by a series of killings that are somehow linked to her birthday. Yet, while Thompson's film lumbered under the veneer of big studio respectability (thus enabling it to have access to a faded star like Glenn Ford), this film has no such pretensions. It plays fair by the rules of the *giallo* and is done with surprising relish.

According to an interview with producer/director/co-writer Ovidio G. Assonitis included on the Dark Sky DVD release of the film, his original function was to have been as producer, but he stepped in to direct when the first-time director suggested by Warner Bros. (who provided the film with its only theatrical release anywhere in the world, in Germany) turned out to be an incompetent. He declines to give the director's name, but alludes to the fact that he was an experienced cinematographer and went on to do better work in later years. Truth be told, this was not an unusual situation for Assonitis to be in. The notoriously hands-on producer is well known for hiring directors with relatively little experience and then proceeding to ghost-direct from the sidelines, or in some cases actually taking over altogether, as was the case here. He would later clash with a first-time director named James Cameron on *Piranha Part Two: The Spawning* (1981) and would end up taking over the picture and supervising the final assembly, though only Cameron's name would be listed in the credits—much to the future Oscar-winner's dismay. In any event, no signs of production difficulties are evident in the film, which is done with considerably more care, style and flair than usual for one of his cash-strapped productions.

The location photography in Savannah, Georgia and (above all else) the use of direct sound recording immediately sets the movie apart from other *gialli* of the period. It should also be noted that the film was the first of the Italian thrillers to be recorded in Dolby Stereo, which adds an extra illusion of gloss to the proceedings. Assonitis does an excellent job of pacing the material, and if he indulges in a few too many cheap scares, he also delivers a number of memorably nasty murder scenes, notably at the end.

Another aspect that stands out is the use of dark humor. Unlike some of the overt *giallo* parodies of the period, this one does not use comedy as a means of undercutting the potential scares; on the contrary, the gallows humor adds an extra layer of queasiness to the proceedings, as the killer indulges in childish bouts of cat-and-mouse with the panic-stricken victims. It proves to be an unexpectedly potent touch which helps keep the viewer off-guard: smiling one moment and wincing the next.

The cast comprises unknown American actors, but they all rise to the occasion. Trish Everly is very good as the heroine, Julia. She is a very sympathetic character who works with deaf children for a living; we take her side early on and are genuinely invested in her safety, which inevitably adds to the film's suspense factor. It would appear that this was

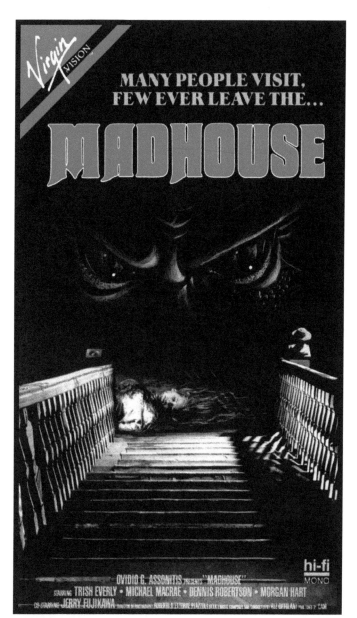

Cover for the American VHS release of *Madhouse* from Virgin Vision; artist unknown.

Everly's only movie appearance. Another standout is Dennis Robertson as her devoted uncle, Father James. The character starts off as a typical pious cleric, but he becomes much more interesting as the story unfolds and ends up playing a major role in the proceedings. Robertson has primarily worked in the theater and on television; he made his small-screen debut in the 1960s and has guest-starred on everything from *General Hospital* and *Gunsmoke* to *M*A*S*H* and *Cheers*. His film work is rather sporadic, but he did appear in the well-remembered made-for-TV horror film *Dark Night of the Scarecrow* (1981) just prior to this one.

Assonitis was born in Egypt in 1943. The son of Greek immigrants, he broke into pictures in the distribution end of the business in the 1960s. By the 1970s, he was working as a producer; he served as an associate producer on Aldo Lado's ***Who Saw Her Die?*** (1972), among many other movies. He began directing with *Beyond the Door* (1974), an *Exorcist* clone that overcame lousy reviews to become a major box-office smash. Assonitis followed it up with the *Jaws* rip-off *Tentacles* (1977) and produced a bizarre horror fantasy—vaguely on *The Omen* lines—titled *The Visitor* (1979); these films were more noteworthy for their casts of slightly embarrassed looking stars (including John Huston, Henry Fonda, Mel Ferrer and Shelley Winters) than for their artistic merit. *Madhouse* is certainly his best work as a director, but its dearth of star power and overall lack of exposure has condemned it to obscurity. Assonitis has been inactive since the early 2000s.

1982

The New York Ripper (Italy)

Aka *Lo squartatore di New York; L'éventreur de New York; El descuartizador de Nueva York; El destripador de Nueva York; Der New York Ripper*

Directed by Lucio Fulci; Produced by Fulvio De Angelis; Screenplay by Gianfranco Clerici, Lucio Fulci, Vincenzo Mannino and Dardano Sacchetti; Director of Photography: Luigi Kuveiller; Editor: Vincenzo Tomassi; Music by Francesco De Masi

Main Players: Jack Hedley (Lieutenant Williams); Paolo Malco (Dr. Davis); Almanta Suska [as Almanta Keller] (Fay Majors); Alexandra Delli Colli (Jane Forrester Lodge); Andrea Occhipinti [as Andrew Painter] (Peter Bunch); Renato Rossini [as Howard Ross] (Mikis Scellenda); Cosimo Cinieri [as Laurence Welles] (Dr. Lodge); Lucio Fulci (Chief of Police)

Home Video: Blue Underground (Region free DVD and All region Blu-ray)

A maniac is slashing up young women in New York, and embittered Lieutenant Williams does not have any leads to follow. He enlists the aid of a brilliant young psychologist, Dr. Davis, in the hopes of generating a profile that may help trap the killer. Meanwhile, the latter begins calling Williams and taunting him on the phone ...

The early 1980s witnessed the death of the *giallo* as an especially viable commercial commodity, but it was not a genre that went quietly into that good night; films like *The New York Ripper* demonstrated that there were still ample buttons to be pushed within the genre.

Lucio Fulci came to this film while riding the wave of success that had greeted his supernatural horror films *Zombie* (1979), *City of the Living Dead* (1980), *The Beyond* (1981) and *The House by the Cemetery* (1981). These films mixed the elegant with the grotesque and served up heaps of *Grand Guignol*, which earned the middle-aged filmmaker the moniker of "The Godfather of Gore" among a generation of gorehounds. What Fulci truly thought of all this is open to speculation, but he went along with it and appreciated the fact that his career, which had been somewhat derailed in the 1970s due to the controversy over some of his more politically committed works like *The Eroticist* (1972), was finally back on course. The gory highlights that endeared his films to some fans alienated him from others and definitely made him a scapegoat for morally-outraged censors the world over. *The New York Ripper* would transpose this emphasis on blood and gore into a more realistic context; things which played out as over-the-top and operatic in the context of the supernatural now would seem sadistic and cruel. The critics tore the film to shreds, censors sought to hack it to bits (the British would ban it outright for many years before passing it with cuts for home video release in 2002), and bewildered fans did not quite know what to make of it. No doubt many of these fans were unfamiliar with Fulci's prolific output prior to *Zombie*, however, and failed to realize that the film built upon groundwork already established by the filmmaker in his *gialli* of the late '60s and 1970s. *The New York Ripper* would not prove to be his final word on the subject in the literal sense—he would helm one more *giallo*, **Murder-Rock: Dancing Death** (1984)—but it may as well have been.

Italian poster for *The New York Ripper*; artwork by Enzo Sciotti.

In a sense, the film can be seen as Fulci's reaction to the enthusiastic reception of his gory horror films. So many of the fans and critics alike spent so much time going on about the excessive violence in these films (in a positive and negative way, inevitably) that very often the other aspects of the films went unappreciated. Critics wrote little about Fulci's artful use of framing, the luscious cinematography by Sergio Salvati, the crisp and efficient editing of Vincenzo Tomassi or the inventive soundtracks by Fabio Frizzi; instead, one review after another dwelled on the films' assorted gory highlights. This was surely not unexpected, but by the same token it must have amused Fulci no end to realize that, at the end of the day, so much of the response these films generated was down to their elaborately choreographed scenes of cannibalism and mutilation. By removing this action from the realm of the "fantastic," where they were somehow more palatable (pardon the expression), Fulci suc-

French lobby card: Jane (Alexandra Delli Colli)'s taste for kinky sex leads her to an appointment with Mikis (Renato Rossini, aka Howard Ross), a prime suspect in *The New York Ripper*.

ceeded in pushing the envelope further than ever before. His *gialli* of the 1970s had moments of potent violence (think no further than the vicious chain-whipping in ***Don't Torture a Duckling***, 1972), but such sequences were more along the lines of punctuation points. In *The New York Ripper*, they would become far more central to the film's gritty and seedy ambience. By pairing the realistic presentation of violent death with sleazy doses of sex and perversion, he concocted a heady cocktail that proved to be a little too potent for its intended audience. Avid gorehounds did not appreciate having their fetish thrown in their face, and many rejected the film outright. On the other end of the spectrum, the apoplectic critics who had long complained that Fulci's work showed a misogynist streak had a field day as they felt this film provided the final and absolute validation of their thesis that Fulci was little more than a vile pornographer who traded on "money shots" of women being brutalized in nauseating detail. In any event, if Fulci's intention was to confront his fans and critics alike on the topic of violence, it was not a discussion people were necessarily prepared to have at the time of the film's original release; time and plenty of weak, watered-down *gialli* and Italian horror films have done much to rehabilitate the film's reputation, though it still remains something of a hot-button topic among fans of the genre in general and of Fulci's work in particular.

Much has been written about *The New York Ripper* down through the years, and a good chunk of it is negative. Stephen Thrower's fine book on the director, *Beyond Terror:*

The Films of Lucio Fulci, made a valiant attempt at evening the scales somewhat, but little of any real thought or sensitivity has ever been attempted on this most misunderstood of *gialli*. In a way, it is easy to see why. To put it bluntly, this is one mean *bastard* of a movie. It opens with a golden retriever finding a severed hand amid the trash of New York City and it closes with a pathetic little girl, lonely and parentless, crying her eyes out as the police prepare to rest on their laurels now that their latest psychopath has been put out of commission. It wallows in scenes of kinky sex: live sex shows in the city's Times Square district (this was long before Mayor Bloomberg turned it into a far less atmospheric tourist trap), illicit motel room hookups and more are detailed in an appropriately sordid manner. On top of that, it presents a cast of characters that can charitably be described as dysfunctional. In the film's embittered *milieu*, innocence is no guarantee of happiness, and the representatives of justice are just a hair's-breadth removed from the criminals they are seeking to apprehend and punish. The question arises: Was Fulci really seeking to provoke his critics into a fit of sputtering rage? If so, he certainly succeeded beyond his wildest dreams.

Even those connected to the film do not all have positive things to say about it. Dardano Sacchetti was one of Fulci's key creative collaborators during this period and he has often spoken with enthusiasm of the work they did together. When it comes to titles beloved by the fans like *City of the Living Dead* or *The Beyond*, Sacchetti is quick to point out that he had a major hand in developing some of the more

Faye (Almanta Suska, aka Almanta Keller), the imperiled heroine of *The New York Ripper*.

outré and outrageous ideas present in those films; when the topic of *The New York Ripper* comes up, however, his response is somewhat different. When asked where the film's scenes of kinky sex sprang from, Sacchetti responded:

> From Fulci's perverse mind! He nurtures a profound sadism toward women. However, he's not an aggressive person—he works it all off in his films! […] He's had such a wretched life that, in the end, he's turned nasty himself."[1]

These are strong words, pregnant with a none-too-subtle suggestion that Fulci's so-called misogyny was deeply etched into his character and therefore spilled out into his art. Even if we ignore the notion of Sacchetti eagerly looking to take credit for the things that the fans liked while distancing himself from those that they did not, it is still dangerous to accept these allegations at face value. *The New York Ripper* is often classified as a textbook example of cinematic misogyny, and in fairness, it is easy to understand why. The

victims tend to be female and the nature of the violence is often directed toward mutilating their beautiful visages or, worse, toward attacking their very sexuality. Matters are not helped by the presence of a hero figure, Lieutenant Williams, who smugly passes moral judgment on the victims while trying to apprehend their murderer. Fulci is banking on his critics forming a knee-jerk reaction, but might he have been hoping that his fans may have been willing to look beneath the surface and examine things more clearly? It is difficult to know for sure just what he was thinking, but it seems hard to reconcile the notion of Fulci, with his liberal social conscience (as evidenced in his earlier works), truly embracing the notion of punishing his female characters for simply exploring their sexual fantasies. In essence, Fulci's intentions here are to provoke the viewer while also telling a tightly plotted and mostly logical thriller scenario. As Stephen Thrower posits in his analysis of the picture, this is a very sophisticated game of cat and mouse, with Fulci losing out in the end by virtue of the fact that so much genre criticism is superficial and reactionary; again, time and reflection are beginning to make the film's more sophisticated elements more evident.

The characters are a deliberately cold and unfeeling lot. Lieutenant Williams is a variation on the tough, cynical detective figures associated with the *noir* genre; he even wears a raincoat with an upturned collar. He may occupy much of the film's narrative space, but is not a conventional hero by any means. Williams is crass, crude and downright inhuman in his dealings with other people and in his reactions to the carnage that is taking place around him; one can argue that he has been hardened by his work and that this is the nature of the job, but he is deliberately shown in a very abrupt and unsympathetic fashion. Even worse, he is a bigot and a hypocrite. He has no problem implying to the grieving husband of one victim that the woman brought about her own death by fooling around, yet his only real relationship outside of his "office" is with the prostitute he beds on a semi-regular basis. There is something rather sad and lonely in this, which serves to make him a little pathetic, but the cold, arrogant and condescending attitude he displays throughout the picture makes the audience keep him at arm's length. Still, if one accepts the notion that he is the hero and that this therefore makes him the film's "moral compass," then his allegations against the victims would indeed be very troubling. This is, again, one of the subtle elements that Fulci and his collaborators (including Sacchetti, whether he likes the film or not) worked into the picture, which has generated so much confused criticism down through the years. To assist in his investigation, Williams enlists the aid of a psychologist/teacher, Dr. Davis. The latter is one of the film's most interesting characters. He is defined by a morbid, ironic sense of humor. This, in itself, sets him apart from Williams, who is presented as completely humorless. Davis also displays a smug, self-satisfied quality, with a healthy ego, yet he has a measure of compassion and empathy that differentiates him from the lieutenant. Interestingly, he is also revealed to be gay. Critics who have argued that Fulci was displaying an overzealous Catholic attitude to sex and sexuality tend to conveniently overlook this aspect; if this were really true, Davis would be marked as aberrant because of his sexuality. True, he hides it from people, and the audience only discovers his sexual preferences by virtue of a brief scene where he is seen picking up a copy of *Blueboy* magazine from a local news stand, but it is a telling moment and is included for good reason. Part of it is to play on the conventions of the genre, which often conflates the "different" with the aberrant; as Fulci demonstrated in earlier works like *Don't Torture a Duckling* and *City of the Living Dead*, it is not the "other" figures who are predisposed to violence and hatred, but rather the bigoted, so-called "normal" characters. *The New York Ripper* remains true to this thesis by presenting Davis as a basically affable and likable character who uses his intellect to help trap the killer. In the film's chilly environment, Dr. Davis is one of the few characters that shows any real humanity. Similarly, the nominal heroine, Faye, is not really all that interesting. Indeed, she is rather a dense and irritating presence overall; she may embody the "Catholic" ideal of the sexually conservative woman (she may even be a virgin, though this is not dealt with in any meaningful detail), but she consistently displays poor judgment and never really engages audience sympathy. By contrast, many of the "earthy" victims have real spunk and are considerably more lively and interesting. For example, Jane Forrester Lodge may fit the profile of the "affluent pervert" one is accustomed to seeing in so many *gialli*, but she still has real humanity and comes across as a sympathetic presence. She is married to a successful doctor, but their relationship seems chilly and distant. She gets off on having sex with random men while he gets his kicks by listening to the audio recordings and masturbating to them in his study (instead of simply having sex with her). Fulci does not pass moral judgment on this character, even if Lieutenant Williams does. Indeed, the scene where she is trying to escape from the Ripper's clutches is one of the most suspenseful in the picture—and it is suspenseful for the best of reasons, because we want to see her escape from his clutches. Here again, if Fulci were really intending to condemn this character, the emphasis and execution of this sequence would be very different; there is no doubt that he is on her side, rather than that of the killer, but this again would prove to be a distinction that was too subtle for many reviewers.

In addition to the film's seedy ambience and graphic sadism, the other controversial element is the killer's duck-like voice. Believe it or not, there is actually a somewhat compelling psychological reason provided for this at the end of the picture, but it understandably threw viewers for a loop and continues to do so to this day. Proceeding on the assumption that Fulci was intelligent enough to realize that this would draw snickers from some viewers, it seems safe to conclude that he was having a little bit of fun with genre convention. Dario Argento had popularized the use of breathless, whispering, vaguely androgynous voices for his killers (largely to keep their identity shrouded in mystery until the end of the film), and Fulci takes things a step further by adopting an even more ludicrous form of subterfuge. Whether the decision was a wise one or not is open to debate, but there is no denying that it is a memorable touch and the final explanation goes a long way toward validating it in context.

The New York Ripper seldom gets its due as a piece of filmmaking, but it is definitely one of Fulci's best, most assured pictures. He directs the movie with energy, style and conviction. The pace is steady throughout and the mixture of police procedural sequences and shocking sensationalism is nicely balanced. The film benefits from its location shooting in New York (with interiors shot in Rome; the old Italian tradition of transforming a setting into something overtly "American" by plastering the Stars and Stripes on a wall as set dressing is in evidence in at least one scene), and Luigi Kuveiller's lighting is superb. The use of color is more naturalistic than in some of Fulci's more stylized '70s thrillers, but there is a marvelous Mario Bava-like moment when one victim is killed in a room suffused with green light. Francesco De Masi's funky score is alternately thrilling and mournful, while Germano Natali's special make-up effects are notable for their queasy realism.

The cast includes a number of familiar faces. English actor Jack Hedley may seem odd casting as the gruff New York cop, but he gives an excellent performance.[2] Hedley resists the urge to soften the character and is admirably committed in showing him as the cold-hearted son of a bitch that he really is. Hedley was born in London in 1930 under the name Jack Hawkins; he changed the name later on to avoid confusion with

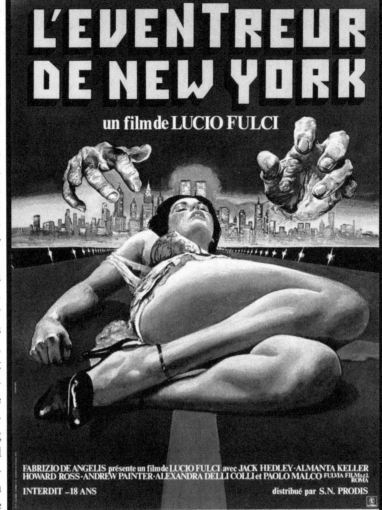

French poster for *The New York Ripper*; artwork by Enzo Sciotti.

credit was *Watch Me When I Kill!* and he would go on to appear in Sergio Martino's **The Scorpion with Two Tails** (1982) and Lamberto Bava's **Midnight Killer** (1986), among others. He is probably best remembered as the father in Fulci's *The House by the Cemetery*, but he remained active in films and Italian television until the mid-2000s. Alexandra Delli Colli, who manages to convey great depth of character in her relatively few scenes, plays Jane Forrester Lodge. Delli Colli was born in 1957 and began appearing in films in the mid-'70s. Her statuesque build and elegant looks made her a natural for exploitation cinema, and she bared all in quite a few films, including Marino Girolami's demented *Zombie Holocaust* (1980). She disappeared from films in the late 1980s. The supporting cast includes *giallo* stalwart Renato Rossini (properly revolting as a Greek immigrant with a passion for fetish sex) and Fulci

the star of British films bearing the same name, best known for his appearances in such blockbusters as David Lean's *The Bridge on the River Kwai* (1957) and William Wyler's *Ben-Hur* (1959). Under the pseudonym of Jack Hedley, he began appearing on British television in the late 1950s and made his film debut in 1958. He played an uncredited bit part in David Lean's *Lawrence of Arabia* (1962, which featured his namesake in a much larger one, with proper billing!) before landing meaty, starring roles in John Gilling's *The Scarlet Blade* (1963) and Don Sharp's *Witchcraft* (1964). He popped up in everything from Roy Ward Baker's *The Anniversary* (1968) to John Glen's James Bond adventure *For Your Eyes Only* (1981) before making his only foray into the world of Italian exploitation cinema with *The New York Ripper*. Hedley spent the rest of the decade into the early 2000s working predominantly in television, before retiring from acting; he is reportedly now living in South Africa. Dr. Davis is very well played by Paolo Malco. His mixture of charm and cynicism helps to make the character a likable one, and he and Hedley have excellent chemistry together. Malco was born in Liguria in 1947 and made his film debut in 1973. His first *giallo*

himself, who cameos as Williams' brusque superior. Other players like Andrea Occhipinti and Cosimo Cinieri would go on to play more significant roles in later *gialli*.

Notes:
1. Palmerini, Luca M. and Gaetano Mistretta, *Spaghetti Nightmares* (Florida: Fantasma Books, 1996), p. 125.
2. Prolific voice actor Edward Mannix dubbed Hedley into English. The latter is one of those names "Euro-Cult" buffs may not recognize—but his voice is certainly recognizable. Among his many English-language dubbing credits are Mario Bava's **Twitch of the Death Nerve** (where he dubbed Luigi Pistilli), Sergio Martino's **Your Vice is a Locked Room and Only I Have the Key** (again dubbing Pistilli), Massimo Dallamano's **What Have They Done To Your Daughters?** (dubbing supporting player Ferdinando Murolo), Fulci's *Zombie* (as the voice of the cop who busts Ian McCullough and Tisa Farrow as they snoop around the deserted boat), Juan Piquer Simón's *Pieces* (dubbing Paul L. Smith) and many, many more.

No Thanks, Coffee Makes Me Nervous (Italy)

Aka *No grazie, il caffè mi rende nervoso; No gracias, el café me pone nervioso*

Directed by Lodovico Gasparini; Produced by Mauro Berardi and Gaetano Daniele; Screenplay by Michael Pergolani and Massimo Troisi; Director of Photography: Pasquale Rachini; Music by James Senese

Main Players: Lello Arena (Michele Giuffrida); Maddalena Crippa (Lisa Sole); Massimo Troisi (Himself); Armando Marra (Dieci Decimi); Carlo Monni (Commissioner); Mimmo Seppe (Journalist)

Michele is a small-time journalist. He is accustomed to being sent to cover puff pieces, so when his editor assigns him to cover the local "First New Naples Festival," it seems to be business as usual. However, a mysterious lunatic who goes by the name "Funiculì Funicalà" takes the story into interesting and unexpected directions, first by making threats and then by killing off the celebrities involved in the festival ...

The *giallo* comes in for another ribbing with this slight but amusing send-up. The decision to set the film against the Neapolitan music scene is an admittedly original concept, and the filmmakers do a nice job of capturing the local flavor.

The story was devised by writer/actor Massimo Troisi, who plays a comic variation of himself in the film. Troisi is not a name one associates with these films, and for good reason. He attained popularity in Italy for his bittersweet comic persona. Born in 1953, he started working in films in the early 1980s as a screenwriter and an actor. He struck a chord with Italian audiences and became a beloved star in short order. Troisi would later achieve his greatest international recognition when he wrote and starred in the hit film *Il postino* (1994), which would also prove to be his last picture. As a child, he had endured rheumatic fever, which left him with a damaged heart. His condition had worsened by the time he started work on *Il postino*, and his doctors advised him against pushing too hard, but his commitment to the project was absolute; he died a matter of hours after completing his last shot on the film, at the age of 41. He would be posthumously nominated for two Oscars for the film: one as Best Actor and one for Best Screenplay. Troisi's role in *No Thanks, Coffee Makes Me Nervous* is not lengthy, but the subplot dealing with his neurotic character is good for a few laughs.

The character of Michele, the down-on-his-luck journalist who finds unexpected success—and far too much excitement—when the killer begins targeting the people connected to the music festival, carries much of the film. Michele is an endearing variation on the type of characters that Bob Hope had played in the 1930s and '40s: the cynical, wisecrack-ing coward. His investigation into the murders is predictably played for laughs rather than suspense, but the final reveal of the killer's identity is genuinely surprising, thus putting this ahead of many other straightforward *gialli* of the period on that level.

The film contains some genuinely funny set pieces. For example, there is the scene where Michele and his blind co-hort do battle with a thug. As the cohort tries to direct his blows in the right direction, Michele is left to struggle furiously with a stubborn bottle that refuses to break and provide him with the desired jagged weapon. There is also a terrific bit where Michele and a would-be assailant go back and forth, using reverse psychology and guilt trips to compel each other to give up the gun they are fighting over.

The assorted murder scenes are very tame, of course, and the film never plumbs the depths of the *giallo*'s propensity for sordid sex, but it manages to send up the genre with style and enthusiasm. The creepy phone calls, which have been a part of the genre since its inception, are parodied very effectively, while the killer's final, demented confession puts one in mind of the films of Dario Argento. The motivation for the crimes is novel too: the killer (who utilizes the moniker Funiculì Funicalà, which is derived from a famous Ne-

Poster for *No Thanks, Coffee Makes Me Nervous*; artist unknown.

apolitan folk song of the same name) is looking to preserve the integrity and sense of tradition among the Neapolitans by killing off the "outsider" elements represented by the music festival; as such, the killer is hoping to keep the culture pure and untainted by contemporary pop culture. Director Lodovico Gasparini paces the film very well, and Pasquale Rachini's cinematography is stylish in an unfussy sort of way. While it is fair to say that comedy is not a genre that always translates well into other cultures—look no further than the phenomenon of Franco and Ciccio in Italy, if evidence is needed—this is one of a handful of comedic *gialli* that proves to be a welcome exception to the rule.

Lello Arena is very good as the put upon Michele. Arena's deadpan approach suits the material beautifully, and he makes the character likable and engaging. He was born in Naples in 1953 and started appearing in films in the early 1980s. Arena and Massimo Troisi (along with Enzo De Caro) comprised the comic trio "La Smorfia," which became immensely popular on Italian television in the 1970s. Arena also worked with Troisi on several film projects, including *Scusate il ritardo* (1983), for which he won the David Di Donatello Award for Best Supporting Actor. Arena also tried his hand at directing with *Chiari di Luna* (1988), which he also wrote. His would-be love interest Lisa is played by Maddalena Crippa, who more than holds her own against the actor. Crippa was born in 1957 and made her acting debut in the late 1970s. She scored her biggest success with her role in Francesco Rosi's *Three Brothers* (1981), for which she was nominated for a "Silver Ribbon" prize through the Italian National Syndicate of Film Journalists; the movie itself would be nominated for an Oscar as Best Foreign Language Film, among other accolades.

Director Lodovico Gasparini was born in Madrid in 1948. *No Thanks, Coffee Makes Me Nervous* marked his debut as a director, though he has gone on to direct nearly two dozen credits, in Italy and Spain, in the ensuing years. This would mark his only brush with the genre.

The Scorpion with Two Tails (Italy/France)

Aka *Assassinio al cimitero etrusco; Il mistero degli Etruschi; Crime au cimetière étrusque*

Directed by Sergio Martino (as Christian Plummer); Produced by Luciano Martino; Screenplay by Ernesto Gastaldi, Jacques Leitienne and Mara Chianetta (as Mara Meryl), from a story by Ernesto Gastaldi and Dardano Sacchetti; Director of Photography: Giancarlo Ferrando; Editor: Daniele Alabiso and Eugenio Alabiso; Music by Fabio Frizzi

Main Players: Elvire Audray (Joan Barnard); Paolo Malco (Mike Grant); Claudio Cassinelli (Paolo Domelli); Marilù Tolo (Contessa Maria Volumna); John Saxon (Arthur Barnard); Van Johnson (Mulligan)

Home Video: Mya Communication (Region 1 DVD)

Archaeologist Arthur Barnard is murdered soon after uncovering an Etruscan tomb. His wife, Joan, has been suffering from recurring nightmares involving the Etruscans and flies from America to Italy to investigate. Her friend, scientist Mike Grant, as well as her father, Mulligan, who has been financing Arthur's expedition, joins her. As they begin looking for clues into what happened to Arthur, the killer strikes again ...

Sergio Martino directed some of the finest *gialli* of the 1970s, but his return to the genre with *The Scorpion with Two Tails* is a major disappointment.

Truth be told, everybody seems to be having a bad day here. Ernesto Gastaldi and his wife, Mara Meryl, contributed to the screenplay, based on a story developed by Gastaldi and Dardano Sacchetti, but it is hardly a feather in their cap. The garbled narrative is far too ridiculous to be taken seriously and very little suspense is generated. Too much time is spent on long, drawn out dialogue sequences, and the characterizations are also on the dull side. Gastaldi's ability to construct a compelling narrative with a surprising but logical conclusion is nowhere in evidence, making this one of his weakest contributions to the genre as well.

Martino's flair and style appears to have deserted him here. Frankly, the director underwent a noticeable and dispiriting decline during this timeframe as he directed a series of action-oriented films (including *Hands of Steel*, 1986, and *American Rickshaw*, 1990) in a decidedly anonymous fashion. The visual inventiveness and kinetic pacing of his '70s films disappeared in the process, and only a handful of his films from this point on would prove to be worth investing much time in. Sadly, *The Scorpion with Two Tails* shows him working at his least inspired. The title promises a return to the glories of his peak period in the 1970s, as it evokes *The Case of the Scorpion's Tail* (1971), but this is simply a case of setting the film up to fail. It could not be any further removed in style and tone. Much of the material plays out in a flat and conventional manner, though in fairness this may have been dictated by the fact that the film was originally made as a TV miniseries. The various would-be shock effects are clumsily handled, making it hard to believe that the same hand responsible for such gems as *The Strange Vice of Mrs. Wardh* (1971) and *Your Vice is a Locked Room and Only I Have the Key* (1972) was responsible for this one as well.

Matters are surely not helped by the fact that the original running time has been greatly reduced in the available feature-length video editions. The film, as noted, was originally aired on Italian television in miniseries format. There were seven one-hour (including commercial breaks) instalments. How this slight and preposterous story could have been stretched out for so long is anybody's guess, but this inevitably would have given the material more room to breathe. The feature-length version, clocking in at a little less than 100 minutes, obviously loses a great deal of material, thus accounting for the choppy story continuity. The original

Spanish lobby card: Ancient Etruscan rites in *The Scorpion with Two Tails*.

miniseries edition is not available on video at this time, however, though its unenthusiastic reception at the time it was aired seems to indicate that it was not appreciably better overall.

Martino utilizes a lot of his favorite collaborators, including cinematographer Giancarlo Ferrando and editor Eugenio Alabiso. Ferrando's cinematography is professional enough but lacks the spark of his earlier collaborations with the director; the editing is harder to judge, given the merciless way in which the material has been whittled down, but what is left onscreen seems very choppy and blunt. The main pleasure to be had is the music score by Fabio Frizzi. He recycles a few themes from his score for Lucio Fulci's *City of the Living Dead* (1980), but the majority of the score comprises new material. It is a rather lush and romantic score, which taps into the setting's sense of mystery far better than anything else in the film.

The final nail in the coffin is undoubtedly the horrific performance by Elvire Audray in the central role of Joan Barnard. Audray appears to have mastered the art of looking clueless in any given situation, but does not succeed in con-

veying any emotion beyond this. With such a catastrophic performance at its core, the film has not much chance of succeeding; the dialogue scenes, already overlong and drawn-out, become interminable thanks to her constant, grating presence in them. Audray was born in 1960 and began appearing in films in 1982; *The Scorpion with Two Tails* was one of her first credits. She would go on to appear in such fare as Umberto Lenzi's *Ironmaster* (1983) and Mario Gariazzo's *White Slave* (1985), but not surprisingly her career never really took off; she died in 2000. John Saxon shows up to collect a paycheck as her husband Arthur; he only appears in a few scenes, and one can only be glad for him that he was spared having to share any scenes with his on-screen spouse. Paolo Malco is his usual reliable self as the ambiguous Mike, while Claudio Cassinelli (who seems to be speaking in English with his own voice on the soundtrack) injects some much-needed vitality when he shows up in the second half as a rival archaeologist who assists Joan in investigating the mystery. Joan's father is played by Hollywood veteran Van Johnson, who phones in his performance with an air of tired disinterest. Johnson was born in Rhode Island in 1916 and made his film debut in 1940. He was placed under contract by MGM and rose to prominence as a popular boy-next-door type in numerous fluffy comedies and musicals, including *Two Girls and a Sailor* (1944), *Easy to Wed* (1946) and *Brigadoon* (1954). He was also cast in heavier fare, including *Battleground* (1949) and *The Caine Mutiny* (1954), before becoming a popular fixture on television in the 1950s and '60s. He began appearing in Italian films in the late '60s, including Enzo G. Castellari's *Eagles Over London* (1969) and Tonino Valerii's *The Price of Power* (1969). One of his last movies was Fabrizio De Angelis' *Killer Crocodile* (1989). Johnson died in 2008 at the age of 92.

Tenebrae (Italy)

Aka *Tenebre; Unsane; Ténèbres; Tenebre – Der kalte Hauch des Todes*

Directed by Dario Argento; Produced by Salvatore Argento; Screenplay by Dario Argento (Note: American prints credit George Kemp as co-writer; presumably he was responsible for the English-language dialogue, as he is not credited on the Italian print.); Director of Photography: Lu-

French poster for *Tenebrae*; artist unknown.

ciano Tovoli; Editor: Franco Fraticelli; Music by Massimo Morante (as Morante), Fabio Pignatelli (as Pignatelli) and Claudio Simonetti (as Simonetti) (Note: The American theatrical version replaced the original end titles music with the track "Take Me Tonight," by Kim Wilde.)

Main Players: Anthony Franciosa (Peter Neal); Daria Nicolodi (Anne); Giuliano Gemma (Detective Germani); John Saxon (Bullmer); John Steiner (Cristiano Berti); Christian Borromeo (Gianni); Ania Pieroni (Elsa Germani); Roberto Coatti [as Eva Robbins] (Girl on Beach); Lara Wendel (Maria Alboretto); Veronica Lario (Jane McKerrow)

Home Video: Anchor Bay (Region 1 DVD); Arrow Video (Region B Blu-ray); Synapse Films (Region A Blu-ray)

Thriller writer Peter Neal travels to Rome to promote his latest book, Tenebrae. *His visit is spoiled when a maniac starts killing off young women and stuffing pages of his book into their mouths. Detective Germani harbors some doubts about Peter's innocence, so the author sets out to clear his name by finding the real killer ...*

Following the success of **Deep Red** (1975), Dario Argento switched gears and started to explore the possibilities of supernatural horror. *Suspiria* (1977) proved to be his biggest hit to date, so a follow-up was inevitable. *Inferno* (1980) became the second part in a proposed trilogy, but the film proved to be a commercial disappointment. When *Tenebrae* was announced, many assumed that it was to be the final installment in the trilogy. The title seemed to allude to the figure of the Mother of Darkness (Mater Lachrymarum), who was part of the "Three Mothers" mythology established in *Suspiria* and *Inferno*, yet it would actually mark his return to the *giallo*—while the trilogy would remain incomplete until *Mother of Tears* emerged to mixed reviews in 2007.

The story is one of the most ingenious in all of Argento's films. It adopts the format of a metacinematic commentary on the *giallo* genre as a whole, with particular focus on Argento's role in it. Peter Neal is an obvious stand-in for the director. He is a successful *giallo* novelist whose books have sold millions of copies worldwide. He faces critics and detractors who accuse him of practicing misogyny in his works and he is also confronted with a deranged fan whose love of his work has turned into an obsession. According to Argento scholar Alan Jones, this last element was based on a real-life scare that had happened to the director. He quotes Argento as saying:

> A more than keen fan had gotten hold of the number where I was staying and made progressively more alarming threats on my life.[1]

Argento went on to explain that while in Los Angeles, he was shocked by the sudden, senseless drive-by shooting of some Japanese tourists in the lobby of the hotel where he was staying. The notion of this kind of senseless, illogical violence is very much at the heart of *Tenebrae*.

The film is renowned for its cool, icy aesthetic. The title, which is Latin for darkness, would seem to promise the kind of shadowy, baroque *mise-en-scène* typical of films like **The Bird with the Crystal Plumage** (1970) and **Deep Red**, but Argento and cinematographer Luciano Tovoli (who had translated the director's extreme visual ideas into a reality in *Suspiria*) decided to go in an unexpected direction. *Tenebrae* is therefore a deliberately bright and over-lit film. Much of the action unfolds in the daytime, and even the nighttime sequences are brighter than usual. The color scheme tends toward cool whites, pinks and pale blues—with the occasional splash of crimson, of course. The look of the film is remarkably consistent and well designed. Argento's use of costuming and décor ensures that the picture does not stray from its meticulous sense of design. The end result seems to shimmer, even if it avoids the clichés one would normally anticipate in a thriller of this sort.

In addition to the film's marvelously detailed design, it also works very well as a character piece. Peter Neal is one of the most interesting protagonists in all of Argento's works. He is something of a yuppie in some respects, but he radiates warmth and charm in a generally hostile landscape. The character has an endearing streak of self-deprecating humor, yet he takes his work very seriously. He is also sharp and astute in his dealings with the police. When he arrives in Rome and is told by Detective Germani that a girl he does not even know has been murdered and that pages of *Tenebrae* were found jammed into her mouth, Neal does not miss a beat. "Tell me, when somebody is killed with a Smith & Wesson revolver, do you go and interview the president of Smith & Wesson?" Neal is seldom at a loss for words, but he does flounder when confronted by the feminist journalist who accuses him of misogyny. Neal retorts with a reminder that he is a full supporter of the equal rights movement, but the journalist refuses to let him off too easily. She continues to press the issue of the sexist, outdated macho posturing attitude of the characters in his books, and his only recourse is to find excuses and make a hasty retreat. Neal's character continues to evolve as the story unfolds, making him one of the more complex and credibly human characters in Argento's body of work. Similarly, Detective Germani is considerably more endearing than the average plodding flatfoot in the *giallo* universe. Germani is elegant and well spoken; he is also a committed *giallo* fan in his own right and is quick to admit that he is a fan of Peter Neal's work. The two men display a somewhat competitive quality in their scenes together, with Neal doing his best to outdo Germani in the detective work, while Germani delights in telling Neal that he guessed the identity of the killer in *Tenebrae* early on in the book. "It's never happened before!" he boasts. The fact that Germani is like this is crucial to the film's appeal; it ensures that the police procedural scenes do not become a deficit, since the audience enjoys being in his company.

Spanish poster for *Tenebrae*; artwork by "Jano"/Francisco Fernández Zarza.

Argento explores the use of doubling in a rigorous fashion in the film. The film builds to a double climax and all of the major characters are presented with *doppelgänger* figures. Actions are echoed throughout, as well. This is not merely an empty gesture, however. Argento skillfully suggests the dual nature of man by showing the good and the bad, the yin and the yang, that exists in each of us. In the film's rather cold and emotionless landscape, nobody is above suspicion; everybody has the capacity to commit murder and even innocuous, seemingly pleasant individuals may well be closet psychopaths.

Still, it is the reflexive nature of the subject matter that proves to be the most interesting. The title of the film is reflected in the title of Peter Neal's latest book—or should that be vice versa—and the conventions of the *giallo* are laid bare in a meticulous fashion. The film is something of a compendium of clichés and tropes in some respects. Everything one may expect from one of these movies is on display, from the killer with black gloves, to the threatening phone calls, to the subjective camerawork, to the elaborately choreographed murder sequences, to the final surprise reveal of the killer's identity, and so on. One almost gets the sense that Argento intended for the film to be his final word on the genre. After all, by the time *Tenebrae* was made, the director had been making films for the better part of 15 years and much of his time had been spent within the confines of the *giallo*. *Suspiria* and *Inferno* allowed him a chance to explore other facets of the horror and suspense genres, but they, too, were infected with aspects of the thriller; despite their emphasis on witchcraft and the esoteric, they also had their black-gloved killers and a string of gory murders. Argento therefore came back to the genre with a vengeance on this film, much as he had with **Deep Red**, which followed up on the failure of his only non-horror/thriller film to date, *Le cinque giornate* (1973). Given that **Deep Red** and *Tenebrae* arguably tower over his other works, it can be argued with some persuasion that the director did well to leave the thriller behind on occasion, thus enabling him to come back to it with his creative juices flowing in a free and enthusiastic fashion. If his goal was to make the *giallo* to end all *gialli*, he came very close to succeeding. The film is as stylish and assured as *Deep Red* in its own unique way, and it offers an intriguing narrative laced with felicitous directorial touches that speak of his peculiar and distinctive approach to such subject matter.

Argento's command of the medium is evident throughout. The most famous sequence is an elaborate crane shot that crawls over the roof of an apartment building before settling on the other side of the building, where the killer is busily breaking in through a window. The shot has no real narrative function. It is grandstanding, pure and simple. And yet, this is the essence of Argento's cinema. On the audio commentary for the Arrow Blu-ray release of the film, critic Kim Newman aptly sums this up as "senselessly brilliant." This may seem a rather flippant remark, but it is very much on the money. Argento's films are often not so much about deep, incisive sociological concerns. Compared to the films of Lucio Fulci, which are often imprinted with a strong social conscience, Argento's work is more concerned with the surface. This is not necessarily a bad thing, by any means. He is first and foremost a stylist and an illusionist. His gift lies in his ability to lure audiences into elaborately worked-out traps, where they are fed bits of visual information in such a way that they fail to see the big picture; the clues are often right out in front, but because of the manner in which they are presented, it is easy to miss them and be misled as a result. Many of his films have clever narrative arcs, but few of them have a great deal of meat on the bone, as it were. On the other hand, it is the sheer giddy enthusiasm of the filmmaking that stands out in his best works. Argento's flair for taking seemingly ordinary sequences and transforming them into magical *tours-de-force* is not something to be taken lightly. More so than many of his contemporaries, he not only understands the formal needs of the cinematic process, but he has the depth of imagination and the good taste to be able to realize his vision with flair and consistency. This is a point worth considering, as it is one of the things that

separates him from many other genre directors of the period. Many were skilled at delivering good set pieces, but the films they made were often routinely executed on the whole. With Argento, on the other hand, this was never a cause for concern. His best work is noteworthy for its robust technical skill and willingness to experiment; whether the sequence in question is a big murder scene or a throwaway bit of visual exposition, Argento handles them all with a good eye. *Tenebrae* is a case in point. There is not a scene in the film that appears to be thoughtlessly executed or out of place. Every scene has its value, whether it be for the way it keys into the story's intricate structure or for how it reaffirms Argento's love of experimenting with the formal aspects of the medium.

The film also ratchets-up the violent content, though it admittedly is not nearly as extreme as some of the more rough-and-ready *gialli* of the period, such as **The New York Ripper** (1982). The violence in **The New York Ripper** is nasty and visceral; the bloodshed in *Tenebrae* is comparatively elegant and well choreographed. Argento's propensity for treating murder scenes like big show-stopping musical numbers is one of his most endearing attributes to his fans, though it is inevitably problematic for knee-jerk critics who equate murdering female characters with a deep-rooted misogyny on the part of the filmmaker. As the debate between Peter Neal and the journalist makes clear, it is not always wise to confuse the artist with the art … and yet, surprises are in store which could arguably muddy the waters of this particular argument, depending on your point of view. In any event, the film's brutal highlights include some memorably nasty throat-slashings and a particularly violent final act, which almost sends the film into the arena of Shakespearian tragedy. One particularly memorable sequence depicts a character having an arm chopped off and literally spraying the brilliantly white walls red with blood. This is precisely the kind of stylistic flourish that sets Argento apart from the rest of the pack. It is also precisely the kind of moment that landed his films in hot water with the censors; in the case of *Tenebrae*, the film would be banned for a period of time in the U.K. as one of the infamous "video nasties" of the 1980s.[2] Now that the furor has died down, however, and with the benefit of some much more uneven work in recent years, it is possible to appreciate *Tenebrae* as one of Argento's best films—as well as a key *giallo* that holds up a mirror and distorts the genre and its excesses in a deliciously sneaky and subversive fashion.

Argento had originally planned for Christopher Walken to play the role of Peter Neal, but he passed on the project, so the part went to Anthony Franciosa instead. According to Alan Jones, in a commentary track with Kim Newman on the Arrow Blu-ray release of the film, Argento and Franciosa were at loggerheads throughout the shoot. The tension does not show onscreen, however. Franciosa's relaxed, charming and intelligent performance seldom gets its due when the film is discussed. True, it is fun to imagine what an actor like Walken would have been like in the film, but the true testimony to Franciosa's effectiveness is that he makes any other casting seem superfluous. Franciosa has a lot of ground to cover with this characterization, and he does not miss a beat. It is a terrific piece of acting from an actor who was not always appreciated as much as he should have been. Born in New York City in 1928, he started off as a theater actor and member of the famous Actors Studio. He started acting on television in 1955 and made his film debut in 1957. Oscar-nominated as Best Actor for his role as Pollo Pope (a role he had originated on stage) in Fred Zinnemann's film of *A Hatful of Rain* (1957), Franciosa quickly established that he was not just another handsome face. He held his own against Paul Newman and Orson Welles in *The Long, Hot Summer* (1958), won a Golden Globe for *Career* (1959), co-starring Dean Martin and Shirley MacLaine and gave a scene-stealing turn in Gordon Douglas' underrated western *Rio Conchos* (1964). Franciosa began appearing in Italian genre fare in 1970 when he top-lined Antonio Margheriti's color remake of his most popular film *Castle of Blood* (1964); titled *Web of the Spider*, it cast Franciosa as a journalist who accepts a wager from Edgar Allan Poe (Klaus Kinski!) to spend the night in a spooky castle with tragic results. He started turning up in a number of TV shows and movies of the week, including Dan Curtis' quirky *Curse of the Black Widow* (1977), in which he gave another winning performance. Good roles were in short supply following *Tenebrae*, but he would revisit the *giallo* with **Fashion Crimes** (1989). He died in 2006 at the age of 77. John Saxon makes a guest star appearance as Peter

Japanese poster for *Tenebrae*; artist unknown, though it utilizes a variation on the same artwork used for the Italian and French posters.

Neal's agent, Bullmer. Saxon does a wonderful job in the role and adds some welcome humor to the proceedings; he and Franciosa play very well off of each other too. Neal's devoted secretary is played by Argento's then-muse Daria Nicolodi. The relationship between director and actress was beginning to fray by this time, and Nicolodi would later recall that she was pressured into playing the role, when she had actually wanted to play the part of the enigmatic girl on the beach who features in the film's recurring flashback scenes. Nicolodi is clearly uneasy in such a bland and functional role and overcompensates by overacting in some scenes. Giuliano Gemma is splendid as Detective Germani. Gemma's natural charisma is evident throughout and he is one of the few actors in the Argento canon who succeeds in turning a representative of the police into a charming and believable human being. Gemma was born in Rome in 1938 and broke into films in the late 1950s as a stuntman. His athletic build and good looks made him an ideal candidate for *pepla*, and he appeared in such films as *My Son, The Hero (1962), Goliath and the Sins of Babylon* (1963) and *Hercules Against the Sons of the Sun* (1964) before rising to fame as a star of Spaghetti Westerns. He starred in *A Pistol for Ringo* and *The Return of Ringo* (both 1965), thus making him one of the key icons of the Italian Western. Gemma also appeared in a small role in Luchino Visconti's magisterial epic *The Leopard* (1963) and top-lined Luciano Ercoli's borderline *giallo The Magnificent Dare Devil* (1973). In his later years, he alternated acting with a new passion: sculpting. Sadly, Gemma's life was cut short when he was killed in a car accident in 2013, at the age of 75; his daughter, actress Vera Gemma, appeared in Argento's *giallo* **The Card Player** (2004). The supporting cast includes memorable roles for John Steiner and Roberto Coatti, appearing under the name of Eva Robins. Steiner is memorably camp as the TV critic

French lobby card depicting Mirella Banti in danger in *Tenebrae*.

who seems fixated on Neal's books, thus making him a reliable red herring. Steiner was born in England in 1941 and began acting in British films and television in the mid-1960s. He made his film debut with a memorable role as one of the inmates in Peter Brook's disturbing *Marat/Sade* (1966) and went on to appear in Peter Sasdy's inept *Rosemary's Baby* clone, *I Don't Want to Be Born* (1976). Steiner ventured to Rome in the late 1960s and appeared in everything from Spaghetti Westerns (*Tepepa*, 1969–with Orson Welles), *poliziotteschi* (*Violent Rome*, 1975) to horror (Mario Bava's *Shock*, 1977—with Nicolodi) to adventure (Lucio Fulci's *White Fang*, 1973) to art house exploitation (Tinto Brass' *Salon Kitty*, 1976). He was among the cast of Brass' infamous *Caligula* (1979) and appeared in Paolo Cavara's *giallo Plot of Fear* (1976). He would go on to feature in another *giallo*, *Mystère* (1983), but as the Italian film industry went into decline and good roles became harder to come by, Steiner elected to change careers; today he has a successful career as a real estate agent in Los Angeles. Coatti/Robins plays the enigmatic girl on the beach, the role that Nicolodi had coveted, and definitely makes a powerful impression. Coatti was born in Bologna in 1958. As a child, Coatti claims that he started to grow breasts and that his body failed to develop in a conventionally masculine fashion; as such, she is androgynous rather than transsexual and identifies herself as a female. Coatti took the name Eva Robin's (the spelling is accurate, though she is billed without the apostrophe in this movie) and launched a career as a transsexual performer on screen. Robin's' sultry looks would be put to use in a number of erotic films which traded on the surprise reveal that she is also equipped with male genitalia. Argento's casting of Robin's is part of the picture's deceptive visual landscape, but it is not exploited as such onscreen; in other words, viewers who do not realize that the performer possesses both male and female characteristics would be none the wiser, but it is there in the background for those who are in on the reference. Robin's would later appear in another *giallo*, *Bad Inclination* (2003).

Notes:
1. Jones, Alan, *Dario Argento: The Man, The Myths & The Magic* (Godalming: FAB Press, 2012), p. 120.
2. British social activist Mary Whitehouse coined the term "video nasty." In the early 1980s, as the home video boom began to enter full swing, a number of films with graphic content came under fire and were pilloried as "video nasties." It was the contention of Whitehouse and her cohorts that these films could have an adverse psychological effect on viewers, in particular children who would have easier access to viewing them in the comfort of their own home as opposed to the cinema where ratings were strictly enforced. Efforts were undertaken to ban these movies outright, without even allowing for censored versions to be offered as an alternative. As censorship in the U.K. began to relax in the 1990s, many of these previously banned titles were finally released in cut editions; *Tenebrae* would be passed in 1999 with a matter of seconds removed, before finally being passed fully uncut in 2003. Among the many films included on the official "video nasties" list were Mario Bava's ***Twitch of the Death Nerve***, Umberto Lenzi's *Cannibal Ferox*, Ruggero Deodato's *Cannibal Holocaust* and *The House by the Edge of the Park* and Lucio Fulci's *Zombie*, *The Beyond* and *The House by the Cemetery*.

1983

A Blade in the Dark (Italy)

Aka *La casa con la scala nel buio; Cuchillos en la oscuridad; La maison de la terreur; Das Haus mit dem dunklen Keller*

Directed by Lamberto Bava; Produced by Lamberto Bava, Mino Loy (uncredited) and Luciano Martino (uncredited) (Note: Rumors abound that the film was partly financed by Dario Argento); Screenplay by Elisa Briganti and Dardano Sacchetti; Director of Photography: Gianlorenzo Battaglia; Editor: Lamberto Bava; Music by Guido De Angelis and Maurizio De Angelis

Main Players: Andrea Occhipinti (Bruno); Anny Papa (Sandra); Michele Soavi (Tony Rendina); Fabiola Toledo (Angela); Valeria Cavalli (Katia); Stanko Molnar (Giovanni); Lara Lamberti (Julia); Giovanni Frezza (Little boy in the film)

Home Video: Blue Underground (Region 1 DVD)

Bruno is hired to score a thriller by his director friend, Sandra. In order to get the right feel for the material, Bruno rents a villa in the country from his wealthy friend, Tony. Bruno sets to work in the ominous surroundings, but it soon becomes apparent that he is not alone ...

A Blade in the Dark marked Lamberto Bava's debut as a *giallo* filmmaker. The offer to make the movie came while he was assisting Dario Argento on **Tenebrae** (1982), so in order to prepare the film—his second as a solo director—he had to be excused from his duties on that picture.

The husband-and-wife team of Dardano Sacchetti and Elisa Briganti penned the screenplay. In the interview included on the Blue Underground DVD release of the film, Sacchetti and Bava recall that their collaboration would be strained; the two men had become friendly years before when they worked with Bava's father, Mario, on **Twitch of the Death Nerve** (1971), but their approaches and temperaments would occasionally prove to be at odds. In any event, the scenario continues the metacinematic trend that had been properly initiated by Argento in **Tenebrae**. While Argento's film dealt with a successful thriller writer who becomes immersed in a real-life *giallo*, Bava's deals with a composer trying his hand at scoring a violent thriller. The final twist is actually a reference to an unusual bit of casting in his father's Gothic masterpiece *Kill, Baby ... Kill!* (1966), but to say too much about that would be to spoil the surprise. Suffice it to say, the story offers its fair share of surprises, and Bava maximizes the claustrophobic potential of the setting and does a fine job of sustaining an eerie mood.

The film stumbles rather badly in some areas, however. For one thing, the English dubbing is some of the worst to be inflicted upon any *giallo*. The stilted English-language dialogue is sometimes painful to listen to ("Is it possible you're such a vacant nerd? Your satisfaction is to sit in the sun like a frog?") and the vocal performances tend to be awkward. Bava also has a hard time sustaining a good pace, though he would certainly improve in this area in later movies. The film starts off well and moves on to some potent set pieces, but there is a little too much talk and a few too many scenes of characters wandering around aimlessly. The murder scenes also range from the memorable to the silly. One character is beaten to death with a wrench, and the exaggerated performances do not do much to sell the illusion; similarly, another scene with a character being menaced by an X-Acto knife is drawn out to the point of absurdity. On the other hand, one memorably vicious murder scene does offer up the kind of tactile flourishes one normally associates with Argento. A victim is interrupted in the process of washing their hair, and the killer pins their hand to a bathroom shelf by means of a nasty-looking butcher knife before covering their head with a plastic bag and smashing it repeatedly against the hard tile; the mixture of soap suds and the crimson blood creates a memorably queasy effect. Nothing else in the picture can quite match the savage impact of that scene.

Part of the problem with the film is its excessive length. Clocking in at 110 minutes, it does not have the kind of intricate narrative or sustained stylistic flourishes to justify lingering for so long. The movie was originally commissioned for Italian television by producer Mino Loy and was to have been aired in four 30-minute segments. As Bava explains in the interview included on the DVD release, the goal was to include a shocking murder during each segment, and the finished film certainly bears this out. It was produced on a very low budget, with co-producer Luciano Martino providing his villa as a cost-effective (but still attractive) location. However, when the film was screened for the television censors, it was found to be far too gory. Sooner than neuter the film altogether, the producers instructed Bava to cut it into a single feature. He would have done well to have cut the flick down by another 10 minutes, at least, because as it stands it is simply too long for its own good.

Despite the low-budget production, the film actually looks quite reasonable. Gianlorenzo Battaglia's cinematography is compromised by the decision to shoot on 16mm

ANDREA OCCHIPINTI · LARA NASZINSKI · ANNY PAPA · FABIOLA TOLEDO dans

LA MAISON DE LA TERREUR

UN FILM DE LAMBERTO BAVA

French poster for *A Blade in the Dark*; artwork by Enzo Sciotti.

and then blow the image up to 35mm for theatrical distribution—this results in a fair amount of grain in the image—but beyond that concession, his lighting is moody and atmospheric. The more classical, Gothic moments display Bava's obvious love for the genre. The music score by Guido and Maurizio De Angelis is also very effective and helps carry the film through some of its lulls.

The cast is not entirely satisfactory, however. Andrea Occhipinti gives a rather flat and listless performance as Bruno. Occhipinti was born in Milan in 1957. He began showing up in films and television in 1979 and had his first brush with the *giallo* in Lucio Fulci's **The New York Ripper** (1982). His good looks made him a somewhat popular actor in the 1980s, and he turned up in everything from Fulci's sword-and-sandal opus *Conquest* (1983) to John Derek's infamous *Bolero* (1984), where he played the love interest to the director's sexpot wife, Bo Derek. In the mid-1990s, he started working more as a producer; he has had a hand in such films as Lars Von Trier's *Antichrist* (2009), Michael Haneke's *Funny Games* (2007) and *The White Ribbon* (2009) and Paolo Sorrentino's *This Must Be the Place* (2011). The supporting cast includes future director Michele Soavi, who gives a rather poor performance as Bruno's layabout friend who rents out his villa for some extra cash. Soavi would go on to direct his own *giallo*, **Stage Fright** (1987).

Lamberto Bava was born in Rome in 1944. The first offspring of the great cinematographer/special effects wizard/film director Mario Bava, he grew up surrounded by his father's work. Despite early warnings from his father against pursuing a career in film, he decided that moviemaking was his calling and started off by assisting his father on *Planet of the Vampires* (1965). In time, he developed a reputation as one of Italy's best assistant directors, and he worked with such practitioners as Ruggero Deodato on *Jungle Holocaust* (1977) and *Cannibal Holocaust* (1980) and Dario Argento on *Inferno* (1980) and **Tenebrae**. In 1980, he made his directing debut with *Macabre*, a disturbing, fact-based tale of murder and insanity in New Orleans, which was co-written by Pupi Avati. The film garnered some good notices—and it would be the only movie he directed that his father would live to see. "After watching it, he said something which has since stuck in my memory, 'Now I can die in peace,' and in fact he died two months later. I think he had spoken unwittingly, because at the time he was fine, poor man!"[1] Sadly, the film failed to find an audience and the frustrated director found himself working as an assistant when his own career should have been flourishing; *A Blade in the Dark* changed things, however, as it proved to be more commercially viable. He directed the immensely popular *Demons* (1985) for producer Dario Argento and its success led to the inferior *Demons 2* (1986). Bava would continue working steadily throughout the 1980s, surviving the collapse of the Italian film industry by working extensively in television. He scored a major hit with the made-for-TV fantasy film *The Cave of the Golden Rose* (1991), which made him one of the most bankable television directors in Italy. Bava would continue to revisit the *giallo* off and on, with such titles as **Midnight Killer** (1986), **Delirium: Photos of Gioia** (1987) and **Body Puzzle** (1992).

Notes:
1. Palmerini, Luca M. and Gaetano Mistretta, *Spaghetti Nightmares* (Florida: Fantasma Books, 1996), p. 22.

Killing of the Flesh (Italy)
Aka *Delitto carnale; Sensual Murder*

Directed by Cesare Canevari; Produced by Antonio Bertuccili; Screenplay by Cesare Canevari and Fulvio Ricciardi; Director of Photography: Vittorio Bernini; Editor: Francesco Bertuccioli; Music by Mimi Uva

Main Players: Marc Porel (Max); Sonia Otero (Lea); Vanni Materassi (Giorgio); Moana Pozzi

Greedy relatives assemble for the reading of their uncle's will. As the relatives plot and scheme, they pass the time by engaging in various affairs with their spouses. Meanwhile, a murderer begins picking them off one by one ...

Cesare Canevari's *A Hyena in the Safe* (1968) is one of the great, unsung quirky *gialli* of the 1960s. Sadly, the same distinction cannot be made for *Killing of the Flesh* in its time frame.

The film fits into the trend toward more and more explicit eroticism. Canevari does not waste much time diving into the cesspool of sexploitation, but the movie is surprisingly reticent in pushing the envelope and is never particularly erotic. Even so, the majority of the running time is comprised of various couplings. There is, for instance, an extremely long and drawn out orgy scene in a nightclub, as the relatives and their spouses get drunk (lots of J&B plugs are in evidence!) and engage in the sort of debauched behavior one might expect to find in one of Canevari's Nazisploitation items. There is an even more bizarre sequence as well, where one of the male characters beats the living daylights out of his lover for showing signs of distress at what is going on ... which merely serves to put the two of them in the mood for a little lovemaking!

The thriller elements are decidedly mild. Indeed, viewers may well wonder if it is even a *giallo* at all on first viewing, since nothing remotely "thrilling" occurs until about the halfway mark. The murders start to happen on a semi-regular basis at that point, but Canevari shows great restraint; the killer favors strangulation, so there is not much of an opportunity to indulge in the genre's other main fetish: blood and gore.

The director's flair for interesting imagery is nowhere to be found here. Whereas earlier works like *Hyena in the Safe* and the bizarre Spaghetti Western *Mátalo!* (1970) showed him to be a craftsman with a flair for the unusual, here he seems to have been working on autopilot. The camerawork

ARMANDO BERTUCCIOLI Presenta

MARC POREL · SONIA OTERO
FULVIO RICCIARDI · MOANA POZZI

DELITTO CARNALE

con
DIRCE FUNARI TONY RACCOSTA DESY e SILVANA RINO FALCONE
e la partecipazione di NICO SALATINO ANGELA MINAFRO e PIPPO VOLPE
con VANNI MATERASSI Regia: CESARE CANEVARI · Musiche di MIMI UVA
Colore della TELECOLOR S.p.A. Produz. A.F.C. CINEMATOGRAFICA · Distrib. IND. REGIONALI

Italian *locandina* for *Killing of the Flesh*; artwork unsigned.

is merely functional and the lighting by Vittorio Bernini ranges from the competent to the downright ugly. Matters are not helped by Mimi Uva's score, which is mostly recycled from **The Sister of Ursula** (1978) and would not be out of place in a conventional porno movie.

The cast is about as unenthused as the director. Marc Porel plays the decidedly fishy Max and, by default, he probably gives the best performance. It is not a patch on his earlier roles in Lucio Fulci's **Don't Torture a Duckling** (1972) and **The Psychic** (1977), however, and it is not one of his more memorable turns. Sadly, it would be the talented actor's last film; he died later that year at the age of 34. The supporting cast includes future adult film superstar Moana

Pozzi, who joins the rest of the female cast by doffing her clothes at the drop of a hat. Pozzi's impressive physique and earthy beauty would make her a favorite among porno fans. She was born in Genoa in 1961 and started off as a model before making her film debut in 1980. She gravitated to erotica early on, and was appearing in hardcore sex films on a regular basis by 1986. She grabbed headlines in the 1990s by publishing a scandalous memoir in which she named some of her most famous lovers, including Robert De Niro, Harvey Keitel and Roberto Benigni. In 1992, she and fellow porn starlet Cicciolina (real name Ilona Staller, who earned her *giallo* stripes in **Calling All Police Cars**, 1975) formed the Love Party of Italy and pushed for the legalization of brothels and increased sex education in schools; the would-be political platform did not take off, but it earned Pozzi and Staller plenty of headlines. She died in 1994 at the age of 33, from liver cancer. Pozzi's presence in a relatively minor role was later played up when she attained XXX stardom and a hardcore edit of the movie was released under the misleading title of *Moana la Pantera Bionda* (*Moana the Blonde Panther*)! According to reviews, very little of Canevari's footage remains in this edit, which is fleshed out (so to speak) with hardcore sex scenes from Pozzi's later sex flicks.

Killing of the Flesh marked the end of Canevari's film career; he died in 2012.

Mystère (Italy)

Aka *Dagger Eyes*

Directed by Carlo Vanzina; Screenplay by Carlo Vanzina and Enrico Vanzina; Director of Photography: Giuseppe Maccari; Editor: Raimondo Crociani; Music by Armando Trovajoli

Main Players: Carole Bouquet (Mystère); Phil Coccioletti (Inspector Colt); Duilio Del Prete (Captain Levi); John Steiner (Ivanov); Gabriele Tinti (Mink); Peter Berling (Reinhardt); Janet Agren (Pamela)

Mystère is a high-class call girl. One night, a German named Reinhardt hires her and her friend Pamela for a threesome. Pamela steals Reinhardt's expensive gold lighter, not realizing that negatives of some scandalous photographs are concealed inside. When Reinhardt and Pamela are subsequently killed, Mystère soon realizes that she is next on the killer's hit list ...

Mystère combines elements of the *giallo* with the espionage thriller and tosses in a little light erotica for good measure. The end result is agreeable, if uneven.

The screenplay by brothers Carlo and Enrico Vanzina is episodic in structure. There is a prologue, the main action is divided into days and there is an irony-laden epilogue. It is not a bad way of structuring the movie as such, but it definitely offers one false climax too many and the filmmakers go a little overboard trying to up the surprise factor.

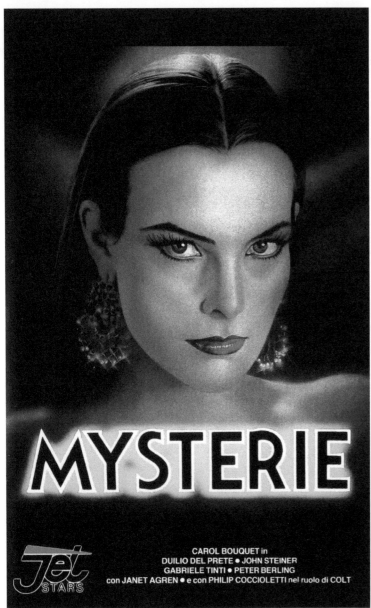

Cover for the Norwegian VHS release of *Mystère*.

CAROL BOUQUET in
DUILIO DEL PRETE ● JOHN STEINER
GABRIELE TINTI ● PETER BERLING
con JANET AGREN ● e con PHILIP COCCIOLETTI nel ruolo di COLT

The *giallo* elements are very muted indeed. There is a string of killings committed by a mysterious black-gloved assassin, but the identity of the assailant is easy to guess and director Carlo Vanzina does not go in for graphic bloodshed during the murder scenes. The thriller element is soft-peddled after the killer's identity is revealed, then it switches gears into a fairly straightforward game of cat-and-mouse as Mystère and her policeman paramour, Inspector Colt, try to outwit the foreign secret agents who are implicated in an attempted political assassination. As such, viewers looking for conventional thrills will likely be disappointed, but the sprightly pace and slick production values help to make it worth a look.

Even the erotic element is strangely subdued, though part of this may have been down to leading lady Carole Bouquet's refusal to disrobe on camera. In an era when so many *gialli* offered up bountiful images of actresses in varying states of undress, this seems especially coy. Indeed, it results in a few awkward images of Mystère, a world-class hooker, having sex with her clients while still partially dressed. There is certainly nothing wrong with leaving a little to the imagination and Bouquet is definitely a stunningly beautiful presence, but it does basically amount to one long joke without a punch line.

Bouquet gives a somewhat one-note performance in the lead, but she is primarily on hand to provide the film with a dash of glamour; she is successful on that level. Born in France in 1957, she made an auspicious film debut with her role as *That Obscure Object of Desire* (1977) for director Luis Buñuel; she "shared" the part with Angela Molina, with both actresses embodying different aspects of the enigmatic girl's personality. The success of the film (which marked the end of Buñuel's career) led to more high-profile assignments. She tested for the female lead in the James Bond film *Moonraker* (1979) but lost out to Lois Chiles; luck was on her side, however, as she snagged its counterpart in the much better *For Your Eyes Only* (1981) instead. She also appeared in films for directors like Dino Risi (*Good King Dagobert*, 1984) and Francis Ford Coppola (the "Life Without Zoe" segment of *New York Stories*, 1989) and recently appeared in the made-for-TV remake of *Rosemary's Baby* (2014). Phil Coccioletti played her on-again/off-again romantic interest, Inspector Colt. His off-putting screen presence combined with the character's narcissistic, absurdly macho attitude makes him one of the least sympathetic would-be heroes in any *giallo*. He was born in Greensburg, Pennsylvania in 1953 and began featuring in guest bits on American television in the late 1970s. *Mystère* was one of his first film appearances, and it would remain his largest movie role. He spent the rest of his career alternating between small parts in films like *Weekend at Bernie's II* (1993) and *It's Complicated* (2009) and doing guest spots on TV shows like *Law and Order* and *Sex and the City*. John Steiner steals the show as the Russian agent who wants to retrieve the photos, but it is a case of petty theft at best.

Director Carlo Vanzina is the son of director Stefano Vanzina (aka Steno; his lone *giallo* credit is the once-presumed-lost ***Il terrore con gli occhi storti***, 1972) and the younger brother of co-writer Enrico Vanzina. He was born in Rome in 1951 and got his start in the late 1960s, initially serving as an assistant to his father before breaking out on his own. He directed his first film in 1976 and worked primarily in comedy (*Figlio delle Stelle*, 1979) before trying his hand at the *giallo*. He scored a hit with ***Nothing Underneath*** (1985), one of the few commercially popular *gialli* of the 1980s, but his attempt at making lightning strike twice with ***Squillo*** (1996) and ***Sotto il vestito niente—L'ultima sfilata*** (2011) were met with apathy. Vanzina remains a prolific director in the Italian film industry.

1984

Murder-Rock: Dancing Death (Italy)

Aka *Murderock—Uccide a passo di danza; Danza mortal; Murderock; Murder Rock; Slashdance*

Directed by Lucio Fulci; Produced by Augusto Caminito; Screenplay by Gianfranco Clerici, Lucio Fulci, Roberto Gianviti and Vincenzo Mannino; Director of Photography: Giuseppe Pinori; Editor: Vincenzo Tomassi; Music by Keith Emerson

Main Players: Olga Karlatos (Candice Norman); Ray Lovelock (George Webb); Cosimo Cinieri (Inspector Borges); Claudio Cassinelli (Dick Gibson); Giuseppe Mannajuolo (Professor Davis); Christian Borromeo (Willy Stark); Geretta Geretta (Margie); Lucio Fulci (Phil)

Home Video: Shriek Show/Media Blasters (Region 1 DVD)

A student at a New York dance academy is murdered and the police try to discover who is responsible. Their investigation reveals that there is much competition and jealousy among the students and faculty alike, thus making it harder to pin down a main suspect. The murders continue, while Inspector Borges decides to follow a hunch in the hopes of bringing the chaos to a close ...

Following the outrage that greeted **The New York Ripper** (1982), Lucio Fulci began making gentler films for a period of time. Perhaps he had been cowed by the backlash against his most extreme picture to date, or perhaps he was just bored with all the excess and decided to pursue other options ... whatever the rationale, he was damned if he did, damned if he did not. Critics and audiences may have felt he went too far with **The New York Ripper**, but they were equally vociferous in stating that *Murder-Rock: Dancing Death* did not go nearly far enough. Fulci himself would later describe the film as representing:

> The end of an era—at that point, I felt the need to renew myself, realizing that such violent, wild horror had had its day.[1]

The movie continues the dialogue about America that started with **The New York Ripper**. In the earlier film, the characters speak of the need to be the best at their particular field; similarly, the characters in *Murder-Rock: Dancing Death* are driven by the desire to be the best in their own field. Fulci's theme here is not exactly anti-American as such, but it does critique the way in which people are often pressured to succeed at all costs within that culture. The dog-eat-dog mentality is very much at the core of this film, whereas it was more subtly integrated into the earlier one. Fulci and his co-writers do not hammer the message home too forcefully, but it does add a bit of subtext that augments interest for those who are willing to dig beneath the surface.

Unfortunately, the plot is pretty generic. The characters are mostly ciphers and suspense is not generated nearly so potently as in the director's earlier *gialli*. That said, the film is hardly the disaster some have painted it to be. It is arguably the last really slick, well-crafted effort the director would make; shrinking budgets and Fulci's own failing health would taint subsequent movies. He still appears to have been in robust form when he made this, and he busts out plenty of stylistic devices to help shore up the shaky narrative. Fulci often spoke of his love of Mario Bava's work, and *Murder-Rock: Dancing Death* allows him to borrow the Bava-esque trope of shooting scenes in half-darkness, with pulsing light illuminating the action from outside the windows. This device was utilized to great effect by Bava in the "Drop of Water" segment of **The Three Faces of Fear** (1963) and in the antique shop murder scene of **Blood and Black Lace** (1964), but Fulci goes it one better. Much of the film is done in this style. The use of exaggerated lighting effects, wide-angle lenses and mobile camerawork gives the movie a kinetic quality that helps to make up for its script issues.

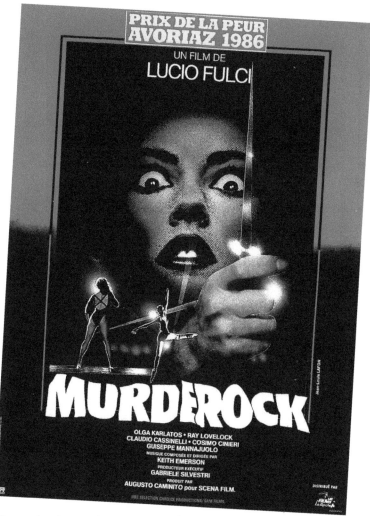

Cover for the Anglo export pressbook for *Murder-Rock: Dancing Death*; artist unknown (possibly Enzo Sciotti?).

If the majority of the characters are noteworthy for being either bland or backstabbing, Fulci seems to find much to love in the figure of Inspector Borges. The character would seem to be an extension of Lieutenant Williams in *The New York Ripper*, right down to the shabby raincoat, but while Williams was a hypocrite and a bit of a bastard, Borges is far more humanistic. He even has a family, which Fulci demonstrates in subtle visual terms via the portrait of him with his wife and children shown on his desk; Fulci does not dwell on this detail and it would be easy enough to miss it, but as is so often the case in the director's work, nothing is arbitrary within the frame. Borges is a cynic who is not afraid to resort to rough tactics in order to get the information he needs, but he is also distinguished by a wry sense of humor. When discussing the case with his psychologist colleague Professor Davis (an older, tenured version of the character played by Paolo Malco in *The New York Ripper*, perhaps?), Davis states that one suspect is a psychopath; Borges snaps back, "He's not a psycho—he's an *asshole!*" Borges' quips and amusingly unorthodox style go a long way toward redeem-

Lobby card for *Murder Rock*.

ing the film's otherwise functional investigation scenes. If only the other characters had been developed with similar wit and sensitivity, the movie would surely have benefitted as a result.

Even so, the film looks great thanks to Giuseppe Pinori's lighting and Fulci's interesting use of framing and camera movement. This would be one of the last times that his flair for the visual would be firmly in evidence. The various murder scenes are bloodless—the killer uses an ornate hatpin (!) to penetrate their breastplate and stop the victims' hearts from beating—but nudity is on the light side, especially when compared to the excesses of Fulci's previous thriller. The use of trippy dream sequences and a female protagonist who dreams of her own demise calls to mind *A Lizard in a Woman's Skin* (1971), and if the title under

review is not worthy of that earlier gem, it is still a solid and enjoyable late-period entry in his filmography. However, the music score by Keith Emerson compromises the overall impact. The popular musician, best known for his work with the progressive rock trio Emerson, Lake and Palmer, had been hired by Dario Argento to score *Inferno* (1980), and he made a very good job of that assignment. However, here he was hired to provide a kitschy sort of soundtrack that was designed to fit into the breakdancing craze spearheaded by the success of Adrian Lyne's *Flashdance* (1983). The film's similarities to that popular piece of schmaltz led to its being referred to as *Slashdance* in some areas. In any event, the breakdancing scenes are mercifully few and far between, but Emerson's songs are bound to inspire a mixture of groans and derision. His more conventional suspense cues are more in keeping with the genre and its codes, but for many viewers, the presence of songs like "Tonight is Your Night" and "Streets to Blame" are hard to forgive, let alone overlook. Fulci would later dismiss the score, while Emerson does not recall meeting with him for the project.

Olga Karlatos gives a rather flat performance as the beleaguered Candice. She is the film's nominal heroine, but she is an ambiguous presence and could have been a rather interesting figure if Karlatos had been up to the demands of the role. Unfortunately, her weak performance puts the film on an uneven keel. Born Olga Vlassopulos in Athens in 1947, she changed her name to Karlatos and began acting in Italian films in the mid-1960s. Her beautiful looks went a long way toward getting her roles, but she was seldom more than adequate in her acting. She appeared in Enzo G. Castellari's superior Spaghetti Western *Keoma* (1976) before first working with Fulci on *Zombie* (1979). She would go on to play a very small role in Sergio Leone's final masterpiece, *Once Upon a Time in America* (1984), and snagged her biggest mainstream role playing the mother (!) of rocker Prince in his vanity project *Purple Rain* (1984). She retired from films in the mid-1980s. The supporting cast includes such reliable genre veterans as Ray Lovelock and Claudio Cassinelli, while Fulci makes a cameo as a talent agent. The best impression is made by Mephistophelean-looking character actor Cosimo Cinieri as Inspector Borges. Cinieri's offbeat performance gives the film a much-needed injection of humor and humanity, and he effortlessly steals the film from his co-stars. He was born in Taranto in 1938 and started appearing in films in 1971. He was something of a favorite of Fulci's, with the director casting him in several films in rapid succession: *The New York Ripper*, *Manhattan Baby* (1982), *The New Gladiators* (1983) and this film. This was certainly the most significant of his roles for Fulci, and he makes the best of it. He remains active in Italian films and television; he recently played the writer Alberto Moravia in Federico Bruno's docudrama *Pasolini, la verità nascosta* (2013).

Sadly, *Murder-Rock: Dancing Death* would mark the end of Fulci's association with the *giallo*. He is seldom lionized in the same way as Argento, but he definitely should be. His *gialli* are remarkably well done on the whole, and if this one marks a weak finale to his career in the genre, it still stands head and shoulders above much of the genre's subsequent output. Lucio Fulci died in 1996 from complications related to diabetes, but his legacy lives on; as the popular fandom slogan would have it, "Fulci Lives!"

Notes:
1. Palmerini, Luca M. and Gaetano Mistretta, *Spaghetti Nightmares* (Florida: Fantasma Books, 1996), p. 62.

1985

Formula for a Murder
(Italy)

Aka *7, Hyden Park: la casa maledetta; Formule pour un meurtre; Das Haus der Verfluchten*

Directed by Alberto De Martino (as Martin Herbert); Produced by Fabrizio De Angelis (as David Colby); Screenplay by Alberto De Martino and Vincenzo Mannino (as Frank Walker); Director of Photography: Gianlorenzo Battaglia (as Lawrence Barkey); Editor: Vincenzo Tomassi (as Vincent P. Thomas); Music by Francesco De Masi

Main Players: Christina Nagy (Joanna); David Warbeck (Craig); Rossano Brazzi (Dr. Sernich); Carroll Blumenberg (Ruth); Andrea Bosic (Father Peter); Loris Loddi (Father Davis)

Home Video: Shamelesss Screen Entertainment (Region free DVD)

As a child, Joanna is paralyzed when she is attacked and molested by a man pretending to be a priest. Joanna blocks this painful memory from her conscious mind as an adult and suddenly finds herself being wooed by the charming Craig. Her friend Ruth is concerned that Craig is only interested in Joanna's money, but the lonely woman welcomes the attention and agrees to marry him. Suddenly, people in Joanna's life begin meeting with violent deaths, and it becomes apparent that Craig may not be all that he appears to be ...

Formula for a Murder harkens back to the "woman in peril" thrillers of the 1960s, which were inspired by Henri-Georges Clouzot's *Les Diaboliques* (1955). As such, it evokes a more "old school" vibe and does not enter into the excessive spirit of the other *gialli* of the period.

Alberto De Martino handles the material with his usual efficiency. The story is not exactly loaded with surprises, but the director sensibly seems to recognize this and does not try to play up the mystery angle for long. It is pretty evident from the get-go that Craig is only interested in Joanna for her money and given that he is never present when she is being

terrorized by the figure of the masked priest, it is a safe bet that he is behind it all. Sooner than milk this blazingly obvious plot point as a "final twist reveal," De Martino sensibly lets the cat out of the bag early on. Thus, the film is not so much a "whodunit" as a "will she get it?" variety of thriller.

The mystery angle may be downplayed, but that does not get in the way of some classical *giallo* thrills. The various murders are surprisingly brutal and bloody, notably one scene where a character is viciously attacked with a shovel. The final showdown between Joanna and Craig is also very well staged and contains some wince-inducing moments as the imperiled heroine fights for her life and gives her assailant a run for his money.

In terms of production values, the film looks as slick and polished as one would expect from De Martino. The exteriors were shot on location in Boston (De Martino was among the few Italian genre filmmakers of the period who really made a concerted effort to pass his work off as *faux*-American) while the Roman interiors are convincingly passed off as American as well. Gianlorenzo Battaglia's cinematography is stylish and moody, with some very effective use of shadows, and Vincenzo Tomassi's editing is as smooth as ever. The music score by Francesco De Masi quotes liberally from his score for ***The New York Ripper*** (1982), which can be a little jarring if you are familiar with Lucio Fulci's superior thriller, but it does not disrupt the mood too badly.

The film also benefits from two excellent central performances. Christina Nagy is in good form as Joanna. It would have been easy to play the wheelchair-bound character for mawkish sympathy, but Nagy and De Martino steer clear of cliché and go to great pains to show her as a strong, re-

Italian newspaper ad for *Formula for a Murder*; artist unknown.

sourceful woman. Nagy evokes sympathy throughout and is also very skillful at conveying the character's growing horror without going over-the-top. Not much is known about the actress, who appears to have enjoyed a very brief career before presumably leaving films to focus on other pursuits. Her other credits were on British TV, suggesting that she likely hailed from that country, and *Formula for a Murder* remains her only brush with the world of Italian genre filmmaking. David Warbeck is every bit her equal as the charming but deranged Craig. Warbeck is an effortlessly likable actor, so he has no problems making the character properly ingratiating early on, but he had less experience playing psychopaths and, as such, his descent into madness and violence makes for an enjoyable change of pace. The actor would later recall in his audio commentary for the Anchor Bay DVD release of Lucio Fulci's *The Beyond* (1981) that he was trying to channel Jack Nicholson in *The Shining* (1980) during his final rampage; whether this comes off as obvious is debatable, but he is appropriately sinister and makes for a good foil to Nagy's resourceful heroine. Warbeck (real name David Mitchell) was born in New Zealand in 1941. He studied acting at the Royal Academy of Dramatic Arts and started off acting for British television in the early 1960s. He made his film debut in 1969 and went on to appear in such diverse films as Freddie Francis' *Trog* (1970), John Hough's *Twins of Evil* (1971) and Russ Meyer's *Black Snake* (1973). Warbeck first ventured to Italy in 1972 when he was cast by Sergio Leone in *Duck, You Sucker* (1972); he did not have any lines, but made an impression as the friend of James Coburn's IRA agent anti-hero. Warbeck loved working in Italy and began making more and more films there from the mid-1970s onward. He performed for such directors as Antonio Margheriti (*The Last Hunter*, 1980) and Giuliano Carnimeo (*Rat Man*, 1988), but found his greatest success among genre fans thanks to back-to-back pictures for Lucio Fulci: *The Black Cat* and *The Beyond* (both from 1981). Warbeck embraced the cult following these movies attained and became a popular presence at fantasy and horror film festivals in Europe and America in addition to continuing his acting career. He revisited the *giallo* with an appearance in **Fatal Frames** (1996), which would prove to be one of his last films. He fell victim to cancer at the too-young age of 55 in 1997.

Formula for a Murder would prove to be Alberto De Martino's swan song; he retired in the mid-1980s and has had the pleasure of seeing his films embraced by a new generation of fans. Alberto De Martino died in Rome on June 2, 2015.

Nothing Underneath (Italy)

Aka *Sotto il vestito niente; Où est passée Jessica; The Last Shot*

Directed by Carlo Vanzina; Produced by Achille Manzotti; Screenplay by Franco Ferrini, Carlo Vanzina and Enrico Vanzina, from a novel by Marco Parma; Director of Photography: Giuseppe Maccari; Editor: Raimondo Crociani; Music by Pino Donaggio

Main Players: Tom Schanley (Bob Crane); Renée Simonson (Barbara); Donald Pleasence (Commissioner Danesi); Nicola Perring (Jessica Crane); Maria McDonald (Margaux Wilson)

Home Video: Another World Entertainment (Region 2 DVD)

Bob and Jessica Crane are twins who share a special bond. When Jessica is abducted in Rome, Bob is assailed by strange sensations in Wyoming and hops aboard a plane to Italy to look into what has happened. He goes to the police, and, while Commissioner Danesi is sympathetic, he finds it hard to believe that Bob could possibly have "sensed" what has happened to Jessica over such a vast distance. When another model is murdered, Danesi begins to take Bob's story more seriously ...

Nothing Underneath (the title alludes to the superficial nature of the modeling world) proved to be one of the few big *giallo* hits of the 1980s. Its mixture of thriller elements with glamor, a dash of eroticism and a bit of horror proved to be a successful one, and it certainly remains director Carlo Vanzina's best contribution to the genre.

Like **Blazing Magnum** (1976) and **Madhouse** (1981), the film is noteworthy for being among the few *gialli* to utilize live on-set sound recording. A brief recap of the Italian tradition of dubbing (or looping) their films is helpful in this context. Italian films were typically dubbed due to a variety of factors. For one thing, the devastation of World War II left many of the production facilities in shambles. The location filming utilized in the Neo-realist movement was therefore born out of necessity, though it would also necessitate the use of post-synched sound. Dubbing became such an integral part of the filmmaking process that it was accepted practice for many years; some directors, like Federico Fellini, even regarded it as an essential component of the unreality of the cinematic process. Things began to shift a bit in the 1980s and gradually even directors like Dario Argento would begin to embrace shooting with live sound, though the heavy accents of some actors would still necessitate some looping, no matter what. Given that the emphasis on the international market resulted in the movies being shot in English, however, the Italian tracks are still created in the dubbing stage. In any event, *Nothing Underneath* is one of the first pictures to employ this technique, and the results are quite well done.

The film was adapted from a novel by Marco Parma by Vanzina and his brother Enrico, with the able assistance of Franco Ferrini. The latter began working extensively on Dario Argento's films during this time; he would have a hand in the writing of **Phenomena** (1985), **Opera** (1987), *Two Evil Eyes* (1990), **Trauma** (1993), **The Stendhal Syndrome** (1996), **The Card Player** (2004) and **Do You Like Hitchcock?** (2005). He also contributed to the screenplays for the Argento-produced **Demons** (1985), **Demons 2** (1986) and *The Church* (1989 and would go on to work again with Vanzina on **Squillo** (1996).

French lobby card for *Nothing Underneath*.

The story is something of a critique of the fashion industry, and its emphasis on the objectification of women. The pressure for these women to live up to an unrealistic ideal is something of a subtext that runs throughout the picture, though the writers do not play it up in an unduly obvious manner. *Gialli* set in the world of *haute couture* can be traced back to the films of Mario Bava, notably ***Blood and Black Lace*** (1964), where the models of a chic fashion house are brutally murdered by a mysterious killer. Bava's ***Hatchet for the Honeymoon*** (1970) also dealt with a fashion *milieu*, while his son Lamberto Bava would go on to make ***Delirium: Photos of Gioia*** (1987) and Argento would follow suit with ***Giallo*** (2009). The emphasis on the glossy surface makes sense in this context: *gialli*, after all, are renowned for their stylish, shimmering surfaces. Underneath this eye-catching exterior, however, there lurks a darker reality. As is so often the case in other films of this sort, the killer in *Nothing Underneath* comes across as a perfectly normal and stable individual; it is only at the end, when the game has been exposed, that the twisted psychology becomes visible.

Vanzina directs the film with style and authority. The pacing is very good and the images are consistently eye-catching. The murders are not as plentiful as in other *gialli* of the period, but the shock effects are well done. The finale makes the most inspired use of ultra-slow-motion photography this side of ***Four Flies on Grey Velvet*** (1971), an effect underscored by Pino Donaggio's beautiful music. Donaggio made his *giallo* debut with this film, and he would go on to score a number of other thrillers. Indeed, his music here is reminiscent of his score for Brian De Palma's "American *giallo*," *Body Double* (1984). He was born in Burano in 1941 and began scoring films in 1973, with Nicolas Roeg's borderline *giallo Don't Look Now*. It was a triumphant beginning for the composer, who would go on to become De Palma's composer of choice after the premature demise of Maestro Bernard Herrmann in 1975. Donaggio's career has encompassed everything from low-budget horror films in America (*Tourist Trap*, 1979) and Italy (Lucio Fulci's *The Black Cat*, 1981) to slick mainstream fare like De Palma's *Dressed to Kill* (1980) and *Passion* (2012). His *giallo* credits include Dario Argento's ***Trauma*** and ***Do You Like Hitchcock?***, as well as Ruggero Deodato's ***Phantom of Death*** (1988) and Vanzina's ***Squillo*** and ***Sotto il vestito niente—L'ultima sfilata*** (2011).[1]

American actor Tom Schanley, who puts in a decent performance as Bob Crane,[2] heads the cast. Schanley embodies the blandly wholesome all-American boy, and this is what is required of him. *Nothing Underneath* marked his film debut following some guest appearances on American television, and it would seem to have remained his only brush with the world of European cult cinema; he has subsequently featured in everything from *T.J. Hooker* and *Murder, She Wrote* to *Get the Gringo* (2012) with Mel Gibson. Jessica Perring plays his sister Jessica. The latter is certainly beautiful, but the character does not get a lot of screen time and she does not have much of an opportunity to stand out beyond that. Her career appears to have died out not long after making this film. The major name in the picture is Donald Pleasence, who puts in a winning performance as Commissioner Danesi. Dodgy Italian accent to one side, Pleasence takes the cliché character—the dogged policeman who is due to retire in short order—and makes him likable. He was born in Nottinghamshire in 1919 and began acting in the theater before making his film debut in 1954. Pleasence initially harbored a desire to be a leading man but later recalled that seeing himself onscreen convinced him that his future lay in character roles. He was an insanely prolific actor, appearing in everything from big-budget mainstream pictures to lowbrow horror movies. Like his contemporaries John Carradine and Christopher Lee, he seems to have had a hard time saying no to script offers, but remaining employed was his goal and he certainly never went through any lean periods as a result. His filmography is chock-full of recognizable titles. To choose but a few, there is John Sturges' *The Great Escape* (1963), Roman Polanski's *Cul-de-sac* (1966), Lewis Gilbert's *You Only Live Twice* (1967), George Lucas' *THX 1138* (1971), John Carpenter's *Halloween* (1978) and Woody Allen's *Shadows and Fog* (1991). Pleasence went on to appear in a number of *gialli*, including Dario Argento's **Phenomena**, Ruggero Deodato's **Phantom of Death** and Al Festa's **Fatal Frames** (1996). The latter would prove to be his last film; he died in 1995 at the age of 75 following open-heart surgery.

Notes:

1. Dario Piana's **Too Beautiful to Die** (1988) was also sold as a sequel to *Nothing Underneath* in Italy, where it was released as *Sotto il vestito niente 2*.
2. One is tempted to theorize that the name is an allusion to the TV actor, of *Hogan's Heroes* fame, who died mysteriously in 1978; his strange life and death was later dramatized by director Paul Schrader in *Auto Focus* (2002). Alternatively, it is more likely a variation on the name of Janet Leigh's character, Marion Crane, in Hitchcock's *Psycho* (1960).

Phenomena (Italy)

Aka *Creepers*

Directed by Dario Argento; Produced by Dario Argento; Screenplay by Dario Argento and Franco Ferrini; Director of Photography: Romano Albani; Editor: Franco Fraticelli; Music by Claudio Simonetti, Goblin, Bill Wyman, Terry Taylor, Simon Boswell and Fabio Pignatelli

Main Players: Jennifer Connelly (Jennifer Corvino); Donald Pleasence (Professor John MacGregor); Daria Nicolodi (Frau Brückner); Patrick Bauchau (Inspector Geiger); Federica Mastroianni (Sophie); Dalila Di Lazzaro (Headmistress); Michele Soavi (Kurt); Fiore Argento (Vera Brandt)

Home Video: Anchor Bay Entertainment (Region 1 DVD); Arrow Video (All region Blu-ray); Synapse (All region Blu-ray)

Jennifer Corvino is sent to a boarding school in Switzerland. She is the daughter of a popular movie star, but the snobbish students are jealous and make her life miserable. Matters are not helped by the fact that she has an unusual connection to the insect world, which entomologist John McGregor, whom she befriends, describes as a form of telepathy. As if that is not enough, there is also a killer on the loose in the area with a penchant for murdering young girls ...

Phenomena marks the beginning of self-conscious self-celebration in Argento's filmography. It also marks something of an attempt to meld the *giallo* with the more supernatural horror films he began experimenting in with *Suspiria* (1977) and *Inferno* (1980).

The frankly ridiculous screenplay by Argento and Franco Ferrini plays out like a grab bag of elements recycled from the director's earlier movies—a sort of "greatest hits" package, if you like. The problem with this approach is it never really gels. The paranormal elements of the story sit uneasily alongside the *giallo* plot and the film lacks the sheer sense of style evident in his earlier efforts. That is not to say that the picture is without its pleasures, however, but it does mark a definite step in the wrong direction. Happily, Argento would get back on track with his next film, *Opera* (1987), but *Phenomena* can be seen as a sign of things to come with regards to his more erratic work of the 2000s, which is similarly marked by a tendency toward self-quotation.

In the context of *Phenomena*, the tendency to rely on previously tried ideas and imagery seems an empty gesture. We are treated to a slow-motion decapitation (à la **Four Flies on Grey Velvet**, 1971), a curious bit of voice-over narration limited to one scene (an idea used far more effectively in *Suspiria*), a strange girl's school presided over by ogre-like staff (also from *Suspiria*), an underwater set piece straight out of *Inferno* and, of course, a maniac with black gloves and an improbably extravagant outfit, which is a holdover from so many of his other *gialli*. Other elements are recycled, as well, but that is sufficient to give one a good idea of the level at which the director is working in this film. The main problem with these quotations is that they do not fit easily into the story itself, which appears to be attempting a more fairy tale–like ambience than usual. Rather, they feel like arbitrary concessions to the audience from a director who has suddenly become aware of his own import and celebrity.

The film also continues Argento's fascination with the animal world. The notion of Professor McGregor's "helper monkey" is played out in an interesting fashion, and when the simian later escapes and starts wielding a razor blade while seeking to avenge her master, the imagery becomes decidedly surreal, even absurd. It is an audacious idea that allows the film to conclude on a literal note of *deus ex machina*—or *deus ex monkey*, if you prefer. There is something almost naïve about the faith Argento had in such bizarre, over-the-top ideas, which are generally played out without the sense of self-conscious irony and tongue-in-cheek humor which would come to typify his later work.

Some elements of autobiography play into the figure of the film's protagonist, Jennifer. She is the daughter of a famous movie star; the heroine also comes from a broken home. It has been said that the story she tells to her roommate, Sophie, about the way in which her mother deserted her and her father was based on the director's own childhood. Argento's complex relationship with his absent mother manifests itself in the form of wicked mothers and stepmother figures in so many of his films and it is definitely a major factor in the structure of this film. Jennifer is also a vegetarian, reflecting Argento's own habits. Sadly, these elements to one side, the character is not nearly as interesting as she should be. She possesses extrasensory perception and has an unusual bond with the insect world, thus putting her in an even more precarious emotional state than the usual angst-ridden adolescent. Argento uses these outré elements to explore the character's growing pains, but given that characterization is seldom his strong suit, it is not surprising that the character remains rather flat and uninteresting.

In general, Argento's flair for creating memorable images and sustaining an off-kilter atmosphere offers its own reward. Sadly, this is only sporadically in evidence in *Phenomena*. A few magnificent scenes remind one of Argento's talent: Jennifer's sleepwalking visions come to mind, as does the opening involving a Danish tourist (played by Argento's eldest daughter, Fiore) who runs afoul of the killer. The film builds to a climax that is as noteworthy for its sadism as for its utter ridiculousness. And therein lies part of the problem: in lieu of a more interesting story or a more seductive style, the director seems content to pile on the agony with a trowel. It is effective enough in its own way, but it seems awfully facile compared to the nightmarish splendor of *Inferno* or the immaculately structured and executed *Deep Red*.

Curiously, Argento elects to film *Phenomena* in a more overtly realistic style than usual. The story would seem to dictate a baroque approach, similar to that of *Inferno*, but Argento defies expectations by going in the opposite direction. There is something to be said for steering clear of the obvious, but it really does not do the film any favors. The cold blue lighting is similar to the chic appearance of *Tenebrae* but it is not nearly as well executed. Some of this is down to the lighting of Romano Albani, which does not succeed in creating the same sustained air of artifice as that of Luciano Tovoli in *Tenebrae*, but much of it is attributable to Argento's unexpectedly functional direction. The director's

Italian *locandina* for *Phenomena*; artwork by Enzo Sciotti.

flair for prowling camerawork is sporadically evident, but too many scenes unfold in a conventional manner. The dialogue-heavy screenplay is another drawback. *Phenomena* was the first of the director's films to rely on on-set direct sound recording and the often stilted dialogue would seem to indicate that he was not fully prepared for this. Argento's films are not exactly renowned for their sparkling dialogue, but the English-language dialogue found in the likes of **The Bird with the Crystal Plumage** (1970), **Deep Red** (1975) and *Tenebrae* (1982) is generally quite effective on its own terms; here, however, there are more than a few howlers, notably Jennifer's testy declaration to the doctor who insists on administering an EEG after one of her sleepwalking spells: "I am not crazy … epileptic … schizophrenic … or stoned!"

The film's uneven, messy structure is reflected in the use of music. Argento's previous films were unified in sound and vision, while this one adopts the mid-1980s trend of mixing and matching popular songs for the benefit of increased soundtrack album sales. In lieu of the driving progressive rock sounds of Goblin, the jangly jazz-fueled work of Ennio Morricone or the elegant piano-based music by Keith Emerson, *Phenomena* mixes original compositions by the likes of Bill Wyman and Claudio Simonetti with heavy metal music by Iron Maiden and other popular groups. The use of

JENNIFER HAS A FEW MILLION CLOSE FRIENDS.
SHE'S GOING TO NEED THEM ALL.

Featuring music by IRON MAIDEN and MOTÖRHEAD

From Dario Argento the master of terror...

Dario Argento

Creepers

It will make your skin crawl

From New Line Cinema

R RESTRICTED

American poster for *Phenomena*, which was released in a retitled, heavily edited version; artist unknown.

A young Jennifer Connelly heads the cast, while an appealing actress, but she struggles with Argento's awkward dialogue and never convinces us as a psychically gifted individual. She was born in New York in 1970 and started off as a child model before making her acting debut with an episode of the anthology series *Tales of the Unexpected* in 1982. She made her film debut when she was cast in the role of the young Deborah (played as an adult by Elizabeth McGovern) in Sergio Leone's epic *Once Upon a Time in America* (1984). Argento caught a glimpse of Connelly while visiting his mentor and decided to cast her in the role of Jennifer, which proved to be the actress' first leading role. She would go on to appear in Jim Henson's popular fantasy *Labyrinth* (1986) before halting her career to concentrate on her studies. She came back to films later on and appeared in the likes of the *Black Swan* precursor *Étoile* (1988), Dennis Hopper's sexy *noir The Hot Spot* (1990), Disney's *The Rocketeer* (1991) and Lee Tamahori's neo-*noir Mulholland Falls* (1996). In the 2000s, she proved her diversity—and earned some of the best reviews of her career—by appearing in such diverse films as Ed Harris' *Pollock* and Darren Aronofsky's *Requiem for a Dream* (both 2000). She followed these up with an Academy Award-winning turn in Ron Howard's *A Beautiful Mind* (2001) and an acclaimed one in Vadim Perelman's *House of Sand and Fog* (2003). Her more recent credits include Edward Zwick's *Blood Diamond* (2006) and Aronofsky's *Noah* (2014). The supporting cast includes Daria Nicolodi, giving her worst performance by far for Argento, and Donald Pleasence, whose Scots accent has taken some criticism but who still gives the warmest, most believable performance in the picture. Special note must also be made of Tanga the monkey, who enters into the spirit of the proceedings with tremendous enthusiasm.

metal would infect Argento's work for a period of time, but it is not always successfully integrated here. The use of Iron Maiden's "Flash of the Blade" during some of the more frenetic moments is a little obvious but it works well enough, whereas a piece by Motörhead is played over what should be a touching, mournful moment for no evident reason. Goblin is credited as contributing, but this is a little deceptive. Their "contribution" is limited to two cues from their *Dawn of the Dead* soundtrack, which can barely be heard as Sophie watches TV at one point.

The already convoluted narrative was impacted even further when New Line acquired the film for theatrical release in the United States. Argento's original Italian release ran 116 minutes, which he had tightened to a more satisfactory 110 minutes for other European provinces (including the U.K.), but New Line saw fit to butcher it, releasing it at a barely coherent 82 minutes. They also retitled the film as *Creepers*, but it did not make much of a ripple; it was, however, the last Argento film to receive any kind of a meaningful theatrical release in America and it proved to be a huge hit in Italy in its original form.

1986

The Killer Has Returned
(Italy)

Aka *L'assassino è ancora tra noi; The Killer is Still Among Us*

Directed by Camillo Teti; Screenplay by Ernesto Gastaldi and Camillo Teti, from a story by Giuliano Carnimeo and Ernesto Gastaldi; Director of Photography: Giuseppe Bernardini; Editor: Delia Apolloni; Music by Detto Mariano

Main Players: Mariangela D'Abbraccio (Cristiana); Giovanni Visentin (Alex); Riccardo Perrotti (Professor); Yvonne D'Abbraccio (Chiara)

Cristiana is a graduate student majoring in criminology; as part of her thesis, she is following the police investigation into a series of murders. The assassin, dubbed "The Couples Killer" because of his M.O. of targeting young lov-

ers while they are at their most vulnerable, has left no clues behind thus far. Cristiana begins working up a profile and soon finds herself in danger as well ...

It is difficult to believe that Ernesto Gastaldi had a hand in the writing of this rather inept thriller. The plot is strictly by the numbers and the production values indicate that the film was thrown together with indecent haste.

Gastaldi and Teti took inspiration from the real-life series of murders committed by the so-called "Monster of Florence." These crimes unfolded between 1968 and 1985 and involved eight sets of killings, all of them apparently couples caught in the act of making love. The identity of the killer (or killers) has never been firmly established, though three men were arrested and charged with the crime in 1996; the ensuing trial became a sensation in Italy. The story would be dramatized more "officially" in the *giallo* **The Monster of Florence** (1986) as well as in a less-sensationalized TV miniseries of the same name from 2009.[1] The film concludes with an onscreen declaration that the film is meant to serve as a warning to young people (against *what*? Parking in secluded areas and necking?) and an appeal to the police to continue doing everything in their power to put a stop to the bloodshed; but, while well-intended, it comes off as vaguely hypocritical in the context of a film that trades on such overtly sensationalized imagery. When one considers that the crimes were still fresh in the minds of the public—and that the wounds suffered by the friends and family of the victims had not even had an opportunity to begin healing—this leaves a very bad taste in the mouth indeed.

The film starts off with a scene that would not be out of place in the average American slasher film. A young couple parks in a deserted area for a little make-out session and is summarily dispatched by a psychopath. The killer tends to go in for blunt efficiency, shooting the victims at point blank range before taking his (or her?) time mutilating the bodies with a knife. This latter element comes into play rather forcefully at the end, which offers up one of the more nauseating bits of sensationalism to be found in any *giallo*, as the murderer slices off a victim's nipple before mutilating her genitals as well. It is a nasty scene, but—ironically enough—it gives the film a sudden jolt of life after the preceding hour or so of tedium. These set pieces are clearly patterned after the crimes of "The Monster of Florence," and they do not skimp on highlighting the more nauseating, sexualized nature of some of the murders.

Unfortunately, much of the film is handled in a lazy, haphazard fashion. The characters are dull and their relationships do not seem credible. Cristiana's work as a graduate student is a novel touch in a genre that was not exactly awash with them during this time, but nothing meaningful is done with this aspect of the plot. She fulfills the function of the dogged amateur detective, it is true, but beyond that she has no depth and does not inspire much sympathy, let alone interest. In a move typical of so many 1980s movies, she meets the police pathologist, Alex, and is in bed with

him a mere hour later; their pillow talk implies that they are falling deep in love after having known each other for a few brief hours, but things turn sour when Alex tries to pressure Christiana into dropping her investigation. It is almost as if director/co-writer Camillo Teti presented Gastaldi with a checklist of clichés and encouraged him to incorporate them all, one by one. The only real flash of imagination comes at the very end, when the film suddenly takes on a self-reflexive quality; it is an unforeseen development that robs the film of its expected *denouement*.

Sensibly, Gastaldi has since distanced himself from the film. In an email interview with writer Roberto Curti he made his stance on the film very clear:

> Bad movie. [Giuliano] Carnimeo was supposed to shoot it, but eventually it was the producer, Teti, who directed it. He was the son of [Federico] Teti

Italian *locandina* **for** *The Killer Has Returned*; **artist unknown.**

who administered Sergio Leone's Rafran company. Probably the script was pretty bad as well; however, it was partially rewritten by the makeshift director, who was also afraid he would be sued because of several references I had made [to the real-life cases].

The entire production is rather carelessly executed. Giuseppe Bernardini's photography is drab and lacks atmosphere, while Teti's direction only comes to life (just barely) when charting the more nauseating aspects of the crimes. Dialogue scenes drag interminably, and, even at less than 90 minutes, the film seems to last much longer. A dull cast and an instantly forgettable music score do not help matters either. On the plus side, Roberto Pace's special make-up effects are noteworthy for their realism.

Director Camillo Teti was born in 1939. He worked extensively as a production manager and assistant through the 1960s and 1970s, but *The Killer Has Returned* marked his debut as a writer and director. He would go on to direct sporadically, including the animated *Titanic: The Legend Goes On ...* (2000), as well as produce films such as Fabrizio De Angelis' *Killer Crocodile* (1989) and Giannetto De Rossi's *Killer Crocodile 2* (1990).

Notes:
1. A more detailed examination of the case is provided in the review for *The Monster of Florence* (1986).

Midnight Killer (Italy)

Aka *Morirai a mezzanotte; Midnight Horror; You'll Die at Midnight*

Directed by Lamberto Bava (as John Old, Jr.); Produced by Lamberto Bava, Massimo Manasse and Marco Grillo Spina; Screenplay by Lamberto Bava (as John Old, Jr.) and Dardano Sacchetti; Director of Photography: Gianlorenzo Battaglia; Editor: Lamberto Bava (as John Old, Jr.); Music by Claudio Simonetti

Main Players: Paolo Malco (Inspector Piero Terzi); Valeria D'Obici (Anna Berardi); Leonardo Treviglio (Nicola Levi); Lara Wendel (Carol Terzi); Eliana Miglio (Monica)

When his wife is murdered, police officer Nicola Levi comes under suspicion. However, psychologist Anna Berardi is of the opinion that it is the work of the so-called "Midnight Killer." The problem with this theory: the Midnight Killer perished in a fire some years ago. Anna refuses to believe that her hunch is wrong and launches her own investigation while Inspector Terzi focuses on trying to find a flesh and blood assassin ...

Lamberto Bava's second *giallo* draws heavily on the works of Dario Argento. It may be derivative, but *Midnight Killer* remains one of the most purely enjoyable *gialli* of the mid-1980s.

Bava directs the film with great flair and economy. In addition to co-writing the script, he also edited the film and maintains an excellent pace and tempo, especially when

Italian *locandina* for *Midnight Killer*; artwork by Enzo Sciotti.

compared to his first thriller, the effective but overlong *A Blade in the Dark* (1983). In addition to serving up some great shock effects, the film sustains a good sense of suspense throughout. The finale may be a little on the incredible side, but let us face it that is part and parcel of the genre. One of the big reveals at the end also works in a specific nod to **The Bird with the Crystal Plumage** (1970), but Bava is not merely aping earlier works here. He draws from some of the genre's most effective iconography and delivers a thriller that can stand on its own merits.

The screenplay by Bava and Dardano Sacchetti is taut and engrossing. The notion of a legendary killer apparently returning from the grave to continue his bloody work is reminiscent of the slasher films of the 1980s, wherein Jason Voorhees, Michael Myers and other unstoppable bogeymen return time and time again to claim more victims. Bava and Sacchetti use this idea as a starting point, but they develop it in a more credible and realistic fashion. Their killer is not a supernatural entity but a very human psychopath with an unstoppable urge to kill.

Structurally, the film is somewhat unusual in that it shifts points of view at several instances. Early on, the emphasis is on the character of Nicola, who is accused of murdering his wife in a jealous rage. The emphasis then shifts to Inspector Terzi, who rejects the notion of the "Midnight Killer" returning to continue his crime spree. Then the film focuses on the character of Terzi's daughter Carol, who may become the killer's latest victim. The shifting focal point throws the viewer off-guard, making it difficult to identify with any one figure as a protagonist, but fortunately the three characters are sufficiently well drawn (and portrayed) to hold one's interest.

Bava would later claim that he was very uneasy making *gialli*—"I find doing scenes where women get stabbed to death repugnant. Dario Argento does it so well, but I feel sick as soon as I see the knife in the murderer's hand."[1] But this is not borne out by the mean-spirited murder scenes in this film. One character attempts to defend herself with a nasty-looking hand mixer with sharp prongs, but the extension cord runs out and she finds herself at the receiving end of the killer's knife; the latter goes a step farther at that point, by using said mixer to mutilate the dead woman's genitals. There is a very vicious shower murder, à *la Psycho* (1960), and the blood flows quite freely in the other murder scenes as well. The film does not just work on the basis of these scenes, however; it is a well-crafted movie, with some striking cinematography courtesy of Gianlorenzo Battaglia (who shot many of Bava's efforts during this period) and a strong story at its core. The music score by Claudio Simonetti is also very effective; the opening title theme, with its blend of techno beats and classical violins, is one of his most impressive compositions.

Paolo Malco delivers a fine performance as the cynical Inspector Terzi. He gives the character a nice dose of sly humor and is believable throughout. Lara Wendel plays his daughter Carol. She is also very effective as the strong-willed criminal psychology major who finds herself up to her neck in murder. Wendel is a likable presence, and this certainly helps to make her worth rooting for when she goes up against the killer; she also displays more cleverness than is the norm in trying to outwit the murderer. The actress was born in Munich in 1965, under the name Daniela Rachele Barnes. She made her debut with a small role in **My Dear Killer** (1972) and also appeared in such borderline *gialli* as Damiano Damiani's *The Assassin of Rome* (1972) and Francesco Barilli's *The Perfume of the Lady in Black* (1974) before a more substantial role in Dario Argento's **Tenebrae** (1982) In addition to Italian horror films like *Zombie 5: Killing Birds* (1987), she also featured in more arthouse-type fare like Michelangelo Antonioni's *Identification of a Woman* (1982) and Federico Fellini's *Intervista* (1987). She stopped acting in the early 1980s. Leonardo Treviglio also puts in good work as Nicola. Treviglio's palpable rage at his wife's infidelity makes one unsure whether or not to accept his claims of innocence, and his performance is appropriately ambiguous. Treviglio was born in Milan in 1949 and made his movie debut playing the title character in Derek Jarman's *Sebastiane* (1976). He would go on to appear in such films as Bernardo Bertolucci's *Stealing Beauty* (1996), Dario Argento's *The Phantom of the Opera* (1998) and Julie Taymor's *Titus* (1999).

Bava's next *giallo* would prove to be his most unusual: **Delirium: Photos of Gioia** (1987).

Notes:

1. Palmerini, Luca M. and Gaetano Mistretta, *Spaghetti Nightmares* (Florida: Fantasma Books, 1996), p. 23

The Monster of Florence
(Italy)

Aka *Il mostro di Firenze; Night Ripper—Das Monster von Florenz*

Directed by Cesare Ferrario; Produced by Mario Giacomini and Bruno Noris; Screenplay by Cesare Ferrario and Fulvio Ricciardi; Director of Photography: Claudio Cirillo; Music by Paolo Rustichelli

Main Players: Leonard Mann (Andreas Ackerman); Bettina Giovannini (Giulia); Gabriele Tinti (Enrico)

FILMART GIALLO EDITION

IL MOSTRO DI FIRENZE

NIGHT RIPPER

REGIE: CESARE FERRARIO

DAS MONSTER VON FLORENZ

MIT LEONARD MANN UND GABRIELE TINTI   #006

A rash of murders shocks Florence. The press dubs the killer "The Monster" and luridly charts every detail of the crimes, but the police have no clues and the murders continue. Andreas, a journalist, sifts through the evidence and attempts to form a portrait of the killer ...

Like **The Pyjama Girl Case** (1977), *The Monster of Florence* is a rare *giallo* that derives explicit inspiration from the newspaper headlines. In this case, the story focuses on the very real mayhem wrought by a psychopath who stalked Florence from 1968 until 1985. A recap of the killer's crimes is more unsettling and perhaps a good deal more interesting than the film itself.[1]

In August of 1968 an unknown assailant shoots Antonio Lo Bianco and his lover Barbara Locci to death. Locci's little boy, who was asleep in the back seat as the two indulged in a quick make-out session, was unharmed and reported the crime to some neighbors. Locci was well known for carrying on numerous affairs behind the back of her husband Stefano

The killer attempts to wash away his sins in *The Monster of Florence*.

Mele, and the authorities became convinced that the cuckolded husband was responsible. Stefano Mele was sent to prison, all the while protesting his innocence.

In September of 1974, another pair of lovers, Pasquale Gentilcore and Stefania Pettini, was killed while having sex in Gentilcore's car. Gentilcore was shot, while Pettini's body was mutilated and violated in a shocking fashion.

In June of 1981, Giovanni Foggi and Carmela Di Nuccio, engaged to be married, parked on a road near their home, were murdered. Once again, the female bore the brunt of the killer's rage. After she had been killed, the murderer used a knife to remove her genitals. A Peeping Tom who was spying on the couple as they made love got more than he bargained for when he bore witness to the crime. Sooner than report what he saw to the police, he started telling his cronies of the incident and eventually the authorities got wind of what he had seen. The man was charged with the murders and sentenced to prison, but the case against him was weak and he was eventually released.

Later that year, in October, Stefano Baldi and Susanna Cambi, also engaged, were murdered while in a nearby park. Cambi's body was mutilated in the same fashion as that of Di Nuccio.

In June of the following year, Paolo Mainardi and Antonella Migliorini were attacked while they were parked on a lonely stretch of road. Migliorini's body was not mutilated, but she died during the attack. Mainardi lived a few hours after being discovered, but died before he could provide the police with any relevant clues.

In September of 1983, German tourists Horst Wilhelm Meyer and Jens Uwe Rüsch were shot to death in their car; in an interesting twist, they were the first couple of male victims, but whether they were involved in a homosexual relationship or were simply killed by chance has never been determined. Given that Rüsch had a slim build and long blonde hair, the theory is that the killer likely mistook him for a woman.

In July 1984, Claudio Stefanacci and his girlfriend Pia Gilda Rontini were stabbed to death while they were parked and making love. Rontini's corpse was horribly mutilated, with the killer removing her genitals and her left breast, presumably as a macabre souvenir.

And in September 1985, French tourists Jean Michel Kraveichvili and Nadine Mauriot were attacked while camping. Mauriot was shot to death and died instantly, while Kraveichvili made an ill-fated run for safety before being dispatched as well. Mauriot's body was sexually mutilated and the killer even went so far as to send a piece of her breast along with a taunting note to the state prosecutor on the case.

In 1994, an elderly farmer by the name of Pietro Pacciani was accused of committing the murders and was sentenced to life in prison. Pacciani's cohorts, Mario Vanni and Giancarlo Lotti, were sentenced to 30 years in prison and life in prison, respectively, for assisting the old man in the crimes. Pacciani appealed the verdict and was released in 1996. He had a long history of perpetrating sexual abuse on his wife and daughters, but his official role in the killings remains debated to this day; he died in 1998, while Lotti followed in 2002 and Vanni in 2009.

As of 2014, the identity of the killer (or killers) responsible for these horrific crimes remains a mystery. The arrests made in 1968 and June 1981 did not stop the killings and, if Pacciani and his cohorts were indeed the guilty parties, this has yet to be definitively proven. In the eyes of the court, the sentences of Pacciani and his friends brought the case to a satisfactory close; others are not so sure, however. Numerous books and journalistic exposes have been written, notably Douglas Preston and Mario Spezi's (who provided the killer with the sensational moniker of "The Monster of Florence" while covering the crimes as a journalist) *The Monster of Florence*, first published in 2008. Cesare Ferrario's film of the same name offers a sensationalized but curiously dull reconstruction of the crimes.

The film opens with the 1985 murder, then shifts back and forth as the protagonist, journalist Andreas Ackerman, obsesses over the killings and tries to crack the case. The majority of the killings are dramatized, but Ferrario does not go in for the more unsavory details in any kind of graphic fashion. He likely worried, and for good reason, that to do so would be upsetting to the relatives of the victims.

In any event, the end result is weak tea as a *giallo* and inadequate as a docudrama. Ferrario's flat, functional direction fails to generate any suspense or menace and the production values are rather cheap, giving the film a somewhat tawdry air. A more gifted filmmaker could probably make a very compelling movie about the mystery surrounding these murders, but as of now they would have to be content with offering up theories and suppositions in place of cold, hard facts; the case remains as muddy and indistinct as ever.

The cast includes *giallo* veterans Leonard Mann and Gabriele Tinti as rival journalists. Mann's performance as the dogged and obsessive Andreas is no more than adequate. He fails to really come to grips with the character's obsessive nature and comes off as a bit of a cipher as a result. Tinti does his best as Enrico, but his screen time is limited and he does not get nearly enough to do.

Director Ferrario entered the industry as an actor in the mid-1970s. *The Monster of Florence* marked his directing and writing debut, but it did not lead to much more work in the long run. He made only a handful of films before retiring in 2001.

The story would get another go-around on Italian TV with the miniseries *The Monster of Florence* (2009); this version would adopt a more sedate approach and does not include the more lurid touches that tilts Ferrario's film into the realm of the *giallo*. Elements of the case also inspired Camillo Teti's **The Killer Has Returned** (1986) and Gianni Siragusa's **28° Minuto** (1991).

Notes:

1. Information on the case is from the revised edition of *The Monster of Florence* by Douglas Preston and Mario Spezi (New York: Grand Central Publishing, 2013).

1987

Delirium: Photos of Gioia
(Italy)

Aka *Le foto di Gioia; Crimenes en portada; Das unheimliche Auge; Photos of Joy*

Directed by Lamberto Bava; Produced by Massimo Manasse and Marco Grillo Spina; Screenplay by Gianfranco

Anglo poster for *Delirium: Photos of Gioia*, highlighting the killer's surreal vision of one of his victims.

Clerici and Daniele Stroppa; Director of Photography: Gianlorenzo Battaglia; Editor: Mauro Bonanni; Music by Simon Boswell

Main Players: Serena Grandi (Gioia); Daria Nicolodi (Evelyn); David Brandon (Roberto); Vanni Corbellini (Tony); Luigi Montefiori [as George Eastman] (Alex); Capucine (Flora); Karl Zinny (Mark); Lino Salemme (Inspector Corsi)

Home Video: Shriek Show/Media Blasters (Region 1 DVD)

Gioia is an ex-model who runs an adult magazine titled Pussycat. *A killer begins targeting her glamorous models. As if that is not bad enough, the killer also poses the corpses in front of enlarged photos of Gioia from her modeling days. Fearing for her life, she turns to the police for assistance but the murders continue, as do the harassing photos. In time, it becomes apparent that Gioia is next on the killer's hit list ...*

Delirium: Photos of Gioia is Lamberto Bava's strangest *giallo*. Whether or not this is to the film's benefit is debatable, however.

The screenplay by Gianfranco Clerici and Daniele Stroppa utilizes the world of fashion as the backdrop. This theme of surface beauty being savagely violated by a deranged mind goes back as far as Mario Bava's **Blood and Black Lace** (1964) in the realm of the Italian *giallo* film and it has certainly been utilized by many filmmakers, including Carlo Vanzina (**Nothing Underneath**, 1985) and Dario Argento (**Giallo**, 2009). In terms of its basic structure, there is nothing really new on display here, but Lamberto Bava brought something decidedly quirky to the mix. In an interview with authors Luca M. Palmerini and Gaetano Mistretta, the director suggests that doing a couple of *gialli* more or less back-to-back sapped his enthusiasm; he never felt a strong affinity for the genre and preferred making fantasy films like *Demons* (1985).[1] In order to dredge up some enthusiasm for the project and impose something of a personal stamp on it, Bava decided to explore the notion of the killer's point of view. Not content with merely rehashing the usual subjective camerawork, the director decided to signal his presence by the appearance of pulsing colored light. In addition, he came up with the idea of showing the killer's perception of his victims by providing them with grotesque, over-the-top visages: one woman's face is dominated by a huge, solitary eyeball; another takes on the appearance of a bee and so forth. It was probably the riskiest move a *giallo* filmmaker had made since Lucio Fulci decided to make his psychopath quack like a duck in **The New York Ripper** (1982), but the result drew more jeers than praise. Some of this is down to the admittedly cheap-looking masks designed by make-up artist Rosario Prestopino and his crew, but the idea itself was tricky at best to realize and it simply does not come off as well as Bava had intended.

In an interview included on the Shriek Show DVD release of the film, Bava indicates that this was one of the few films he made where he had sufficient time and money to get the results he was looking for. Beyond the lovably bizarre but shoddy "killer's POV" gimmick, it is easy to see why he felt this way. The production values are very slick and there is some lovely cinematography from Gianlorenzo Battaglia. Most of the effects work is pretty well done and the story is engaging enough, even if it fails to bring any new twists to the tried-and-true formula. Bava directs the film with economy and style and if the softcore sex scenes look a little hokey, thanks to some ill-advised slow-motion photography, the various shocks are nicely achieved and integrated into the finished product.

The film was designed as a showcase for its beautiful leading lady, Serena Grandi. Her spectacular physique had made her a favorite in the Italian erotica scene, but with *Delirium: Photos of Gioia* she was looking to establish herself as a more serious actress. Sadly, she is not up to the challenges of the role. Her background as a model and erotic film star keys into the movie's examination of the fashion world, but she lacks the acting chops to make the character come to life. The star spends much of the film appearing to pose rather than emote and, while this adds to the subtext in an unintentional manner, it does not really do the picture any favors beyond that. Grandi was born in Bologna in 1958 and made her film debut in 1980. One of her first credits was the infamous Joe D'Amato gorefest *Anthropophagus* (1980), where she was billed under the name of Vanessa Steiger and participated in the movie's most infamous moment, when her pregnant character is dispatched by the monster (played by Luigi Montefiori, who also appears here) who proceeds to tear the fetus from her womb and feast on it. After this, she tended to focus more on sexy, comedic roles. Tinto Brass cast her as *Miranda* (1985), which catapulted her to stardom, while Luigi Cozzi made use of her in *The Adventures of Hercules II* (1985). She would go on to appear in such *gialli* as **Crime of Passion** (1994) and **The Strange Story of Olga O** (1995). She recently appeared in Paolo Sorrentino's Oscar-winning *The Great Beauty* (2013). The supporting cast includes En-

Italian *locandina* for *Delirium: Photos of Gioia*; designer unknown.

glish actor David Brandon (real name David Haughton) as a photographer who comes under suspicion. He was born in 1940 and started acting on the stage before making his film debut in Derek Jarman's *Jubilee* (1978). He began appearing in Italian films in the early 1980s and has since alternated his career between working there and in the U.K. Brandon's flair for playing shady types would be put to good use in other *gialli*, including the aforementioned *The Strange Story of Olga O* and *Stage Fright* (1987), but his movie career has slowed down in recent years as he has elected to focus on writing and directing for the theater. Daria Nicolodi puts in a good performance as Gioia's devoted assistant, while, as already stated, Luigi Montefiori is on hand to play one of Gioia's former lovers, who comes back into the picture and rekindles their romance. Montefiori was typically cast as brutes and thugs, so it is fun seeing him in a more romantic context, but his character is poorly developed and his scenes feel like a subplot that goes nowhere. Born in Genoa in 1942, he started off as an artist before being lured into a life in the cinema. His imposing height (6'9") and muscular build made him an ideal candidate for Spaghetti Westerns and he soon made appearances in the likes of *Django Kills Silently* (1967) and *The Last Killer* (1967). Federico Fellini caught sight of him and cast him as the Minotaur in his ancient Roman epic *Fellini Satyricon* (1969), while Mario Bava gave him arguably his best role as the psychotic criminal Thirty-Two (so named because of his impressive member; do not forget the Italians use the metric system!) in his gritty kidnapping thriller *Rabid Dogs* (1974). Montefiori also featured in such films as Enzo G. Castellari's *1990: The Bronx Warriors* (1982), Sergio Martino's *2019: After the Fall of New York* (1983) and Bruce Beresford's *King David* (1985), in which he played Goliath. Often billed under the alias of George Eastman, he would appear under his real name in films of which he was more proud, including *Fellini Satyricon*, *Rabid Dogs* and *King David*. Montefiori is also a prolific screenwriter; among his credits in that field are the aforementioned *Anthropophagus*, in which he also played the cannibalistic killer, and Michele Soavi's *Stage Fright*. He has also tried his hand at producing and directing but has been inactive in films since the early 2000s. The boyish Karl Zinny plays Gioia's crippled neighbor. He does a decent job though the character's propensity for pulling silly pranks wears a little thin. Zinny was born in 1964 and began appearing in films in the late 1970s. Lamberto Bava cast him in several efforts in rapid succession—the others being *Demons* (1985) and *Graveyard Disturbance* (1987)— but his career never really took off. Another familiar face from Bava's unofficial repertory company, Lino Salemme, is on hand to play the police inspector. Salemme, with his hulking build and shifty appearance, is unusual casting in the part and he seems ill at ease. Bava also used him in *Demons* and *Graveyard Shift*, in addition to *Demons 2* (1986), but like Zinny his career never caught fire and he has been

inactive since playing a minor role in Mel Gibson's scandalous *The Passion of the Christ* (2004). Former international film star Capucine plays Flora, who runs a rival erotic magazine and covets not only ownership of the *Pussycat* empire but of Gioia herself. Born Germaine Lefebvre in 1928, the French actress changed her name to the more mysterious and elegant-sounding Capucine and made her mark as a fashion model before breaking into movies in 1948. She earned a Golden Globe nomination for her English-language debut *Song Without End*, appeared opposite John Wayne in *North to Alaska* (both 1960) and played the wife of Peter Sellers' bumbling Inspector Clouseau in *The Pink Panther* (1963). She followed these up with roles in Clive Donner's *What's New Pussycat* (1965), Federico Fellini's *Fellini Satyricon* (1969) and Terence Young's *Red Sun* (1971). Capucine also enjoyed a lengthy affair with actor William Holden (with whom she had appeared in *The Lion*, 1962, and *The 7th Dawn*, 1964) but her constant struggle with bipolar disorder would permanently impact her personal life. She made her *giallo* debut with a guest star role in Sergio Corbucci's *Atrocious Tales of Love and Death* (1979). Her star had waned by the time she appeared in *Delirium: Photos of Gioia*; it would prove to be one of her last roles before she grabbed headlines one last time by jumping from the window of her apartment and plummeting to her death in 1990.

Notes:

1. Palmerini, Luca M. and Gaetano Mistretta, *Spaghetti Nightmares* (Florida: Fantasma Books, 1996), p. 23.

Delitti (Italy)

Directed by Giovanna Lenzi and (uncredited) Sergio Pastore; Screenplay by Giovanna Lenzi and Sergio Pastore (as Serge Vidor); Director of Photography: Domenico Paolercio; Editor: Gianfranco Amicucci; Music by Guido and Maurizio De Angelis

Main Players: Saverio Vallone (Bob Rowling); Giorgio Ardisson (Chief Inspector); Michela Miti (Betty); Tony Valente (Inspector Sanders); Solvi Stubing (Harriet); Gianni Dei (Harry); Linda Christian (The Announcer)

A killer targets various victims and stabs and strangles them to death, after which he (or she) uses a rare snake to bite the bodies; this has a decidedly horrific effect on their faces. Brash Inspector Sanders is called in to investigate, but his unconventional techniques land him in hot water with his superiors. Meanwhile, the killings continue ...

Delitti is of note as the first *giallo* to be directed by a woman. Sadly, the end result can hardly be seen as a positive step in the women's liberation movement, though it does prove that women can direct every bit as poorly as their worst male counterparts.

To say that the screenplay is a hackneyed mess would be an understatement. The plot, such as it is, rambles from

Bland advertising for the abysmal *Delitti*; artist unknown.

ably. The characters are a dismal and dreary lot, from the clichéd rogue police inspector to the various vaguely defined female victims, and the story could not possibly be any less involving. The actors seem to be aware of just how hopeless their situation is, with veterans like Giorgio Ardisson phoning it in. Even the killer's *modus operandi* is ludicrous. The notion of carrying such a deadly serpent around in one's pants pockets (no other explanation is proffered, so we are led to assume that this is the case) is unbelievably daft. The attempt at demonstrating the horrific effects that the snake's bite has on the victims is done in by some less-than-special make-up effects work. Similarly, the various murders are so listlessly staged as to be risible. The victims barely seem to put up any kind of a struggle and the stingy doses of gore barely have a chance to register. The music score by Guido and Maurizio De Angelis draws heavily from their score for Lamberto Bava's ***A Blade in the Dark*** (1983), which merely serves to remind one of what a good *giallo* ought to be like. Ultimately, the film may not sink as low as ***The Killer Has Returned*** (1986) in terms of sheer bad taste, but it remains one of the shoddiest and most tedious *gialli* of its period.

The film marked the directing debut of Giovanna Lenzi. Even allowing for her inexperience behind the camera, it is still difficult to forgive her utterly inept work on this picture. According to the credits, the "supervising director" was one Serge Vidor; this was, in fact, a pseudonym for Lenzi's then-husband, director Sergio Pastore. The latter, whose credits included the *giallo* ***The Crimes of the Black Cat*** (1972), died from a stroke he suffered while at the premiere for the finished film. Just how much of the picture was informed by his guidance is open to speculation. Lenzi was born in Rome in 1943 and started off as an actress in the 1960s. Among her credits in this capacity were the early *gialli* ***A ... come assassino*** (1966, where she was credited as Barbara Penn) and ***Deadly Inheritance*** (1968, where she was billed under her more common pseudonym, Jeannette Len). She also appeared in ***The Crimes of the Black Cat*** and this movie as well. She would direct one more film, *La Tempesta* (1988), from a screenplay she wrote with Pastore, before making a brief return to acting. She retired in 1990.

Giallo: la tua impronta del venerdi
(TV Series) (Italy)

TV series produced by Dario Argento; TV series created by Enzo Tortora; Series Director of Photography: Pasquale Rachini; Series Editor: Piero Bozza

Recurring players: Antonella Vitale (Calypso 9); Matteo Gazzolo (Rosso 27); Lea Martino (Loredana); Franco Cerri (Tango 28); Stefano De Sando (Inspector Argentini)

Giallo: la tua impronta del venerdi was the brainchild of Italian television mogul Enzo Tortora. According to Luigi

one inept set piece to the next. Suspense is non-existent. Attempts at shock effects fall laughably flat. There is a lot of sex on display, but even this is handled in a perfunctory and downright timid fashion. It is one thing to have oodles of hardcore groping, as in ***Play Motel*** (1979); it is quite another to linger on the spectacle of actors awkwardly simulating intercourse while still wearing their underwear. The most horrific thing on display, truth be told, is some very poorly judged comic relief, notably in the form of the inspector's pursuit of a dwarf suspect (whom he proceeds to beat the hell out of) and a bizarre vignette in which a red herring appears poised to strike and then ... breaks into a cheesy dance routine. Not quite as bad, but still groan inducing, is the final warning from an on-screen narrator to mind who you become friends with ... and to steer clear of people who like snakes!

The production values are extremely cheap, giving the film something of the same seedy vibe as ***Giallo a Venezia*** (1979), but it lacks that film's willingness to embrace the more lurid aspects of the genre. If the idea was to aim for a more old-fashioned approach to suspense, it fails miser-

Cozzi, Tortora devised the series following a major personal scandal where he was accused of being a drug dealer and sent to prison; the accusations were eventually proven to be false, however, and he was released after serving only part of his sentence.[1] The RAI network took advantage of the scandal and offered the TV veteran a chance at redeeming his ruined career by coming up with a new program to fill an open Friday night slot. Tortora devised the idea of a *giallo*-themed series and wasted no time in securing the services of Dario Argento. The format of the series, which ran from October 1987 until January 1988, was somewhat convoluted. The first part of the show was hosted by Tortora and focused on the *giallo* in literature and the cinema, sometimes with an emphasis on real-life mysteries as well; the next part of the show, titled "Dario Argento's Nightmares," allowed the director to come on and discuss a thriller scenario, which he would dramatize in the form of a three-minute short film he directed; this would segue into a segment wherein Argento would interview pop culture personalities about their art (the guests would include the likes of genre-related actors like Anthony Perkins and musicians who interested the director, such as members of the group Pink Floyd) while providing some behind-the-scenes glimpses into the making of his own films; after that, Tortora would come back and introduce a short thriller featurette, which would pause before the final revelation of the killer's identity, thus enabling Tortora to invite members of a studio audience to take a crack at guessing the ending—those who succeeded could win a cash prize. As Cozzi explained, "These mini-movies were all supervised by Dario and given the title *Turno di notte*. […] We shot them in two days prior to airing and it was an enormous

undertaking. The show failed because it was considered too talky although most people did watch the first part because of Dario's involvement and then switched to another channel when Tortora's section took over."[2]

The show has since slid into obscurity and there have been no official DVD releases. One can imagine that Argento is only too happy for this as the series does not show off his talents to their fullest. Given the hectic production schedule and the episodic nature of the series, this is hardly surprising. The segment devoted to Argento's "nightmares" is generally hackneyed. Hosted by a haunted-looking Argento (perhaps a sleep-deprived Argento would be more appropriate), with actress Coralina Cataldi-Tassoni lurking around in the background, staring like a mad woman, they traded on the notion of the director as a celebrity. This was why Tortora reached out to him in the first place, as his participation would likely draw viewers who might otherwise not be inclined to explore Tortora's interest in crime stories (doubtlessly rooted in the scandal which ruined his name for a period of time). The stories range from the pointless to the absurd, but one vignette does stand out from the rest of the pack: "The Worm," which deals with a young woman who realizes that she has been infected by a deadly parasite. The segment has nothing to do with the *giallo*, but it builds to a memorably gruesome finale and lingers in the mind in a way that the other vignettes he directed decidedly do not.

The main "meat" of the show is to be found in the *Turno di Notte* (or *Night Shift*) segment, which offers up a new *giallo* subject in every episode. The same cast of characters unites the segments: a group of taxicab drivers working the night shift. The main problem with the set-up is that it strains

credulity early on and only succeeds in getting more contrived as things proceed. The introduction of a supernatural element—the so-called Ghost Taxi—sits uneasily in the mix, and the notion of a group of fresh-faced young cab drivers working hand-in-hand with the police department is too absurd to be taken seriously. One is reminded of the pitfalls that befell Carl Kolchak, the character created by writer Jeff Rice and dramatized by Richard Matheson and Dan Curtis in the form of two memorable 1970s TV movies, *The Night Stalker* (1972) and *The Night Strangler* (1973). The notion of the cynical reporter uncovering a vampire in Las Vegas was simultaneously fresh and amusing. The idea of the reporter relocating to Seattle, where he discovers a strange creature that is killing off the populace in order to prolong its immortality, began to strain believability a little. But it still worked well enough. Inevitably, the popularity of the two films resulted in a weekly series: *Kolchak: The Night Stalker* (1974-1975). It flopped, largely because the idea of Kolchak doing battle with a new supernatural entity every week just became silly and turned the whole thing into a piece of self-parody. The same principle applies here. Argento's first foray into television *gialli*, **Door into Darkness** (1973), benefitted from telling a separate, stand-alone story every week. Here, the contrivance of a link between the various stories wears out its welcome early on. Worse, each episode builds toward a finale to end the series on a fantastic note that is not in keeping with the overall tone of the project.

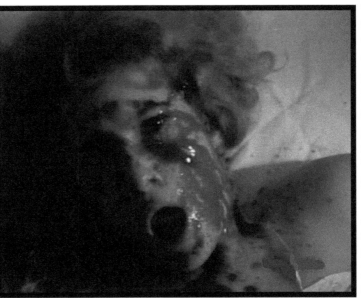

A gruesome image from one of the "Dario Argento's Nightmares" segments from the TV series *Giallo: la tua impronta del venerdi.*

The various stories have their moments, but none of them are particularly memorable. Lamberto Bava provides a sure and steady hand in guiding the first six segments, while Luigi Cozzi brings a different, more film buff-oriented sensibility to the remaining nine installments. In "*È di moda la morte,*" a model jumps to her death and another is stabbed to death before driver Rosso 27 (the drivers are nicknamed based on the names of their respective cabs) is able to uncover the culprit; David Brandon guest stars. "*Heavy Metal*" begins with Calypso 9 picking up a punk rocker and nearly ending up mincemeat when the youth leads her into a murder plot; Bava makes good use of moody lighting in this segment, while the use of metal standbys like Iron Maiden's "Flash of the Blade" and Saxon's "Fast as a Shark" recalls its usage in other Argento projects like **Phenomena** (1985) and *Demons* (1985). "*Buona fine e miglior principio*" deals with a murder committed at a crowded New Year's party; *giallo* veteran

Maurice Poli (who appeared in Mario Bava's **Five Dolls for an August Moon**, 1970) is among the red herrings and the music quotes from Goblin's score for **Deep Red** (1975). "*Giubbetto rosso*" begins with Rosso 27 being flagged down by a hysterical woman who claims to have escaped from the clutches of the so-called Red Jacket Killer, who has been terrorizing the region. He takes the girl back to the scene of the crime, where he makes a surprising discovery. "*Il bambino rapito*" gives some decent screen time to the otherwise ill-used Tango 28, who gets mixed up in a kidnapping scenario and helps the police in discovering the identity of the culprit. Bava's final installment, "*Babbo Natale,*" deals with Rosso 27 trying to keep the Christmas spirit while investigating the murder of a man in a Santa Claus outfit. Cozzi's contributions kick off with "*L'impronta dell'assassino,*" which tells of a murder that takes place in the gym where Calypso 9 formerly worked out; Brett Halsey (Mario Bava's *Four Times That Night*, 1969) and Mirella D'Angelo (Dario Argento's **Tenebrae**, 1982) are among the suspects. "*Ciak si muore*" borrows its name from an obscure 1974 *giallo* (**Clap, You're Dead**) and tells the more-clever-than-usual story of Calypso 9 picking up celebrity fare Corinne Cléry and taking her to film a thriller at Cinecittà. The star-struck cabbie sticks around to observe and is on hand when Cléry is unexpectedly butchered during a take. Cozzi's film buff leanings are evident as he seems to relish the behind-the-scenes atmosphere of the famous Roman film studio and the soundtrack is awash with (presumably unlicensed) cues by John Williams from *Star Wars* (1977) and *Raiders of the Lost Ark* (1981). "*Sposarsi è un po' morire*" begins with Rosso 27 picking up a bride-to-be who is running away from the altar; as he carts her to her uncertain destination, she is shot and killed in the back seat … it is up to Rosso to figure out who could have done it. Cozzi again lays on the library music, this time with an over-generous helping of Bernard Herrmann's iconic score for *Psycho* (1960). "*Delitto in Rock*" features Calypso 9 as she helps a friend in locating a tape the woman had left behind in the cab which contains a rare, unpublished song by Jim Morrison; the problem is, the person who has it is not ready to give it up and somebody is ready to commit murder in order to covet it. Calypso 9 is back for "*L'evasa,*" in which she is forced at gunpoint to take an escaped convict on the run; the soft-hearted cabbie believes the woman when she says that she is innocent and that she is trying to catch the person who is really guilty of the crime of which she is accused; some of Ennio Morricone's music for **The Cat O'Nine Tails** (1971) is on display in this segment. "*La casa dello Stradivari*" puts the luckless Rosso 27 in danger when his cab is stolen and he goes to a secluded villa for assistance; while waiting for Calypso 9 to come to the rescue, he bears witness to a crime. "*Giallo Natale*" has a cast and a set-up to die for (at least for the initiated): Daria Nicolodi plays a woman who vows to kill her ex-husband, while her real-life daughter Asia Argento is on hand to play her little girl, who tries to avert tragedy; one can only imagine the atmosphere on set with Argento supervising the production. Renato Rossini is also on hand, again billed as Howard Ross, and the segment is enjoyable in a silly sort of way, but it does not quite live up to expectations. "*Via delle streghe*" is the most stylish of Cozzi's contributions, and it deals with a costume party in which everybody is done up as a recognizable horror or sci-fi icon: the Invisible Man, the Creature from the Black Lagoon, etc. Goblin's iconic score for *Suspiria* (1977) is included, as are some snatches from Ennio Morricone's score for John Carpenter's *The Thing* (1982). The series limps to a very uninspiring ending with "*Il taxi fantasma*," which seeks to wrap-up a running reference to a mysterious Ghost Taxi, which Rosso 27 is particularly fixated on. That the series wraps up with a half-hearted foray into the supernatural and the paranormal suggests that everybody involved had grown tired of the *giallo* format.

Not surprisingly, the series failed to make much of an impression and it was not renewed for a second season.

Notes:
1. Jones, Alan, *Dario Argento: The Man, The Myths & The Magic* (Godalming: FAB Press, 2012), p. 50.
2. *Ibid*, p. 50.

Opera (Italy)

Aka *Terror at the Opera; Ópera; Terreur à l'opéra; Terror in der Oper*

Directed by Dario Argento; Produced by Dario Argento; Screenplay by Dario Argento and Franco Ferrini; Director of Photography: Ronnie Taylor; Editor: Franco Fraticelli; Music by Claudio Simonetti, Brian Eno, Roger Eno and Bill Wyman

Main Players: Cristina Marsillach (Betty); Ian Charleson (Marco); Urbano Barberini (Inspector Alan Santini); Daria Nicolodi (Mira); Coralina Cataldi-Tassoni (Giulia); William McNamara (Stefano); Antonella Vitale (Marion); Francesca Cassola (Alma)

Home Video: Blue Underground (Region free DVD); Eclipse (All region blu-ray from Japan, which includes the English soundtrack)

Betty is a young understudy for the famed opera singer Mara Czekova. When Mara is struck down in an accident, Betty gets her chance at stardom by singing the role of Lady Macbeth. It transpires that a maniac is orchestrating these events in order to further her career. The killer also targets the people closest to Betty, and forces the girl to watch as he butchers various victims by taping needles underneath her eyelids. Betty tries to fight back and uncover the identity of the maniac, but the murders continue and the police seem powerless to do anything about it ...

Following the uncertainty of **Phenomena** (1985), Dario Argento got back on *terra firma* with *Opera*. The film would be his most ambitious production to date; unfortunately, it would also be marked with personal tragedy and loss, making it a none-too-popular topic with its mercurial filmmaker.

The story of *Opera* is essentially a variation on Gaston Leroux's *The Phantom of the Opera*. Leroux was born in Paris in 1868. Despite attaining a law degree, he was something of a spendthrift and a lay-about as a young man. He received a sizable inheritance following the death of his parents, but he squandered it and soon lost interest in the legal profession.[1] He turned his energy to journalism before striking out on his own as a novelist. He found his niche writing mysteries, striking paydirt with a series of books centered on

One-sheet poster for *Opera*: design by Renato Casaro.

Media press material for *Opera.*

detective Joseph Rouletabille. The character made his debut in *Le mystère de la chambre jaune*, or *The Mystery of the Yellow Room*, as it is known in English. Rouletabille's adventures would prove as popular in French culture as Edgar Allan Poe's C. Auguste Dupin had been in America or Sir Arthur Conan Doyle's Sherlock Holmes had been in England. Though basically forgotten today, these stories helped make Leroux an immensely popular writer of pulp fiction. There is little doubt that Leroux's most popular creation remains *Le Fantôme de l'Opéra*, or *The Phantom of the Opera*. It was first published in book form in February of 1910, though it had previously been serialized in the French newspaper *Le Gaulois* between September of 1909 and January of 1910.[2] It would make its English-language debut in 1911. Surprisingly, it was not an immediate hit with the public, and its popularity at the time waned in comparison to the much more profitable adventures of Rouletabille.[3] Indeed, its reputation as a classic stems less from its merits as a book than from its impact on popular culture.

Leroux's story made a powerful impression on Argento. For years he would claim that he was not interested in film-ing any of the old horror warhorses like *Dracula*, but that he would love to have a crack at Leroux's story.[4] Collaborating with Franco Ferrini, he managed to concoct a script which distilled the essence of Leroux's twisted melodrama into a properly ferocious *giallo*. The director would also draw inspiration from the fears that were gripping society at the time. In *Opera*, love is haunted by the spectre of AIDS, he would claim. "In fact, nobody loves in this film … Betty doesn't want and can't have sexual relations, and relations between people are generally cold; people are distant with each other. This is surely the personification of the AIDS nightmare."[5] The film that emerges is vicious in its violence and deliberately cold in its emotions; this potent cocktail proved a little too off-putting for many viewers when the film emerged in 1987, but it is now recognized as one of Argento's key works. Indeed, for many viewers, it marks the end of the director's peak period. Interestingly, Argento would later revisit the story for the more straightforward (albeit very idiosyncratic) *The Phantom of the Opera* (1998).

The story adopts the basic outline of Leroux's book. A maniac is fixated on a young understudy and takes it upon himself to ensure that she rises to the top by removing obstacles from her path. Beyond this, the two stories are very different. Whereas Christine, the young ingénue in Leroux's story, is a wholesome and psychologically stable character, Betty is far from it. She is marked, like so many Argento protagonists, by a childhood trauma that she is unable to come to grips with. Betty alludes to dreams and memories, but they seem vague; for her, they are best forgotten. She is taken aback when Mara's "accident" pushes her toward the limelight, and she is unsure how to react. Adopting the old theatrical maxim that "the show must go on," she makes her debut in properly triumphant form. What should be a happy, joyous occasion is soon tainted by a series of bizarre occurrences. When Betty becomes aware of the negative influence of her deranged admirer, she attempts to fight back, but her inability to trust or confide in others makes it difficult for her to open up and admit to what is going on. For Betty, the killings and the unwanted attentions of the psychotic admirer recall memories of the past, and as she tries to sort out the past from the present, she finds herself trapped in a nightmare from which there may be no awakening.

In the film's deliberately cold and unemotional universe, normal, loving relationships have no meaning. Betty is frigid. The director, Marco, is a sadist who seems to derive satisfaction from the chaos that erupts around his latest production. Inspector Santini is odd, to say the least; he seems sincere in his desire to unmask the killer, yet his halting, self-conscious interactions with the other characters imply a stunted emotional growth. Betty has a nominal boyfriend in handsome stage manager Stefano, but she seems completely disinterested in him. Stefano showers her with praise and wants to make love with her, but Betty makes excuses to put him off. Similarly, Marco has a glamorous lover in the form of Marion, but he seems totally disconnected from her. When Marion suggests to Marco that he is interested in getting Betty into bed, he can only smirk. His reaction speaks volumes, yet he is never overtly lecherous toward his star discovery. For Marco, physical expression is less interesting than voyeurism. He gets off on looking, not on touching.

The character of Marco has some interesting connections to Argento himself. If anything, it is one of the least flattering self-portraits ever committed to film. Marco is a director who specializes in gory horror films. *Macbeth* is the second of his attempts at doing a "modern" take on a popular opera staple, following a poorly received staging of *Rigoletto*. Argento had caught some headlines in Italy in 1985 when he was courted by the Sferisterio Theater to stage a new version of *Rigoletto*; when Argento's radical ideas, full of blood and vampirism, were rejected as too outré, he left the production and decided to incorporate some of his observations about the world of opera into his next *giallo*.[6] When Inspector Santini grills Marco about his background in horror films, one cannot help but think of Detective Germani's interrogation of author Peter Neal in *Tenebrae* (1982). In common with both films is a tendency toward the self-reflexive. Marco

may lack the charm and elegance of his counterpart in the earlier effort, but his comeback is no less well judged: "I think it's a little unwise to use movies as a guide to reality, don't you, Inspector?" Santini is not impressed, however: Marco's flippant demeanor coupled with his proclivity toward violence in his work marks him out as an ideal suspect. Other connections come to mind as well, including the fact that Antonella Vitale, the actress who plays Marion, was actually Argento's companion at the time of filming. And the circle of references would close quite neatly in October of 2013 when Argento made his long-delayed opera-directing debut with … *Macbeth*.

Opera is very much in the same spirit as ***Tenebrae***, albeit in a slightly different key. Whereas ***Tenebrae*** was somewhat light and nimble in its allusions, *Opera* is considerably darker and more disturbing. Even so, the two films share a similar fixation with examining the link between art and reality. Argento makes it quite clear that he recognizes the voyeuristic component of his profession throughout the film. His bravura use of tracking shots is powerfully evident and the emphasis on eyes and sight is a major motif. The killer induces Betty—and by extension, the audience—to be complicit in his crimes by forcing her to watch. He literally gets off on her reactions. The killings are savage, largely because the killer makes a point of making a grand show out of them for the benefit of his captive audience. This is in itself a commentary on Argento's role as a director. He would later recall that the idea of pinning Betty's eyes open came to him when he was musing over the way in which audiences averted

Cristina Marsillach as Betty, the complex heroine of *Opera*.

Renato Casaro stands proudly holding the Ciak D'Oro advertising award which he won for the Italian poster for Dario Argento's *Opera*, 1987.[11]

their eyes during the scary moments in his films. "For years I've been annoyed by people covering their eyes during the unspooling of the gorier moments in my films […] I film these images because I want people to see them and not avoid the positive confrontation of their fears by looking away."[7] Adopting a variation on the "Ludovico Treatment" utilized in Anthony Burgess' *A Clockwork Orange* (1962), or more precisely the Stanley Kubrick film version from 1971, Argento devised a devilishly clever scheme. The killer would tape needles beneath Betty's eyes, thus forcing her to keep looking while he serenades her with his twisted display of love and fidelity. The link between the killer's sadism and Argento's desire to compel audiences to confront their fears removes hypocrisy from the scenario; the director makes it vividly clear that he knows that audiences are fascinated with these films because of their elaborate murder scenes, and he sees no reason not to confront and even celebrate this by making *Opera* into his most vicious and gory film to date. The end result is nasty and can be difficult to swallow on first viewing, but the film's intelligent use of audience manipulation pays off upon repeat viewings.

From a *technical* perspective, *Opera* is Dario Argento's masterpiece. Even more so than *Deep Red* (1975) and *Suspiria* (1977), it shows the director at the absolute peak of his powers. The camera seldom stops moving. The fetishistic close-ups of the killer's instruments, so much a part of *Deep Red*'s visual landscape, are back in full force, and the roving dolly and Steadicam shots allow the audience to get inside the killer's head. Argento goes a step further by literally showing the inner workings of the deranged mind, with shots of the murderer's throbbing gray matter on gaudy display whenever the urge to kill becomes too overpowering to resist. Ronnie Taylor's lush cinematography helps to make *Opera* into one of the most visually stunning of all *gialli*. The production values are impeccable throughout and the special make-up effects by Rosario Prestopino and animatronic effects by Sergio Stivaletti are truly state-of-the-art. Argento's desire to push the imagery to the extreme results in such memorable flourishes as a dizzying traveling shot from the point of view of some crows looking to get revenge on the killer and a truly dazzling sequence involving an eye, a peephole and a gun. Argento's artful use of music manifests in another patchwork soundtrack, à *la* **Phenomena**. Claudio Simonetti, Brian Eno, Bill Wyman and Terry Taylor composed some splendid original pieces of music for the film, and plenty of Verdi and Puccini is worked in as well. Argento's fascination with heavy metal continues, and the contrast between the frenetic modern music and the stately elegance of the setting is effective without being too overdone.

Unfortunately, the story itself does not always hold water. The most problematic aspect of the script is the final act, which was admittedly hastily rewritten at the 11th hour to accommodate production overages.[8] Even so, it is hard to excuse—let alone, forgive—the sloppy, totally illogical solution Argento devised, which smacks of complete disregard for the carefully constructed mood and atmosphere he had worked so hard to maintain. The ending is not entirely ruinous, mercifully, but it does dock the film a few points and helps to prevent it from quite matching the overall brilliance of **Deep Red** and **Tenebrae**.

Spanish actress Cristina Marsillach heads the cast. Argento's conflicts with the fiery, strong-willed Marsillach is the stuff of legend among fans. The director has often cited her and **Tenebrae** star Anthony Franciosa as being the performers he least liked working with, and things came to a head when the director forced the actress to do take after take of a dangerous scene involving fire, during which she received some minor burns.[9] Marsillach has often been criticized for her rather cold and "unnatural" performance, but this actually suits the character very well. She is very much a woman who seems uneasy in her own skin and this cuts to the very heart of the character and her awkward relations with the other characters. Marsillach was born in Madrid in 1963. She started off as a model and TV actress before making her film debut in 1981. She appeared in a number of Spanish films before landing a small role in Giuseppe Patroni Griffi's steamy melodrama *The Trap* (1985), co-written by Lucio Fulci; her sister Blanca also featured in the film. Following this, she appeared opposite Tom Hanks in the World War II tearjerker *Every Time We Say Goodbye* (1986). *Opera* marked her only foray into the world of the *giallo*; she would continue acting until the mid-1990s. Scottish actor Ian Charleson plays Marco. His marvelous performance does not always get its due, either, which is a great shame. He brings tremendous weight and irony to the role and succeeds in making the character engaging. The actor would admit to writer Alan Jones that he based a lot of the character's mannerisms on Argento, which certainly seems highly appropriate in context.[10] Charleson was born in Edinburgh in 1949. He did plenty of work in the theater and on British television before making his big-screen debut in 1978. Charleson attracted much acclaim for his work in the Oscar-winning *Chariots of Fire* (1981) and went on to appear in Sir Richard Attenborough's Oscar-winning *Gandhi* (1982). *Opera* was an unusual foray for the actor into the world of European cult cinema, but he approached the role of Marco with commitment and earned the respect of his director. Sadly, by the time he made the film he had already been diagnosed with AIDS; Argento was aware of his condition but hired him anyway, and steps were taken to conceal his condition from the production. *Opera* would be his last film role; he completed work on two projects for British TV in 1988, after which his condition worsened. He died in 1990 at the age of 40. Urbano Barberini plays Inspector Santini. He is arguably too young for the role, but gives a good performance and effectively taps into the character's neuroses. Born in Rome in 1961, he made his film debut in 1984. He first worked with Argento on *Demons* (1985), a massively popular exercise in shock horror co-written and produced by Argento and directed by Lamberto Bava. He would go on to appear in Bava's *Until Death* (1987) and Luigi Cozzi's *The Black Cat* (1989), in addition to more mainstream fare like *Casino Royale* (2006). *Opera* also marked the termination of the working relationship between Argento and Daria Nicolodi. Nicolodi did not enjoy playing Betty's agent/mother figure Mira, but she is far better here than she was in **Phenomena**. She and the director differed on some issues during the filming and Nicolodi would later claim that she was fearful that he was seriously trying to kill her during the filming of her death scene in the film. They would finally reunite years later for *Mother of Tears* (2007), but for all intents and purposes *Opera* marked the end of an era.

For Argento, *Opera* remains a problematic topic. Part of this is down to the fact that his father, Salvatore, passed away during pre-production on the picture. Then there was his unhappy experience in working with Marsillach. And as he later admitted in an interview included on the Blue Underground DVD release of the film, much of this turmoil is due to painful memories of a breakdown he suffered once the film was finished. Even so, the lavish production proved to be a big hit with audiences, and it remains one of his most popular titles—and for good reason.

Notes:

1. Riley, Philip, *The Making of The Phantom of the Opera (Including The Original 1925 Shooting Script)* (New Jersey: MagicImage Filmbooks, 1999), p. 21.

2. *Ibid*, p.34

3. *Ibid*, p.34

4. He may well have done better to have stuck to his guns on that point; his version of Bram Stoker's classic tale, *Dracula 3D* (2012), would not become a feather in his cap.

5. Palmerini, Luca M. and Gaetano Mistretta, *Spaghetti Nightmares* (Florida: Fantasma Books, 1996), p. 16.

6. Jones, Alan, *Dario Argento: The Man, The Myths & The Magic* (Godalming: FAB Press, 2012), p. 159.

7. *Ibid*, p. 158.

8. In an interview with authors Luca M. Palmerini and Gaetano Mistretta in the book *Spaghetti Nightmares* (Florida: Fantasma Books, 1996, p. 51), Ferrini reveals: "In the screenplay, a scene was envisioned in which the killer took a corpse and brought it into the theater, as if hinting at what would happen. There were two things he could do with this body. It could have been either the 'masked' character that had fallen from the stalls and been disinterred, like in *The Phantom of the Opera*, or a tramp who'd been killed and then thrown onto the fire; but in both cases the films have gone on too long, so Dario opted for the dummy."

9. *Ibid*, p. 160.

10. *Ibid*, p. 161.

11. (page 136 caption) www.filmonpaper.com

Japanese poster for *Opera*.

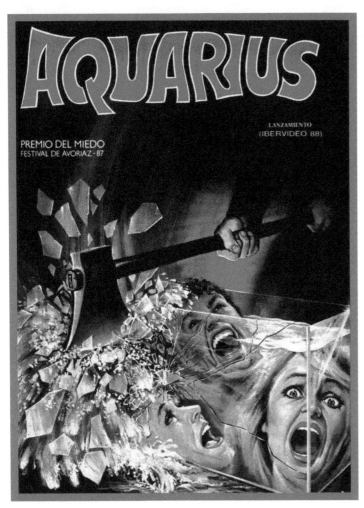

Cover to the French pressbook for *Stage Fright*; artwork by Jean-Louis Lafon.

Stage Fright (Italy)

Aka *Deliria; Bloody Bird; Aquarius; Aquarius—Theater des Todes; StageFright: Aquarius*

Directed by Michele Soavi (as Michael Soavi); Produced by Aristide Massaccesi and Donatella Donati; Screenplay by Luigi Montefiori (as Lew Cooper); Director of Photography: Renato Tafuri; Editor: Kathleen Stratton; Music by Simon Boswell

Main Players: David Brandon (Peter); Barbara Cupisti (Alicia); Giovanni Lombardo Radice [as John Morghen] (Brett); Robert Gligorov (Danny); Jo Ann Smith (Sybil); James E.R. Sampson (Willy); Domenico Fiore [as Don Fiore] (Police Chief); Mickey Knox (Older Cop); Michele Soavi (Younger Cop); Piero Vida (Ferrari); Loredana Parrella (Corinne); Clain Parker (Irving Wallace)

Home Video: Blue Underground (Region 1 DVD and All region Blu-ray)

A small time theatrical troupe is busy rehearsing an avant-garde musical involving a murderer. Art blends with reality when a lunatic named Irving Wallace escapes from a local insane asylum and makes his way to the theater. Locking everybody inside with him, Wallace goes on a killing spree ...

Part slasher film, part *giallo* and part dark comedy, *Stage Fright* is undoubtedly one of the key Italian thrillers of the 1980s. It also marks a very auspicious debut for director Michele Soavi.

The screenplay by actor Luigi Montefiori is surprisingly clever. Within the confines of a modest production such as this, Montefiori and Soavi take the time to examine some of the tropes of the genre. They also send up some of the more cliché-ridden conventions, though their enthusiasm admittedly gets the better of them in the end. The film suffers from one false ending too many, and the attempt at sending up the genre with a final wink at the audience is out of place and ends the film on a very sour note.

That being said, the film is brilliantly executed overall. The story bears some superficial similarities to Argento's *Opera* (1987), on which Soavi acted as a second unit director and bit-part actor. In common with both films is the character of a sadistic director who pushes his actors to the limit and seems to derive some perverse pleasure out of the murder and mayhem that is taking place around him. Yet, while Marco in *Opera* has some redeeming qualities, Peter in this film has none to speak of. He is a sadist and a despot who treats his collaborators like garbage. When the killings begin, his cynical response is to work the tragedy into the production and play it up in the press in the hopes of selling some extra tickets. Montefiori and Soavi use the character to poke fun at the more sensational aspects of the genre. For example, one of his "artistic" additions to the play is the notion of the victim raping her attacker. When questioned about the logic in this, he petulantly replies that it has nothing to do with logic and everything to do with creating a sensation. This certainly sums up the genre rather neatly, and with a good dose of humor. Peter's role in the proceedings takes on its most perversely satisfying twist when he finds himself directing the masked killer—thinking it is the actor hired to play the role—to murder an actress on stage. True, it is an unintentional act of complicity, but one cannot help but get the impression that it is the sort of sensational "happy accident" that he would be only too pleased to play up for the publicity. He is not above using his companions in an effort to save his own hide, either, thus highlighting his essential cowardice. The basic similarity of the theatrical *milieu* and the figure of the tyrannical director cannot help but make one compare the two films, even if their tone is very different. Whereas *Opera* was dark and despairing, *Stage Fright* is considerably more tongue-in-cheek in its sensibilities. Curiously, both the Argento and Soavi movies suffer from uncertain final acts, but they both manage to overcome this deficit through the sheer forcefulness of their filmmaking.

Considering that this was Soavi's first time directing a feature, it is amazing just how confident and sure-footed the film is on the whole. Some of this is down to Montefiori's taut, sensibly scaled-down scenario. As he explained in an interview:

He had no fixed ideas about the sort of story he wanted, but he knew what he didn't want. [...]

I wrote what I thought would be a good story for him. I wanted a closed set, so that as a director, he could concentrate and keep everything under his control and I came up with the idea of building up a story around a theater company rehearsing a horror musical in a film studio.[1]

Whether Montefiori drew upon memories of seeing the similarly claustrophobic *The Killer Reserved Nine Seats* (1974) is open to speculation, but the material proved to be ideally suited to Soavi's sensibilities. The director does a splendid job of building tension and suspense, and his flair for baroque imagery is evident throughout. The film is not as lavish as *Opera*, for example, but within its more modest limitations it is loaded with ambitious camerawork and stunning visuals. Renato Tafuri's lighting is gorgeous and the score by Simon Boswell effectively underlines the suspense and adds energy to the frenetic shock sequences.

The film is also noteworthy for its wonderfully outré presentation of the killer. Instead of the usual black gloves and fedora, Soavi has the killer outfitted in a black costume topped off with a giant owl's head. Critics took this as a reference to *The Bird with the Crystal Plumage* (1970), but Soavi would later say that he drew inspiration from the macabre art work of Max Ernst.[2] The whodunit aspect of the film is non-existent, given that we know the identity of the maniac from the get-go, but in place of the usual sting-in-the-tail plot reveal, Soavi chooses to emphasize an almost unbearable tension as the killer methodically goes about his work. The various murders are incredibly bloody and brutal and Soavi works in some nice nods to Argento's imagery, including the scene where a character bends down to pick something up, thus revealing the killer standing directly behind him; Argento used this visual to great effect in *Tenebrae*, on which Soavi acted as second assistant director in addition to playing two small acting roles. The scenes of the killer arranging the corpses on stage, as a sort of macabre still life, is yet

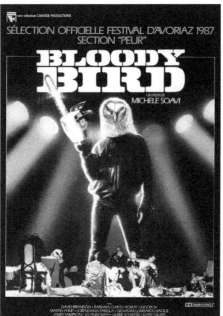

French poster for *Stage Fright*; artwork by Jean-Louis Lafon.

another sardonic riff on the genre's tendency to emphasize the "design" aspect of the murder scenes. The humor does not detract from the killer's presence, however; he is one of the most memorably vicious and frightening psychopaths in the genre's extensive history.

David Brandon gives an excellent performance as Peter. He is the type of character audiences truly love to hate, and Brandon presents him in an unapologetic manner as the bastard he really is. The role gives him far more to do than had

been the case in Lamberto Bava's *Delirium: Photos of Gioia* (1987), and it is clear that he is having a ball. Barbara Cupisti plays the heroine, Alicia. She is very likable and helps to make the character worth rooting for. The script does not provide her with any real backstory or depth, but this is to be expected in such a taut scenario. Cupisti's appealing performance adds greatly to the film's suspense, since the audience is firmly on her side throughout. She was born in Tuscany in 1962. She made her debut as Paolo Malco's assistant in *The New York Ripper* (1982) and also made a brief appearance in *Opera*. She would go on to feature in *Eyewitness* (1990) and the borderline *giallo Dark Bar* (1988), and she played a leading role in Soavi's next directing effort, the Dario Argento-produced *The Church* (1989). She also had a part in Soavi's *Dellamorte Dellamore* (1994), but has been inactive since the early 2000s.

Michele Soavi was born in Milan in 1957. He became a film buff early on and studied to become an actor. He started appearing in movies in the mid-1970s, and by the end of the decade was experimenting with working behind-the-scenes as well. As an actor, he appeared in the likes of Lucio Fulci's *City of the Living Dead* (1980) and Lamberto Bava's *A Blade in the Dark* (1983). He worked his way into Dario Argento's entourage and became his assistant on *Tenebrae* and *Phenomena* (1985) before being entrusted with the extensive second unit work on *Opera*; he also appeared in these films in small acting roles, making him something of a bargain. In addition he assisted Lamberto Bava on *Blastfighter* (1984) and *Demons* (1985) and worked as Terry Gilliam's second unit director on *The Adventures of Baron Munchausen* (1988) and *The Brothers Grimm* (2005). Following the success of *Stage Fright*, his directing career took off. He made *The Church* and *The Sect* (1991) for Dario Argento before achieving his greatest success with the highly unusual "living dead" flick *Dellamorte Dellamore*. The picture drew enthusiastic responses from the likes of Martin Scorsese, but his ascension up the ladder of the Italian film industry was interrupted when he needed to take a break from making movies to look after his ailing son. Soavi returned to the director's chair with the superior made-for-TV crime films *Ultimo 2—La sfida* (1999) and *Uno Bianca* (2001) and then earned some of his best reviews with the gritty *noir The Goodbye Kiss* (2006). He remains active in the Italian TV scene, but sadly has yet to revisit the *giallo*.

Notes:
1. Palmerini, Luca M. and Gaetano Mistretta, *Spaghetti Nightmares* (Florida: Fantasma Books, 1996), p. 110.
2. *Ibid*, p. 148.

Sweets from a Stranger
(Italy)

Aka *Caramelle da uno sconosciuto*

Directed by Franco Ferrini; Produced by Claudio Bonivento; Screenplay by Franco Ferrini and Andrea Giuseppini; Director of Photography: Giuseppe Bernardini; Editor: Franco Fraticelli; Music by Umberto Smaila

Main Players: Barbara De Rossi (Lena); Marina Suma (Angela); Athina Cenci (Nadine); Mara Venier (Stella); Laura Betti (Jolanda); Anny Papa (Monica); Ilaria Cecchi (Valentina)

A serial killer is targeting prostitutes. The women decide to band together in the hope of protecting themselves, but their efforts are only partially successful and the killer continues to strike. The police are unable to turn up any clues, but the resourceful working women eventually uncover some leads themselves...

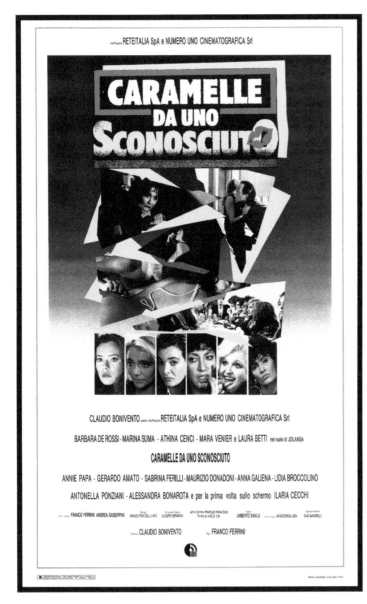

Italian *locandina* for *Sweets from a Stranger*; artist unknown.

There is no other *giallo* quite like *Sweets from a Stranger*. The film is in some respects more of a social document than a proper thriller, but it warrants inclusion here for its novel variations on a standard formula.

Writer/director Franco Ferrini used Fritz Lang's classic *M* (1931) as one of his models. In place of the thieves and vagabonds who band together in order to trap a killer, here the focus is on prostitutes. Ferrini's research into the world of prostitution, with its own special codes and ethics, is put to very good use, giving the film an air of realism. The tone vacillates between the humorous and the tragic, but Ferrini resists the urge to condemn the profession outright; indeed, he seems to understand that for some people, it is a necessary way of life brought about by adversity and circumstance.

The *giallo* elements are somewhat muted, but Ferrini opens the film with an extended stalking sequence which climaxes in a bloody murder. Compared to the films that Ferrini's sometimes-partner Dario Argento was making during this time, *Sweets from a Stranger* may seem somewhat tame. Indeed, given its emphasis on the world of prostitution, it is not even interested in pushing the envelope in the exploitation direction, either. Instead, Ferrini observes his characters with empathy and a wry sense of humor as they set aside their differences (notably over the issue of "turf," with one set of prostitutes being very possessive of one area of town, etc.) and work together in order to trap the maniac who is targeting members of their profession. Ferrini avoids the hypocrisy found in other, more exploitative films by steering clear of bad taste eroticism and phony moral posturing. He seems to have tremendous affection for his characters, and the audience follows suit.

The emphasis on the social aspect of the film will likely be off-putting for some of the more thrill-hungry viewers, but the movie is by no means staid or boring. Ferrini paces the material very well and the actors all give very credible performances. True, blood and gore are kept to a minimum, but the various murder scenes have a nasty edge just the same. The way the film details the lives of the prostitutes, each of whom has a different attitude toward their work, only serves to enrich the drama as a whole. By creating a group of characters worth caring about, Ferrini ensures that the film is engaging as both a drama and a thriller. The final unmasking of the killer's identity is sure to come out of left field and makes for one of the more legitimately shocking reveals in the genre, but to say too much about this would be to rob the film of its surprise factor. Suffice it to say, the story is logically plotted and comes to its natural conclusion.

Technical credits are all up to par. Giuseppe Bernardini's cinematography is slick if unexceptional and the editing by Argento's then-regular collaborator Franco Fraticelli[1] is up to his usual excellent standards. Umberto Smaila's score is probably the film's weak point. The score is not bad *per se*, though one cue manages to rip off Elmer Bernstein's iconic theme for *The Great Escape* (1963) to distracting effect, but it does not really stand out in the way that the best *giallo* soundtracks do. Special effects are kept to a minimum, but the assorted razor-slashings are convincingly realized.

Director Franco Ferrini was born in La Spezia in 1944. He was a passionate cinephile from an early age and wrote books and essays on directors like Pier Paolo Pasolini, Sergio Leone and John Ford while still in college. His admiration for Leone led him to contact the great director and ask for a chance to work with him on the screenplay for *Once Upon a Time in America* (1984). The film took many years to finally reach the screen, during which time its screenplay underwent many radical changes, so Ferrini's first official screenwriting credits came in the mid-1970s. He had his first *giallo* credit on the troubled production **Rings of Fear** (1978), but would go on to work on more lighthearted fare. According to Ferrini, his friendship with Dario Argento began in 1983 when he sent the director a script for a thriller he had written. "[It] later formed the basis for *Dial: Help* (1988), directed by Ruggero Deodato.[2] Dario read it, and although he showed a certain interest, he decided to let the idea go."[3] Even so, the two men got along and decided to work together on the screenplay for **Phenomena** (1985). Their collaboration would continue for many years, though Ferrini also struck out on his own upon occasion. *Sweets from a Stranger* marked his directing debut, and, though he was pleased with how the film turned out, it would mark the end of his directing career. Ferrini's other *giallo* credits include **Opera** (1987), **Trauma** (1993), **The Stendhal Syndrome** (1996)[4], **Sleepless** (2001), **The Card Player** (2004) and **Do You Like Hitchcock?** (2005) for Argento, as well as **Nothing Underneath** (1985), **Squillo** (1996) and **Sotto il vestito niente —L'ultima sfilata** (2011) for director Carlo Vanzina.

Notes:

1. The same year's **Opera** would mark the end of the Fraticelli-Argento collaborations, at least so far as the films directed by Argento are concerned; he would subsequently edit Michele Soavi's *The Church* (1989) and *The Sect* (1991), both co-written and produced by Argento.
2. Ferrini's script was completely overhauled, and Ferrini only received a "story" credit.
3. Palmerini, Luca M. and Gaetano Mistretta, *Spaghetti Nightmares* (Florida: Fantasma Books, 1996), p. 49.
4. Ferrini helped develop the story with Argento but is not credited on the release prints.

1988

Delitti e profumi (Italy)

Directed by Vittorio De Sisti; Produced by Claudio Bonivento; Screenplay by Oreste De Fornari, Franco Ferrini and Francesco Massaro; Director of Photography: Giuseppe

One-sheet poster for *Delitti e profumi.*

Maccari; Editor: Claudio Di Mauro; Music by Umberto Smaila

Main Players: Jerry Calà (Eddy); Umberto Smaila (Vice Commissioner Turoni); Simonetta Gianfelici (Ambra Altar); Marina Viro (Marina); Nina Soldano (Mairi)

Security guard Eddy becomes mixed up in a series of murders when a model dies mysteriously. It turns out that the murderer is sending prospective victims bottles of a special perfume that is highly flammable; when the victim sprays it on their body and is exposed to direct light, they burst into flames. Eddy launches an investigation in competition with his rival Vice Commissario Turoni, but the two inept sleuths are unable to prevent further bloodshed ...

Franco Ferrini co-wrote this *giallo* spoof, which is more of a vehicle for the comedy stylings of Jerry Calà and Umberto Smaila. Even so, the killer's gruesome method of revenge and the lip service paid to genre conventions makes it one of the more successful send-ups.

The story is slight, even incidental, and much of the emphasis is on slapstick and the like. The inept protagonist played by Calà is a small-time security guard who is quite

141

content in the doldrums of his job. When the series of killings begin happening more or less under his nose, it is as much of a nuisance as anything else for him to investigate. Unlike the amateur detectives of a typical Dario Argento thriller, Eddy is not obsessed with finding the truth; he is simply thrown head-first into the thick of things and wants to upstage his pompous rival, Turoni.

Ultimately, the source of all the problems is once again rooted in childhood trauma. The murders are appropriately vivid, as the victims burst into flames when they are hit with a light source, and other *giallo* tropes are on display as well: the killer in black gloves, subjective camerawork, plenty of red herrings, etc. Ferrini's dual background in both thrillers and comedy serves the film well, as he recognizes the need to leave plenty of room for the comedy routines to play out, while still building up a credible thriller scenario with an appropriately surprising final twist.

Whether the film is successful as comedy, however, is down to one's affinity for Calà and Smaila. The two performers were part of a comedy troupe called *I Gatti di Vicolo Miracoli*, along with Giandrea Gazzola, Mallaby Spray and Nino Salerno.[1] The troupe rose to prominence in the 1970s and was extremely popular in Italy; they disbanded in 1985. Calà was born in Catania in 1951 and started off performing in cabaret acts, culminating in *I Gatti di Vicolo Miracoli*, where he also composed and performed a number of popular songs. He started appearing in films sporadically in the late 1960s but his film career did not really begin to take off until the 1980s. *Delitti e profumi* was his only brush with the *giallo* genre. Calà also directed a handful of movies in the 1990s and remains a presence in Italian films and television to this day. Smaila was born in Verona in 1950. He started appearing in films in the 1970s and has also worked extensively as a composer; in addition to scoring this picture, he also scored Franco Ferrini's **Sweets from a Stranger** (1987). He has been relatively idle in the new millennium,[2] so far as film work is concerned. The two comedians do their usual shtick here. Calà is bumbling and cowardly, but with a sweet, romantic streak, while Smaila is all bluff and bluster, doing his best to look cool in very 1980s fashions, while proving to be a total washout as a policeman.

Director Vittorio De Sisti was born in 1940 and began making films in the late 1960s. He specialized in comedic subjects and worked extensively in Italian television until his death in 2005.

Notes:
1. Gazzola and Spray soon left the group and were replaced by Franco Oppini for the rest of the troupe's run.
2. Between 1987 and 1991, Smaila hosted the hit late night quiz show *Colpo grosso*, which featured topless girls as a particularly saleable feature. The gimmick was that Smaila's curvaceous assistants would strip as the game unfolded, thus encouraging viewers to stick around to see how far they would go.

Obsession: A Taste for Fear
(Italy)

Aka *Pathos (Un sapore di paura); Pathos–Segreta Inquietudine; Rausch der Begierde*

Directed by Piccio Raffanini; Produced by Jacques Goyard; Screenplay by Piccio Raffanini and Lidia Ravera; Director of Photography: Romano Albani; Editor: Mario Morra; Music by Gabriele Ducros

Main Players: Virginia Hey (Diane); Gérard Darmon (Georges); Gioia Scola (Valerie); Dario Parisini (Lieutenant Arnold); Carin McDonald (Kim); Teagan Clive (Teagan Morrison)

Diane works in the world of high fashion as a photographer. Her fashion spreads are highly erotic, with an emphasis on S/M imagery. When one of her models is killed, Diane becomes a suspect. In time, another model is killed and it becomes apparent that the killer is targeting Diane's lovers. She soon realizes that the killer has something special in store for her as well ...

Dario Argento has often alluded to **Tenebrae** (1982) as being set in the future, but this is only vaguely apparent in

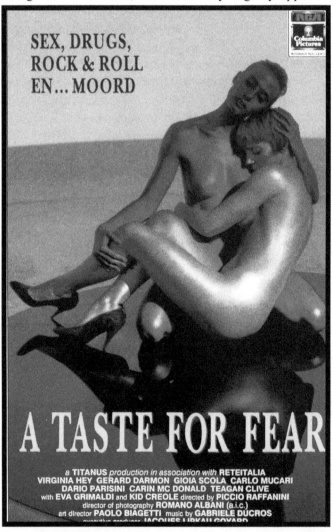

Cover for the Dutch VHS release of *Obsession: A Taste for Fear* from RCA Columbia Pictures.

the film itself and it does not play a noteworthy role in the film's plot. Thus, *Obsession: A Taste for Fear* can take the prize for being the first truly "futuristic *giallo*."

The screenplay by Lidia Ravera and director Piccio Raffanini again makes use of the fashion *milieu* popularized by Mario Bava in **Blood and Black Lace** (1964). Raffanini takes things a step further, however, by making the fashion shoots overtly sexualized and sadistic in nature. Unfortunately, that is about as far as the film goes with regards to introducing new elements to the game. The remainder of the plot is as ho-hum and predictable as they come, with a "shocking" final twist that can be guessed early in the picture.

Raffanini's direction is flat and functional, despite the very 1980s music video aesthetic. Cinematographer Romano Albani gets to play with colored lighting in a way that recalls his work on Dario Argento's far superior *Inferno* (1980), but his efforts do not amount to much. In lieu of interesting characters and suspense, the film simply moves from one posed still life to another. The emphasis on surface gloss fits the subject matter, but whether this was an intentional bit of commentary or a happy accident is open to speculation.

The emphasis is on softcore erotica, regardless. The genre's fixation on sordid sex became more and more apparent in the 1980s, thanks to gradually relaxing censorship standards. *Obsession: A Taste for Fear* does not delve into the extremes of films like **Play Motel** (1979) or **Giallo a Venezia** (1979), but it spends more than a little bit of time on its various sexual encounters. The protagonist favors both male and female partners, so this opens the door for different combinations, and the fashion shoots themselves are presented in a highly sexualized manner. Unfortunately, the actors have no genuine chemistry and the end result looks like yet another stiff, obviously posed tableau in which no real heat is ever generated.

The use of a futuristic setting seems wholly arbitrary and only succeeds in making the film appear dated. Raffanini and company clearly had Ridley Scott's *Blade Runner* (1982) on their mind, but their comparatively paltry budget does not allow for the same amazing sights and ideas. There are plenty of outré fashions and hairstyles on display, but they seem awfully '80s, truth be told, while the depiction of futuristic cars and other bits of hardware look decidedly quaint by today's standards. It would be easier to forgive this if there was any real sign of creativity at the heart of it all, but this is not the case; much like virtually everything else in the film, it is all surface gloss ... and tacky surface gloss, at that.

Raffanini's sluggish, uninspired direction is a constant sore spot, as are the listless performances. Australian model-turned-actress Virginia Hey (born 1952) would seem to be an ideal piece of casting as Diane, but she makes for a dull protagonist. Diane's voracious sexual appetites dominate much of the film, and she is ultimately a rather petulant and unsympathetic figure. Hey looks good, but that is about it; her acting is distinctly one-note. She made her film

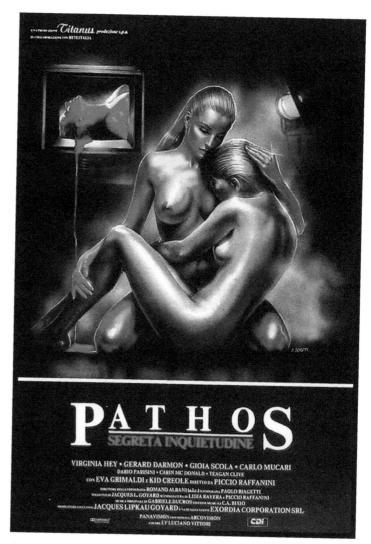

One-sheet Italian poster for *Obsession: A Taste for Fear* under an alternate title; artwork by Enzo Sciotti.

debut with an appearance in George Miller's *Mad Max 2: The Road Warrior* (1981) and later featured in the James Bond thriller *The Living Daylights* (1987), but she is better known for her modeling work. Dario Parisini plays the cliché cop on the case, Lieutenant Arnold. His "hip" posturing extends to the same growth of designer stubble throughout the picture and the main twist is his lack of interest in taking Diane to bed, despite her many overtures. Parisini was born in 1965 and his short-lived acting career dried up in the mid-1990s. The supporting cast includes American body builder-turned-actress Teagan Clive, who plays one of the luckless models. Clive's imposing physique is prominently featured in her various scenes, but she does not have a lot to do beyond posing and flexing her muscles. She was born in 1959 and made her film debut with a small role in the John Candy comedy *Armed and Dangerous* (1986); her film career came to a halt in the early 1990s.

Not much is known about Raffanini; if extant filmographies are to be believed, *Obsession: A Taste for Fear* remains his only directing credit for the big screen, though he appears to have worked in Italian television and music videos as well.

Ruggero Deodato's Off Balance aka

PHANTOM OF DEATH

LET THE SYMPHONY OF SLAUGHTER BEGIN!

Shameless Screen Entertainment   18

Phantom of Death (Italy)

Aka *Un delitto poco comune; Bestia asesina; Le tueur de la pleine lune; Off Balance – Der Tod wartet in Venedig; Off Balance*

Directed by Ruggero Deodato; Produced by Gianfranco Clerici, Pietro Innocenzi and Vincenzo Mannino; Screenplay by Gianfranco Clerici, Vincenzo Mannino and Gigliola Battaglini; Director of Photography: Giorgio Di Battista; Editor: Daniele Alabiso; Music by Pino Donaggio

Main Players: Michael York (Robert Dominici); Edwige Fenech (Hélène Martell); Donald Pleasence (Inspector Datti); Mapi Galán (Susanna); Fabio Sartor (Davide); Antonella Ponziani (Gloria Datti); Giovanni Lombardo Radice (Father Giuliano)

Home Video: Shameless Screen Entertainment (Region free DVD)

Robert Dominici is a successful pianist. His idyllic existence is turned upside-down when he is diagnosed with a rare disease that causes rapid aging. The disease also affects his mind, leading to terrifying fits of rage during which he kills. Inspector Datti investigates the killings but is unable to make sense of them. Robert begins taunting the inspector with phone calls, hoping that he will put a stop to him before he kills again ...

Phantom of Death is a horror-*giallo* hybrid. The film starts off as a proper thriller, but it shows its hand about half an hour in and reveals its mystery early on. This may seem to discredit it from this context, but it still contains enough elements to make it worthy of inclusion as a proper *giallo*.

The screenplay (co-written by genre veterans Gianfranco Clerici and Vincenzo Mannino, whose other credits include Lucio Fulci's **The New York Ripper**, 1982) contains some novel ideas. In place of the usual mystery scenario, they place more emphasis on characterization, with much of the attention given to its tragic protagonist, Robert Dominici. Robert's glittering universe is completely shattered when it is revealed that he suffers from the rare disease, progeria or Hutchinson-Gilford progeria syndrome. In essence, this is a genetic condition that results in rapidly accelerated aging. It is typically diagnosed in children, many of whom die by the age of 13.[1] In making use of a rare (but real) condition such as this, Clerici and Mannino ensure that the audience will feel some empathy for the character. Even so, it is "science" of a distinctly fanciful nature. The notion of a grown man being suddenly stricken with the illness is not supported by existing research, while the idea of the disease leading to fits of homicidal fury is similarly fanciful. Even so, the implication is that these fits of rage come from the character's frustration and grief over his ever-deteriorating physical state, so this can be excused as a bit of dramatic license. Robert is given far more depth and nuance than is usual in a thriller like this; the scenes of him befriending an old dog which has been abandoned by its own kind may be a little "on the nose" in terms of symbolism, but they help to humanize him and give the audience some insight into his loneliness and sense of isolation. Even when the character lashes out and kills innocent people, it is still possible to feel some pity for him as his condition continues to worsen and he begs the somewhat slow-on-the-uptake Inspector Datti to put a stop to his activities. Interestingly, director Ruggero Deodato would later complain that the sympathetic portrayal of the killer "softened" the film's impact.[2]

Deodato directs with a sure hand. The early section of the film that conforms more closely to the *giallo* is slick and suspenseful; the latter sections, which are closer to a traditional horror film, prove to be compelling and appropriately shocking where necessary. Much of the pleasure in the film stems from the prolonged game of cat-and-mouse between Robert and Inspector Datti. The latter is a warm and humane figure, much more so than usual for a policeman in one of these films, but his inability to see the truth when it is right under his nose can be a little vexing at times. Robert derives great satisfaction from pushing the veteran policeman's buttons, and the audience shares in this perverse pleasure. Given Deodato's reputation for extreme imagery, the film is surprisingly tame, but a few gory moments pop up along the way and the make-up and special effects work is generally very good. Fabrizio Sforza deserves special credit for making York's transformation from handsome young man to the shriveled shadow of his former self-credible.

The film benefits from an outstanding central performance by Michael York. His sensitive portrayal makes Robert into the most pitiful killer in the *giallo* canon; he is a sensitive, artistic man who has so much to live for, only to have it cruelly yanked away by the sudden onslaught of the disease. He was born (as Michael York-Johnson) in England in 1942. After earning his stripes as an actor at Oxford, he joined Sir Laurence Olivier's National Theatre Company. He began appearing in films in the late 1960s, impressing with supporting turns in Joseph Losey's *Accident* and Franco Zeffirelli's *The Taming of the Shrew* (both 1967) and *Romeo and Juliet* (1968). He was nearly cast in the lead of Dario Argento's **Four Flies on Grey Velvet** (1971) and was considered for the lead in the cult occult hit *The Wicker Man* (1973), but his career did not suffer from these losses. Among many successful credits, he appeared in Bob Fosse's *Cabaret* (1972), Richard Lester's *The Three Musketeers* (1973), *The Four Musketeers* (1974) and *The Return of the Musketeers* (1989), Sidney Lumet's *Murder on the Orient Express* (1974) and Michael Anderson's *Logan's Run* (1976). He achieved some later success playing Basil Exposition in the hit comedy *Austin Powers: International Man of Mystery* (1997), as well as its sequels *Austin Powers: The Spy Who Shagged Me* (1999) and *Austin Powers in Goldmember* (2002). Sadly, around 2009 he began to undergo a real-life horror story of his own when he started suffering from some unexplained health issues; his still youthful features began to suffer and his condition would be misdiagnosed until it was finally revealed to be a rare blood condition known as amyloidosis. He underwent a stem cell transplant procedure and chemotherapy to combat the illness. After a period of losing his voice and his hair, he has been rallying and began accepting more acting assignments now that his health is on the rebound. Inspector Datti is played by Donald Pleasence, who puts in a good performance. He teeters on the edge of hammy overstatement in some scenes (notably when he rushes through the streets exclaiming "Bastard! You bastard! You fucking bastard!" after Robert gets the upper hand on him once again), but he is generally relaxed and low-key. Robert's love interest is played by *giallo* queen Edwige Fenech, making her first thriller appearance since the 1970s. Interestingly, Deodato would later complain that her presence in the film was something of a hindrance:

> She is good but she has nothing to do with the film. […] But I do not want to be misunderstood, Fenech is an excellent professional; it is simply that she was not right for that particular role.[3]

Deodato's reservations to one side, Fenech acquits herself well and it is nice to hear her actual voice on the soundtrack for once—like so many other *gialli* of the period, the film makes extensive use of on-set sound recording (though many supporting players are dubbed), thus preserving the vocal work by York, Pleasence and others as well.

Robert (Michael York) ages rapidly due to a mysterious illness in *Phantom of Death*; **tragically, actor Michael York's handsome looks would be devastated by a real-life disease in later years.**

Deodato was born in Potenza in 1939. He entered film as an assistant to director Roberto Rossellini, working on such films as *Il generale Della Rovere* (1959) and *Escape by Night* (1960). He also assisted filmmakers Riccardo Freda (*Romeo and Juliet*, 1964) and Antonio Margheriti (*Castle of Blood*, 1964) before making his directing debut on *Hercules, Prisoner of Evil* (1964), which he took over from Margheriti. He was not credited with directing that *pepla*, however, and would not begin his directorial career in earnest until 1968. He would direct superhero films (*Phenomenal and the Treasure of Tutankamen*, 1968), Spaghetti Westerns (*In the Name of the Father*, 1969), *poliziotteschi* (*Live Like a Cop, Die Like a Man*, 1976) and erotic thrillers (*Waves of Lust*, 1975) before venturing into the "cannibal" subgenre with *Jungle Holocaust* (1977). He directed his best known (and most notorious) film in that genre with *Cannibal Holocaust* (1980), and the firestorm of controversy which surrounds its excesses (including some instances of real animal killing on-camera) sometimes obscures its many merits as a piece of filmmaking. Deodato would never quite recapture its savage impact and spent the 1980s directing a number of pictures unworthy of his talents (including the sword and sorcery entry *The Barbarians*, 1987), as well as such stylish but silly efforts as the borderline *giallo Dial: Help* (1988). He would revisit the genre with **The Washing Machine** (1993), but much of his subsequent work has been on Italian television.

Notes:
1. F. Scott Fitzgerald's short story *The Curious Case of Benjamin Button* (1922) made use of a reversal of the illness, by having its protagonist born as an old man who ages backwards, ultimately dying as a "newborn" baby; the story was filmed in 2008 to middling effect by director David Fincher.
2. Fenton, Harvey, ed., *Cannibal Holocaust and the Savage Cinema of Ruggero Deodato* (Godalming: FAB Press, 2nd edition, 2011), p. 98.
3. *Ibid*, p. 27

ACHILLE MANZOTTI
PRESENTA

SOTTO IL VESTITO
NIENTE II

UN FILM DI **DARIO PIANA**

Italian *locandina* for *Too Beautiful to Die*; artist unknown.

Too Beautiful To Die (Italy)

Aka *Sotto il vestito niente 2; Demasiado bellas para morir; They Only Come Out at Night*

Directed by Dario Piana; Produced by Achille Manzotti; Screenplay by Sergio Donati, Claudio Mancini, Achille Manzotti and Dario Piana; Director of Photography: Alan Jones; Music by Roberto Cacciapaglia

Main Players: Françoise-Eric Gendron (David); Florence Guérin (Melanie Roberts); Randi Ingerman (Lauren); Giovanni Tamberi (Alex Conti); Nora Ariffin (Leslie)

A model is raped by a perverse millionaire, aided by several other models who hold her down. She subsequently dies in an accident, and then the people responsible for the rape start dying in mysterious circumstances, as well ...

In Italy, this was sold as a sequel to the successful **Nothing Underneath** (1985). In truth the two films have virtually nothing in common beyond the thriller trappings and the fashion *milieu*.

The hackneyed scenario by director Dario Piana and producer Achille Manzotti brings nothing new to the table. There is the expected emphasis on softcore sex, typical of *gialli* of the era, and plenty of catty in-fighting and bitchy dialogue among the competitive models. The traumatic rape is handled in a leering fashion and the actual *giallo* elements seem to take forever to come into play. Piana seems more interested in staging music videos and fashion shoots within the film than he is in exploring the potential for suspense, and the end result is badly dated. Italian sources indicate that the gifted Sergio Donati had a hand in concocting this grab bag of clichés, but he is not credited on the English-language prints. If he truly did have a role in it, one can only assume (or hope) that his ideas were largely ignored.

The film has the usual over-slick, atmosphere-killing aesthetic that dogs so many *gialli* of the period. It looks more like a slick fashion shoot than a proper thriller, and this only serves to undermine any potential for suspense. As mentioned before, Piana has no sense of pacing and the film seems much longer than it really is. The characters are dull, the actors phone in their performances and the cinematography by Alan Jones (not to be confused with the Argento film scholar) is stylish in an anonymous sort of way, which perfectly sums up the film's overall aesthetic in a nutshell.

Director Dario Piana was born in Milan in 1953. He started off as a comic book artist, then broke into films drawing storyboards. He has largely worked in advertising, directing hundreds of commercials, for which he has won many awards. *Too Beautiful to Die* marked his debut as a writer/director of features, and he would not return to directing films until he contributed to the 2007 "8 Films to Die For" direct-to-video series in the U.S. with *The Deaths of Ian Stone. Too Beautiful to Die* remains his only *giallo* credit.

1989

Arabella, Black Angel (Italy)

Aka *Arabella l'angelo nero; Angel: Black Angel; Black Angel*

Directed by Stelvio Massi (as Max Steel); Produced by Paolo Di Tosto, Armando Novelli and Francesco Vitulano; Screenplay by R. Filippucci; Director of Photography: Stelvio Massi (as Stefano Catalano); Editor: Cesare Bianchini; Music by Serfran

Main Players: Tinì Cansino (Arabella); Valentina Visconti (Inspector Gina Fowler); Francesco Casale (Francesco Veronese); Ida Galli [as Evelyn Stewart] (Marta Veronese); Carlo Mucari (De Rosa)

Arabella is married to successful novelist Francesco, who has been wheelchair-bound as a result of a traffic accident. Francesco's lack of attention prompts Arabella to enact kinky sexual fantasies with random strangers. When these people start turning up dead, their bodies horribly mutilated in a sexual manner, Inspector Fowler is assigned to investigate ...

Stelvio Massi's first crack at the *giallo*, **Five Women for the Killer** (1974), was by no means a classic of its kind; however, it certainly looks like one compared to the director's ill-advised attempt at an "erotic *giallo*."

The film continues the genre's downward spiral into vanilla softcore porno. There is plenty of sex on display, but little of it is genuinely sexy. Massi's flair for kinetic action scenes does not lend itself to this type of material, and he seems to have been thoroughly bored by the assignment; one can hardly blame him, really.

The ridiculous screenplay leaves very little room for logic. In essence, Arabella is something of a nymphomaniac, but she claims to still be deeply in love with her moody husband. Francesco ignores her in general, but when he gets wise to her extramarital flings this seems to fire-up his imagination and removes his writer's block. He begins incorporating her flings into his new novel, but when the series of killings begins to unfold and he decides to make the surrogate Arabella (the novel's "black angel") into the killer, this is simply too much for her to bear. Never mind that the husband is downright abusive and gets his jollies writing about her extracurricular activities—this is apparently tolerable, but the notion of his transforming her into a murderer on page is just going too far! The investigation is spearheaded by a female, Inspector Fowler, whose masculine hairdo and propensity for wearing suits codes her as a lesbian; in the film's simple-minded, provincial universe, only "unnaturally tough" women could possibly hold down such a position. The revelation of her own childhood traumas seeks to explain her lesbianism as if it is a mental aberration of sorts, while her connection to the suspects is unveiled late in the game in an attempt to offer up a halfhearted twist. None of the attempts at generating suspense prove to be successful really, and the film seems more concerned with luridly detailing "shocking" sexual acts (which seem to extend no further than a male escort who insists on wearing a boxing glove while doing the deed or a shadowy suggestion of "pegging" in another sequence) than focusing on the mystery elements.

Massi's direction is a far cry from his glory days as a top-notch helmer of *poliziotteschi* like *Emergency Squad* (1974) and *The Iron Commissioner* (1978). His flair for staging action scenes and making the most of meager production resources through dynamic staging and framing is nowhere to be seen here. *Arabella, Black Angel* may well be one of his most anonymous works, and if one were to buy the credited pseudonym of Max Steel, there would be little to indicate that a craftsman of Massi's caliber had anything to do with it.

The cast appears to have been assembled for their looks rather than their thespian skills. Tinì Cansino puts in a rather stiff performance as Arabella, though she is certainly game when it comes to disrobing. Cansino was born in Greece in 1959 and made her way to Italy in the 1980s, where she enjoyed a brief and undistinguished film career. Valentina Visconti plays Inspector Fowler. Her one-note performance fails to make sense of an admittedly clichéd character. Visconti is a beautiful actress and she also gets to bare all for her "art," but she fails to make much of an impression beyond

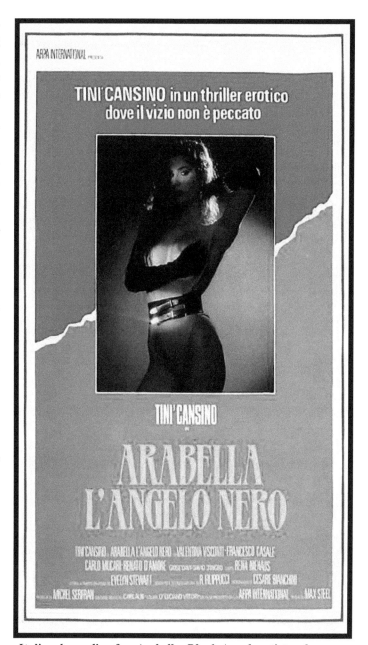

Italian *locandina* for *Arabella, Black Angel*; artist unknown.

that. Her film career appears to have been short-lived, with extant filmographies indicating only a handful of appearances between 1987 and 1997.

Fashion Crimes (Italy)

Aka *La morte è di moda; Crimes sur mesure*

Directed by Bruno Gaburro [as Joe Brenner]; Screenplay by Luciano Appignani; Director of Photography: Sergio Rubini; Editor: Alessandro Lucidi; Music by Filippo Trecca

Main Players: Anthony Franciosa (Commissioner Rizzo); Miles O'Keeffe (Dr. Gianmarco Contini); Teresa Leopardi (Gloria); Marina Giulia Cavalli (Dr. Olga Bioni); Giancarlo Prete [as Timothy Brent] (Giorgio)

Gloria witnesses a murder and reports it to the police. Commissioner Rizzo investigates, but the story does not add up. The villa in which she claims to have witnessed the crime has been abandoned for years, and there is no sign of a body.

Gloria remains insistent, but her friends are skeptical. When somebody starts making attempts on her life, however, Commissioner Rizzo comes to believe her story ...

In an era marked by more and more graphic bloodshed and eroticism, *Fashion Crimes* stands out as an uncommonly timid thriller. It is not without its pleasures, but the film is simply too staid to really make much of an impression.

Like some other *gialli* of the era, including **Nothing Underneath** (1985) and **Delirium: Photos of Gioia** (1987), the film makes use of a fashion backdrop. Yet, despite the title, this aspect does not play much of a role in the narrative. Gloria is a model and the final revelation of the killer's motivation is linked to the world of design, but viewers expecting another seamy exploration of the backstabbing and bitchiness behind the profession will be sorely disappointed. Like so much of the film, this aspect is in place as a means of paying lip service to genre conventions, but it does not add anything new to the fray.

Indeed, the film is most noteworthy for its air of utter reticence. Whether director Bruno Gaburro was looking to "take the high road" and avoid the genre's seedier excesses or was simply making the film with an eye toward its eventual television release is open to speculation, but audiences will not find a more low-key *giallo* made for theatrical exhibition than this one. The killings are sparse and are handled with great restraint; there is barely any blood to speak of and none of the more sadistic, sexualized violence typical of other thrillers of the era. The fashion setting would seem to promise some salacious views of the models switching in and out of their costumes, at the very least, but there is nary a bare breast on display. This is not necessarily a bad thing in itself. The constant repetition of boring, unimaginatively staged sex scenes and blunt, nasty murder set pieces did salvage many of the lesser *gialli* of the period after all. On the downside, there is a general sense that Gaburro and company simply could not be bothered to embrace the genre properly at all, resulting in a curiously muted and unexciting end product. If one did not know better, it would be easy to mistake the film for a made-for-television picture, not just due to its lack of excess, but because of its blandly efficient approach in general.

The film's saving grace is the performance of Anthony Franciosa as Commissioner Rizzo. He is not a particularly deep character. He is the usual seasoned, slightly cynical police authority figure who follows his gut instinct when the facts seem to point him in a different direction. Franciosa's charismatic, winning performance makes him into a character worth caring about. The actor's flair for filling out poorly developed characters with improvised bits of business is evident throughout. For example, there is a charming scene where Rizzo is interviewing a janitor. For no particular reason, Rizzo takes the man's broom and starts cleaning up the garbage on the floor. It may well have been a scripted moment, but there is something wonderfully spontaneous about Franciosa's performance that it feels very much spur-of-the-moment and adds a welcome touch of humor to an otherwise uninteresting scene. Franciosa easily steals the film, and the fact that his role is substantial helps to make the otherwise ho-hum proceedings bearable. The supporting cast includes Miles O'Keeffe. He makes for an unlikely psychiatrist and his stiff performance helps to kill his scenes dead in their tracks. Born in Tennessee in 1954, O'Keeffe (whose surname is typically misspelled, as it is in the opening credits of the film, as O'Keefe) dabbled in athletics and psychology (hey, maybe his casting is not so strange after all) before entering films as an extra, almost as a lark. He made his debut opposite Bo Derek in the notorious *Tarzan, the Ape Man* (1981), in which he played the title role. He would go on to appear in a number of B-films and became surprisingly popular for a period of time, considering that his performances were seldom anywhere outside the realm of the wooden. He appeared in some Italian-made sword-and-sorcery items, including Aristide Massaccesi's *The Blade Master* (1984) and Alfonso Brescia's *Iron Warrior* (1987), but *Fashion Crimes* would remain his only *giallo*. O'Keeffe has been relatively inactive in recent years, but still pops up on occasion.

Director Gaburro was born in 1939. He started writing and directing films in the late 1960s but never established much of a reputation despite dabbling in different genres. His handling of *Fashion Crimes* is professional enough but never displays a real flair for the material. He remains active, mostly in Italian television.

Italian *locandina* for *Fashion Crimes*; artist unknown.

As a final point of trivia, the children of filmmaker Antonio Margheriti both worked on *Fashion Crimes*: Edoardo (who would later become a director in his own right; his credits include *Negli occhi dell'assassino*, 2009, and two episodes in the TV miniseries *6 passi nel giallo*, 2012) acted as production manager, while his sister Antonella served as script supervisor.

1990

Eyewitness (Italy)

Aka *Testimone oculare*

Directed by Lamberto Bava; Produced by Lamberto Bava and Andrea Piazzesi; Screenplay by Massimo De Rita and Giorgio Stegani, from a story by Lamberto Bava; Director of Photography: Gianfranco Transunto; Editor: Piero Bozza; Music by Simon Boswell

Main Players: Barbara Cupisti (Elisa); Stefano Davanzati (Commissioner Mara); Alessio Orano (Department Store Manager); Giuseppe Pianviti (Karl); Mary Sellers (Tiziana); Loredana Romito (Mara); Antonella Angelucci (Lucy)

Elisa and Karl are at a local department store looking to steal some items. The mall closes and they are left behind, but unknown to them, so is a worker named Mara. The store manager, who is actually a sex fiend and a sadist, kills the latter. Elisa witnesses the act, hides and goes unnoticed until a security guard stumbles on the scene. The police are called to investigate and discover that their witness is blind, though she insists that she would recognize the killer if he were in front of her again. When the manager gets word that there was a witness, he sets out to silence her ...

This made-for-TV thriller from Lamberto Bava borrows a page from thrillers like Terence Young's *Wait Until Dark* (1967) and Richard Fleischer's *See No Evil* (1971) by using a blind character as its damsel-in-distress.

The screenplay was co-written by veteran scenarist Massimo De Rita, who worked on the production end of Mario Bava's *Black Sunday* (1960), *Erik the Conquror* (1961) and *The Girl Who Knew Too Much* (1963), in addition to co-writing Alberto De Martino's *The Man With Icy Eyes* (1971). Lamberto Bava devised the story and it works in some very clever touches and unexpected twists. Despite being made for television, there is a little bit of nudity and some mild blood and violence in the murder sequences. The film builds to an effective climax, recalling Tod Browning's *Freaks* (1932), as assorted handicapped characters join forces to give the killer a well deserved taste of his own medicine.

The identity of the killer is revealed from the get-go, so the "whodunit" angle is non-existent, but Bava skillfully builds tension and suspense by virtue of putting a very likable and strong-willed protagonist in danger. The cunning killer hides behind a mask of civility and respectability, but he is actually another in a long line of socially affluent deviants whose sexual fixations have exploded into a homicidal fury. Elisa is similar to the character of blind Franco Arno in Dario Argento's *The Cat O'Nine Tails* (1971), in that she is a "cripple" who refuses to be defined by her handicap. She may lack the ability to see but compensates for this by having remarkably acute senses in other areas. She is strong-willed, determined and reacts with anger when people act condescendingly toward her or show pity. The contrast between these two strong characters is very interesting and helps to build a real sense of menace. The viewer is well

DVD art for the Italian release of *Eyewitness*.

aware that the department store manager (who is deprived of a name) is not going to give himself away through foolish behavior, while being simultaneously sure that Elisa is too proud and determined to prove herself to rely on the help of the hot-headed but well-meaning Commissioner Mara.

Bava's direction is polished throughout. He makes good use of shadowy lighting (courtesy of cinematographer Gianfranco Transunto) and mobile camerawork, all of which helps to belie the film's small-screen origins. He made some of his best films during this period but, unfortunately, few of them are as readily available as his more popular (but frankly inferior) *Demons* films for producer/co-writer Dario Argento. Bava's reputation as a hack unworthy of being compared with his father is therefore more than a little unfair; given a script he believes in and enough time and resources to do a good job, he is more than capable of delivering a satisfying picture, as he does here. The film also benefits from an excellent score by Simon Boswell.

The cast includes *giallo* veterans Barbara Cupisti as Elisa and Alessio Orano as the killer. Cupisti (**Stage Fright**, 1987) puts in a very strong performance. She avoids cliché by emphasizing the character's intelligence and determination, and makes for a very likable protagonist. Orano (**The Killer Must Kill Again**, 1975) is positively chilling as the sociopathic murderer, and is more than capable of holding his own against Cupisti. The finale works as well as it does because both actors really do go for broke in playing up their game of cat-and-mouse; in an era of thrillers overrun with softcore garbage, it is a real treat seeing something more plot-driven and suspenseful like this.

Scandal in Black
(Italy/Germany)

Aka *Appuntamento in nero; Appointment in Black; Naked Rage; Blind Date*

Directed by Antonio Bonifacio (as Anthony Bonifacio); Produced by Andrea Angioli and Remo Angioli; Screenplay by Daniele Stroppa (as Daniel Brados); Director of Photography: Pier Luigi Santi; Editor: Carlos Pulera; Music by Mark Ross

Main Players: Mirella Banti (Angela Baldwin); Andy J. Forest (John Baldwin); Mary Lindstrom (Eva); Daniele Stroppa (Davide); Franco Citti (Projectionist); Sonia Viviani (Inspector)

Home Video: Mya Communication (Region free DVD)

Angela is the wife of respected politician John. One day, she goes to the cinema and is attacked in the ladies' room. John has the incident covered up to avoid a scandal, but Angela is terrified that the attacker will return. An inspector is called in to investigate when Angela starts receiving strange phone calls, and what she uncovers is not what was expected...

Scandal in Black is a throwback of sorts to the sexy *gialli* of the late 1960s popularized by Romolo Guerrieri's **The Sweet Body of Deborah** and Umberto Lenzi's **Orgasmo** (both 1968), but the relaxed censorship standards result in less plotting and more softcore groping.

The film starts with its protagonist, Angela, dressed to the nines and going to a squalid movie theater that is advertising the borderline *giallo Fatal Temptation* (1988). All hopes for self-reflexive cleverness are soon thrown out the window as she enters the (remarkably well-lit) theater and stands for an eternity as she watches a topless blonde on the cinema screen gyrating and appearing to be doing neck exercises as an unseen partner presumably pleasures her. Things go from bad to worse as she is attacked and the dim-witted theater

staff clumsily attempts to deal with the situation. One would be tempted to view the proceedings as tongue-in-cheek, but there is nothing to support this hypothesis. Instead, we are simply bearing witness to clumsy and witless filmmaking.

The plot contains plenty of twists and turns, but once it becomes apparent that the film is following the *Les Diaboliques* (1955) template, it is a little too easy to guess what is going to happen next. The emphasis is firmly on sex however: lots of sex and lots of nudity. On that level, the film can be considered a success. The women are attractive and they do not seem to have any qualms about stripping on camera. Sadly, director Antonio Bonifacio is less than inspired and much of the action is handled in a clumsy and unimaginative fashion; one "hot and heavy" session literally unfolds in a static master shot, and dialogue scenes are similarly listless and basic in their coverage.

The *giallo* elements include mysterious phone calls, a shower attack, games of double-cross and plenty of sexual blackmail, but these things take a back seat in favor of softcore erotica. The attempts at building suspense are unsuccessful, and Bonifacio's effort at aping John Carpenter

DVD cover art for *Scandal in Black*.

by utilizing a similar POV shot to the one found at the opening of *Halloween* (1978) only serves to remind one of what a superior filmmaker Carpenter is. Production values are generally slim, and Pier Luigi Santi's lighting is a working definition of uninspired efficiency. Mark Ross' sleazy score offers up plenty of bad jazz; this is especially evident in the laughter-inducing scene wherein a drunken Angela encourages the cheesy DJs at her husband's latest soiree to play some "sexy" music, inspiring them to unleash the full fury of their Casio keyboards.

Mirella Banti and Mary Lindstrom are about equally insipid in the roles of Angela and Eva, respectively. Angela's backstory involving childhood rape should mark her out as a sympathetic figure, but Banti's one-note performance results in more posturing for the camera than genuine emoting. Lindstrom is similarly stunning to look at but fails to make the ambiguous Eva into a credible three-dimensional character. The gifted character actor Franco Citti is on hand to play the sleazy projectionist who blackmails Angela, but his role is small and his talents are completely wasted in such a squalid film. Daniele Stroppa, who wrote the script, plays a small role in full-blown red herring mode. Stroppa would go on to collaborate on the screenplay for Lucio Fulci's *The House of Clocks* (1989) and *Voices from Beyond* (1990) and also had a hand in what was to have been Fulci's comeback vehicle before his untimely death, *The Wax Mask* (1997), which was ultimately directed by Sergio Stivaletti.

Director Antonio Bonifacio was born in Cosenza in 1957. He entered films in the late 1970s as an actor, and then started working as an assistant director before becoming a director in his own right. *Scandal in Black* was his debut as a director, and he has gone on to a not-very-prolific career, which also includes another erotic *giallo*, **The Strange Story of Olga O** (1995).

1991

28° Minuto

Directed by Paolo Frajoli [actually Gianni Siragusa]; Screenplay by Paolo Frajoli, Francesco Panfili; Director of Photography: Sandro Grossi; Music: Paolo Rustichelli; Editor: Alessandro Perrella.

Main Players: Corinne Cléry (Poggi's lover); Marzio Honorato (Commissioner Mauro Poggi); Christian Borromeo (Fabrizio); Antonella Sperati (Patrizia); Mimmo Palmara (Chief Commissioner); Paul Muller (Psychiatrist)

A maniac who targets young couples in secluded areas terrorizes an Italian city. Commissioner Mauro Poggi is dedicated to bringing the killer to justice, but leads are few and far between and the series of killings continue ...

28° Minuto takes inspiration from the gruesome real-life case of the "Monster of Florence." As such, it is in "good"

company with such similarly tasteless and exploitative items as **The Killer Has Returned** and **The Monster of Florence** (both 1986).

The film is nothing short of a disaster, bluntly speaking. The warmed-over true crime scenario is riddled with clichés

Corinne Cléry is about the only reason to see *28° Minuto*.

and is burdened with one stultifying sequence after another. The investigating Commissioner bickers with his lover. Cozy couple Fabrizio and Patrizia dance the night away in a nightclub, where Fabrizio looks on admiringly as Patrizia does a dance routine. The young lovebirds take in a showing of a horror film (thus providing an excuse for an extended clip from Tonino Ricci's *Panic*, 1982) while the Commissioner (in bed) makes up with his lover. Fabrizio looks on again as Patrizia rehearses her dance moves ... well, you get the idea. To cap it all off, the film simply ends quite suddenly and most unsatisfyingly. It does, however, provide the wonderfully incisive solution (and motivation) that the killer was an impotent mama's boy; one wonders if the policemen on the actual case ever looked to this bit of armchair psychology for inspiration!

If there was any desire to present anything resembling a credible examination of the real-life mystery scenario, it certainly does not come off that way in the finished product. The film is slowly paced, the characters are flat to the point of being completely forgettable and the filmmaking is indescribably crude and lazy. The aforementioned movie theater sequence affords glimpses of posters for Dario Argento's *Inferno* (1980) and **Phenomena** (1985) and Ruggero Deodato's slasher film *Body Count* (1986), but this merely serves to remind one of what a decent Italian horror film is all about. The end result is unremittingly dull and cheap, with nary an element worthy of recommendation.

Indeed, the film is more interesting for its convoluted production history. It was shot in 1986 and designed to compete with the other, above-referenced films on the "Monster of Florence" case. However, the production was hit with some legal woes and the unfinished film was shelved. In

1991 Aristide Massaccesi acquired the footage, and he decided to update it and play down the "Monster of Florence" angle. All explicit references to the case were removed, though the murder scenes are comprised of re-edited scenes from *The Killer Has Returned*. Massaccesi also padded the film with the lengthy quotation from *Panic*, thus explaining the presence of such a protracted film clip. Even so, it still came in at a very short length, running less than 80 minutes; not that one would be able to guess this given the film's glacial pacing. Original director Gianni Siragusa is not credited; instead, editor Paolo Frajoli, who helped to "revise" the material with Massaccesi, took the "honors." The film was never granted a theatrical release, nor has it ever been officially issued on any format beyond a long out-of-print Italian VHS in 1991.

The cast includes the lovely Corinne Cléry, who does her best with a dull role. Christian Borromeo and Antonella Sperati play the bland young lovers. Borromeo had previously given a winning performance as Anthony Franciosa's young assistant in Argento's *Tenebrae* (1982), as well as appearing as a red herring in Lucio Fulci's *Murder-Rock: Dancing Death* (1984), but he seems somewhat out of his depth here. Given that he has relatively little to do but fawn over his onscreen love interest, it is easy to understand why the material failed to bring out his best; in any event, he ends up playing a significant role in the proceedings. Sperati is similarly uninspiring, though she does have several nude scenes along with numerous way-too-long dance routines. "Euro-Cult" cinema fixture Paul Müller shows up for one scene as a police doctor; the filmmakers would have done well to cast him in a larger role.

Murder in Blue Light (Italy)

Aka *Omicidio a luci blu*

Directed by Alfonso Brescia; Produced by Gianluca Curti and Stefano Curti; Screenplay by Alfonso Brescia; Director of Photography: Louis Lucky; Editor: Charly Chandler; Music by Gianluca Bacconi and Stefano Curti

Main Players: Florence Guérin (Starlet Dubois); David Hess (Sergeant Flanagan); Brian Peterson (Ted Harris); Joseph Misiti (Mike); Wendy Windham (Blonde Prostitute); Sonia Topazio (Prostitute)

A serial killer is stalking the streets of New York and leaving an unusual calling card by the bodies: a toy hand grenade. Model Starlet Dubois decides to go undercover as a prostitute in the hopes of catching the killer, but her investigation clashes with that of hot-headed NYPD Sergeant Flanagan ...

Director Alfonso Brescia's third *giallo*, following *Il tuo dolce corpo da uccidere* (1970) and *Naked Girl Killed in the Park ...* (1972), is a lesson in the law of diminishing returns.

The film seems to take its inspiration from the glossy Hollywood thrillers of Brian De Palma. The use of slick lighting, often filtering into scenes through venetian blinds

Italian advertising art for *Murder in Blue Light.*

or with a foggy ambience, is a typical De Palma touch, and the contrast between the world of high fashion and of low flesh-peddling is also something one might expect to see in a film like *Dressed to Kill* (1980) or *Body Double* (1984). Unfortunately, Brescia is no match for De Palma and the end result is very poor indeed.

The remarkably unimaginative screenplay by Brescia offers up plenty of warmed-over situations we have already seen in better thrillers. Likable or (at least) engaging characters might have taken the curse off of the material, but Brescia strikes out in this regard as well. The protagonist/ model/undercover hooker Starlet is bitchy and disagreeable from the start. If the idea was to establish her as spunky and independent, it does not materialize as intended; she simply comes off as a spoiled brat, and her motivation for wanting to catch the killer is never persuasive. Similarly, the tough, no-nonsense Sergeant Flanagan might as well have wandered in from a 1930s Warner Bros. gangster film. He is the typical streetwise cop with a heart of gold, and that is about all there is to it. The other characters pretty much disappear into the background, though there is something a little touching and pathetic about Starlet's duped pimp Mike, who fails to see through her subterfuge.

The *giallo* elements are very subdued following an appropriately atmospheric opening scene depicting the killer at work. Brescia spends more time focusing on the behind-the-scenes squabbles of the modeling world, contrasting it with the world of prostitution and coming to the not-terribly-profound conclusion that the two worlds ultimately have much in common. There is a bit of sex, but the film is not nearly as sleazy as some of the other thrillers of the period. The murders themselves are handled not so much with tact as an air of utter disinterest; apart from the opening scene, most of them take place off-camera and very little blood is spilled in the process. The killer's fondness for whistling "Greensleeves" while stalking his prey is one of the film's few inspired flourishes, and cannot help but recall Peter Lorre's whistling pedophile in Fritz Lang's groundbreaking masterpiece *M* (1931).

Leading lady Florence Guérin gives a rather wooden performance, which hardly helps in making the character more interesting. Guérin has the right look for the part, but beyond that she is pretty much all surface and never catches fire. She was born in France in 1965 and started showing up on French television and cinema screens in 1980. She appeared in the *giallo* **Too Beautiful to Die** (1988) and also (as herself) in Jess Franco's slick shocker *Faceless* (1987). Following a flurry of activity in the 1980s, her career slowed down from the 1990s onwards. Cult favorite David Hess plays Flanagan. He does the best he can with such a hokey character, but all the wild-eyed shenanigans in the world can only inject so much life into his scenes. Hess easily steals the film, but it is by no means one of his more memorable performances. He was born in New York City in 1936 and got his start as a songwriter before making his film debut in 1972—and what a debut it was! Cast as the psychopathic Krug in Wes Craven's directorial debut, *The Last House on the Left*, Hess established himself as a premier purveyor of screen villainy. The success/controversy of the film sent him on a long road of playing various psychos and perverts in pictures of varying quality. He ended up in Italy, where he offered variations on this persona in such movies as Pasquale Festa Campanile's tense kidnapping thriller *Hitch Hike* (1977) and Ruggero Deodato's over-the-top *The House on the Edge of the Park* (1980). He remained active in films and television in the U.S. and Europe until his sudden death at the age of 75 in 2011.

1992

Body Puzzle (Italy)

Aka *Misteria; Puzzle mortal; Body Puzzle – Mit blutigen Grüßen*

Directed by Lamberto Bava; Produced by Mario Bregni and Pietro Bregni; Screenplay by Lamberto Bava, Teodoro Corrà [as Teodoro Agrimi] and Bruce Martin; Director of Photography: Luigi Kuveiller; Editor: Piero Bozza; Music by Carlo Maria Cordio

Main Players: Tomas Arana (Michele); Joanna Pacula (Tracy); François Montagut (Abe); Gianni Garko (Police Chief); Erika Blanc (Dr. Corti); Bruno Corazzari (Professor Busco); Giovanni Lombardo Radice (Morangi)

Home Video: Raro Video (Region free DVD)

A maniac sets his sights on various victims who received organ transplants from the same donor. It transpires that the killer has taken on the personality of his late lover, who died in a motorcycle accident and whose organs these donors claimed. Intrepid Inspector Michele (Tomas Arana) must get to the bottom of the mystery before it is too late ...

Following a series of smaller-scale made-for-TV films, Lamberto Bava returned to the big screen with *Body Puzzle*. For Bava, it was a genre for which he had mixed feelings. "I find doing scenes where women get stabbed to death to be repugnant. [...] I'm better off doing something else."[1] Hap-

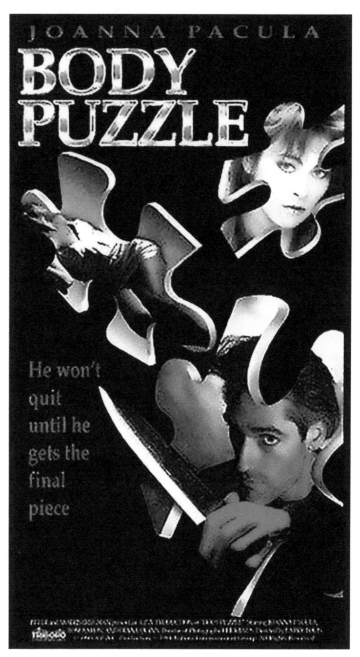

U.S. advertising for *Body Puzzle*; artist unknown.

153

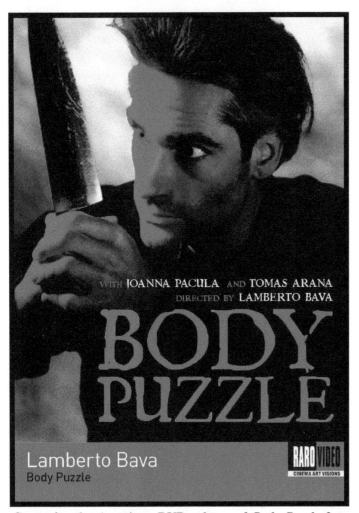

Cover for the American DVD release of *Body Puzzle* from Raro; artist unknown.

pily, none of the director's ambivalence shows in the finished product. Bava came to *Body Puzzle* following the ambitious TV miniseries *The Cave of the Golden Rose* (1991), which would become a major ratings winner in Italy. A tale of fantasy and chivalry, it was apparently far closer to the type of subject matter he yearned to direct, so he must have approached *Body Puzzle* with some measure of ambivalence. In fact, he would go directly from finishing this film to directing three sequels to *Cave* (*The Cave of the Golden Rose 2*, 1992, *The Cave of the Golden Rose 3*, 1993 and *The Cave of the Golden Rose 4*, 1994), and their combined success would make him a much-sought-after director for the small screen in Italy. As such, *Body Puzzle* may well have been a paycheck gig more than anything else, a means of passing the time in between his preferred fantasy work, but if he had any misgivings about the material and its violent content, it certainly is not evident in the finished product. Indeed, the film is distinguished by a cheerfully audacious touch that borders on bad taste. The murder scenes are staged with flair and élan, whether it be the bathroom assault which ends up with a woman losing her hand (literally) in a public toilet (which allows Bava to indulge in a bit of Dario Argento-style camerawork, with the camera being placed inside the commode); or, most memorably, when the killer slays a young

teacher in front of a schoolroom full of blind children—the latter is capped off with one angelic child getting a splash of blood right in the face!

For his return to the *giallo*, Bava was well served by producers Mario and Pietro Bregni, who gave him an adequate budget and shooting schedule to work with. The production company, Produzioni Atlas Consorziate (P.A.C.), had previously produced *Five Dolls for an August Moon* (1970) for Bava's father, Mario Bava. Indeed, the co-writer and production manager on this film, Teodora Corrà, had appeared in that earlier film in the juicy supporting role of George Stark. American prints credit the screenplay to Bruce Martin, but Corrà devised the story with Domenico Paolella and wrote the final scenario with Lamberto Bava. The script is not without its flaws, including the usual contrivances one expects in these films to help keep the plot rattling along. For example, the psychiatrist who feels free to share the case history of her patients without so much as a subpoena being waved under her nose (does patient confidentiality not apply in Italy?) and the pace slowed down by the gratuitous and wholly arbitrary love affair between Tomas Arana's Inspector and Joanna Pacula's panic-stricken victim-to-be. The latter pays off in some soft-focus groping on a stair case, but by the end of the picture it appears to have been forgotten altogether, as Arana walks away from the carnage to catch up on some much needed sleep.

The cast is loaded with familiar "Euro-Cult" faces. Tomas Arana dominates the proceedings as the cynical and quick-tempered Inspector. American-born Arana gravitated to Italian films in the late 1970s, making an unbilled cameo appearance in Sergio Corbucci's comic *giallo Atrocious Tales of Love and Death* (1979), but he rose to prominence in the 1980s thanks to an appearance as Lazarus in Martin Scorsese's controversial passion project *The Last Temptation of Christ* (1988). He followed that film up with his first appearance for Lamberto Bava in the made-for-TV horror item *Prince of Terror* (1988), in which he played a horror director with the irresistible name of Vincent Omen. He would go on to play juicy roles in the Michele Soavi-directed Dario Argento productions *The Church* (1989) and *The Sect* (1991) before reteaming with Bava on this film. Arana would later feature in the *giallo Bugie rosse* (1993) but has spent recent years appearing in higher-profile productions like *L.A. Confidential* (1997), *Gladiator* (2000) and *The Bourne Supremacy* (2004). Arana's laconic, sardonic take on the role of Michele helps to ground *Body Puzzle* in reality. The character may be a cliché, but Arana believes in it; the audience cannot help but follow suit. Polish-born Joanna Pacula plays the role of Tracy, who fulfills the narrative function of damsel-in-distress. A fling with director Roman Polanski resulted in her getting an early break in the film *Gorky Park* (1983), though she had been acting in films of various pedigrees since the late 1970s. Pacula's striking good looks and piercing blue eyes made her a desired (and desirable) presence, but she could sometimes register as wooden. She acquits herself very well as *Body Puzzle*'s imperiled heroine, even if her relationship with Arana comes off as forced at best. The supporting cast includes choice cameos by the likes of Gianni Garko (all grit and clenched teeth as an ill-tempered Police Commissioner, as if there is any other kind), Erika Blanc (still looking glamorous as a psychiatrist), Bruno Corazzari (dubbed in the English track by Nick Alexander) and Giovanni Lombardo Radice, who gets all the best lines in his role as a bitchy homosexual who knows a thing or two about the killer.

Bava handles the material with conviction, and the production values are well above average for a *giallo* of this vintage. Luigi Kuveiller handled the cinematography, whose earlier encounters with the genre included the likes of Dario Argento's **Deep Red** (1975), Lucio Fulci's **A Lizard in a Woman's Skin** (1971) and **The New York Ripper** (1982) and Corbucci's **Atrocious Tales of Love and Death**. His lighting is not quite as stylized and lush as it was on those earlier films, but then again it is not that type of movie. Kuveiller and Bava go for a more mainstream, commercial aesthetic, perhaps inspired by the director's recent work in television and the general trend to gearing films toward the small screen in Italy at that time. That is not to say that the film lacks style, however. As noted above, the murder set pieces are audacious and over-the-top, while the roving camerawork and clever angles help give the film a stylistic boost during even the most dialogue-heavy sequences. Sadly, the decision to employ fast-motion during the picture's two key chase scenes only serves to undercut their impact, making them appear more comedic than thrilling. This minor irritant to one side, the film emerges as one of Bava's strongest thrillers and one of the last truly satisfying contributions to the genre since the mid-'80s. Sadly, the film's release was poorly handled, resulting in middling box-office. For Bava, it would remain his last run-in with the genre until 2012, when he contributed to the TV series **6 passi nel giallo**.

Two final points of trivia worth noting include a change imposed on the film in post-production, whereby the killer's favored choice of background music was changed from Carl Orff's *Carmina Burana* to Modest Mussorgsky's *Night on Bald Mountain*. Bava complained

Italian advertising art for *Circle of Fear*; artist unknown

that the change weakened the savage impact of the killings, but a rights issue overrode his objections. Secondly, it is worth noting that the character of the cemetery worker is identified as Mario Fulci. Bava has certainly worked many explicit references to his late father into his work (including the demonic mask which triggers the infections in *Demons*, 1985), while the surname would appear to pay homage to one of the other past masters of the *giallo*.

Notes:
1. Palmerini, Luca M. and Gaetano Mistretta, *Spaghetti Nightmares* (Florida: Fantasma Books, 1996), p. 23.

Circle of Fear (Italy)

Aka *Alibi perfetto; Jugando con fuego; Wendekreis der Angst*

Directed by Aldo Lado; Screenplay by Paola Bellu, Roberto Brodie Booth, Aldo Lado and Dardano Sacchetti; Director of Photography: Luigi Kuveiller; Editor: Peter Money; Music by Romano Mussolini

Main Players: Michael Woods (Tony Giordani); Kay Rush [as Kay Sandvik] (Lisa Bonnetti); Annie Girardot (Countess); Burt Young (Mancini); Philippe Leroy (Police Chief); Bobby Rhodes (Pathologist)

Home Video: Madacy (Region free DVD)

Narcotics agents Tony Giordani and Lisa Bonnetti take part in a botched drug sting. Their chief is furious because the head of the drug operation has escaped, but they did manage to snag a large amount of pure heroin, which the drug ring is anxious to get back. When Tony is attacked and his wife is murdered, the police figure it is a vendetta from the Mafia, but it is soon revealed that a serial killer, long thought dead, has come back and is looking to resume his work ...

Aldo Lado's **Who Saw Her Die?** (1972) was something of a flawed gem which stands out as a key *giallo* of the golden age of Italian thrillers. His return to the genre with *Circle of Fear* is far less accomplished, but it is not without its charms.

The first half of the film plays like a typical American police program. There are no overt *giallo* elements, and indeed the opening scenes detailing the sting-gone-wrong are very ropey, setting the viewer up for a major disappointment. Then the unexpected happens. Not only does it suddenly transform into a *giallo*, but it becomes much more engaging in the process. It could be that Lado and Dardano Sacchetti were less than enthused by the narcotics angle, but they certainly appear to have had a rush of enthusiasm for the serial killer angle and the ensuing game of cat-and-mouse that the psychopath plays with the police.

The main characters are dull and appear to have been based on viewings of imported American cop shows, but audiences can forgive this once the mystery elements begin to crop up. The sure and steady hands of Sacchetti and Lado ensure that some surprising plot twists develop and the finale comes as a genuine surprise. Lado directs the film with brisk efficiency, with an eye toward action and pacing. The various action scenes are well staged; considering the low budget and the slick cinematography by genre veteran Luigi Kuveiller (**Deep Red**, 1975), things remain interesting to look at throughout. The effect is badly let down by a ghastly music score by Romano Mussolini, which makes one yearn for the days of soundtracks by Goblin or Ennio Morricone. If the film represents a major comedown compared to Lado's promising work of the 1970s, it still stands out in relief as an enjoyable and well-crafted thriller compared to so many other *gialli* of its era; just stick with it beyond the ultra-generic opening scenes.

Michael Woods puts in a decent performance as Tony Giordani. He is the usual tough narcotics agent one would expect to see on a cop show. He has got a temper and a strong moral code, and his determination to bring down the cartel is something of an obsession. Woods brings a little charisma to the role, however, and this helps make him a tolerable protagonist. The younger brother of actor James Woods, he was born in Detroit in 1957. He never enjoyed his brother's popularity, but this is as much a question of talent as anything else. He started acting in TV films in 1980 and began racking-up movie appearances in the 1990s. Woods' film career never really took off, and *Circle of Fear* is certainly his only leading role. He appears to have been inactive since the mid-1990s. Kay Rush plays his partner/lover Lisa. Rush does the best she can under the circumstances; it is another clichéd role, but she invests it with some humanity and makes the character sympathetic. She was born in Wisconsin in 1961 and gravitated to Italy in the 1980s, where she embarked on her brief acting career. Rush appeared in a number of Italian films and TV miniseries until the early 2000s, at which point she seems to have abandoned the profession. The supporting cast includes the always-welcome Philippe Leroy (properly pissed-off as the apoplectic police chief) and American character actor Burt Young. He plays the Mafia goon who is quick to switch sides when he is caught with his hand in the cookie jar. It is the type of role the actor could have played in his sleep, but he brings a welcome dash of humor to the proceedings. Born in New York City in 1940, he trained under Lee Strasberg at the legendary Actors Studio. He broke into films in 1970, and his early credits include small but memorable roles in Barry Shear's *Across 110th Street* (1972),

Roman Polanski's *Chinatown* (1974) and Karl Reisz's *The Gambler* (1975). He found his greatest success playing Paulie, the brother-in-law of Sylvester Stallone's idealized boxer, in the box-office smash *Rocky* (1976); he even netted an Oscar nomination for the role, while the film itself somewhat improbably won Best Picture. He would go on to reprise the role in the various sequels made in 1979, 1982, 1985, 1990 and 2006. He also featured in Damiano Damiani's *Amityville II: The Possession* (1982) and Sergio Leone's *Once Upon a Time in America* (1984), and would go on to appear in Pupi Avati's borderline *giallo The Hideout* (2007). He remains an active presence in films and television.

Masquerade (Italy)

Aka *Private Detective; Bassi istinti; Teri & Rocco Mysterie; The Black Gloves*

Directed by Silvio Bandinelli; Produced by Silvio Bandinelli; Screenplay by Silvio Bandinelli and Ernesto de Pascale; Director of Photography: Franco Taccola; Editor: Massimo Pratesi; Music by Marco Lamioni

Main Players: Raven [as Nellie Marie Vickers] (Linda Forrester); Joey Silvera (Captain Guido Morante); Teri Weigel [as Teresa Weigel] (Sandra); Rocco Siffredi [as Rocco Tano] (Roberto Onorati); Eva Orlowski [as Eva Pistarino] (Anna)

An antique dealer in Florence is murdered just as he is on the point of revealing all about an art-smuggling ring. Undercover cop Linda Forrester is sent to Italy to investigate. Working with Captain Guido Morante, who becomes her lover, she narrows down the field of suspects as a mysterious killer in black continues eliminating those implicated in the case ...

Beginning in the late 1970s, Italian filmmakers started exploring the potential of mixing thriller elements with hardcore sex. It proved to be an uneasy marriage for many reasons, but the trend continued into the 1990s with this film.

Truth be told, the movie is more indebted to American models like Paul Verhoeven's massively popular *Basic Instinct* (1992)—indeed, the film was even made available in a hardcore edit under the title *Bassi istinti*, thus making the lineage all the more obvious. Yet Verhoeven's effort, for all its scandalous and salacious content, managed to tell an engaging story with some surprising twists and turns; it was a good example, if one were needed, of a skilled filmmaker combining sex and suspense in a way that felt organic. In the hands of first-time director Silvio Bandinelli, *Masquerade* feels very much like an indifferently plotted bit of fluff spiced up with lots of sex. The end result is a mishmash that fails to capture the kinetic energy of its American model.

The story is a mixture of thriller, *noir* and erotica. Sadly, none of the elements are very successfully rendered, though the sexual aspects are at least handled with more gusto in the XXX edit of the film. The thriller angle feels very half-hearted, while the *noir* trappings are dispensed with early on. Surprises are few and far between, and the assorted murder scenes are so listlessly staged as to be unintentionally funny. It really is not clear when watching the film just what Bandinelli had in mind, as the disparate mixture of various exploitable elements never gels together to create a unified whole.

At the very least, the film pays lip service to the familiar *giallo* tropes (right down to the killer in a black raincoat and fedora) that allows it to rate mention here at all. Many of the erotic thrillers of the period could not even be bothered to do this, making their inclusion on the lists compiled by some fans all the more perplexing. It may not work as a *giallo*, but at least *Masquerade* has the look and feel of one.

Logic and character motivation take a back seat to the all-important goal of getting the characters to engage in as many sexual encounters as possible. The fact that the film is largely set in Italy, with bookend scenes set in the U.S., is almost incidental. True, Bandinelli spends a good deal of time indulging in travelogue views of Florence, but with so much of the action confined to various bedrooms the story could have been set just about anywhere. Linda is established as a tough and free-spirited protagonist early on, yet she falls into flat out damsel-in-distress mode in key scenes. No doubt the filmmakers felt that this would "feminize" her somewhat, but it only serves to make nonsense of her character. Her Italian contact, Captain Morante, is similarly defined by two key elements. He is good in the kitchen and in the bedroom. Beyond that, the film does not really bother to define the characters or their relationships very well. They are chiefly there to stab each other in the back and screw.

The cast includes a number of familiar porno actors of the era. Nellie Marie Vickers, better known as Raven, plays the role of Linda. She acquits herself reasonably well, but the inconsistent nature of the character does not do much to help her efforts. Even so, she at least comes off as professional, which is more than can be said of some of her co-stars. Born in 1964, she entered the porno side of the industry in 1983. She established herself as a "cool" type, elegant but not prone to getting as down and dirty as some of her contemporaries. She appeared in quite a few films before taking a respite in the late 1980s; she then returned in the early 1990s and remained active for the better part of the decade before retiring for good. Joey Silvera plays her Italian partner/lover. He does a decent job under the circumstances, but his rather sleazy appearance makes him an odd piece of casting for a police captain. Born Joseph Nassivera in Rochester, New York in 1951, Silvera entered adult films in the early 1970s and racked up over a thousand credits as a performer; he is still active on camera to this day. He is also a prolific director of adult videos, making nearly 300 since the mid-1990s. Teri Weigel overacts rather badly as a child-like nymphomaniac who is mixed up in the killings. Weigel's tendency to go over-the-top is compensated for by her

Linda (Raven, aka Nellie Marie Vickers) "cools off" in the shower on this foreign poster for *Masquerade*.

statuesque figure and eager performing in her various sexual trysts. She was born in Fort Lauderdale in 1962 and began appearing in adult films in the mid-1980s. She quickly established herself as a popular presence in the porno scene and crossed over on occasion to the mainstream thanks to appearances in *Predator 2* and the Steven Seagal film *Marked for Death* (both 1990). Weigel stepped away from porn in 2004 but returned as a "mature" performer later in the decade for a period of time. Italian porn stud Rocco Siffredi is also on hand as one of many suspects, but his main function in the plot is less apparent in the "soft" edit of the film as opposed to the hardcore edit, so to speak. Born in Ortona in 1964, he started appearing in adult films in the mid-1980s. To date, he has appeared in about 450 hardcore sex films, as well as the odd "mainstream" title (which still trade on his porno legacy) like *Romance* (1999). Siffredi is also a prolific director of adult films and has helmed over 200 videos since the mid-1990s.

Director Silvio Bandinelli was born in Tripoli in 1954. *Masquerade* marked his debut as a director. He would go on to specialize in porn subjects, as well.

1993

Bugie rosse (Italy)

Directed by Pierfrancesco Campanella; Screenplay by Pierfrancesco Campanella; Director of Photography: Mario Vulpiani; Music by Natale Massara

Main Players: Tomas Arana (Marco); Gioia Scola (Adria); Lorenzo Flaherty (Andrea); Alida Valli (Caterina); Natasha Hovey (Lucia)

Journalist Marco goes undercover to explore the homosexual underworld. Meanwhile, a killer with a vendetta against homosexuals begins targeting some of his contacts. Marco comes under suspicion and decides to investigate on his own in order to clear his name. As he delves deeper into the milieu, he begins to change ...

For a genre that trades on images of sex, the *giallo* has always been remarkably skittish where homosexuality is concerned. Many *gialli* have traded on sensationalized images of lesbian lovemaking, but where male-on-male contact is concerned, it is something of a no-no. On this level, *Bugie rosse* deserves a lot of points for boldly going where no other *giallo* has gone before.

Italian *locandina* for *Bugie rosse*; artist unknown.

The screenplay by director Pierfrancesco Campanella seems to have been inspired by William Friedkin's *Cruising* (1980). Friedkin's thriller ignited a firestorm of controversy for its frank depiction of the S/M leather bar scene, and many wrongly targeted it as a homophobic portrayal of gay life; on the contrary, it offered a wonderfully ambiguous account of a rookie cop (Al Pacino) who is assigned to investigate a series of murders in the homosexual community. To that end, he goes undercover and in the process learns a great deal about himself that he has kept repressed. Campanella's scenario is very similar. Marco is not a cop, but he is still investigating a series of gay-themed murders while doing an exposé of the gay nightclub and prostitution scene. Another similarity emerges when it becomes apparent that he is starting to be drawn to the *milieu*, suggesting that his own contradictory emotions indicate a serious repression, which is finally coming to light.

The refreshing thing about the film is its non-judgemental approach to what could have been a scenario in very bad taste. Campanella does not stigmatize the gay characters as "fairies," nor does he use the film as an opportunity to belittle them or depict them as deviant. Some very well drawn and sympathetic characters add to the drama, while stereotypes are downplayed in favor of a more realistic approach. Some *gialli* have been accused of adopting a hypocritical stance, condemning sexuality on the one hand while playing it up through lurid imagery, but this is not a charge that can be leveled against *Bugie rosse*.

The thriller elements are not as prominent as the sociological dimension of the story, but they are successfully integrated and intelligently worked out. The final reveal of the killer's identity is not terribly surprising, but the finale manages to offer up a twist or two. The murders are handled with tact but still pack a wallop, largely because many of the characters affected have managed to win over the sympathy of the audience. This last aspect is something worth considering, as it is something that appears to have been lost on many *giallo* filmmakers. In establishing and developing characters who are worthy of audience interest and empathy, Campanella succeeds in building real suspense; he therefore does not have to go overboard with the blood and gore during the killings, since they affect the viewer on a different level.

The film is undoubtedly one of the best *gialli* of the period; admittedly, this is damning the movie with faint praise when one considers the competition. Campanella directs with a mature sensibility. The sex is actually somewhat erotic for once, and the depiction of the marginalized homosexual community makes for a very interesting backdrop. Mario Vulpiani's cinematography is moody and stylish, avoiding the trend toward overlit, music video aesthetics that handicapped so many thrillers of the period. Natale Massara's score reflects something of his longstanding association with Pino Donaggio; Massara has conducted a great many of Donaggio's scores since *Carrie* (1976).

The cast does a splendid job. Tomas Arana again proves himself to be one of the genre's most compelling and engaging leading men since the days of George Hilton and Jean Sorel. Arana's slightly ambiguous moral character comes in very handy since his motivations remain suspect at different points in the narrative. Lorenzo Flaherty gives a strong performance as Andrea, a young escort who becomes involved with Marco. He initially seeks to use Andrea for information, but is clearly drawn to the handsome young man and develops a genuine affection for him. Flaherty makes the character sympathetic and he has great chemistry with Arana. He was born in Rome in 1967 and made his debut as one of the partygoers in Lamberto Bava's *Demons 2* (1986). He has enjoyed a prolific and successful career in Italian film and television and remains in demand to this day. The supporting cast includes another alum of the *Demons* franchise. Natasha Hovey, who plays Marco's videographer assistant, played one of the leads in the original *Demons* (1985). The Lebanese actress remains active in Italian films as well. Alida Valli makes a guest star appearance and adds real class to the proceedings, though her role is rather small.

Director Campanella got his start in films writing and appearing in a bizarre Italian film called *Transgression* (1988). The movie includes some thriller elements, but is ultimately an anti-drug message flick with the usual erotic elements thrown in for good (?) measure. He began directing in the early 1990s and would remain busy through the early 2000s, but his output was never very prolific. He has been inactive since 2007.

Private Crimes (Italy)

Aka *Delitti privati; Mord in der Toskana*

Directed by Sergio Martino; Produced by Edwige Fenech and Pietro Innocenzi; Screenplay by Franco Marotta and Laura Toscano; Director of Photography: Giancarlo Ferrando; Editor: Eugenio Alabiso; Music by Natale Massara

Main Players: Edwige Fenech (Nicole Venturi); Ray Lovelock (Commissioner Stefano Avanzo); Victoria Vera (Anna Selpi); Paolo Malco (Massimo Pierboni); Gabriele Ferzetti (Doctor Guido Braschi); Alida Valli (Matilde Pierboni); Annie Girardot (Ada Roversi); Lorenzo Flaherty (Paolo Roversi); Gudrun Landgrebe (Daniela Pierboni); Cinzia de Ponti (Magistrate Castelli); Silvia Mocchi (Chiara); Maja Maranow (Milena Bolzoni); Laurent Terzieff (Professor Carlo Mauri); Vittoria Belvedere (Sandra Durani)

Marco Pierboni is assassinated and his body is found stuffed in the trunk of his car. Down the road 20 year-old Sandra Durani is also found murdered. It transpires that the two victims were involved in an affair. Sandra's journalist mother, Nicole Venturi, sets out to unmask the murderer and discovers all manner of shady back-room dealings, affairs and other sundry unpleasantries lurking beneath the surface of the little town...

Sergio Martino's return to the *giallo* comes in the form of another TV miniseries. Unlike **The Scorpion with Two**

German DVD cover for *Private Crimes*; artist unknown.

Tails (1982), however, *Private Crimes* is not without points of interest.

On the downside, the miniseries format results in far too much material to sift through. The film was originally broadcast in four 90-minute instalments, resulting in a final runtime of approximately six hours. In order to pad the plot out for that duration, writers Franco Marotta and Laura Toscano adopt an episodic approach similar to a soap opera. Everybody in the town has a secret of some kind, it would seem, and just about everybody has been involved in an illicit affair with one of the other characters. The piling-on of revelations becomes a little ridiculous after a while, but Martino handles the material with such conviction that it ends up working in spite of its excesses.

Admittedly, the thriller elements are not particularly well played up. The mysterious killer is on hand, along with point of view shots, anonymous typewritten letters and threatening phone-calls, but the film never goes full blast with regards to exploring the more lurid aspects of the genre. The killings are few and far between and they are toned down to suit the television medium. Even so, Martino's expertise in the genre is evident as he builds suspense and builds to a credible but surprising finale in which all is finally revealed. Perhaps if

159

It has nothing to do with *Private Crimes*, but this cover for *Blitz* magazine from 1985 makes it clear that star Edwige Fenech had lost none of her luster in the years since her heyday as the Queen of the Giallo in the 1970s.

the series had been done in four one-hour segments it would have worked better. As it stands, it has much to recommend for the patient viewer; just do not go in expecting all kinds of sleazy and gory mayhem.

The scenario wallows in revelations about various extramarital affairs, but the film itself is very chaste in its approach. This was undoubtedly a result of the TV format, but it is amazing just the same to see how coy it is compared to so many other thrillers of the era. The revelation about a prostitution ring being run under the guise of a respectable business recalls aspects of Mario Bava's **Blood and Black Lace** (1964) and Massimo Dallamano's **What Have They Done To Your Daughters?** (1974), but Martino's film feels far more old-fashioned than either of those trail blazers. The over-arching theme of so-called respectable society concealing a seedy reality is a classic *giallo* theme, and the film definitely explores it to the hilt.

Martino's direction is polished and assured. Following a run of mostly indifferent erotic thrillers, including *Foxy Lady* (1992) and *Craving Desire* (1993), the prospect of returning to the genre in which he first established himself seems to have energized him. While those other titles were much too indebted to American cinema and were more concerned with T&A action than anything else, *Private Crimes* allows him

to take his time in telling an intricate and twist-laden thriller scenario. Working with longstanding collaborators like cinematographer Giancarlo Ferrando and editor Eugenio Alabiso, he delivers a film that is stylish and engaging, though admittedly much too long-winded for its own good. A more sensible running time and a less verbose screenplay would have helped, but even so, this is an enjoyable thriller that manages to hit the right notes where it counts.

The cast includes a number of *giallo* veterans. Edwige Fenech dominates the series with her heart-felt performance as the single mother consumed by grief and a desire for justice. Fenech, still looking as radiant as ever, handles the different emotional components of her characterization very well, and again proves that she has real acting chops in addition to good looks. Ray Lovelock is good as the Police Commissioner, whose frustration over the case leads him to rethink his future with the department. Lovelock effectively conveys the character's mounting frustration and dogged devotion to the law, but the character does not undergo many interesting developments and he is kept sidelined as a result. Guest stars Alida Valli and Gabriele Ferzetti are both in excellent form, while Paolo Malco adds another nicely shaded ambiguous characterization to his filmography.

Trauma (Italy/USA)

Aka *Dario Argento's Trauma*

Directed by Dario Argento; Produced by Dario Argento, Chris Beckman, T. David Pash and Andrea Tinnirello; Screenplay by Dario Argento and T.E.D. Klein; Director of Photography: Raffaele Mertes; Editor: Bennett Goldberg; Music by Pino Donaggio

Main Players: Christopher Rydell (David Parsons); Asia Argento (Aura Petrescu); Piper Laurie (Adriana Petrescu); Frederic Forrest (Dr. Judd); James Russo (Captain Travis); Laura Johnson (Grace Harrington); Dominique Serrand (Stefan Petrescu); Brad Dourif (Dr. Lloyd)

Home Video: Anchor Bay (Region 1 DVD)

When her parents are murdered by the so-called Head Hunter killer, Aura Petrescu takes to her heels. She meets up with graphic designer David Parsons, a recovering drug addict who wishes to help the young woman. As they investigate the killings, Aura is haunted by the feeling that she saw something important which may help to identify the killer ...

Following the release of **Opera** (1987), Dario Argento decided the time was ripe for world domination ... well, for pushing his name further into the international marketplace, in any event. He concocted the idea of an Edgar Allan Poe anthology to be shot in the U.S. and ultimately decided upon filming in Pittsburgh, Pennsylvania, due to the collaboration of his friend and colleague George A. Romero. The resulting movie, *Two Evil Eyes* (1990), was a disappointment that did little to further the director's reputation. Still determined to make a go of it in the American marketplace, he decided to regroup and go back to his old standby the *giallo*. *Trauma* would therefore find the Italian master of horror trying to connect with an American Cineplex audience, while going down memory lane with his most self-referential effort to date.

The film is largely written-off as a failed experiment by many Argento fans, but just as his segment of *Two Evil Eyes* ("The Black Cat") is now starting to be appreciated as the fine piece of work it always was, nobody seems to be in a huge rush to defend *Trauma* as yet. This is indeed a pity, as the picture has much to recommend and is one of the director's most purely enjoyable outings.

Many critics seem determined to dismiss the film on the grounds of its being an American production. The suggestion is made that the process of shooting in America resulted in Argento's quirky voice and vision being effectively neutered. This is patently absurd. The movie is loaded with weird, off-the-wall touches and sequences that could only have sprung from Argento's unorthodox imagination. Even the set-up is far from conventional. A teenage anorexic[1] and a 20-something recovering heroin addict fall in love while investigating a series of gruesome murders. Far from representing Argento succumbing to the bland and cookie-cutter mentality of American genre filmmaking, *Trauma* shows the director exploring his favored terrain in an altogether more emotional manner.

As Argento explained to Alan Jones, he saw *Trauma* as:

Deep Soul, my **Deep Red** for a new generation. Usually my stories come from articles in newspapers or things I hear on the streets. Not this time. It's from deep down inside myself.[2]

The idea for the film reportedly grew out of the problems encountered by the eldest daughter of Daria Nicolodi, who was the product of the actress' first marriage. Argento channeled his frustrations over her struggles with anorexia into the screenplay for *Trauma*, giving it a more personal dimension than usual in his work. This perhaps explains why the film is much warmer in tone than so many of his other thrillers. The characters of Aura and David are well developed and make for an appropriately quirky love story in the midst of a typical *giallo* scenario.

The screenplay developed in a tortuous fashion. Argento devised the story with the collaboration of Franco Ferrini and Gianni Romoli, but when the decision was made to make the film in America, the director decided it was necessary to hire an American collaborator. Horror novelist T.E.D. Klein came onboard and helped to polish the dialogue and tone down some of the wilder excesses. Argento reportedly planned to go overboard with the blood and gore, but Klein rightly reckoned that this would not sit well with the American marketplace. Argento went along with the advice and decided to tone down the violence in hopes of finally scoring an American hit. He really need not have bothered. Even with the toned-down bloodshed, the film is still much too

outré and bizarre to pass for anything resembling a mainstream American movie.

The major problem Argento faced in his quest for establishing himself in the American marketplace was one of name value. In Italy, Argento is an institution in himself—even when his films fail to draw audiences (and this has increasingly become the case in recent years), he is still a bona fide celebrity; in a sense he is that rarest of creatures: the star-as-director. His reputation is not nearly so well known

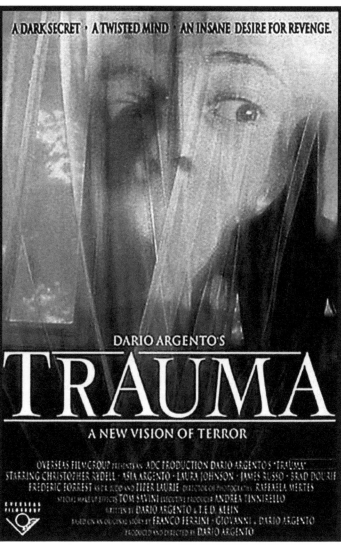

U.S. art for *Trauma*.

in America, however, outside of genre circles. Argento's desire to make himself into a John Carpenter type (that is, a brand name) extends to putting his name above the title for the first time in his career, but the very elements that make him so beloved among cult movie buffs are the ones that will inevitably scare off a major mainstream audience. His thrillers are too convoluted and chaotically plotted, too loaded with bizarre elements and contrivances that they simply do not sit well with audiences accustomed to more "traditional" plotting. Similarly, his baroque style and fixation on images of violent death will forever mark him as an "outsider" figure, as films of this sort have never meant big business at the American box-office; sure, horror films will turn a profit, but the critics sneer at them and most "average" moviegoers regard them with a smirk and a condescending laugh. For Argento, however, the genre is an art form—and his inability to connect with an American audience would inevitably send him back to Italy, where he had more to prove, but there he had an easier time getting the sort of financing and exposure he desired.

Trauma has a number of problems, many of which can be blamed on the director's over-eager desire to please a wide audience. The story is intriguing, but it succumbs to cliché when it should go for the unexpected. The notion of the Head Hunter killer is played out in an arbitrary and conventional manner. Argento's flair for "hidden in plain view" clues comes into play at the end, but the mystery is somewhat haltingly developed. The presence of too many cooks (i.e., writers) in the kitchen may well have overcomplicated things somewhat. Argento's work with Ferrini has never been as effective as his collaboration with Bernardino Zapponi on **Deep Red** (1975), for example, but the addition of American collaborator Klein merely serves to water things down to some extent. Argento's intention of exploring the psychological aspects of eating disorders proved to be a major casualty, with Klein arguing that American audiences would not respond to this aspect; therefore, this angle is rather muted in the film and is basically dropped altogether after the halfway point. It seems likely that, in his desire to appease the audience, Argento lost sight of some of his own goals in the process, reminding one of his oft-parroted criticisms of **The Cat O'Nine Tails** (1971), which he often referred to as his least favorite of his own pictures.

That said, there is still much to love in *Trauma*. The director's stylish *mise-en-scène* is one of the film's major strengths. Working with cinematographer Raffaele Mertes, Argento makes use of soft, misty interiors and cold, harsh exteriors to contrast the love story with the brutality of the world at large. His balletic use of moving camera is still much in evidence as the camera swoops, turns, gyrates and glides along of its own accord. The use of the widescreen frame is artful throughout and again shows him to be a director who makes the most of the frame at all times. The love story between Aura and David is genuinely moving. The scene in which David frantically looks for Aura, believing her to have killed herself, is a heartbreaking moment for a director not known for pulling at the heart strings. Some welcome humor is also introduced in the form of a subplot involving an inquisitive little boy who lives next door to the killer. The scenes of the child engaging in his hobby of watching butterflies even allows the director to indulge in a bit of "butterfly point of view" action which cannot help but remind one of the crows in **Opera**.

The murders may be muted in terms of gore, but they are still remarkably well staged and executed. The film opens with the slaying of a chiropractor, who is taken by surprise when she turns her back on the killer. The use of tight close-ups, gruesome sound effects and artful shadowplay gives the sequence a visceral punch, even though very little is actually seen. Similarly, a later scene depicting the death of a doctor who holds the key to the mystery is beautifully staged in a creepy, rundown tenement building. The killer's preferred use of an electric contraption (dubbed the "noose-o-matic" by the film crew) is stymied when the machine runs low on power, so the hapless doctor is dragged to an elevator shaft and his head is positioned so that the descending elevator can do the decapitating instead. It is all wonderfully over-the-top and theatrical, and Argento knows it; far from aiming for stuffy realism, he indulges these flights of fancy with an eye for the decorative. The surprisingly shoddy severed heads created by make-up wizard Tom Savini dilute their impact, however. Savini (born in Pittsburgh in 1946) first worked with Argento on *Two Evil Eyes* and looked forward to continuing their collaboration on *Trauma*.

> I think the only problem with *Two Evil Eyes* […] is that it was Dario's first time working in America and it seems to me to be his most inhibited film. Whereas, I think, with *Trauma*, Dario is completely at his ease![3]

However, he would later change his tune when it became clear that Argento was going for a less-is-more approach.

> I've done a lot less on *Trauma* than I expected to and I am upset about that. Inventive murders usually set Dario's films apart so it was just my luck to work with him on a movie where he wanted twisted surprise to drive the narrative more than the murders themselves.[4]

It is probably just as well that Argento did not dwell on the severed heads more, truth be told, as they do not represent a feather in Savini's cap. Savini became fixated on filmmaking and special effects (or as he likes to call them, magic tricks) at an early age when he saw the saccharine Lon Chaney bi-opic *Man of a Thousand Faces* (1957), starring James Cagney. Following a stint in Vietnam as a combat photographer, he hooked up with George A. Romero and worked with him as an actor and make-up artist on *Martin* (1977). The two men got along well and went on to collaborate on *Dawn of the Dead* (1978), *Knightriders* (1981), *Creepshow* (1982), *Day of the Dead* (1985) and other films. Savini's flair for realistic gore effects made him into a full-fledged icon of the horror genre in the 1980s, but as the trend toward computer-generated effects took hold later, he started to focus more on acting and on teaching make-up effects to eager students in Pittsburgh. As an actor, Savini has appeared in such titles as Robert Rodriguez's *From Dusk Till Dawn* (1996) and Quentin Tarantino's *Django Unchained* (2012). He has also directed some films, notably a Romero-scripted remake of *Night of the Living Dead* (1990).

Italian lobby card for *Trauma*, featuring star-crossed lovers Christopher Rydell and Asia Argento on the right.

Argento was able to assemble a notable cast, but sadly not everybody was inspired to do their best work. Asia Argento is very impressive in the role of Aura. The actress would grow irritated with whisperings among the crew that nepotism secured her the role, but she brings tremendous energy and sincerity to the part. If she never succeeds in sounding convincingly Romanian, she can hardly be faulted; acting in English in such a prominent role was a challenge in itself, and she was not the only one who failed to convince in the accent department. Born in Rome in 1975, she is the only offspring of Dario Argento and Daria Nicolodi; Nicolodi's daughter Anna had been born to another father, while Argento's daughter Fiore was the product of his first marriage. Asia debuted on Italian television in the mid-1980s and began acting in her father's productions with back-to-back appearances in *Demons 2* (1986) and a segment of ***Giallo: la tua impronta del venerdi*** (1987). *Trauma* marked the first time she was directed by her father, however, and they would go on to collaborate on ***The Stendhal Syndrome*** (1996), *The Phantom of the Opera* (1998), *Mother of Tears* (2007) and *Dracula 3D* (2012). Asia also acted in such films as Patrice Chéreau's *Queen Margot* (1994), Peter Del Monte's *Traveling Companion* (1996), Abel Ferrara's *New Rose*

Hotel (1998), George A. Romero's *Land of the Dead* (2005) and Sofia Coppola's *Marie Antoinette* (2006). In addition to becoming a fixture in the Italian gossip columns, she also developed into a major sex symbol and graduated to directing her own films, commencing with the partly autobiographical *Scarlet Diva* (2000). As of 2014, she has announced her intention to leave acting behind in favor of focusing on other pursuits. Christopher Rydell plays David effectively. His somewhat bland persona is well suited to the awkward outsider trying to make good, and he and Argento have very good onscreen chemistry together. The son of actor-turned-director Mark Rydell (*On Golden Pond*, 1981), he was born in 1963 and began appearing in his father's films as a child actor in the early 1970s. He worked sporadically in movies in the 1980s and '90s, but his career never really caught fire and he has been relatively inactive in recent years. Piper Laurie puts in a barnstorming performance as Aura's mother, the medium Adriana Petrescu. Laurie's theatrical accent and mannerisms make her into an overt monster from the get-go, and she never takes things down a notch for variety. Laurie would later confide to Alan Jones that she simply did not take the project seriously.[5] Born in Detroit in 1932, she started taking acting lessons as a teenager and was put under contract to Universal when she was 17 years old. Her early film work was standard studio fodder, but she established herself as a serious actress in the burgeoning medium of television thanks to stellar performances in hard-hitting dramas like *Days of Wine and Roses* (1958). She appeared opposite Paul Newman in *The Hustler* (1961), netting an Oscar nomination in the process, but took a break from films from the mid-1960s until 1976, when she was cast by Brian De Palma in his hit Stephen King adaptation *Carrie*. Laurie's frightening performance as Carrie's religious fanatic mother earned her her second Oscar nomination. She has remained active in recent years, notably on television. The sinister Dr. Judd is played by Frederic Forest, another fine actor who allows his contempt for the material to manifest in a very weird, mannered performance. Born in Texas in 1936, Forrest made his film debut in the late 1960s. He became a favorite of director Francis Ford Coppola, who cast him in such films as *The Conversation* (1974), *Apocalypse Now* (1979) and *One from the Heart* (1982). Forrest was Oscar-nominated for his supporting role in Mark Rydell's *The Rose* (1979), co-starring Bette Midler and Alan Bates, and he also appeared in such pictures as Wim Wenders' *Hammett* (1982, produced by Coppola), Jack Nicholson's *The Two Jakes* (1990) and Joel Schumacher's *Falling Down* (1993), in which he gives a terrifying yet darkly funny performance as a skinhead shopkeeper. He has been inactive in films since 2006. James Russo plays the plodding police inspector on the case. His flat performance appears to have been in response to the dull role, as he had expressed enthusiasm over the prospect of working with Argento. Born in New York City in 1953, he made his film debut in 1981 and would appear in everything from *Fast Times at Ridgemont High* (1982) and *Beverly Hills Cop* (1984) to Sergio Leone's *Once Upon a Time in America* (1984) and Gus Van Sant's *My Own Private Idaho* (1991). More recently he has been seen in Michael Mann's *Public Enemies* (2009) and Quentin Tarantino's *Django Unchained* (2012). The ever-reliable Brad Dourif puts in a brief appearance as a drug-addled doctor implicated in the killings, and he gives more in his brief scenes than his other "name" co-stars manage combined. Dourif was born in West Virginia in 1950 and earned an Oscar nomination with one of his first film appearances, playing the tragic mental patient Billy Bibbitt in Milos Foreman's Oscar-winning *One Flew Over the Cuckoo's Nest* (1975), starring Jack Nicholson. A powerful, eccentric performer, he would go on to appear in films by John Huston (*Wise Blood*, 1979) and Michael Cimino (*Heaven's Gate*, 1980), as well as William Peter Blatty's troubled/underrated *The Exorcist III* (1990), but Hollywood never seemed quite sure what to do with him. He found popularity voicing the kill-

German poster art for *Trauma*; designer unknown.

er doll Chucky in the *Child's Play* franchise and later impressed with his understated work as the town doctor in HBO's hit series *Deadwood* (2004-2006).

The commercial disappointment of *Trauma*—it received only a limited release in 1994 in America and performed poorly in Italy as well—did not deter Argento from planning another American *giallo*, but by the time **The Stendhal Syndrome** went before the cameras, he had relocated to Italy.

Notes:
1. Actually there seems to have been some confusion on the part of Argento and his co-writers with regards to anorexia; the condition Aura seems to be suffering from is far closer to bulimia, an admittedly similar eating disorder which nevertheless carries its own specific set of symptoms and behaviors.
2. Jones, Alan, *Dario Argento: The Man, The Myths & The Magic* (Godalming: FAB Press, 2012), p. 215.
3. Palmerini, Luca M. and Gaetano Mistretta, *Spaghetti Nightmares* (Florida: Fantasma Books, 1996), p. 133.
4. Jones, Alan, *Dario Argento: The Man, The Myths & The Magic* (Godalming: FAB Press, 2012), p. 221.
5. *Ibid*, p. 218.

The Washing Machine
(Italy/France/Hungary)

Aka *Vortice mortale; Die Waschmaschine*

Directed by Ruggero Deodato; Produced by Alessandro Canzio, Corrado Canzio, André Koob and Aron Sipos; Screenplay by Luis Spagnol; Director of Photography: Sergio D'Offizi; Editor: Gianfranco Amicucci; Music by Claudio Simonetti

Main Players: Philippe Cairot (Inspector Alexander Stacev); Ilaria Borrelli (Maria 'Sissy' Kolba); Katarzyna Figura (Vida Kolba); Barbara Ricci (Ludmilla Kolba); Yorgo Voyagis (Yuri Petkov); Claudia Pozzi (Irina)

Home Video: EVS Entertainment (Region free DVD)

Ludmilla Kolba claims to have found the body of a man cut up and stuffed into her washing machine. The police come to investigate, but there is no sign of a body. Her sisters Maria and Vida claim that Ludmilla was drinking and just imagined the incident. Soon Inspector Stacev is bewitched by the three sisters, and it becomes apparent that they have something sinister up their sleeves ...

A hopelessly generic title to one side, *The Washing Machine* is one of the most satisfying thrillers of the decade. It also represents a determined return to form for director Ruggero Deodato, whose work of the period (barring **Phantom of Death**, 1988) tended toward the anonymous.

The screenplay by Luis Spagnol is wonderfully complex and engaging. The plot twists and turns a great deal, but Deodato's precise direction ensures that it never becomes confused or jumbled. The fragmented approach, with dreams giving way to flashbacks and then resuming with the present, requires the viewer to remain alert. The film's intricate structure could easily have become confusing or even annoying, but it plays out in a genuinely gripping fashion and builds to a splendid, macabre finale.

Like so many *gialli* of the period, the film is heavy on sex and eroticism. Unlike many of these films, however, this one actually generates real heat during its sexy *longueurs*, and the director has the good sense to not allow these scenes to unbalance the movie. The film is first and foremost a thriller, and Deodato does not lose sight of this; however, the concession to the front office does not prove ruinous, since the sex is actually an integral part of the plot.

The movie was shot on location in Budapest, Hungary and the exotic locale definitely adds to the film's appeal. Deodato makes great use of the locations. Sooner than go for typical picture-postcard imagery, however, the coldness of the locales actually serves to underline the flick's rather bleak and cynical tone. This is a film in which people use each other continuously and wherein love is merely an abstract concept; sex and power games are the order of the day, and anybody who is too sensitive to adhere to this notion is in for a very bad time of it.

Surprisingly, Deodato would later dismiss the film as a failure.

> I wasn't very happy with *The Washing Machine* because I was never convinced that the casting was correct, and the film was made too quickly.[1]

In another interview, he would expand on this:

> I can only say that I am not at all pleased with the final result because it's a very intimate movie and it should have had well-known actors […] I am very sorry to have to say this because the setting is extraordinarily good and finding the body inside the washing machine at the beginning of the movie is an unusual and interesting start.[2]

Deodato's feelings on the hectic shooting are not supported by the film itself, which seems very carefully constructed, while his feeling that the material would have been better realized with "name" actors does not necessarily bear close scrutiny. Certainly better-known actors would have helped to market the film to a wider audience, but the small ensemble play their roles very well, and it is hard to imagine bigger names being any more credible or convincing in their place. Regardless, Deodato's dismissal of the film as a failure should not deter his fans from seeking it out, as it is certainly one of the few genuinely accomplished efforts from this stage in his career.

Deodato directs with the energy typical of his best works. As noted above, the sex scenes actually have some conviction to them, but the film is also noteworthy for its ghoulish streak, which manifests during the more horrific moments. There are some surprisingly gory moments along the way, and one nasty set piece cannot help but evoke memories of the savage imagery of his most notorious film, *Cannibal Holocaust* (1980). All of this is a far cry from the comparatively vanilla thrills of the stylish but hopelessly dopey borderline *giallo Dial: Help* (1988), for example, and validates the notion that the director had lost none of his edge in his later years. Deodato can also be seen in a quick cameo as Inspector Stacev's nosy neighbor. The cinematography by the veteran Sergio D'Offizi (**Don't Torture a Duckling**, 1972) steers clear of the over-slick music video aesthetics that in-

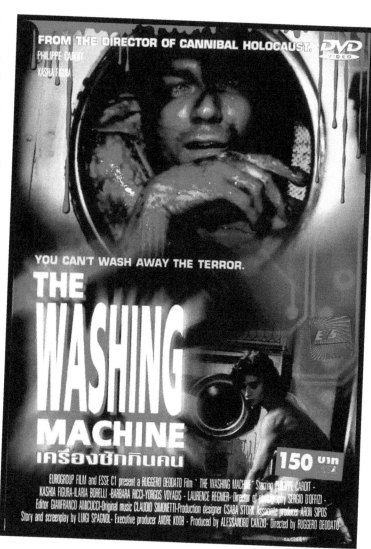

Cover for the Russian DVD release of *The Washing Machine*.

fected the genre during this time, while Claudio Simonetti contributes an effective soundtrack.

The cast is headed by Philippe Cairot, who puts in a good performance as the straight-arrow police inspector who succumbs to temptation. Cairot initially seems cut from the same mold as other bland young actors of the period who attempted to play "tough" by growing some designer stubble and donning a trenchcoat, but he gives a sincere and effective performance and is more than capable when it comes to conveying the character's deteriorating moral sensibility. He was born in Paris in 1959 and began appearing in films in the early 1980s. Most of his pictures were made in France, but he started making the odd Italian film and miniseries in the 1990s. Ilaria Borrelli, Katarzyna Figura and Barbara Ricci play the three seductive sisters. Borrelli and Ricci are both Italian and have worked mostly in Italian films and television, but Polish actress Figura (born in 1962) appeared in some noteworthy "prestige" pictures like Robert Altman's *Prêt-à-Porter* (1994) and Roman Polanski's Oscar-winning *The Pianist* (2002). All three actresses show a commendable enthusiasm for the material and manage to be simultaneously sensuous and frightening. Yorgo Voyagis is also very good as the sleazy and manipulative Yuri, who has his way with the sisters and makes the mistake of thinking that he is in control. Voyagis was born in Athens in 1945 and made his film debut (under the name George Voyadjis) in *Zorba the Greek* (1964). He went on to appear in such films as Franco Zeffirelli's star-studded TV miniseries *Jesus of Nazareth* (1977), George Roy Hill's *The Little Drummer Girl* (1984), Roman Polanski's *Frantic* (1988) and Guy Ritchie's unfortunate remake of *Swept Away* (2002). His Euro horror credentials include Ugo Liberatore's *Damned in Venice* (1978) and Augusto Caminito's *Nosferatu in Venice* (1988).

Notes:
1. Fenton, Harvey, ed., *Cannibal Holocaust and the Savage Cinema of Ruggero Deodato* (Godalming: FAB Press, 2nd edition, 2011), p. 29.
2. Palmerini, Luca M. and Gaetano Mistretta, *Spaghetti Nightmares* (Florida: Fantasma Books, 1996), p. 44.

Crime of Passion (Italy)

Aka *Delitto passionale*

Directed by Flavio Mogherini; Produced by Andrea Angioli and Remo Angioli; Screenplay by Flavio Mogherini and Daniele Stroppa; Director of Photography: Luigi Kuveiller; Editor: Adriano Tagliavia; Music by Gianni Ferrio

Main Players: Serena Grandi (Tania); Paul Martignetti (Inspector Ivan Zanev); Florinda Bolkan (Julia Yancheva); Fabio Testi (Peter Doncev); Anna Maria Petrova (Milena Radeva)

Home Video: Mya Communication (Region free DVD)

Peter Doncev's wife is killed following a tryst with her lover. The police investigate and discover that the marriage was on the rocks, that Peter was also being unfaithful and that the wife was planning a divorce. The plot thickens when it becomes evident that Peter has several mistresses; when one of them turns up dead, it seems likely that he is the culprit, but all may not be as it appears ...

Crime of Passion is Flavio Mogherini's second attempt at a *giallo*. It is not as accomplished as his first, **The Pyjama Girl Case** (1978), but it is still one of the more engaging thrillers of the period.

The film contains some erotic elements, but the overall emphasis is on plotting and characterization. The script by Mogherini and Daniele Stroppa (who also appears in the movie) leans a little too much toward melodrama, but it is intricately plotted and builds to a surprising finale. Sooner than bog the film down with too much softcore action, Mogherini only takes time out for a little bit of groping, and even this has legitimate relevance to the plot; many of the directors who started delving into the realm of "erotic *gialli*" would have been wise to have followed a similar path.

The location shooting in Bulgaria gives the film plenty of color. Mogherini's background as an art director and production designer manifests itself with the many striking set-ups and compositions, often employing eye-catching architecture and other "found" attributes. The movie looks great thanks to cinematographer Luigi Kuveiller, who works in harmony with Mogherini to give the picture a stylish sheen.

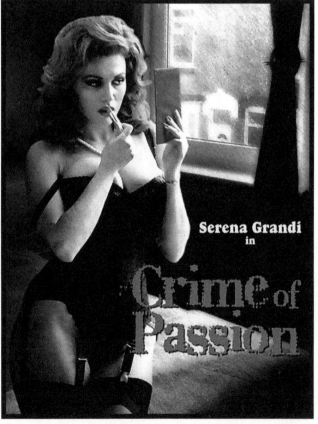

Cover for the American DVD release of *Crime of Passion* from Mya.

As noted above, too much melodrama dooms the film. The various reveals of the assorted characters' affairs reminds one a little too much of a soap opera, though the attention to characterization helps to take some of the curse off of this element. The character of Inspector Zanev, a rookie who is making his first major investigation on his own, drives the narrative. Zanev is an appealing character. His wide-eyed, somewhat naïve outlook is ultimately compromised when he delves deeper and deeper into the case. He forms a romantic interest in the main suspect's handicapped daughter, and this element inevitably plays out in a bittersweet fashion that gives the film an emotional kick. His relationship with his superior, Chief Inspector Costa, is good for some sly humor, as the older man takes glee in testing his young pupil and occasionally setting him up as the butt of a joke.

Mogherini does a decent job of keeping the material moving. His somewhat unorthodox approach to the *giallo* again manifests itself, as he avoids the usual excesses—the violence is muted and the erotic ingredients deliberately, even perversely, underplayed—in favor of focusing on developing the story and the character relationships. The end result may seem awfully tame if approached as a piece of exploitation, but it makes for a quietly effective thriller.

Serena Grandi is somewhat misleadingly billed as the star, though she gives a better performance here than she had in Lamberto Bava's ***Delirium: Photos of Gioia*** (1987). Grandi's presence no doubt helped to sell the film on the promise of sex, but she only has one such scene and remains covered up for much of the film. Even so, she gives an effective performance as one of Peter's mistresses. Peter is well played by Fabio Testi, making his first *giallo* appearance since ***Rings of Fear*** (1978), while another veteran of the golden age of the *gialli*, Florinda Bolkan (***Don't Torture a Duckling***, 1972), shows up as a bitchy diva with red herring written all over her. Paul Martignetti puts in a winning performance as Inspector Zanev. With his long hair done up in a ponytail, he makes for an unusual-looking policeman, but he brings an emotional vulnerability to the part which is unexpectedly moving. His movie career began with this film and does not appear to have lasted for very long.

The Girl From Cortina
(Italy)

Aka *La ragazza di Cortina*

Directed by Giancarlo Ferrando (as Maurizio Vanni); Produced by Sergio Martino; Screenplay by Maurizio Rasio and Piero Regnoli; Director of Photography: Giancarlo Ferrando; Editor: Eugenio Alabiso; Music by Luciano Michelini

Main Players: Vanessa Gravina (Mara); Isabel Russinova (Uba); Lorenzo Flaherty (Marco); Stefano Abbati (Carlo); Paolo Calissano (Sergio)

Italian *locandina* for *The Girl from Cortina*; artist unknown.

Home Video: Mya Communication (Region free DVD)

Mara runs away from her abusive husband Carlo. She fakes her own death and goes to a small village to live incognito, where she falls in with a sexually voracious couple, Uba and Sergio. Mara begins getting used to a happier existence when, suddenly, the past comes back to haunt her ...

This lame thriller is chiefly of note as one of the few modern attempts at the *Les Diaboliques* (1955) formula.

Veteran *giallo* filmmaker Sergio Martino and his brother, Luciano Martino, had a hand in developing the project: Sergio served as executive producer, while Luciano concocted the story. They entrusted directing duties to their longtime collaborator, cinematographer Giancarlo Ferrando, who hides behind the pseudonym of Maurizio Vanni on the picture. The end result is not entirely worthless, but it fails to bring anything new to the formula and feels particularly old-hat in this modern *milieu*.

Another film can be seen as an influence: Joseph Ruben's *Sleeping with the Enemy* (1991). This very mainstream hit stars Julia Roberts as a woman who escapes from abusive lover Patrick Bergin (chewing the scenery and easily walking away with the film), only to have him crop back up in her life just as she is on the verge of finding happiness. The film was one of several generally mediocre American thrillers that found unexpected box-office favor at the time (*Single White Female*, 1992, being another); needless to say, they do not really hold up very well today—and it is hardly surprising that a film looking to copy its basic set-up would suffer the same fate.

Truth be told, the film starts off promisingly enough, if one can get past the laughable pixie-cut wig that leading lady Vanessa Gravina is saddled with in the early scenes, but it soon wears out its welcome. There is far too much dreary chatter and the supporting characters are far too boring—and transparently manipulative—to engender much interest or empathy. The surprises are telegraphed from a mile off and the finale borders on the ludicrous.

Ferrando's direction is blandly efficient, but nothing more. He creates the occasional arresting set-up, but much of the picture is shot like a TV movie of the week. Luciano Michelini's score works hard to try and create an air of suspense, but it only comes off as strained.

The dull cast is headed by pretty but vapid Vanessa Gravina. Her somewhat stiff performance deprives the film of an engaging heroine. The character of Mara is all surface glamour. She poses and pouts, but never succeeds in getting the audience to understand her or feel for her plight. She was born in Milan in 1974 and made her movie debut in 1985. She has been a prolific presence in Italian films and television but is generally celebrated more for her great beauty as opposed to her thespian skills. Isabel Russinova plays Mara's partner in crime. The latter is saddled with some hideous looking fake tattoos (at least one *hopes* that they are fake!) and is similarly vapid in her portrayal; the role called for a bit of shading, but Russinova is ill-equipped for the task, making her role in the plot much too obvious from the get-go. She was born in Bulgaria in 1958 and emigrated to Italy, where she made her film debut in 1982. In addition to her role in this one, she also appeared in Lamberto Bava's made-for-TV horror flick *Dinner with a Vampire* (1987). Russinova has

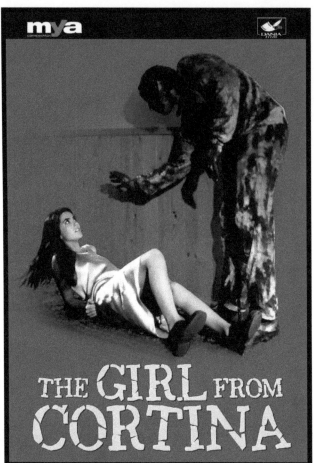

Cover for the American DVD release of *The Girl from Cortina* from Mya; artist unknown.

been relatively inactive in the new millennium, but Gravina remains a familiar presence in the Italian film and television scene.

Director Ferrando, as previously noted, is the longtime cinematographer of choice for Sergio Martino. They collaborated on such efforts as *All the Colors of the Dark* (1972), *Your Vice is a Locked Room and Only I Have the Key* (1972), *Torso* (1973), *The Suspicious Death of a Minor* (1975) and *Mountain of the Cannibal God* (1978), among others. Ferrando got his start as a production manager in the 1950s, and then became a camera operator in the 1960s; he made the transition to cinematography in 1972 and continues to work in that capacity to the present day. *The Girl from Cortina* is his only effort as a director.

Madness (Italy)

Aka *Occhi senza volto*

Directed by Bruno Mattei (as Herik Montgomery); Produced by Mimmo Scavia; Screenplay by Lorenzo De Luca; Director of Photography: Luigi Ciccarese; Editor: Bruno Mattei; Music by Flipper Music (Library)

Main Players: Monica Seller (Giovanna Dei); Gabriele Gori (Nico Vannelli); Emy Valentino (Emy); Achille Brugnini (Marzio Mannino); Fausto Lombardi (Lorenzo Calligari)

A maniac is killing babysitters and gouging out their eyes. The press and the police blame Giovanna Dei for inspiring the killings, as they seem to be modeled after the exploits of her controversial comic book character "Doctor Dark." Giovanna is pressured to end the publication but refuses to do so, and the killings continue ...

The Italian title evokes Georges Franju's masterpiece *Eyes Without a Face* (1960), but nothing could be further removed from it than this flea-bitten *giallo* by exploitation guru Bruno Mattei.

The screenplay by Lorenzo De Luca contains seeds of promise, but the film is so poorly made and acted that it ends up making no impression whatsoever. It continues the thematic argument initiated by Dario Argento's *Tenebrae* (1982), albeit in a rather clumsy way. One exchange between Giovanna and an eager reporter is an almost direct copy of a similar moment in Argento's film: "If they kill someone with an electric drill, do you take it out on Black and Decker?" This echoes a virtually identical moment in Argento's meta-*giallo* where Peter Neal (Anthony Franciosa) asks Detective Germani, "When somebody is killed with a Smith & Wesson revolver, do you go interrogate the president of Smith & Wesson?" But while Argento's film was slick and playful, Mattei's is merely tedious.

The real-life controversy over violent/sexy comic strips (*fumetti neri*) forms part of the plot, as the heroine, Giovanna, is responsible for one titled "Doctor Dark." The *fumetti neri* scandal came to a head in the 1960s, thanks to such comic-strips as *Kriminal* and *Diabolik*, but this was undoubtedly too esoteric a reference on the part of the filmmakers. Instead, it seems likely to have been inspired by the more prescient (for the time) backlash against the popular series *Dylan Dog*, which was flying off the shelves at Italian newsstands at the time this film was in production—indeed, the character of Doctor Dark even shares the same initials as this character. Doctor Dark is a psychopath dressed in black who goes around slashing-up young women and gouging their eyes out. This spills into reality when the killer begins adopting a similar *modus operandi*. The press wastes no time crucifying Giovanna for this, but the theme is only superficially explored. Any attempt at probing into the genre's excesses are done in by the lethargic filmmaking, suggesting that there may have been a better movie to be made from the material, but that Mattei simply was not capable of delivering the goods.

The film is very much up (or rather, *down*) to Mattei's usual standards. The cinematography is flat and ugly. The actors either overact like mad or are so wooden that they seem to disappear into the scenery. The pacing is slow. The special effects work is less-than-special. Shock effects are clumsily staged. The score comprises stock cues from older Italian flicks, including Mel Welles' *Lady Frankenstein* (1971), but this merely serves to remind one of better films from a better era of Italian moviemaking.

Bruno Mattei was born in Rome in 1931. He grew up in a cinema environment; his father was an editor who owned an editing studio. The younger Mattei started off as an editing room assistant before becoming a cutter in his own right, making his official debut in the early 1960s. He edited numerous Italian productions and also did the Italian edits of numerous international co-productions, including Jess Franco's *Count Dracula* (1970). He began directing in 1970 and utilized a number of pseudonyms, including Jordan B. Matthews, Jimmy Matheus and Vincent Dawn. He tried his hand at various genres, including Nazisploitation (*Private House of the SS*, 1977), women-in-prison flicks (*Women's Camp 119*, 1977) and softcore (*Emanuelle and the Erotic Nights*, 1978), but connoisseurs of the "so

bad it's good" school of cinema have enshrined him for his *Dawn of the Dead* rip-off *Hell of the Living Dead* (1980) and his post-apocalyptic shocker, *Rats: Nights of Terror* (1984). Amazingly, he did not start to dabble in the *giallo* until the 1990s. *Dangerous Attraction* (1993) contained elements of the genre, but was closer to the trend of softcore erotic thrillers indebted to the success of films like *Basic Instinct* (1992). His next and final *giallo* was **Omicidio al telefono** (1994). Mattei continued making movies into the 2000s, though his final works were shot on video. He died in 2007 at the age of 75.

DVD cover art for *Madness*; artist unknown. Director Bruno Mattei is billed as Herik Montgomery on this release.

The Room Next Door (Italy)
Aka *La stanza accanto*

Directed by Fabrizio Laurenti; Produced by Antonio Avati and Aurelio De Laurentiis; Screenplay by Pupi Avati; Director of Photography: Cesare Bastelli; Music by Carlo Siliotto

Main Players: Mark Benninghoffen (Martin Yakobowsky); Thomas Patrick (Ray Watts); Mary Sellers (Grace Watts); Heather Prete (Kate); David Ghilardi (Konrad); Coralina Cataldi-Tassoni (Nurse)

Export poster art for *The Room Next Door*; artist unknown.

1940: Martin Yakobowsky is sent to a small suburb in Iowa to defend some Polish immigrants who are in danger of losing their land to an unscrupulous congressman. His return to the town inspires mixed feelings among the locals, as he is originally from the area and was mixed up in a murder case that resulted in the execution of a man many believe to have been innocent. As Martin begins digging into the past, he discovers some things which threaten to push him into madness ...

Some viewers have compared *The Room Next Door* to Pupi Avati's masterpiece **The House with Laughing Windows** (1976). There are certainly points of comparison that make this inevitable. After all, Avati co-wrote the screenplay and the film shares a similar slow-burn pace which flies in the face of genre convention.

The movie explores some interesting thematic terrain. Like Avati's **Tutti defunti ... tranne i morti** (1977) and Francesco Barilli's **Pensione paura** (1978), it is one of the relatively few *giallo* period pieces; all three films are set during the era of World War II, though the war itself is downplayed in all three. *The Room Next Door* comes closest to explicitly examining the way in which the conflict was tearing communities apart, however. The story is set in a small rural populace mostly comprising displaced Polish immigrants.

The specter of the war looms in the background, given that the action unfolds prior to the involvement of the U.S., but the tight-knit community is surviving in its newfound environment largely because of its own devotion to one another. In this new land of hope and opportunity, the community finds oppression and bigotry. The local politicians seek to take advantage of the people, and they are willing to stop at nothing in order to secure another plot of land for their own profit. This serves to undermine the romanticized image of the American Dream but proves to be merely a subtext and does not dominate much of the picture.

The narrative thrust is on the mysterious murder and the gradual mental disintegration of its protagonist. Martin Yakobowsky is a skilled attorney, but when it is revealed that he had a role (however marginal) in a gruesome killing 15 years earlier, this threatens to destroy his credibility. Martin has long since suppressed his memories of the incident, so his investigation has as much to do with self-discovery as anything else. The film focuses on the accumulation of details, which become increasingly macabre, finally culminating with his grisly discovery of a bottled-up fetus, which the killer had ripped from the womb of the victim. As Martin comes to question his own sanity and innocence, the film becomes more akin to the *giallo*. The early scenes would seem to have nothing to do with the realm of Italian thrillers, but as the story unfolds it certainly begins to delve into the genre. As usual for Avati, even though he did not direct this time around, the film manages to play with conventions as a means of catching the audience off-guard. Just as one begins to believe that the movie could not possibly be connected to the *giallo*, all bets are off and things build to a memorably macabre finale.

Avati's presence is felt in the slow steady pace and the attention to detail, but director Fabrizio Laurenti favors a somewhat stodgy approach that saps the film of some of its impact. Laurenti was clearly aiming for something classy here, and while it makes for a welcome contrast to the more over-the-top sleazy and exploitative thrillers of the period, it does make the end result a little heavy going at times. The American locales are appropriately bland, emphasizing the notion of the banality of evil, but the film does not come close to replicating the ever-increasing sense of claustrophobia that marked **The House with Laughing Windows**. Even so, it is a well-crafted picture with some nice cinematography from Cesare Bastelli and a subtly effective soundtrack courtesy of Carlo Siliotto.

Mark Benninghoffen heads the cast in the role of Martin. Benninghoffen's wholesome, slightly boring exterior recalls Lino Capolicchio in Avati's earlier film, but he fails to come to grips with the darker attributes of the character. He started off as a theater actor, then made his film debut in the early 1990s. He would later guest star on a number of popular American TV shows, including *The Larry Sanders Show* and *Frasier*, before going into the world of advertising; today he works primarily as a voice-over actor. The supporting cast includes a few *giallo* veterans, including Mary Sellers (whose genre credits number among them ***Stage Fright***, 1987, and ***Eyewitness***, 1990) and Coralina Cataldi-Tassoni (***Opera***, 1987).

Director Fabrizio Laurenti was born in Rome in 1956. He broke into films as a writer and director in the mid-1980s. His earlier credits include *Witchery* (1988) and *Creepers* (1993). *The Room Next Door* is almost certainly his best work as a director, and some of this can undoubtedly be attributed to Avati's input. His recent (sporadic) work has been in Italian television.

Avati, incidentally, would later direct a very fine horror film titled *The Hideout* (2007). Often bracketed as a *giallo*, it is more of a Southern Gothic with an old-fashioned locked room mystery theme. It, too, was set in Iowa and can be seen as expanding on some of the themes found in this earlier film.

1995

The Killer Wore Yellow Shoes (Italy)

Aka *L'assassino è quello con le scarpe gialle*

Directed by Filippo Ottoni; Produced by Guido De Laurentiis, Fulvio Lucisano and Leo Pescarolo; Screenplay by Roberto Ciufoli, Francesca Draghetti, Tiziana Foschi, Pino Insegno and Filippo Ottoni; Director of Photography: Raffaele Mertes; Editor: Enzo Meniconi; Music by Stefano Mainetti

Main Players: Roberto Ciufoli (Roberto); Francesca Draghetti (Francesca); Tiziana Foschi (Tiziana); Pino Insegno (Pino); Dario Cantarelli (Otto)

Roberto is a failure, and his aunt, just about to turn 100, decides to motivate him. In order to inherit her vast fortune, he will have to succeed in re-opening the family theater, which has been closed for years, and put on a successful stage play. Roberto hires a theatrical troupe to mount a performance of Hamlet, *but as they rehearse, a killer begins knocking the various players off...*

The *giallo* comes in for another ribbing with *The Killer Wore Yellow Shoes*. Like so many parodies, however, it falls short due to a tendency toward overkill ... if you will pardon the expression.

Profucer/co-writer/actor Roberto Ciufoli developed the film as a vehicle for the popular comedy quartet "Premiata Ditta," of which he was a member along with Francesca Draghetti, Pino Insegno and Tiziana Foschi. The troupe was formed in 1986 and enjoyed lasting popularity until 2006. Chrome-domed Ciufoli takes center stage as the cowardly Roberto, while the other members of the group fill the other major roles. Insegno is the would-be private eye who

watches too many old *noir* films, Draghetti plays a plucky reporter and Foschi is the actress cast as Ophelia, who is determined that her character should not die in act four. Humor is inevitably one of the more subjective arts, so it comes as no surprise that their propensity for mugging for the camera can be as off-putting for some as it is amusing for others. Chances are if the troupe had been reined-in a little more for some of the film, their manic antics might have come off more successfully in the long run. Sadly, all four of them are operating at an extreme level from the get-go ... and things only get worse as the film unfolds.

The story certainly displays a familiarity with the genre and its trappings, which is no small wonder given the presence of director/co-writer Filippo Ottoni. Born in 1938, the latter co-wrote the screenplay for Mario Bava's ***Twitch of the Death Nerve*** (1971), and while he was not exactly as well versed in the tradition as, say, Ernesto Gastaldi, he nevertheless had the experience of working on one of the genre's key titles. The comically overstated brutality of Bava's film finds its way into this one as well, notably during one of the movie's few genuinely funny vignettes, where a hapless production worker is accidentally beheaded in place of the inept Roberto; the blood spurting from the obvious dummy as it flaps its arms in despair also recalls a marvelous

Italian DVD cover for *The Killer Wore Yellow Shoes.*

moment in Paul Morrissey's horror spoof *Flesh for Frankenstein* (1973), as well as a comparable scene in the brilliant *Monty Python and the Holy Grail* (1975).

Unfortunately, the humor is geared so much toward broad overstatement that it soon becomes grating. Everything from the music score by Stefano Mainetti to the performances of the entire cast scream "this is funny," but a more low-key approach would have been appreciated. The only thing lacking is a laugh track—and thank goodness for that. That said, there are a few chuckles, some in the form of sight gags (the attempts at killing Roberto invariably end up with somebody inadvertently stepping in the way and getting killed themselves) and some through verbal humor (the similarity between the name Otto and the Italian word for eight, "*otto*," results in some amusing miscommunication during the final performance of *Hamlet*). A few more giggles and a little less strained overacting may have made the film one of the more successful *giallo* send-ups; as it stands, however, it is pretty much only recommended for the diehard completists.

Omicidio al telefono (Italy)

Directed by Bruno Mattei (as Frank Klox); Produced by Ninì Grassia; Screenplay by Ninì Grassia and Bruno Mattei; Director of Photography: Luigi Ciccarese; Editor: Bruno Mattei; Music by Ninì Grassia and Aldo Tamborelli

Main Players: Carla Salerno (Lorena); Stefania Mega (Consuelo); Antonio Zequila (Massimo); Pascal Persiano (Dante)

A homicidal maniac in a clown mask targets the women who work at an erotic telephone service. The police are stymied, so they send in two of their female detectives to work undercover. As they become entangled in various relationships as a result of the nature of their undercover work, the killings continue ...

Bruno Mattei strikes again with *Omicidio al telefono*. The title looks back at one of the granddaddies of the genre, "The Telephone" from Mario Bava's **The Three Faces of Fear** (1963), but it is unlikely that Bava could have foreseen where the genre was headed when he made that film!

Like Mattei's previous thriller **Madness** (1994), the film is noteworthy for its utter lack of finesse. Mattei displays absolutely zero skill when it comes to building mood and suspense. Dialogue scenes drag on and on, and the attempts at shock effects again fall flat, partly because the make-up effects are not very effective, as Mattei dwells on things for far too long. The overall impression is of trying to pad the film out to an appropriate feature length, which merely serves to make it feel much longer than it really is.

The seedy backdrop makes room for plenty of would-be steamy encounters. The problem with this is simple—the sex is simply not all that sexy. A director with a little more feel for the erotic and the sensual may have been able to inject a little spice into this kind of material, but given Mattei's "point and shoot" aesthetic, this simply does not work. The emphasis on sex threatens to drown the *giallo* elements, but the presence of the masked killer, the murder set pieces and the final surprise reveal ensures that it remains true to the genre as a whole. The film also has some slasher elements, with the killer's clown mask quoting the opening of John Carpenter's *Halloween* (1978); but the film seems to have a hard time settling on what it really wants to be. Other *gialli* had a similar crisis of identity, but *Omicidio al telefono* is all the more frustrating because it fails in doing justice to any of its disparate elements.

Ultimately, Mattei's lack of feeling for the genre is evident from the get-go, and as such it should not come as a surprise that he would not continue to mine this particular field. The popularity of the format was already very much on the wane anyway, and his own attempts certainly were not going to do anything toward reviving its favor with audiences. Mattei would spend the rest of his career exploring seedier excesses in various shot-on-video productions. His two genre efforts do not represent the nadir of his career—or of the *giallo* in general—but fans of his work will likely find them lacking the inspired lunacy of his more popular titles like *Hell of the Living Dead* (1980).

DVD cover art for Italian release of *Omicidio al telefono*; artist unknown.

The Strange Story of Olga O (Italy)

Aka *La strana storia di Olga 'O'*

Directed by Antonio Bonifacio; Produced by Andrea Angioli and Remo Angioli; Screenplay by Mario Cociani and Daniele Stroppa, from a story by Ernesto Gastaldi; Director of Photography: Luigi Kuveiller; Editor: Adriano Tagliavia; Music by Marco Rossetti (as Mark Ross)

Main Players: Serena Grandi (Olga Roli); Stéphane Ferrara (Inspector Michael Manning); Florinda Bolkan (Sheila Altman); Daniela Poggi (Isabel); David Brandon (Paolo Roli); Dobromir Manev (Dr. Carlo Ferranti)

Former exotic dancer Olga finds herself being terrorized by a psychopath who knows about her tragic past. Her husband, Paolo, attempts to comfort her, but the line between fantasy and reality begins to blur as she becomes more stressed. As if the harassment is not enough, the psychopath also begins killing off the people Olga is close to ...

The *Les Diaboliques* (1955) formula gets another going-over in *The Strange Story of Olga O*. True to the general tone of the era, there is plenty of emphasis on sex and sleaze, and once one understands what direction the plot is headed, surprises are few and far between.

Ernesto Gastaldi developed the story, but the finished script lacks his customary finesse. Writers Mario Cociani and Daniele Stroppa play up the soap opera angle of the plot as Olga deals with ex-flames, bitchy former colleagues and grief over a childhood trauma. Unfortunately, the characters are a dull lot. Olga is a prima donna who inspires no audience empathy, her husband is so transparently shifty that he is either an obvious red herring or an even more obvious villain and her ex-lover, Inspector Manning, is a stereotypically macho American TV-style policeman. In lieu of interesting characters worth investing some time in, one would hope for strong plotting and good narrative twists; sadly, these elements are also in short order. The finale packs in quite a few would-be surprises, but they are far from earth shattering, and anybody with much of a background in watching these types of films will likely figure it out all before the testosterone-heavy Inspector does.

Director Antonio Bonifacio was, of course, no stranger to this type of erotic thriller. His previous *giallo*, **Scandal in Black** (1990), also borrowed heavily from Clouzot's masterpiece and was similarly underwhelming. He piles on the typical 1990s aesthetics, with plenty of venetian blind lighting and unduly dramatic (and overly drawn out) slow-motion imagery, but it does not add much punch to the proceedings. Luigi Kuveiller provides some professional photography, but it is a far cry from his atmospheric work on such *giallo* classics as **A Lizard in a Woman's Skin** (1971) and **Deep Red** (1975). Marco Rossetti's score is bland and would not sound out of place in a typical direct-to-video piece of softcore.

Italian DVD cover for *The Strange Story of Olga O*; artist unknown.

The cast includes a number of familiar faces, but nobody really rises to the occasion here. Serena Grandi once again relies on striking poses and baring her breasts in the role of Olga, while David Brandon plays up his character's more ambiguous traits. Florinda Bolkan shows up to play one of Olga's friends, but this sort of film really is not worthy of her talents.

Ultimately, *The Strange Story of Olga O* is far from the worst of the erotica-heavy thrillers of the 1990s, but it does serve as a depressing reminder of how low the standards had slipped by this stage in the game; sadly, there would still be worse to come.

1996

Fatal Frames (Italy)

Aka *Fatal frames: Fotogrammi mortali*

Directed by Al Festa; Produced by Stefania Stella; Screenplay by Alessandro Monese; Director of Photography: Giuseppe Bernardini; Editor: Maurizio Baglivo; Music by Al Festa

Main Players: Stefania Stella (Herself); Rick Gianasi (Alex Ritt); David Warbeck (Commissioner Bonelli); Donald Pleasence (Professor Robinson); Ugo Pagliai (Commissioner Valneti); Alida Valli (Countess Alessandra Mirafiori); Geoffrey Copleston (Mr. Fairbrain); Linnea Quigley (Wendy Williams); Rossano Brazzi (Dr. Lucidi); Ciccio Ingrassia (Beggar)

Home Video: Synapse (Region 1 DVD)

American music video director Alex Ritt is hired to helm the latest Stefania Stella video in Rome. While there, he witnesses a brutal killing. The police are called, but by the time they arrive on the scene the body has gone and there are no traces of blood evident. Commissioner Bonelli thinks Alex is going insane, but tries to placate him as best he can. When Alex witnesses another murder and the same thing happens again, it becomes evident that something is amiss ...

Fatal Frames was hyped as the next big thing in *gialli*, but the film failed to live up to expectations. It has a devoted cult following in some circles, but for most viewers it remains something of a tolerance test.

Music video director Al Festa and his wife Stefania Stella conceived the movie. The two had already collaborated on

Foreign DVD release of *Fatal Frames*; artist unknown.

numerous music videos but were looking to make a splash in the film market. Looking back over the back catalogue of Italian *gialli* and realizing that the genre was in a slump, they decided to pool their resources and come up with a film that would reflect the style and tone of the classics of the 1970s, while still incorporating their own background in the music scene. It would prove to be an uneasy alliance, and the picture feels very much like a vanity project designed to show off Stella as the next big sex symbol of Italian cinema.

The hackneyed story, devised by Festa himself but executed in screenplay form by Alessandro Monese, is something of a grab bag of ideas culled from earlier thrillers. The notion of the American in Rome dates all the way back to Mario Bava's ***The Girl Who Knew Too Much*** (1963), as does the concept of the protagonist seeing a murder and not being able to convince anybody (especially the police) that it really took place. The murderer's garb is explicitly modeled on the classic *giallo* image of the killer in black, complete with a mask and an oversized fedora. The murder set pieces ape the designer deaths featured in the films of Dario Argento. Festa also draws some stylistic touches from the hit Italian miniseries *Il segno del comando* (1971), a more conventional mystery story (not a proper *giallo*) which was filmed on some of the same scenic locales in Rome and had a similarly dreamy ambience. Unfortunately, all the references in the world are not enough to make for a compelling thriller. Festa and Monese apparently forgot to include interesting characters, since the ones on display here are anything but. The bizarre casting does not help matters either, but more on that in a bit.

Festa stuffs the film with well-known cult movie actors, but he gives them very little to do. One is reminded of director Rob Zombie's affinity for casting actors familiar from 1970s genre cinema. It is all well and good to put these people in the picture, but to squander their talents rather defeats the purpose. The film is carried (if one can even say that) by Stefania Stella and Rick Gianasi, but neither of them come close to giving a satisfactory performance. Festa is clearly taken with his wife and expects the audience to feel the same, but she makes a very poor impression indeed. The proceedings occasionally screech to a halt to indulge in some music videos of Stella, thus furthering the impression that Festa is truly trying to sell her as a major creative presence, but these irritating vignettes do nothing but slow down the already glacial pacing. Whether she is making love or strutting her stuff while singing or being menaced in a decorative fashion, Stella does nothing but pose and make faces; her attempts at emoting are often laughable and her awkward delivery suggests that she was not entirely comfortable acting in English. American actor Gianasi is every bit as hopeless. With his beefy physique and flowing locks, he looks like having just stepped off of the cover of a Harlequin romance, and, like Stella, he does not appear to know the difference between posing for the camera and giving a real performance. He wanders through much of the film in a daze, but when he is required to cut loose and show some real emotion, the results are … less than convincing. The supporting cast promises much, but this is where the film is really at its most unforgivable. Apart from David Warbeck, who has plenty of screen time, the likes of Donald Pleasence, Rossano Brazzi, Ciccio Ingrassia, Angus Scrimm, Alida Valli and Linnea Quigley have virtually nothing to do. Warbeck appears to have been wise to what he was appearing in, and he responds with an over-baked performance. He frowns a lot and shouts many of his lines, desperately trying to add a little life to the film, but it is all for naught. Pleasence has very little to do, and most of his lines are dubbed by another actor (though one gratuitous flashback appears to have had usable onset dialogue recording, as it sounds like his real voice), while Valli, Brazzi, Ingrassia and the rest appear to have filmed their scenes in a day or two, tops.

Festa's direction is laughably overstated. He tries his best to ape the aesthetics of Dario Argento, Mario Bava, Lucio Fulci and other past *giallo* masters, but he comes up way short. The film is lit and edited very much like a music video, and this should not be too surprising, given his background in that field. Festa's attempts at jazzing things up with shock cuts, quick zooms and rapid camera movement come off as an affectation, and his sense of pacing and tempo is way off. Some of the images are striking, thanks largely to cinematographer Giuseppe Bernardini's admittedly overzealous use of colored lighting, but much of the film has all the mood and atmosphere of a TV commercial. Festa goes for some gory shock effects during the various murder scenes and the special effects are admittedly well-done, but these scenes are too few and far between. Much of the film is comprised of boring dialogue exchanges between vapid characters, and when we get to the numerous music video clips or the laughable attempt at eroticism in one love scene (in which Stella quite visibly keeps her underwear on), it is more than evident that things are not likely to improve much. The absolute nadir of the film, however, occurs when Pleasence's character is called back to the United States to work on another killing spree; as the veteran actor (or rather, his double) shuffles off, it is accompanied by a bit of John Carpenter's iconic theme music for *Halloween* (1978). Whether Carpenter was paid for this little bit of homage is unknown, but it is an embarrassing moment for all concerned.

Indeed, the film is much more interesting from a production standpoint. The film began production in 1993 and continued filming into 1994; at that point, financing dried up and the production had to be shut down while additional funds were secured. During that lull in filming, Brazzi passed away in late 1994; Pleasence followed him in early 1995. Festa and Stella were able to secure the financing needed to complete the film from Silvio Berlusconi's Mediaset production company, but with so much of the material involving Brazzi and Pleasence unfinished, some rewriting needed to be done. Their plan involved creating a new character that could be in charge of the investigation; David Warbeck was drafted at this stage in the game to basically cover up the damage and play the scenes originally marked for the two late actors. The film was finally released in 1996 to blistering reviews and some sources listed it as Pleasence's last film. In point of fact, while it was his last released film, he had crammed in a couple of other titles prior to his death, including *Halloween: The Curse of Michael Myers* (1995), which would prove to be his "official" final credit. Festa dedicated the film to the memory of Pleasence and Brazzi, a nice gesture, but it is not likely that either actor would have regarded the project as a feather in their caps. The film also marks the swansong for Ciccio Ingrassia (who cameos as a bum), while Warbeck

Lobby card for *Fatal Frames*: An atmospheric view of the killer stalking his latest victim.

and Valli would only go on to appear in a few more films; Warbeck would die in 1997 from cancer, while Ingrassia and Valli followed in 2003 and 2006, respectively. Festa's original edit of the film ran in the range of 2 hours and 20 minutes (far eclipsing the length of any other *giallo*, unless we count the full-length miniseries versions of such titles as **The Scorpion with Two Tails**,1982 and **Private Crimes**, 1993) but was cut down to a still-excessive but more manageable 2-hour-and-5-minute edit, which is the one that is most commonly available.

Al Festa was born in Rome in 1958. He started off as a musician and began scoring films (including Claudio Fragasso's *Zombie 4: After Death*, 1989) in the late 1980s. He made his debut as a director with *Gipsy Angel* (1990), but his hopes for the success of *Fatal Frames* did not pan out and he walked away from directing movies for a number of years; he recently completed a film called *The Hermit* (2012).

Squillo (Italy)

Directed by Carlo Vanzina; Produced by Giovanni Di Clemente; Screenplay by Carlo Vanzina, Enrico Vanzina and Franco Ferrini; Director of Photography: Luigi Kuveiller; Editor: Sergio Montanari; Music by Pino Donaggio

Main Players: Jennifer Driver (Maria); Raz Degan (Tony); Paul Freeman (Marco); Bianca Koedam (Eva); Antonio Ballerio (Fabio); Alessandra Chiti (Sonja)

Home Video: CDI (Region 2 DVD)

Eva and Maria are sisters from a poor farm family in Poland. Eva immigrates to Italy, where she becomes a successful high-class callgirl. Maria comes to visit, unaware of her sister's line of work. When Eva goes missing, Maria goes undercover to find her. Meanwhile, the people who try to help her in her quest begin to die mysteriously as well ...

Carlo Vanzina's *Squillo* (the title translates to "ring," which has a nice double meaning once one has seen the film) continues the director's trend toward mainstream-style thrillers with a classy veneer. It does not work nearly so well as his best film in the genre, **Nothing Underneath** (1985), but it is preferable to his other *gialli*.

In a weird coincidence, the film continues the theme of Polish immigrants floundering in a new environment, which informed Fabrizio Laurenti's **The Room Next Door** (1994). The socio-political commentary of that earlier film is not explored in much depth here, but it is nevertheless part of the film's narrative. Eva leaves Poland in search of success and finds it as a prostitute. She seems happy in her work, but is careful to shield the reality from her naïve younger sister. Describing herself as an interpreter for wealthy businessmen, she sells her body for high prices and becomes accustomed to a lavish lifestyle. This is

DVD release for *Squillo*; artist unknown.

not the subject of derision on the part of the filmmakers, but the implication is that in the movie's cold and harsh *milieu*, sex is simply a commodity and emotional attachments are fleeting at best. In one scene, Eva is being taken by taxi to an appointment—a street person tries washing the windshield, much to the driver's consternation, but Eva recognizes the young man as a fellow Pole and pays him handsomely for his efforts. Eva's newfound lifestyle may be lavish, but she remembers the lengthy period of struggle and hardship that she endured, and she is not about to turn her back on others who are going through similar troubles. This helps to humanize the character, thus making the audience emotionally invested in her disappearance. Similarly, the younger sister,

Maria, is equally sympathetic. She carries herself with a wide-eyed *naïveté*, but she is not incapable of looking after herself either. When she goes undercover to find her sister, she initially does not realize the reality of what she is getting herself into, but her strength and determination compel her to push forward. The film therefore provides an outsider's view of life in bucolic Italy. The glittering surfaces and ancient architecture are appropriately seductive, but as the story unfolds it is revealed to be a mere façade covering a seedier reality.

The actual thriller elements are extremely muted, and it could be argued that the film is more of a borderline example of the genre, but things do ramp up considerably in the last act and there are some good surprises in store. Vanzina does not dwell on the more sensational or exploitative dimensions of the material either. Nudity is kept to a bare minimum, sex is merely hinted at and the low body count steers clear of gory excess. Instead, the director—working from a screenplay he co-authored with his brother Enrico and seasoned *giallo* scribe Franco Ferrini—focuses more on characterization and building suspense. Happily, he is largely successful in his aim, making the film an enjoyable diversion.

Jennifer Driver gives a good performance as Maria. The beautiful actress dazzles as she undergoes the transformation from "normal" country girl to undercover hooker, and she is good at conveying the character's mixed emotions. Born in Spain in 1973, Driver made her film debut with *Squillo*, though she had already posed for *Playboy* in the September 1993 issue. Her later credits were relatively sparse and include guest spots on some American TV shows and an appearance as Axl Rose's girlfriend in a Guns N' Roses video. Raz Degan plays the Italian policeman who puts his neck on the line to help Maria. If one can get past his hopelessly dated 1990s pretty boy appearance (designer stubble, ponytail and earring), Degan actually gives a decent performance. The character is something of a cliché—the renegade cop who plays by his own rules and flies in the face of his superiors—but the actor humanizes him. He was born in Israel in 1968 and got his start as a male model before entering the film industry. *Squillo* marked his big-screen debut as well, and he would go on to appear in Claudio Fragasso's borderline *giallo Coppia omicida* (1998), Julie Taymor's *Titus* (1999) and Oliver Stone's *Alexander* (2004), among other films. Paul Freeman plays the distinguished businessman who gets mixed up in the plot. His screen time is limited, but he lends a touch of class and gives a convincing performance. Born in Hertfordshire in 1943, he got his start as a stage actor before starting to show up on British television in the 1960s. He made an appearance in John Mackenzie's *The Long Good Friday* (1980) before beating out Giancarlo Giannini to play his most iconic role, the villainous Belaq in Steven Spielberg's *Raiders of the Lost Ark* (1981). He remains active in films and television.

The Stendhal Syndrome
(Italy)

Aka *La sindrome di Stendhal; El síndrome de Stendhal; Das Stendhal Syndrom; Le syndrome de Stendhal*

Directed by Dario Argento; Produced by Dario Argento and Giuseppe Colombo; Screenplay by Dario Argento; Director of Photography: Giuseppe Rotunno; Editor: Angelo Nicolini; Music by Ennio Morricone

Main Players: Asia Argento (Detective Anna Manni); Thomas Kretschmann (Alfredo Grossi); Marco Leonardi (Marco Longhi); Julien Lambroschini (Marie); Paolo Bonacelli (Dr. Cavanna); Luigi Diberti (Inspector Manetti); John Quentin (Anna's father); Sonia Topazio (Victim in Florence)

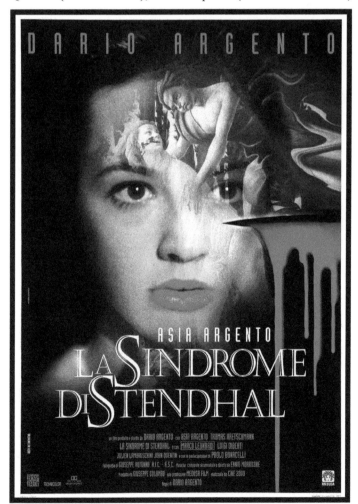

Italian poster for *The Stendhal Syndrome*; artwork by Immagine e Strategia.

Home Video: Blue Underground (Region 1 DVD and All region Blu-ray)

Detective Anna Manni goes to Florence to investigate a series of rapes which have culminated in a murder. While there, she succumbs to an unusual psychological disorder known as The Stendhal Syndrome. The psychopath, Alfredo Grossi, takes advantage of her weakened condition and kidnaps and rapes her. Anna is able to escape, but the combination of the psychological condition and the trauma of her attack threaten to push her into madness ...

Trauma (1993) had been designed to be Dario Argento's entry into the American filmmaking scene, but it ended up becoming a disappointing experience for the director and it underperformed (badly) at the box-office. Even so, Argento plugged along and originally planned for his next project, *The Stendhal Syndrome*, to be shot in Phoenix, Arizona with Bridget Fonda tapped to play the lead. Disagreements and a growing air of resentment on Argento's part toward the American method of filmmaking caused him to change his mind, however, and the movie would be heavily publicized as Argento's return to basics. As he told Alan Jones:

> I don't really like American movies. They're too soft and always deal with the obvious. [...] I also got tired of being told by American casting directors that no American actress would play the "Woman-in-Peril" scenes as written. Well, fuck the lot of them! America can screw itself. Italy is where I belong, where my fans want me to be and where I'm staying.[1]

The Stendhal Syndrome therefore grew out of a feeling of rebellion. Having been constrained by censorship concerns on his two American projects—the other being the Edgar Allan Poe potpourri *Two Evil Eyes* (1990), co-directed by George A. Romero—the director elected to cut loose with this picture. He originally devised the story (with Franco Ferrini) with an eye toward again "coloring within the lines" of the American filmmaking system, but once he made the final decision to return to home base, all bets were off.

> *The Stendhal Syndrome* is a return to the type of strong material I used in the seventies. As shooting has progressed, my gut feeling has made me think this will be as gory and as hardcore as **Tenebrae**.[2]

If anything, Argento was underestimating himself: *The Stendhal Syndrome* would outdo his earlier films and emerge as the darkest, most despairing and most unsettling effort he had made to date.

Argento drew inspiration from a book of the same title by Graziella Magherini, which was published in 1989. The director claims to have become aware of it while working in the U.S., and he recognized in it a good set-up for a thriller. The book is not a narrative, *per se*, but rather an examination of the fanciful-sounding but quite real psychological disorder that affects people who have an adverse reaction to great works of art. Magherini, a psychologist based in Florence, traced the condition back to the French writer Stendhal (real name Henri-Marie Beyle, 1783-1842), who described the phenomenon in his diary. Psychologists recognize that the condition existed long before Stendhal's time, but given that he was the first to put it into words in printed form, it has become inextricably linked to him. In an interview included on the Blue Underground Blu-ray release of the film, Argento claims to have suffered from a bout of the syndrome as well, when he visited Athens with his parents as a child in the 1940s. In essence, the syndrome can be described as an overwhelmingly emotional reaction to works of art; it can trigger such conditions as dizziness, nausea, hallucinations and even personality changes. Magherini observed thousands of such cases while working in the psychiatric hospital of Florence and first wrote about the condition (and gave it the name of The Stendhal Syndrome) in 1979. The condition is debated among clinicians to this day. On the one hand no scientific data exists to back up the notion that works of art have the ability to trigger such extreme reactions, but on the other hand it seems likely that the specific brain chemistry of

French DVD artwork for *The Stendhal Syndrome*; artist unknown.

those who suffer these reactions make it possible for them to undergo such a traumatic event. Scientifically kosher or not, Argento recognized it as a theme that was right up his alley and set about developing a scenario around the illness.

The theme of art having a profound psychological impact is nothing new in Argento's body of work. One could argue that it has been a part of his films since *The Bird with the Crystal Plumage* (1970), with its art gallery setting and artwork that provides a clue to the murderer's identity. Argento would continue this theme in *Deep Red* (1975), where a childhood drawing provides Marcus Daly with the final piece of the puzzle. Similarly, *Tenebrae* (1982) deals with a writer of *giallo* stories who becomes immersed in a real-life thriller of his own, while *Opera* (1987) focuses on violence and sexual aberration connected with the world of classical music. *The Stendhal Syndrome* takes things a step further by rooting itself in a psychological condition that appears to have some real validity. The film does not argue that art is dangerous however; on the contrary, the implication is that it can be a transformative and euphoric experience for most people. But that those people predisposed to mental illness may derive a very different message from it. At its core, this idea is not very different from *Tenebrae*, where a deranged fan of Peter Neal's books uses his works as a template to commit murders. Argento is not suggesting that this is something that is typical among well-balanced individuals, but recognizes that this can potentially be the case among the more unbalanced people in the audience.

The film features one of Argento's finest screenplays and points to a growing maturity that seemed to promise a new direction in his work. If the director's earlier movies were about the thrill of the kill, then this one is very much about the psychological scars of violence. It plays very much like a baroque version of Roman Polanski's classic *Repulsion* (1965), which told the story of a sexually repressed French immigrant in England who succumbs to insanity. Argento adopts a similarly clinical approach, though the nature of the story is inevitably very different. In a sense, the film picks up where many of his earlier ones left off. Titles like *Four Flies on Grey Velvet* (1971), *Deep Red* and *Inferno* (1980) concluded with the implication that their protagonists have been adversely affected by the violence and mayhem to which they have been subjected. Whether they ultimately succumbed to insanity is left vague and ambiguous, but there is little doubt that their lives will never be the same. *The Stendhal Syndrome* focuses on a protagonist who undergoes two traumatic events in rapid succession. The Stendhal Syndrome (it results in temporary amnesia, for one thing) momentarily disables her and then she is completely debilitated by being raped and tortured by a psychopathic killer. Anna Manni is one of the most complex characters in Argento's legacy. She is young and ambitious and has worked her way up the ladder to become an Assistant Police Inspector while still in her 20s. She is sent to Florence to gather information, but her desire to catch the killer gets the better of her and she puts herself in harm's way. Anna pays for her egotism in a big way, and spends the rest of the film in a state of perpetual uncertainty. She believes that Alfredo, the rapist, is still after her—but all signs point to the fact that he is dead from the wounds she inflicted upon him. As she succumbs more and more to paranoia, she only finds relief in a relationship with a French art student named Marie (the name being a homage to Stendhal's real name). For a brief period, things turn almost bucolic—but the threat is never far away and the stress and strain continue to take its toll on Anna. She remains very sympathetic throughout, and the final scene (visually quoting Michelangelo's *Pietà*) is one of the most haunting in the director's *oeuvre*.

Curiously, the film did not go over terribly well with Argento's fanbase. Some of it was undoubtedly down to the director's decision to play up the movie's brutality and fantastic imagery in interviews. Yes, the film is brutal—but it is a different type of savagery compared to the more fanciful excesses of his earlier works. Similarly, the imagery is gorgeously rendered, but it is in a more realistic style than usual. Many fans that expected an over-the-top bloodbath with plenty of acrobatic camera trickery were put off. Its dark, morose tone is difficult to take. Argento's tendency to pepper his pictures with comic relief is nowhere to be found here; this is very grim stuff, and that is as it should be. Nevertheless, it is easy to understand why the film failed to really connect with audiences. *The Stendhal Syndrome* is not easy to warm to. It is not the fun, stylized, over-the-top thrill ride audiences would normally expect from Argento. In fact, it is more of a psychological case study, and a very dark and despairing one at that.

The *giallo* elements are in some respects incidental here. The identity of the rapist-murderer is revealed early on. He is a handsome sociopath by the name of Alfredo Grossi. Unlike the pasty-faced, neurotic psychopaths of Argento's earlier films, he does not look remotely like a killer—and this makes him all the more frightening. Alfredo rapes his victims not because he is unsuccessful with women. The common misconception is that rape is about lust; in fact, it is very much an act of control. Alfredo is handsome, charming and at his ease around people. His crimes are motivated by a desire to control and destroy, pure and simple. He is the most frightening form of psychopath simply because he has no logical motive. He has money, a beautiful wife, a lovely home signifying an apparently stable and ordinary life … but the mental aberration which compels him to destroy beautiful women, psychologically and physically, is overpowering and results in some of the most disturbing sequences to be found in any of Argento's films. The second half of the picture focuses on Anna's growing paranoia and personality changes, and the mystery of who is stalking her is relatively easy to figure out. Argento's expertise in plotting such thrillers indicates that he was less interested in playing-up the mystery angle than he was in exploring the characters' warped psyches. As such, *The Stendhal Syndrome* is only a middling success if

Fan art for *The Stendhal Syndrome*, designed by Malleus for Dark City.

viewed as a conventional *giallo*—but as a character study, it is definitely in the top-tier of his work.

For his return to the comfort and support of the Italian film industry, Argento was given a healthy budget and access to some top-flight collaborators. Giuseppe Rotunno, the brilliant, Oscar-winning director of photography, renowned for his work with *auteurs* like Federico Fellini *(Fellini Satyricon*, 1969), Bob Fosse *(All That Jazz*, 1979), Terry Gilliam *(The Adventures of Baron Munchausen*, 1988) and Luchino Visconti *(The Stranger*, 1967), was brought onboard to lens the film. Rumors abound that the cinematographer and the director clashed at times due to their differing approaches, but Argento would later recall it as a "beautiful relationship" when interviewed for the Blue Underground home video release. Rotunno's lighting is artful and gritty at the same time. He manages a rare feat in conveying an earthy realism while still doing justice to the artistic leanings of the subject matter. Rotunno does not go in for the same stylization as Luigi Kuveiller had done on **Deep Red** or Luciano Tovoli did on **Tenebrae**, but the results are no less striking. Argento's propensity for a mobile camera is in evidence, but he sensibly keeps things on a more even kilter during the more intense dramatic scenes. The opening sequence is rightly celebrat-

Anna (Asia Argento) in *The Stendhal Syndrome.*

ed as a small *tour-de-force*, accomplished through artful imagery and use of sound and music rather than dialogue. However, the entire film is gripping and shows the director working at the top of his game. The music score is by Ennio Morricone, reuniting with the director for the first time after their fall-out over the score for *Four Flies on Grey Velvet*, and it can definitely be ranked among his best soundtracks. The make-up effects by Franco Casagni are realistic, while the digital effects by Sergio Stivaletti are comparatively hit-or-miss. In fairness, *The Stendhal Syndrome* was the first Italian film to utilize CGI, and the technology simply was not as well developed as it would become in later years, but the ropey quality of some of the effects admittedly plays into the surreal nature of the titular disease.

Asia Argento gives her finest performance as Anna Manni. The actress had matured since her appearance in *Trauma*, and if she seems a little youthful to be playing a Police Inspector, she sells the idea through the sheer force-fulness of her acting.[3] It is a very complex role and Argento responds with a fierce, emotionally naked performance that lingers in the mind long after the film is over. The notion of Argento casting his daughter in a role that required her to be raped on camera has inevitably raised many eyebrows, but in fairness the rape scenes are handled with tact, though they are upsetting by necessity. German actor Thomas Kret-schmann plays the psychotic Alfredo. He is brilliant in the part, and, while he does not get to appear throughout the entire film, makes a profound impression just the same. Born in 1962, he had hoped to become an Olympic swimmer but changed career paths and began acting in the mid-1980s. He first appeared with Asia Argento in the historical epic *Queen Margot* (1994), though much of his role was cut down in the editing. He would go on to appear in Guillermo del Toro's *Blade II* (2002), Roman Polanski's *The Pianist* (2002), Oliver Hirschbiegel's *Downfall* (2004) and Peter Jackson's

King Kong (2005) before reuniting with Argento father and daughter to play the title role in the ill-fated *Dracula 3D* (2012). In an odd casting coincidence, he would then be cast as the vampire's arch-nemesis, Professor Van Helsing, in the NBC miniseries *Dracula*, which aired from late 2013 until early 2014. The supporting cast includes Paolo Bo-nacelli, who gives a good performance as the psychiatrist who tries to cure Anna of the Stendhal Syndrome. Born in Rome in 1939, he began appearing in films in the 1960s. His most (in)famous role is as one of the wealthy deviants in Pier Paolo Pasolini's scandalous *Salò, or the 120 Days of Sodom* (1975). He also appeared in Francesco Rosi's *Illustrious Corpses* (1976), Alan Parker's *Midnight Express* (1978), Tinto Brass' *Caligula* (1979), Asia Argento's *Scarlet Diva* (2000) and Anton Corbijn's *The American* (2010).

Argento would follow up *The Stendhal Syndrome* with one of the biggest flops of his career—a lavish, tongue-in-cheek version of *The Phantom of the Opera* (1998), again starring Asia—before revisiting the *giallo* with *Sleepless* (2001).

Notes:
1. Jones, Alan, *Dario Argento: The Man, The Myths & The Magic* (Godalming: FAB Press, 2012), p. 226.
2. *Ibid*, p. 225.
3. As Asia Argento explained to Alan Jones in his book *Dario Argento: The Man, The Myths & The Magic* (p. 232), "I'm not too young for the role because in Italy you are given a great deal of power at the age of 18 when you are fresh out of police training [...]"

1999

Mozart is a Murderer (Italy)
Aka *Mozart è un assassino*

Directed by Sergio Martino; Screenplay by Francesco Contaldo and Sergio Martino; Director of Photography: Bruno Cascio; Editor: Eugenio Alabiso and Giovanni Ballantini; Music by Luigi Ceccarelli

Main Players: Enzo De Caro (Commissioner Antonio Maccari); Daniela Scarlatti (Daniela Onelli); Augusto Fornari; Azzurra Antonacci; Emanuela Garuccio

A student at a music conservatory is brutally murdered and the killer leaves a calling card in the form of a cross etched onto the victim's stomach. Commissario Antonio

Maccari is assigned to investigate, but his own personal demons relating to the unsolved murder of his wife threaten to weaken his judgment at every turn. As the murders continue, Maccari uncovers plenty of dirt on the people connected to the conservatory, and no shortage of suspects ...

Given that he had contributed toward popularizing the genre in the 1970s, it is perhaps fitting that Sergio Martino helped to usher out the *giallo* as the century drew to a close. Indeed, *Mozart is a Murderer* remains his last foray into the thriller to date, and if it does not represent one of his stronger entries in the field, it is still above average compared with much of the competition of the period.

Martino devised the convoluted scenario himself, and if it has a major failing it is that it is too focused on being a police procedural. This is surprising in a sense, given that the story has no shortage of potentially salacious material (drugs, incest, youthful sexual trysts, etc.), but Martino opts to downplay these aspects. The mystery is cleverly plotted and builds to a satisfying resolution, but it could have used a little more of the outré elements that helped to make the director's *gialli* of the 1970s so memorable. Truth be told, the film is simply a little too stuffy and serious for its own good.

The plot focuses on the character of *Commissario* Maccari. Like the detective figures played by Frank Wolff in **Death Occurred Last Night** (1970) and Giancarlo Giannini in **The Black Belly of the Tarantula** (1971), he is distinguished by his flaws and also by the fact that the script allows him something of a personal life. The trauma that haunts him is the stuff of cliché (bureaucratic red tape prevented him from acting in time to save his wife from a deranged kidnapper), but he is allowed to be more humane and prone to self-doubt than the usual one-dimensional flatfoot found in these films.

As noted above, some decidedly unsavory elements are worked in, notably a subplot involving a pedophile instructor at the academy. Martino steers clear of bad taste and handles this with sensitivity and restraint. Like so many *gialli*, the film seeks to explore the darker side of the upper classes. The teacher is clearly represented as an affluent individual with strong connections to "important" people. Maccari's superiors bristle at the idea of trying to pursue legal action against him for this reason, but the detective's strong moral compass compels him to persist and the truth is eventually brought to light. However, the impact this has on the teacher's life and professional standing is left ambiguous, and the viewer has every reason to believe that he will escape with a slap on the wrist, with his crimes being swept under the rug thanks to the intervention of his friends in power. As is so often the case in the world of the *giallo*, justice is an abstract concept and is seldom doled out as one might hope.

Martino's direction is slick and professional but lacks the flair he displayed in his 1970s films. He keeps the material moving at a decent pace and indulges in a few stylistic flourishes—notably a variation on the "inside the mind of

Cover for the Dutch DVD release of *Mozart is a Murderer*; artist unknown.

the killer" gimmick from Dario Argento's **Opera** (1987)—but overall the movie feels curiously impersonal. Martino's work from the 1980s onwards tended toward this kind of stylistic anonymity, so this is not entirely surprising. Even so, the film is well crafted and looks polished throughout. The cinematography by Bruno Cascio admittedly has a bland look one associates with television productions of the period, and this coupled with the overall restraint in the sex and gore department would seem to point to this being earmarked for small-screen distribution.

The cast does not include any particularly well-known international names, but the actors do a fine job regardless. Enzo De Caro is excellent as the tormented Commissioner. De Caro is sympathetic throughout and conveys a dogged determination that crosses over into obsession when his superiors try to have him removed from the case. De Caro was born in Portici in 1958 and began appearing in films in the early 1980s. In addition to dabbling in writing, composing and directing, he is also a prolific actor in Italian films and television, and remains in demand to this day.

2000

Almost Blue (Italy)

Directed by Alex Infascelli; Produced by Vittorio Cecchi Gori and Elisabetta Olmi; Screenplay by Sergio Donati, Alex Infascelli and Luca Infascelli, from the novel by Carlo Lucarelli; Director of Photograpy: Arnaldo Catinari; Editor: Valentina Girodo; Music by Massimo Volume (Vittoria Burattini, Emidio Clementi and Egle Sommacal)

Main Players: Lorenza Indovina (Grazia Negro); Claudio Santamaria (Simone Martini); Rolando Ravello (Alessio Crotti); Andrea Di Stefano (Vittorio Poletto); Dario D'Ambrosi (Matera)

Home Video: Cecchi Gori (Region 2 DVD)

Detective Grazia Negro investigates a series of murders involving college students. The murderer appears to be able to change his identity, leading members of the press to dub him The Iguana. Simone, a blind computer whiz, gleans a clue to his identity when he accidentally overhears a video chat between him and his latest victim. He teams up with Grazia to bring the killer to justice, but more killings will take place before any progress is made ...

After floundering off-and-on for the better part of a decade, the *giallo* got off to a good start in the new millennium with the release of *Almost Blue*.

The film is based on a bestseller by author Carlo Lucarelli. Born in Parma in 1960, Lucarelli rose to prominence in the 1990s as the most successful and renowned of the new generation of *giallo* writers. *Almost Blue* (the title comes from the Elvis Costello song which the character Simone is obsessed with) was published in 1997 and continued the adventures of Inspector Grazia Negro, which had begun with *Lupo mannaro* (1994), already filmed for Italian television and released to that format several months before this film. He would revisit the character later on with *Day After Day* (2000), *Acqua in bocca* (2010) and *Il sogno di volare* (2013). Lucarelli also created a trilogy of books built around

the character Inspector De Luca: *Carte Blanche* (1990), *The Damned Season* (1991) and *Goose Street* (1996). The De Luca stories were set against the backdrop of Fascist Italy and are very serious in tone, while the comparatively humorous adventures of Inspector Coliandro (e.g., *Nikita*, 1997) have been adapted to Italian television as a popular tongue-in-cheek series. The multi-talented Lucarelli would also try his hand at screenwriting (he collaborated on the scenario for Dario Argento's *Sleepless*, 2001), in addition to working as a TV presenter (he hosted a popular true crime series titled *Blu notte misteri d'Italia*) and singing in a punk band named Progetto K. Lucarelli would later turn his energies to directing with an adaptation of one of his thrillers, ***L'isola dell'angelo caduto*** (2012), but the end result was said to be so disappointing that it disappeared after a screening at a Rome film festival and as of now it is not available on home video in any format.

In adapting the book to the screen, *giallo* veteran Sergio Donati and director Alex Infascelli and his brother Luca streamlined the material and delivered a taut, well-paced thriller. Some genre sticklers do not count the movie as a *giallo* because of the emphasis on police procedural and the fact that the killer's identity is almost beside the point. True, the film does not seek to function as a whodunit and it does not work hard at concealing the killer's identity, but the disturbing nature of his crimes is far more potent than any mystery angle, and the story points to the general trend toward a more procedural-based narrative structure which would come to dominate the genre in the new millennium. Even Dario Argento would not be immune to this, as evidenced by the likes of ***The Card Player*** (2004), for example.

Despite the lack of twists and turns, the film is memorably tense and contains some shocking sequences. The killer is a total psychopath, condemned to a life of psychosis and violence due to his horrid upbringing, and no attempt is made at humanizing him or making him the least bit sympathetic. Villains are often more compelling when they have a human streak, but happily the killer in this flick is a welcome exception. With his bizarre appearance and propensity for self-mutilation, he is very much a lost cause; the only course of action is to lock him up and keep him from harming anybody else ever again. The killer's *modus operandi* of taking on the identity of his victims results in some chilling imagery and disturbing details, notably toward the end of the picture when he goes to shocking extremes.

The filmmakers also pay lip service to Lucarelli's attention to detail. His background researching the Italian police force and its various subsidiaries and their methodology pays off with an air of verisimilitude that is unusual in these movies. Lucarelli's decision to focus on the police also had the side effect of helping to eliminate the cliché of the amateur detective. As far back as

Alessio Crotti (Rolando Rovello) loses his sanity and his identity in *Almost Blue*.

Mario Bava's **The Girl Who Knew Too Much** (1963), *gialli* typically focused on hapless heroes and heroines who go it alone (for all intents and purposes) against a deranged psychopath. Bava, of course, took his cue from Hitchcock, who famously observed that nobody called the police in his films because they were too boring. This would become something of a mantra in the flood of *gialli* that spread across the screens throughout the '60s and beyond. Often the weakest link in some of these were their police procedural sequences, which seemed to detract from "the fun stuff" (i.e., sex and violence) and merely served as a mechanical device to advance the plot. Not so in Lucarelli's universe: his police characters are multi-faceted and above all else display real competence at their job.

The film also establishes the theme of the old guard versus the new guard, which is typical of Lucarelli's work. Grazia and her partners represent the new way of doing things. They embrace technology and use it to help trap the killer. The older policemen view this technology with suspicion and mockery, preferring to rely on "tried and true" methods to which they have become accustomed. This theme would later be incorporated into Dario Argento's **Sleepless**, which, perhaps due to Lucarelli's involvement, would be the first of his thrillers to lean toward the procedural format.

Alex Infascelli directs with an eye toward detail and pacing. The film hits the ground running and never really lets up, but sufficient time is afforded to give the characters their due. He avoids some of the more questionable stylistic traits of his contemporaries and gives the movie a rich, cinematic texture, which occasionally calls to mind the *gialli* of the past while still asserting its place as a modern variation on the theme. He and cinematographer Arnaldo Catinari create some memorable images and make excellent use of the widescreen format. Still, it is his attention to little details that lingers in the mind the most, whether it be the shot of the killer sliding his bare feet covered with blood into a pair of sneakers or the ghastly sight of his blood-caked hands typing away at a keyboard. The finale is equal parts exciting and emotionally exhilarating, thanks in no small measure to the sympathetic characters being trapped in an intense situation.

Lorenza Indovina is excellent as Grazia Negra. She is very good at conveying the character's inner struggle while still doing her best to assert her authority with her sexist peers. Like Asia Argento's Anna Manni in **The Stendhal Syndrome** (1996), she is notable as one of the first truly complex female police characters to be found in the *giallo*. Indovina entered films in the early 1990s; one of her first credits was a supporting role in Ricky Tognazzi's excellent crime thriller *La Scorta* (1993). She remains much in demand in Italian films and television and has also dabbled with directing, helming two short subjects to date. Claudio Santamaria gives a moving performance as the blind Simone, who helps Grazia in her quest. Santamaria steers clear of cheap sentimentality and makes the character into a fully

DVD cover art for *Almost Blue*; artist unknown.

realized human being. He starts off as an ambiguous sort, but gradually becomes more sympathetic, and the audience cannot help but feel for him as his attempts at helping the police land his own life in jeopardy. The Italian National Syndicate of Film Journalists nominated Santamaria (born in Rome in 1974) for his work in the film. He made his movie debut in 1997 and established himself as a popular star in Italian cinema thanks to such hit films as *The Last Kiss* (2001), for which he was again nominated as best supporting actor. He has gone on to appear in such titles as Dario Argento's **The Card Player** and the James Bond outing *Casino Royale* (2006).

Infascelli was born in Rome in 1967. He came from a film background, his father was the producer/writer/director Roberto Infascelli (*The Great Kidnapping*, 1973), his uncle, Paolo Infascelli, also worked on the production side of the business (he was a production manager on **The Sunday Woman**, 1975) and his grandfather was prolific producer Carlo Infascelli. While still in his 20s, he relocated to the U.S., where he hoped to make it big in the rock music scene. As he later explained in an interview:

In 1989 I met Courtney Love and, during three days and three nights of sex, drugs and rock and roll spent together at the Roosevelt Hotel, I began to snort cocaine with her. Courtney had just met Kurt Cobain and was officially with Billy Corgan, while I had an affair with the wife of Perry Farrell, who had left him for me. A beautiful mess.[1]

Infascelli eventually returned to Italy where he started pursuing a movie career. He made his debut with a segment of the horror anthology *DeGenerazione* (1994). *Almost Blue* marked his official solo directing debut, and it netted him a David di Donatello award as Best New Director. Sadly, the future did not pan out as brightly as anticipated. His follow up feature, **The Vanity Serum** (2004), failed at the box-office and his later horror film *Hate 2 O* (2006) more or less stopped his career dead in its tracks. As Infascelli explains it:

My professional disintegration began in 2006 with *Hate 2 O* , the horror film that […] we made and distributed independently through newsstands […][2]

According to Infascelli, the success of the venture put him in the doghouse with the production system, and he found himself unofficially blacklisted as a result. He would secure some sporadic work on Italian television, but left with virtually no money in the bank and a family to support, he took to working as a waiter in an Italian restaurant.[3] One can only hope that his fortunes revive, as he has great potential as a filmmaker and appears to understand the genre very well.

Notes:
1. https://it.cinema.yahoo.com/blog/gossip-e-celebrity/alex-infascelli-io-non-ho-paura-di-fare-163219628.html
2. *Ibid.*
3. *Ibid.*

Lupo mannaro (Italy)

Directed by Antonio Tibaldi; Produced by Ivan Fiorini and Domenico Procacci; Screenplay by Carlo Lucarelli and Laura Paolucci, based on the novel by Carlo Lucarelli; Director of Photography: Luca Bigazzi; Editor: Carlotta Cristiani; Music by Aldo De Scalzi and Pivio

Main Players: Gigio Alberti (Police Commissioner Romeo); Maya Sansa (Police Assistant Grazia Negro); Stefano Dionisi (Rago); Bruno Armando (Engineer Velasco); Ninni [Antonino] Bruschetta (Pathologist)

A serial killer is targeting prostitutes, leaving a strange bite mark on their backs as a sort of signature; this earns the killer the nickname of "werewolf" in the press. Commissioner Romeo and his young assistant, Grazia Negro, launch an investigation, which leads them to the respected engineer Velasco. Romeo is convinced of Velasco's guilt, but he is pressured to drop the investigation due to the engineer's po-

litical clout. Meanwhile, the killings continue and Romeo's determination to catch the killer blossoms into a full-blown obsession ...

This made-for-TV thriller is closer in style to an American cop show, but it is worthy of inclusion here for being the first adaptation of Carlo Lucarelli's *Grazia Negro* series; the subsequent **Almost Blue** (2000) would hit theaters later the same year and took things much further into the *giallo* realm.

Lucarelli's story has a decidedly political bent. The character of Velasco, the so-called citizen above suspicion, was openly modeled on Italian politician and media mogul Silvio Berlusconi. The latter started his business empire in the automotive field before moving into television and setting up his own network; by the late 1970s he had struck it rich with his media company Fininvest, which helped to break down the monopoly that the RAI network had on Italian television. Accusations of shady business dealings were already very much part and parcel of his empire, but this did not stop him from entering the world of politics in the 1990s. He was elected Prime Minister in 1994 and served until 1995, after which he was re-elected from 2001 until 2006 and then again from 2008 until 2011, when he finally resigned from office. He has since launched campaigns to reclaim his office, however, and has shown no sign of slowing down. During the course of his political career, he was involved in numerous scandals ranging from extortion and fraud to allegations of underage sexual relations and ties with the Mafia. A true example of "fact is stranger than fiction," his tumultuous public life has made his name notorious across the globe. Lucarelli's decision to skewer him in fairly explicit terms in his book was a gutsy move, but unfortunately the filmmakers failed to follow suit. In the movie, Velasco is more emblematic of a pampered upper class and is not explicitly compared to the notorious Italian politician. Given that Lucarelli was involved in the adaptation, it was presumably agreed that taking this aspect of the story that far might have caused

Behind the scenes of *Lupo mannaro*, with (from left to right) writer Carlo Lucarelli, director Antonio Tibaldi and actors Gigio Alberti, Maya Sansa and Stefano Dionisi.

too many problems, so a less controversial alternative was reached.

Director Antonio Tibaldi does a competent job, but the film never escapes from its small-screen origins. It plays out like a fairly conventional cop thriller and little of the more macabre elements from the book are left in the finished product. The killings are alluded to rather than seen and the sexual kinks of the murderer are likewise left fairly ambiguous. The end result is by no means worthless but it lacks the energy and conviction of **Almost Blue**, and could just as easily be discounted as a proper *giallo* thanks to its inability to commit to the genre and its tropes.

Even so, the actors do a very nice job. Maya Sansa is not as effective in the role of Grazia Negro as Lorenza Indovina was in the Infascelli film, but she still gives a good performance. The character of Commissioner Romeo carries much of the film. Gigio Alberti chain-smokes and wears a hangdog expression but manages to find the character's moral center. Romeo's determination to see justice done pushes him to the brink of madness, and Alberti is effective in playing the different facets of the character. Stefano Dionisio, who plays another policeman on the case, would go on to assume one of the lead roles in Dario Argento's **Sleepless** (2001).

Antonio Tibaldi has worked in various capacities beyond directing and writing; he also has credits for cinematography, editing and other technical disciplines. He made his debut in 1991 with the Australian co-production *On My Own*, starring Judy Davis. After that, he directed the unusual Southern-fried Gothic *Little Boy Blue* (1997), with Nastassja Kinski and Ryan Philippe. *Lupo mannaro* is his only *giallo* credit, though he remains sporadically active directing short subjects.

2001

Sleepless (Italy)

Aka *Nonhosonno; Le sang des innocents; Insomnio*

Directed by Dario Argento; Produced by Claudio Argento and Dario Argento; Screenplay by Dario Argento, Franco Ferrini and Carlo Lucarelli; Director of Photography: Ronnie Taylor; Editor: Anna Rosa Napoli; Music by Goblin

Main Players: Max Von Sydow (Ulisse Moretti); Stefano Dionisi (Giacomo Gallo); Chiara Caselli (Gloria); Gabriele Lavia (Mr. Betti); Roberto Zibetti (Lorenzo Betti); Rossella Falk (Laura de Fabritiis); Paolo Maria Scalondro (Inspector Manni); Barbara Lerici (Angela)

Home Video: Edition Tonfilm (Region B Blu-ray); Medusa Video (Region 2 DVD); Arrow Video (Region 2 DVD)

In 1983 a serial killer targets several victims; Police Commissioner Moretti makes a vow to Giacomo, the young son of one of the victims, that he will find the culprit. The case appears to be resolved when a dwarf suspected of the

Cover for the UK DVD release of *Sleepless*; designer unknown.

killings commits suicide. Seventeen years later, a similar string of killings commences, and Moretti is lured out of retirement by the now-adult Giacomo, who reminds him of his vow ...

Dario Argento's standing in the Italian film industry took a beating in the 1990s. Several of his productions flopped at the box-office, including his own American-made films *Two Evil Eyes* (1990) and **Trauma** (1993) and the Michele Soavi film *The Sect* (1991), which he had produced. His return to Italy with **The Stendhal Syndrome** (1996) was successful enough to net him the biggest budget of his career to make a bizarre version of *The Phantom of the Opera* (1998), but critics and audiences reviled the end result. *Sleepless* therefore bears all the signs of having been made for the sole purpose of getting the director back into the good graces of the public.

The director told Alan Jones:

I know people haven't liked my recent work, but that's their problem. It's important to discover new things and explore different avenues.[1]

It is certainly hard to argue with Argento on this point, but there is very little "new" in *Sleepless*. The film plays like a flabby greatest hits package, with the director self-consciously plowing over the same basic ground as in his earlier triumphs.

Sleepless is one of Argento's least interesting films. Much of its problem stems from its rather stagnant air of self-celebration. Argento began dabbling in self-quotations in **Phenomena** (1985) and took it a step further in **Trauma**, but in *Sleepless* this aspect is out of control. The sense is of a director revisiting previous triumphs hoping to win back his audience. The tactic proved successful to a degree, as the film was popular at the box-office and is often held up as one of his better late-period efforts, but the film does not support such praise. It would take far too long to cite all the visual and thematic references to his previous movies, but some of the allusions to **Tenebrae** (1982, notably a crane shot which serves absolutely no purpose and does not even impress by virtue of its sheer technical virtuosity) and **Deep Red** (1975, notably the use of a dummy) are especially forced and hollow. While nothing is inherently wrong with referring to past works, it helps if some fresh new elements are added to the mix. *Sleepless* fails to do this and comes off as one of the least inspired pictures in the director's *oeuvre* as a result.

Argento's films were never noted for their adherence to logic, but this one goes off the deep-end in terms of sheer idiocy. Despite the director's claims that he felt the script was "one of the best I've ever come up with,"[2] there are simply too many groan-inducing moments to even consider forgiving. The all-important aural clue that haunts Giacomo from childhood makes absolutely no sense. Are we to believe that the killer stopped to use an inhaler while butchering Giacomo's mother? The use of a dummy to throw the victims off-guard is similarly strained, while Moretti's genius as an investigator is undone by having him form certain conclusions years after the fact which he surely could have arrived at when the case was new in 1983. This only scratches the surface, but should provide some insight into how carelessly and haphazardly plotted the film really is. The presence of Carlo Lucarelli, who is credited with providing "additional material," seems to be confined mostly to the technical jargon thrown about by the police—but even this aspect is uncomfortably shoehorned into the narrative. The very fact that the Inspector has to explain the notion of DNA evidence to his superior does not exactly fill one with confidence with regards to the competence of the Italian police system. It seems likely that Argento worried that some of this material might go over the heads of the viewer, so he committed the cardinal sin of taking time out to explain it. Even so, Lucarelli's influence on the script helps make *Sleepless* into a transitional work. It still utilizes the notion of the amateur sleuth, but the emphasis on police bureaucracy and methodology indicates that a change is in the air. Most *gialli* from this point on would reject the classical set-up of the innocent protagonist launching his or her own investigation, and would focus instead on the police as they work together to stop further bloodshed. In that sense, then, the film can be seen as a farewell to a bygone era.

Argento's direction is uncommonly slack and uninspired. He indulges in a little creative camerawork here and there, but much of the film is executed with all the flair of a made-for-TV movie. Ronnie Taylor's lighting tends to be flat and ugly, which is especially surprising given the lush look he had lent to **Opera** and *The Phantom of the Opera*. Sergio Stivaletti's gore effects range from the effective to the laughable, while Anna Napoli's sloppy editing does not do the material many favors. Argento's propensity for dwelling too long on effects shots is particularly damaging here. The various murders are noteworthy for their brutality, but by lingering too long on Stivaletti's ropey prosthetic effects he only serves to undercut their effectiveness. The film's big show-piece is a protracted dolly shot, at foot level, following the killer as he stalks one of his victims; it culminates with the decapitated head of the victim plopping to the ground. The shot was enthusiastically received by some reviewers as reflecting the inventive visual gimmicks of his earlier works, but compared to the likes of the "crow point-of-view" shot in **Opera** or the fetishistic extreme close-ups of the killer's mementos in **Deep Red** or the aforementioned crane shot in **Tenebrae**, it comes off as a very empty gesture; what is supposed to be so special about a shot of a carpet, pray tell? All of this is a far cry from the artfully executed mayhem of **Deep Red** or **Opera** and makes one question Argento's belief in the project. On the upside, the director was able to

French DVD cover for *Sleepless*; artist unknown.

coax Goblin into reuniting long enough to score the film. Their pulsating, exciting soundtrack helps to make up for the often-uninspired imagery.

The cast is also uneven, to say the least. On the plus side, the veteran actor Max Von Sydow is brilliant as Moretti. Argento reportedly had the part earmarked for one of three actors (Sir Richard Attenborough and Rod Steiger being the other two) but held out hopes that Von Sydow, the star of so many films directed by one of his idols, Ingmar Bergman, would accept the part. Fortunately, there was a lull in the actor's schedule and he accepted the offer. Von Sydow's warm and believable performance is a master class in good screen acting—but it sits in a vacuum in the film itself. He injects the role with some sly humor, and Argento enthusiastically accepted some of his suggestions. In the script, the character was often seen talking to himself, so Von Sydow suggested having a pet parrot that he could talk to instead. His interactions with Marcello the bird are funny without being too precious and point to the character's loneliness and isolation. Moretti is an admittedly interesting character. He seems to have been modeled somewhat after the character played by Ray Milland in *The Pyjama Girl Case* (1977), though if this is true, the director has never openly acknowledged it. He is also very much in line with the tradition of brilliant rationalists like Sherlock Holmes and Hercule Poirot. An old-fashioned, no-nonsense policeman who trusts his instincts and has nothing but contempt for modern police methods, he helps to anchor the narrative and gives it something it is otherwise lacking: a heart. Von Sydow is so good and engaging that he helps to distract one from the film's narrative hiccups and some of the lame dialogue he is given (a victim is stabbed to death with a pen and he muses, "Blue blood? Ink!" which again hardly serves to bolster his powers of deduction), but sadly he is the exception rather than the rule. Born in Sweden in 1929, Von Sydow took an interest in acting while still in high school. He made his film debut in 1949 and rose to stardom with his role as the weary knight who engages in a game of chess with the even wearier figure of Death in Ingmar Bergman's masterpiece *The Seventh Seal* (1957); he and Bergman continued to collaborate on such films as *Wild Strawberries* (also 1957), *The Magician* (1958), *The Virgin Spring* (1960), *Through a Glass Darkly* (1961), *Hour of the Wolf* (1968) and others. The multi-lingual actor was able to capitalize on this arthouse success by appearing in some major international productions. He played Jesus in George Stevens' *The Greatest Story Ever Told* (1965), a missionary in George Roy Hill's *Hawaii* (1966) and a neo-Nazi in Michael Anderson's *The Quiller Memorandum* (1966). He was even considered for the title role in the first James Bond film, *Doctor No* (1962), though the part eventually went to Joseph Wiseman; he would later play the ultimate Bond villain, Ernst Stavro Blofeld, in the "unofficial" Bond film *Never Say Never Again* (1983), which featured Sean Connery in an ill-advised return to the part after a long absence. Next to his roles for Bergman, he

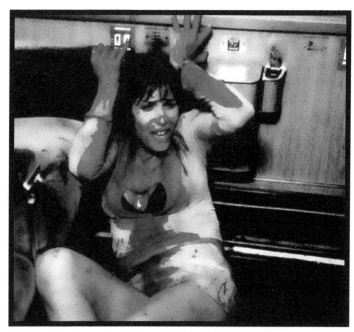

Angela (Barbara Lerici) comes to a bad end aboard a train in the opening scenes of *Sleepless*.

achieved his highest visibility as the frail Father Merrin in William Friedkin's blockbuster *The Exorcist* (1973). He reprised the role (albeit briefly) in John Boorman's underrated sequel *Exorcist II: The Heretic* (1977) and went on to play his favorite of his own roles in Billie August's *Pelle the Conqueror* (1987), for which he was nominated for his first Oscar. Other noteworthy credits include Mike Hodges' *Flash Gordon* (1980, in which he is marvelously camp as Ming the Merciless), the cult comedy *Strange Brew* (1983), Woody Allen's *Hannah and Her Sisters* (1986), Fraser Heston's *Needful Things* (1993, giving a brilliant performance as the Devil, thus making him one of the few screen actors to have played both Christ and Satan), Julian Schnabel's *The Diving Bell and the Butterfly* (2007) and Martin Scorsese's *Shutter Island* (2010). If only the rest of the cast were up to his standards. Stefano Dionisi gives a flat, listless performance as Giacomo. The character has potential for drama, but Dionisi's mopey, one-note performance completely saps it of any potential. He literally disappears into the scenery when he is onscreen with Von Sydow. When he takes center-stage at the end of the picture, the film suffers accordingly. Dionisi was born in Rome in 1966 and started appearing on Italian television in the mid-1980s; he made his big-screen debut in 1990. He won some enthusiastic notices for his role as the castrato singer in Gérard Corbiau's *Farinelli* (1994) and gave a good performance in Pupi Avati's elegant horror film *Arcane Enchanter* (1996), thus making his vapid performance here all the more surprising. Chiara Caselli, who is so boring that she fails to make any kind of impression, be it good, bad or indifferent, plays his love interest. Some of this is down to the character, which could easily have been jettisoned altogether, but Caselli's dull screen presence does not help matters. She was born in Bologna in 1967 and began her career in the late 1980s. One of her better-known credits is Gus Van Sant's *My Own Private Idaho* (1991), but she also appeared in Michelangelo Antonioni and Wim Wenders's *Beyond the Clouds* (1995) and Liliana Cavani's *Ripley's Game* (2002). Roberto Zibetti plays Giacomo's childhood friend Lorenzo and he gives a truly indescribable performance. His bizarre expressions and line readings grate on the nerves early on, and it only gets worse as the film goes on; his final scenes are so broadly overplayed that they turn the film into an involuntary parody. He was born in New Jersey in 1971 and began showing up in films in the early 1990s. He featured in Bernardo Bertolucci's *Stealing Beauty* (1996) and would go on to appear in the miniseries *6 passi nel giallo* (2012). Genre veterans like Gabriele Lavia (*Deep Red*) and Rossella Falk (*The Black Belly of the Tarantula*, 1971) are also on hand, but they have little to do. Matters are not helped by an appalling English-language track, which makes use of generally post-synchronized vocal performances. Von Sydow (mercifully) and Zibetti (sadly) are represented by their own voices, but the voices used for much of the supporting cast are grating and help to cheapen an already dispiriting enterprise.

As a final note of trivia, Argento's daughter Asia penned the nursery rhyme which plays such a significant role in the narrative. The sequence in which Moretti reads the pleasantly morbid ditty aloud is illustrated with pop-up animation and represents one of the few playful touches that really works in the film. Otherwise, attempts at humor courtesy of a scruffy bum named Leone (a nod to Argento's mentor, Sergio Leone) or worse, a scene wherein a number of dwarves are rounded up for questioning, makes one pine for the comparatively sophisticated humor found in the likes of **The Bird with the Crystal Plumage** (1970) or **Four Flies on Grey Velvet** (1971).

Argento's next *giallo* was **The Card Player** (2004).

Notes:
1. Jones, Alan, *Dario Argento: The Man, The Myths & The Magic* (Godalming: FAB Press, 2012), p. 283.
2. *Ibid*, p. 284.

2003

Bad Inclination (Italy)

Aka *Cattive inclinazioni*

Directed by Pierfrancesco Campanella; Produced by Enzo Gallo; Screenplay by Pierfrancesco Campanella, Gianluca Curti and Enzo Gallo; Director of Photography: Giovanni Ragone; Editor: Gianluca Quarto; Music by Alberto Antinori

Main Players: Roberto Coatti [as Eva Robin's] (Nicole Cardente); Mirca Viola (Rita Facino); Florinda Bolkan (Mirta Valenti); Elisabetta Cavallotti (Otilia); Antonio Petrocelli (Visconti); Elisabetta Rocchetti (Donatella); Franco Nero (Vagrant)

Home Video: Shriek Show/Media Blasters (Region 1 DVD)

A serial killer targets the residents of a posh boarding house. His (or her) weapon of choice is a drafting tool known as a set square. Inspector Rita Facino is assigned to investigate and uncovers a lot of dirt on the tenants, but solid leads prove difficult to come by. Meanwhile, the killings continue while various characters plot to use the murders to their own benefit ...

"I wonder why the killer used a set square?" "It's a lethal weapon. If used by an expert, there is no escape." Yes indeed, this is going to be one of *those* films.

Bad Inclination is a well-intended but hopelessly clumsy throwback to the decorative *gialli* of the 1970s. The film is chock-full of red herrings, perverse sex, over-the-top fashions and bitchy dialogue, but it simply never comes together. For all the seediness and violence, it is also curiously dull and uninvolving.

Director Pierfrancesco Campanella does his best to ape the aesthetics of earlier Italian thrillers, but the film looks cheap. The goal seems to have been to meld the "killer in black" style of *gialli* with the more softcore-oriented ones

Cover for the American DVD release of *Bad Inclination* from Shriek Show/Media Blasters.

Italian poster for *Bad Inclination*; artist unknown.

Campanella's direction is slack and does not succeed in generating any real atmosphere or tension. The cinematography by Giovanni Ragone is slick enough, but it has the same bland, made-for-TV look to it that dogged so many *gialli* of the previous decade. Natale Massara's score once again copies the work of Pino Donaggio, while gore effects range from the passable to the laughable; tighter editing would have compensated for this, but really this is the least of the movie's problems. The actors tend to overact like crazy, with veterans like Florinda Bolkan and Franco Nero (in a pointless cameo as a homeless man who drums up public outrage over the killings) looking as if they are well aware of the quality of the film they are appearing in. Transsexual performer Roberto Coatti (aka Eva Robin's) plays a much larger role here than he had done in Dario Argento's *Tenebrae* (1982), but this is not necessarily a good thing. His mannered, one-note performance is less than convincing and shows that Argento was wise to use him in a more sparing (and dialogue-free) manner in that earlier *giallo* classic. Add in the worst English dub job this side of Argento's *Sleepless* (2001) and the picture is at least good for a chuckle, but that is certainly not what the filmmakers had in mind.

2004

The Card Player (Italy)

Aka *Il cartaio; El jugador; The Card Player—Tödliche Pokerspiele*

Directed by Dario Argento; Produced by Claudio Argento and Dario Argento; Screenplay by Dario Argento and Franco Ferrini; Director of Photography: Benoît Debie; Editor: Walter Fasano; Music by Claudio Simonetti

Main Players: Stefania Rocca (Anna Mari); Liam Cunningham (John Brennan); Silvio Muccino (Remo); Claudio Santamaria (Carlo Sturni); Adalberto Maria Merli (Police Commissioner); Fiore Argento (Lucia Marini); Cosimo Fusco (Berardelli)

Home Video: Anchor Bay Entertainment (Region 1 DVD); Edition Tonfilm (Region B Blu-ray)

A serial killer, "The Card Player," challenges Inspector Anna Mari to an unusual game. Each time he abducts a victim, she is to play against him at a game of online poker; if she wins, the victim goes free, if she loses, the victim dies. When a British tourist is kidnapped, Detective John Brennan from Interpol is brought in to collaborate. The police enlist the aid of an online poker whiz named Remo to help beat the killer at his own game, but he is not so easily defeated ...

Sleepless (2001) may have marked something of a nadir for Dario Argento's creative career (at least until that point), but that did not stop it from performing well at the Italian box-office. Energized by the film's success, he set out to create another thriller. *The Card Player*

of the 1990s, but even with this combination the film comes up short. The killings are appropriately brutal, but they are too few and far between—and Campanella tends to take the blunt approach, allowing them to arise out of nowhere, without much in the way of a suspenseful build-up. Similarly, the sexy elements promise much but deliver little. Too many *gialli* of the '90s admittedly spent far too much time on carnal encounters, but in the context of a would-be erotic thriller such as this, one expects a little follow-through. *Bad Inclination*, however, is one big tease. This is particularly disappointing since the director's earlier thriller, ***Bugie rosse*** (1993), was one of the better efforts of its period and seemed to indicate that he had a feel for this sort of material. By contrast, this more conventional thriller seems half-hearted, even amateurish. It could be that the pressures to "play by the book," so to speak, sapped his enthusiasm for the project. Regardless, it marks a major step backwards for him.

The script by Campanella, Gianluca Curti and producer Enzo Gallo contains a few nice ideas, but they are not properly exploited. Too much time is spent on melodramatic backstabbing and soap opera machinations and too little on the actual thriller component. The characterizations are superficial, as well, and there really is not a single character worth caring about in the entire film.

DVD cover art for *The Card Player*; artwork by Rick Melton.

and economical narrative suggests that the rush to get something into production may have prevented the director from exploring the subject matter as thoroughly as usual. Continuing the more realistic aesthetic introduced in *The Stendhal Syndrome* (1996) and carried through to *Sleepless*, Argento and cinematographer Benoît Debie (one of the key figures of the Dogme movement, thanks to films such as Gaspar Noé's *Irreversible*, 2002) create some striking imagery. The film is not nearly as stylized as his earlier works, and has often been unfairly criticized for this, but the approach seems to suit the subject matter very well.

Like *Opera* (1987), the movie is about characters that are isolated and have difficulty communicating their emotions. As such, it is only fitting that the film utilizes the *milieu* of the Internet. The protagonist, Detective Anna Mari, is socially awkward and has a hard time getting close to people on an emotional level. She is devoted to her job, however, and has established a reputation as being one of the top detectives on the force. When she begins an affair with John, it loosens her up somewhat, but the idyll is not destined to last long. Anna and John are both wounded souls and together they find happiness, but in the film's cold ambience this is the exception rather than the rule. A frustrated romantic interest, which also harkens back to *Opera*, results in the killer's fixation on her. In Argento's socially dysfunctional world, the line between love and violence is unusually thin.

One of the film's major handicaps lies in the identity of the killer. It does not give away too much to say that the killer's identity is pretty obvious early on in the picture. Argento later revealed that he elected to change the identity of the killer from one character to a different one; he may have been better off sticking with his original concept. There are a few nice twists and turns and the final revelation certainly does not jar as being illogical, but a little more creativity with trying to keep the identity under wraps would have been appreciated.

Argento's decision to downplay the violence also irked a number of his fans. Truthfully, after the unintentional laughs provided by the ropey prosthetic effects in *Sleepless*, this seems to have been a wise move. The killings are suggested rather than graphically depicted, and at least two of them have a real emotional resonance because they happen to characters that the audience has grown to care about. Sergio Stivaletti's prosthetic corpses are not very convincing, but the clinical attention to queasy details like the mucus and other bodily fluids gives some of the autopsy room scenes a gruesome impact.

The film's most memorable set piece involves Anna relaxing at home; suddenly she catches sight of a reflection in a glass bowl on her coffee table. Realizing that it is the killer lurking outside of her apartment, she thinks fast and turns out all the lights and retrieves her gun. The killer manages to break in and the ensuing game of cat-and-mouse, replete with a marvelous overhead view of the characters slinking

would be his most unusual *giallo* to date, and, while it is not without serious flaws, it represents a determined return to form.

The movie underwent a complicated development. Argento initially put his energies into developing a project called *Dark Glasses* (about a blind woman who teams up with her adopted child to track down a killer targeting prostitutes), but the film fell apart when producers Vittorio and Mario Cecchi Gori went bankrupt and Vittorio was imprisoned on drugs charges. As the Cecchi Goris still owned copyright on the script, even though they lacked the means to produce it, Argento had to abandon the project.[1] *The Card Player* was therefore developed in an abnormally rushed manner and went before the cameras with a lower-than-usual budget for Argento. With this in mind, one may well approach it expecting the worst.

So long as one can overlook some absurd plot elements and even more absurd dialogue (especially in the film's English track), there is much to enjoy in *The Card Player*. The more fanciful elements of the plot are not necessarily any more ludicrous than some of the more improbable plot points in Argento's earlier films, truth be told, but the lean

through the dimly lit apartment, recalls the style and vigor of Argento's best work. The finale, on the other hand, has come in for plenty of criticism. The killer kidnaps Anna and challenges her to one last game of video poker, with her own life on the line this time; in order to make things more interesting, he handcuffs them both to a railroad track ... and the train is due to arrive at any moment. It is ridiculous and absurd as all hell, but there is something charmingly audacious about this *"Perils of Pauline"* finale—and given the film's emphasis on surveillance, technology and a seemingly omnipotent criminal mastermind, it cannot help but recall the silent thrillers of Fritz Lang, whom Argento has often alluded to as one of his idols.

The Card Player may be flawed, but it at least represents an attempt by the director to try something new. Apart from downplaying the violence—which truly flies in the face of all expectations, making it a bit like a Busby Berkeley film without dance numbers—it is also his first true blue police procedural film. The emphasis on the police has led some less-than-enthused reviewers to refer to it as *"CSI: Rome,"* but it is a different approach that works well enough in context. The look of the film is also very different from Argento's earlier films. Debie's lighting avoids the artificial look one associates with Argento's pictures, but his artful use of light and shadow still yields some impressive images. Walter Fasano's editing is tight and the pace is considerably tauter than had been the case in *Sleepless*. Claudio Simonetti's techno-flavored soundtrack is very effective and suits the tone and subject matter.

The cast is generally effective. Stefania Rocca gives a fine performance as Anna. She is adept at suggesting the character's closed-in, socially awkward attributes but also comes across as a strong-willed and highly competent professional. The character is not as well delineated as that of Anna Manni in *The Stendhal Syndrome*, but the two women share certain similarities—no surprise, given that Argento initially had hoped to cast his daughter in the film. Rocca is more than adequate as a replacement, and it frankly makes better sense to have a new character involved in the story as opposed to awkwardly explaining how Anna Manni could possibly have recovered well enough to resume active duty. Rocca was born in Turin in 1971. She began appearing in movies in the mid-1990s

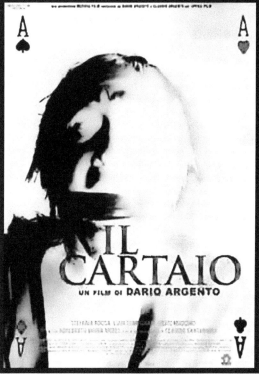

Cover for the American DVD release of *The Card Player* from Anchor Bay; artist unknown.

and rose to prominence with award-nominated performances in films like Donatella Maiorca's psychological thriller *Viol@* (1998) and Alessandro D'Alatri's romantic comedy *Casomai* (2002). She achieved international exposure with her role in Anthony Minghella's *The Talented Mr. Ripley* (1999) and would go on to appear in Abel Ferrara's *Go Go Tales* (2007), along with Asia Argento. Liam Cunningham also does good work as John, though Argento's script bogs him down with the usual drunken Irishman routine. Cunningham has good chemistry with Rocca, however, and their burgeoning love story is more credible because of this. Having such sympathetic characters at the core of the story gives the film a dramatic pull, which was largely lacking in *Sleepless*. Cunningham was born in Dublin in 1961. After deciding to abandon his original career choice as an electrician, he took up acting and began appearing in films and television in the 1990s. His early films include Mike Newell's *Into the West* (1992) and Jerry Zucker's *First Knight* (1995), but he came to the attention of genre fans with his role in Neil Marshall's werewolf film *Dog Soldiers* (2002). More recently he scored a success with a recurring role on the hit HBO series *Game of Thrones*. Silvio Muccino is likable as the computer whiz, Remo, who is brought in by the police for assistance. Muccino plays him very much as a kid out of his depth and this lends the character a touching vulnerability. He was born in Rome in 1982 and made his film debut with a lead role in the critically acclaimed coming-of-age comedy *But Forever in My Mind* (1999), directed by his brother Gabriele Muccino. He also appeared in *The Last Kiss* (2001) for his brother (along with his co-star in this film, Claudio Santamaria) as well as Roman Coppola's *CQ* (2001). In more recent years, he has turned his energy to writing and directing. As for Claudio Santamaria, his character is not as interesting as it had been in *Almost Blue* (2000), where he was so touching as the blind Simone, but he still gives a decent performance. His character is one of several who suffer from some ropey English dubbing unfortunately, but he is properly intense and ambiguous as one of Anna's peers. The supporting cast includes small roles for Argento's daughter Fiore and Vera Gemma, the daughter of Spaghetti Western icon Giuliano Gemma, who played the role of Detective Germani in *Tenebrae* (1982).

Notes:

1. Jones, Alan, *Dario Argento: The Man, The Myths & The Magic* (Godalming: FAB Press, 2012), p. 301.

Italian poster for *Eyes of Crystal*; artist unknown.

Eyes of Crystal
(Italy/Spain/U.K./Bulgaria)

Aka *Occhi di cristallo; Ojos de cristal; Anatomie des Grauens*

Directed by Eros Puglielli; Produced by Marco Chimenz, Giovanni Stabillini and Riccardo Tozzi; Screenplay by Gabriella Blasi, Franco Ferrini and Eros Puglielli, based on a novel by Luca Di Fulvio; Director of Photography: Luca Coassin; Editor: Mauro Bonanni; Music by Francesc Gener

Main Players: Luigi Lo Cascio (Inspector Amaldi); Desislava Tenekedjieva (Lucia); Simón Andreu (Agent Ajaccio); José Ángel Egido (Frese); Eusebio Poncela (Professor Civita)

Home Video: 01 Distribution (Region 2 DVD)

A young couple and a peeping tom are brutally murdered in a remote locale. Inspector Amaldi investigates and soon discovers that it is the work of a serial killer. The latter has a passion for taxidermy and begins taking "souvenirs" from the bodies ...

Eyes of Crystal manages to combine the classical *giallo* tropes with the burgeoning trend toward police procedural thrillers. In many respects, it is also one of the more satisfying latter-day *gialli*.

The screenplay was co-written by Dario Argento's sometime-collaborator Franco Ferrini, and it definitely shows off his expertise in crafting this sort of material. The plot is clever and builds to a surprising but mostly logical finale. The clues are interspersed throughout the narrative, and the savvier *giallo*phile may be able to guess where the story is going to end up. But that should not suggest that it is a strictly by-the-numbers affair. Ferrini and his collaborators, including director Eros Puglielli, work in some macabre material as well, notably an occult subplot which threatens to pull the film into the realm of the supernatural.

The movie seems to have been chiefly influenced by David Fincher's hit serial killer thriller *Se7en* (1995). Puglielli adopts a similarly dank and dreary aesthetic, with dimly lit interiors contrasting with bright exteriors and the occasional storm tossed in for added atmosphere. As in the American model, the game of cat-and-mouse between a psychologically fragile protagonist (in this case, Inspector Amaldi) and a clever, resourceful murderer takes center stage. The killer gets off on leaving clues behind as a means of tormenting the Inspector, and their final showdown threatens to remove the last vestige of the anti-hero's decency and self-respect.

Amaldi is an interesting character. He is highly skilled at his job on the one hand, but on the other he is marked by a hair-trigger temper. This is established early on when he and his level headed partner corner a criminal; the Inspector's outrage over his quarry's demeanor prompts him to shoot the man in the leg, an action that appalls his partner. Amaldi is basically yet another cop on the edge of crossing over to the "dark side," but his relationship with a student named Lucia seems to stabilize him somewhat. When she too becomes endangered, this pushes the Inspector to the brink of insanity, leading to a properly intense final showdown.

Director Puglielli directs with a sure and steady hand. Apart from overdoing it with the shaky-cam during some of the chase scenes—fortunately this is his only notable concession to the empty stylistic mannerisms which have been dogging contemporary cinema—he seems to have confidence in his material and allows it to play out at a good pace. The film is arguably a little overlong, but this is a minor quibble. The cinematography by Luca Coassin is stylish while still remaining true to the grimy aesthetic of its American model, while Francesc Gener contributes an effective soundtrack.

The various murder scenes are remarkable. Puglielli's flair for grisly details really shines through during these scenes and in their aftermath: the drool dripping from one victim's mouth as she is propped up like a macabre statue on the beach, or the young girl's bare feet being sprayed with her own blood as she is riddled with bullets in the opening attack come to mind. The killer's fetish for stuffing his victims and treating them like trophies is a marvelously unsettling touch. One macabre nightmare sequence features one of the victims pulling back the flesh on her bare breast to reveal the stuffing underneath; it is a gruesome image, well-rendered by some convincing make-up effects.

Luigi Lo Cascio is generally effective as Amaldi, though he arguably goes a little overboard with the bug-eyed theatrics when he loses his cool. Beyond that caveat, he successfully conveys the character's fractured soul and manages to hold the viewer's interest. He was born in Palermo in 1967 and got his start in the Italian theater scene. He made his film debut in 2000; he also appeared in the borderline *giallo Don't Tell* (2005). Lo Cascio recently tried his hand at directing with *La città ideale* (2012). The supporting cast includes a welcome appearance by Simón Andreu, making his first *giallo* appearance since the 1970s. He is in good form as a man dying from cancer, who is subject to visions related to the murders.

Director Eros Puglielli was born in Rome in 1973. He made his debut as a writer and director in 1995 and soon established himself as a promising talent with his features and short subjects. *Eyes of Crystal* is his only *giallo* to date, but one hopes that he will revisit the genre at some point; the film definitely shows that he has an affinity for the form.

The Vanity Serum (Italy)

Aka *Il siero della vanità*

Directed by Alex Infascelli; Produced by Marco Poccioni; Screenplay by Niccolò Ammaniti and Alex Infascelli; Director of Photography: Stefano Ricciotti; Editor: Esmerelda Calabria; Music by Marco Castoldi (as Morgan)

Main Players: Margherita Buy (Lucia Allasco); Barbora Bobulova (Azzurra Rispoli); Valerio Mastandrea (Franco Berardi); Francesca Neri (Sonia Norton); Ninni [Antonino] Bruschetta (Vittorio Terracciano); Marco Giallini (Michele Benda)

Home Video: 01 Distribution (Region 2 DVD)

A number of small-time celebrities are drugged and abducted. The police are baffled and have no idea what has become of them. Inspector Lucia Allasco, who barely survived a run-in years before with a maniac, is assigned to the case. She discovers a link between the victims and tries desperately to rescue them before it is too late ...

Alex Infascelli followed up **Almost Blue** (2000) with another *giallo*. Though reportedly based on the novel *Il libro italiano dei morti* by Niccolò Ammaniti, the screenplay by Ammaniti and Infascelli is actually an original property that offers an interesting variation on the thriller formula.

At its core, the film is a searing indictment of the media. The talk-show host, Sonia Norton, is arguably the real villain of the piece. Her desire to fill her show with sensationalism leads to the tragedy that sets the plot in motion. Later in the film, she attempts to exploit the series of kidnappings as a means of boosting ratings. Sonia is crass, superficial and utterly unsympathetic. By contrast, the deranged kidnapper is presented as rather pathetic. He fits the usual *giallo* murderer template—traumatized as a child, he keeps reliving the terrible event over and over again—but in most other respects he is decidedly different from the norm. Infascelli and Ammaniti stress the tragedy of the character, however, thus transforming him into a far more sympathetic figure. In many respects, he is actually preferable to the victims he is targeting.

The film also skewers the notion of celebrity, as the various kidnap victims are all mid-level celebrities who have allowed their egos to spiral out of control. The petty, self-centered people the psychopath elects to kidnap do not engender much sympathy, nor are they intended to. In the movie's bitter landscape, they are representative of a bigger problem: apathy. This comes through particularly strongly in a tense scene when one of them breaks free from their prison and, thinking only of themself, runs off without even trying to help his fellow prisoners. These people present themselves to the public as having compassion, sensitivity and civic spirit, but in reality they are only interested in their own vices.

Cover for the Italian DVD release of *The Vanity Serum*; artist unknown.

Detective Lucia Allasco, who is "marked" like the killer owing to a traumatic event, carries the narrative. Allasco's promising career was sidelined by a botched attempt at apprehending a psychopath; her partner was killed and she was badly injured when the quarry tackled her and they fell from a window. Saddled with a lame leg and a propensity for numbing her pain (psychological and physical) with alcohol, she has a tumultuous relationship with her teenage son and has to endure the annoyance of working with her ex-husband. As the kidnappings continue, Allasco sees the opportunity of salvaging her reputation, but things blow up in her face and she is disgraced yet again. Allasco is fully-realized, full of faults and virtues, and it is the complexity of the character that makes her so endearing.

Infascelli fulfills the promise shown by **Almost Blue** here. The film is stylishly directed and very well paced. It is not loaded with a great deal of action *per se*, but the material is strong and holds one's interest throughout. *The Vanity Serum* is stylishly photographed in bright pop-art colors by Stefano Ricciotti and is tightly edited by Esmerelda Calabria. Marco Castoldi's soundtrack includes a song, *"Una storia d'amore e vanità,"* which would be nominated for a Silver Ribbon by the Italian Syndicate of Film Journalists. The eccentric composer was for a time involved with Asia Argento, a relationship that yielded a daughter in 2001.

If the film has a "downfall" for the traditional *giallo* enthusiast, it is this. Apart from the opening scene involving a decapitation, very little violence is on display in the film. The psychopath is not interested in killing his victims. His goal is merely to imprison them and force them to relive the incident which provoked his trauma over and over again. He dotes on his prisoners and nurses one of them back to health. This provides a very interesting variation on the usual formula, but viewers looking for the typical killer in black gloves routine may be let down. It certainly did not do the film any favors at the box-office, despite some positive reviews; it was a disappointment and began the decline of Infascelli's promising career.

Margherita Buy is excellent in the role of Lucia Allasco. She plays the character as a strong-willed but emotionally vulnerable woman. Buy manages to make the character sympathetic without resorting to sentimentality; she is a tough, bullheaded character from beginning to end, but her desire to see justice done (as opposed to merely looking to further her career) marks her out as an uncommonly decent person in an otherwise cold-blooded environment. Buy was nominated for a Silver Ribbon for her efforts, and deservedly so. She was born in Rome in 1962 and began her career in the early 1980s. Her big breakthrough came with her role in Nino Bizzarri's *La seconda notte* (1987), for which she won an Italian Golden Globe. She went on to earn acclaim for her work in such films as Carlo Verdone's *Maledetto il giorno che t'ho incontrato* (1992), Pasquale Pozzessere's *An Eyewitness Account* (1997), Ferzan Ozpetek's *His Secret Life* (2001) and Maria Sole Tognazzi's *A Five Star Life* (2013),

among others. Francesca Neri is also a standout as the crass talk-show host, Sonia Norton. Neri is fearless in exploring the character's heartless determination for increased ratings—at any cost. It is she rather than the psychopath who ends up being the most unsympathetic presence in the film, and Neri does not shy away from this. She was born in Trento in 1964 and started showing up in films in the mid-1980s. She earned raves for her role in Massimo Troisi's *Pensavo fosse amore invece era un calesse* (1991) and worked for top Spanish directors Bigas Luna, Carlos Saura and Pedro Almodóvar. In subsequent years, she played the wife of Giancarlo Giannini's character in Ridley Scott's *giallo*-esque *Hannibal* (2001) and more recently won critical acclaim for her role in Paolo Genovese's *Una famiglia perfetta* (2012).

Unfortunately, Infascelli's career went on the decline soon after this film. His unusual horror film *Hate 2 O* (2006) was released straight to video and is sometimes erroneously listed as a *giallo*. If his fortunes ever revive, hopefully he will revisit the genre; he definitely has a flair for it.

2005

Do You Like Hitchcock?
(Italy/Spain)

Aka *Ti piace Hitchcock?; T'agrada Hitchcock?; Vous aimez Hitchcock?*

Directed by Dario Argento; Produced by Carlo Bixio, Joan Antoni González and Fabrizio Zappi; Screenplay by Dario Argento and Franco Ferrini; Director of Photography: Frederic Fasano; Editor: Walter Fasano; Music by Pino Donaggio

Main Players: Elio Germano (Giulio); Chiara Conti (Federica Lalli); Elisabetta Rocchetti (Sasha Zerboni); Cristina Brondo (Arianna); Iván Morales (Andrea); Edoardo Stoppa (Inspector)

Home Video: Anchor Bay Entertainment (Region 1 DVD)

Giulio is a film student working on a dissertation on Expressionism and Alfred Hitchcock. He becomes fixated on his sexy neighbor, Sasha, who is prone to strutting about in the nude. One night, he gets more of a view than he bargained for when he sees a murder occurring in her apartment. Might Sasha be responsible for the crime? ...

If **Sleepless** (2001) was Dario Argento's shoddiest *giallo* to date, then *Do You Like Hitchcock?* would prove to be the blandest. Even with its abundant in-jokes cropping up to stave off boredom, the film shows Argento coasting by while yet again quoting from his past successes.

According to Alan Jones, the film was originally designed to be part of a series of thrillers produced by Argento for Italian television; however, the plans eventually fell through and only this initial effort would make it out of the starting gate.[1] The film underwent some behind-the-scenes travails, including a slash in the budget, but emerged looking polished and professional enough, but despite the glossy appearance, precious little inventiveness is on display here. In any event, it did not hit the Italian airwaves until 2007, by which point the public responded with apathy.

The notion of Argento paying explicit homage to the cinema of Alfred Hitchcock and the German Expressionist filmmakers of the 1920s has some promise. The director allows his inner film geek to run amok as everything from Fritz Lang's *M* (1931) and F.W. Murnau's *Nosferatu* (1922) to Hitchcock's *Strangers on a Train* (1951) and *Rear Window* (1954) get referenced in one way or another. He even throws in visual nods to the work of his friends and family, with posters for Bernardo Bertolucci's *The Dreamers* (2003) and Asia Argento's *Scarlet Diva* (2000) seen as set decoration. Never one to shy away from a little self-promotion, the director even uses a fairly prominent ad for **The Card Player** (2004) in the video shop set. Familiar names like Bava and Sirio Bernadotte also crop up for the eagle-eyed viewer. But all the references and tips of the hat in the world are not enough to override the general air of *ennui* that handicaps the proceedings. If Argento were genuinely motivated to pay tribute to his cinematic mentors, he would have done well developing a better script to go along with it.

The film begins with a flashback scene that can best be described as pointless. Argento's decision to shoehorn a bit of black magic into an otherwise strictly realistic thriller merely points to his desire to pay lip service to his entire back catalogue; the two witches glimpsed

Cover for the American DVD release of *Do You Like Hitchcock?* from Anchor Bay; artist unknown.

Giulio (Elio Germano)'s propensity for spying on his sexy neighbor lands him in hot water in *Do You Like Hitchcock?*

at the beginning are poor stand-ins for the Three Mothers, however. It then picks up in the present day, with a dreary film geek serving as our protagonist. Giulio is one of the least interesting protagonists to be found in any of Argento's work, but he sets the tone for what is to come. He bickers with his on-again/off-again girlfriend Federica, and this is presumably Argento's take on the screwball comedy genre, but it does not come off well at all. Giulio is a dud and Federica comes off as far too variable in her moods. All the references to *Strangers on a Train* rather give the game away that a double climax is in the offing, and, sure enough, it develops as expected. Plot twists are relatively sparse and never as effective as they might have been. If Argento had developed the story a bit more slyly, it may have come off better—but as it stands, the film simply limps from one dull set piece to the next, before finally arriving at a would-be ironic fadeout.

As if that is not bad enough, the film is seldom more than routine in its execution. Argento's flair for mobile camerawork and arresting compositions is only sporadically in evidence. Frederic Fasano's cinematography is accomplished but lacks the requisite atmosphere. There is a memorably nasty death by pestle, and the bathtub attack quotes the memorably protracted murder scene in Hitchcock's *Torn Curtain* (1966) by emphasizing just how hard it is to kill a person. Beyond that, there is too much soap opera in the character relationships, and assorted oddball touches

195

like the homeless woman who pops up sporadically at key points in the narrative fails to gel; it does not help, too, that she looks every inch like central casting's idea of a bag lady rather than the real deal. Pino Donaggio's playful score tries hard to set the right tone, but the film itself is curiously joyous.

Elio Germano in the role of Giulio heads the rather boring cast. Germano does not have much in the way of screen presence, though he is convincing enough as a film student. It does not help that Argento's script gives him very little to work with. His character does not have much of a background. And apart from his voyeuristic tendencies, he lacks depth. He does not disgrace himself in the part by any means, but neither does he make much of an impression. Germano was born in Rome in 1980. He began his career as a teen actor in the 1990s and would go on to prove that he was a more accomplished actor in Daniele Luchetti's *La nostra vita* (2010), which would net him a Best Actor award at the Cannes Film Festival. The supporting cast includes Elisabetta Rocchetti in the role of the *femme fatale* Sasha. Rocchetti is rather good in her limited screen time and makes a better impression than most of her cast-mates. The actress, born in Rome in 1970, was becoming a familiar face in *gialli* around this time. In addition to this film, she also appeared in **Sleepless** (2001), **Bad Inclination** (2003) and **The Vanity Serum**

Italian poster for *La notte del mio primo amore*; artist unknown.

(2004). She made her debut with a small role in Peter Del Monte's critically acclaimed *Traveling Companion* (1996), starring Asia Argento and Michel Piccoli, then went on to appear in such films as Sergio Stivaletti's *The Wax Mask* (1997; co-written and produced by Argento himself), Gabriele Muccino's *The Last Kiss* (2001) and Gabriele Albanesi's *The Last House in the Woods* (2006), among others. She has also tried her hand at directing.

Argento's next thriller would be the notoriously troubled **Giallo** (2009).

Notes:
1. Jones, Alan, *Dario Argento: The Man, The Myths & The Magic* (Godalming: FAB Press, 2012), p. 331.

2006

La notte del mio primo amore (Italy)

Directed by Alessandro Pambianco; Produced by Rossella Belli and Pierluca Neri; Screenplay by Rossella Belli, Pierluca Neri, Alessandro Pambianco and Germano Tarricone; Director of Photography: Daniele Baldacci; Editor: Alessandro Corradi; Music by Gels

Main Players: Luca Bastianello (Andrea); Giulia Ruffinelli (Chiara); Valentina Izumi (Marina); Lucio Mattioli (Serial Killer); Joanna Moskwa (Vanessa)

A small town is shocked by a series of gruesome murders of young women. Chiara, who comes from an already-strict family, finds herself virtually under house arrest due to the fear over the killings. Her boyfriend Andrea, tired of the rules imposed by her family, issues an ultimatum: either she sneaks out to join him or he is breaking up with her. Chiara manages to keep the appointment, but soon undergoes an ordeal that will affect her for the rest of her life ...

The ironically titled *La notte del mio primo amore* (The Night of My First Love) is closer in tone to an American slasher film.

The screenplay by director Alessandro Pambianco and his collaborators is a pretty generic affair. There is a murderer on the loose, but this does not get in the way of young love. The teenage characters do not have any more depth than the ones found in the comparable American fare, and attempts at transforming the story into a whodunit are not very persuasive. The film soon tips its hand that the killer is a completely separate entity, wearing a mask over his face and favoring power tools (in this case, a nail-gun) like Leatherface in Tobe Hooper's *The Texas Chain Saw Massacre* (1974) and its many sequels and variations. The killer is admittedly eerie. Silent and deadly, prone to fits of psychotic anger, he stalks through the narrative with one goal: to kill.

Sadly, there is not much interest generated for the characters or their plight. Chiara is somewhat sympathetic, given the unduly strict nature of her upbringing (on the other hand, if only she had listened to her parents …), but Andrea is a manipulative and unpleasant sort. Chiara's friend, Marina, is much too sketchily developed, and the other characters more or less disappear into the scenery. The actors do a competent job, but nobody really stands out.

Pambianco's direction favors some irritating stylistic devices. The lighting is much too dark and murky. It would appear he and cinematographer Daniele Baldacci were trying to ape the *noir*-ish look attained by David Fincher and Darius Khondji on *Se7en* (1995), but they do not come close to emulating the effect. Whereas the American film kept things shadowy and eerie, this one simply seems under-lit and muddy. Pambianco also gives in to the trend toward overly shaky camerawork as a means of conveying an air of hysteria and nervous energy. This unfortunate stylistic quirk has dogged many movies in recent years, but skilled filmmaking can suggest this emotional effect without having to resort to such an obvious ham-fisted device. The picture has a slightly cheap quality to it that suggests it was filmed in haste, and it is possible this necessitated the need for hand-held camerawork, but it is still overdone on this level and becomes headache inducing.

Alessandro Pambianco got his start as a sound recordist, working on such films as Roberto Benigni's Oscar-winning *Life is Beautiful* (1997) and Dario Argento's **Sleepless** (2001). *La notte del mio primo amore* marked his directing debut, and to date it remains his only stint as a director.

2008

Darkness Surrounds Roberta (Italy/USA)

Directed by Giovanni Pianigiani; Produced by Joe Zaso; Screenplay by Bruno Di Marcello and Giovanni Pianigiani; Director of Photography: Alexander Birrell; Music by Marco Werba

Main Players: Yassmin Pucci (Roberta Parenti); Leandro Guerrini (Sandro); Raine Brown (Dora Miller); Joseph Zaso (Derek)

Home Video: Cinema Image Productions (Region 1 DVD)

A former painter named Roberta has undergone a terrible trauma and now leads a lonely and loveless existence. In order to spice things up a bit, she gets involved in some sex games with her friend Dora, but when photographs of

Cover for the CD release of Marco Werba's soundtrack for *Darkness Surrounds Roberta* from HeXacord; artist unknown.

one of her assignations surface, it threatens to cause a scandal for her husband. Making things even worse, a killer is making threats against her life and eventually kidnaps her, hoping that she will paint for him a perfect canvas ...

Darkness Surrounds Roberta is an earnest, well-intentioned tribute to the *gialli* of the 1970s. Unfortunately it is also utterly inept on every level, and may well take the prize as the worst of the films reviewed in this study.

As producer/co-star Joseph Zaso admits on the extras found on the DVD release from Cinema Image Productions, he and director Giovanni Pianigiani took more inspiration from the *gialli* of Umberto Lenzi and Sergio Martino than from the work of Dario Argento. Indeed, the film plays very much like an updated version of one of Martino's vehicles for Edwige Fenech. Roberta is a frustrated artist who is sidelined by a horrific rape. In her mind the link between the violent attack and her artwork is quite clear and made even clearer to her by her social climber of a husband, who forbids her to exorcise her feelings by painting. She eventually finds herself being targeted by a psychopath with a fondness for slicing up young models. At this point, the film becomes a sort of sexed-up, low-rent version of *The Phantom of the Opera*, as the masked lunatic locks Roberta away and compels her to paint a picture for him. The upside of this is that it allows Roberta to confront her past and be at peace with herself; the downside is, well … she is at the mercy of a vicious psychopath. This does not prevent her from willingly having sex with him however. The final reveal of the killer's identity is too daft to be believed, but this is in keeping with the lack of logic that dominates the entire production.

Apart from suffering from a cheap shot-on-video aesthetic, the film is terribly paced. Scenes drag on for far too long—nowhere is this more evident than in the opening murder scene, which goes from being suitably shocking to just flat-out ridiculous as it supplies a half-dozen gory close-ups too many. Pianigiani does not appear to understand that tempo is crucial in this sort of film, so he feels free to drag even the most innocuous of scenes out to the bitter end. The various sexual encounters are clearly meant to be kinky and erotic, but the implication of auto-asphyxiation and assorted other deviant thrills really is not enough to be shocking, and the actors over-emote their reactions so badly that the scenes quickly wear out their welcome.

On the other hand, the movie is rife with plenty of genuinely funny moments—the problem is, they are not intended to be funny. The killer's muffled voice evokes the sexless ones used in many *gialli* of the past, but the effect does not come off very well here. Action scenes are clumsily staged and edited. One scene depicting a woman being run down by a car is so protracted that it becomes utterly comical; all it is missing is a cry of "*Noooooooooo!*" on the soundtrack. There is also the dialogue to contend with … at least the dialogue that is intelligible. The film was shot with live sound and the Italian actors struggle gamely, but the accents are sometimes very difficult to cut through. Even with an easier to understand audio track, there would not be much to recommend here.

The film came about because producer Zaso was involved in another *giallo* homage titled *5 Dead on the Crimson Canvas* (1996). Shot for peanuts in the United States, the flick was produced by Zaso and was originally to have been titled *Darkness Surrounds Gloria*. The title was changed to better reflect the colorful *giallo* titles of the past, but Zaso decided he would hold onto the title in the hopes of someday making a "true" *giallo* in Italy. This film provided him with such an opportunity, and it is clear that his heart was in the right place, but that does not salvage the end product at all. Pianigiani's direction is strictly amateur-hour and the harsh cinematography by Alexander Birrell attempts to ape the color schemes of Mario Bava and Dario Argento without the benefit of their good taste and artistic eye. Marco Werba's soundtrack varies from the effective to the overstated, and the less said about the actors, the better.

Simply put, the *giallo* does not get any worse than this.

2009

Giallo
(Italy/USA/U.K./Spain)

Directed by Dario Argento; Produced by Adrien Brody, Rafael Primorac and Richard Rionda Del Castro; Screenplay by Jim Agnew, Dario Argento and Sean Keller; Director of Photography: Frederic Fasano; Editor: Roberto Silvi; Music by Marco Werba

Main Players: Adrien Brody (Inspector Enzo Avolfi / Giallo) [Note: Brody plays Giallo under the pseudonym Byron Deidra, which is an anagram of his own name.]; Emanuelle Seigner (Linda); Elsa Pataky (Celine); Robert Miano (Inspector Mori); Valentina Izumi (Keiko); Sata Oi (Midori)

Home Video: Maya Home Entertainment (Region 1 DVD)

A killer with a yellow complexion is abducting, torturing and murdering young women. When Linda arrives to visit her sister Celine, she discovers that the girl is missing.

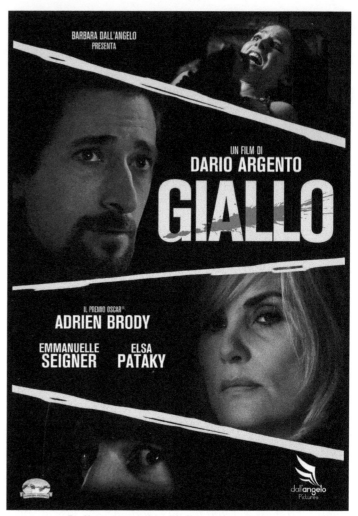

Italian poster for *Giallo*; artist unknown.

In desperation, she reports the disappearance to the police, who do not take her fears very seriously. The exception is renegade cop Enzo Avolfi, who is working on the case of the murdered women. He teams up with Linda and attempts to find Celine and stop the killer before any more blood is spilled ...

In theory, *Giallo* would seem to offer Dario Argento an opportunity to neatly summarize his past in the thriller genre, while allowing him to take a step in a different direction. That is the theory. In practice, it did not quite pan out that way.

The movie originated with a screenplay by the writing team of Sean Keller and Jim Agnew. The latter (a producer of low budget direct-to-video films who decided to try his hand at screenwriting) and Keller (an actor-turned-writer) had formed a fast friendship, and decided to write a horror picture together. The result of their efforts, an off-the-wall genre homage titled *LA Gothic*, ended up in the lap of director John Carpenter, who expressed some interest in making it. Unfortunately, the project stalled after a lengthy prep period and during that time the two decided to try their luck with a different subject. They concocted the idea of a killer terrorizing Turin as a bit of homage to the *gialli* of the 1970s and '80s and were overjoyed when Dario Argento expressed a desire to make the film. For Argento, the flick represented something of a challenge. It marked his first time directing a feature that he did not write himself (though his recent credits on the Showtime *Masters of Horror* series, "Jenifer" and "Pelts," were likewise penned by other writers) and it dealt with the thriller genre in a different manner than usual. His initial feelings about the project were optimistic, almost to a naïve degree:

> It's a moment in my career. It's a step. It's something a bit different from the *giallo* films in my past, but also a bit different from the horror genre. It's something in the middle. […] I was very comfortable with it.[1]

Argento's optimism would soon fade, however. In an interview with Derek Botelho, Keller explained:

> This was meant as an homage to Argento, Bava and Martino and all these other fantastic, stylized directors, so we could do something scary and horrific and also kind of make a comment on that genre at the same time.[2]

According to Keller, however, it soon became apparent that Argento was not interested in recycling too many elements of past thrillers.

> As soon as we hooked up with Dario, which was just amazing, he sort of dropped the bomb that "I don't want to do that style anymore. I want it to be more realistic."[3]

This attempt at realism prompted the director to work with his writers on toning down a lot of the more excessive elements in the story; as fate would have it, other factors would have a significant impact on the development of the material as well.

The project originally was set to star Ray Liotta in the role of the cop, Vincent Gallo in that of the killer and Asia Argento as the heroine. This dream lineup would remain in the realm of fantasy as, one by one, the selected stars dropped out of the project. The casting of Elsa Pataky as the kidnapped Celine gave the production access to a name replacement. Oscar-winner Adrien Brody was Pataky's boyfriend at the time and he expressed interest in working with Italy's reigning master of horror. Brody entered into the film with enthusiasm and was even given co-producer status on the project as well. One of the things he requested was to also play the role of the demented murderer, albeit under heavy make-up and under the pseudonym of Byron Deidra. The goal was to keep his casting in two roles as secretive as possible, but many viewers would see through the subterfuge and it did not remain much of a secret for very long. Brody's casting also led to securing the services of French star Emanuelle Seigner for the role originally earmarked for Asia Argento. Seigner, the wife of the great director Roman

Polanski, knew Brody from when he worked on her husband's Oscar-winning Holocaust drama *The Pianist* (2002), and she accepted the part. Thus, while the film did not have quite the lineup it was originally pegged to have, it still offered some legitimate American (Brody) and European (Seigner) star power, something which Argento's recent works had been lacking.

The cast in place, the movie proceeded smoothly up to a point, but it soon became apparent that the producers were writing checks they could not cash. Neither Brody nor Ar-

French poster for *Giallo*; artist unknown.

gento were paid their contracted salaries and Brody would eventually take the producers to court to secure the balance of his pay. Given that he had contractual rights over the film, this resulted in the picture being temporarily withdrawn from circulation until the matter was settled. The producers eventually ponied-up the cash and Brody allowed the film to go into release … but it did not amount to much. *Giallo* made its belated Italian premiere on DVD in 2010; it would be released briefly to theaters the following year, where it failed to make so much as a ripple. Elsewhere, the film was generally shuffled off straight to video, and when the critics got around to reviewing it, it was met with the worst reviews of Argento's career. Fans were quick to point to the fact that the director lost control of the flick in post-production and

Academy award-winner Adrien Brody toplines *Giallo* as the morally ambiguous Enzo.

that the film's failure as a whole could not be blamed entirely upon him. Even so, it proved to be a dispiriting experience for Argento, who has more or less disowned the film. He told Alan Jones:

I will never talk about it; I just can't bring myself to.[4]

The question becomes, is it really as bad as all that? The answer is complicated. On the one hand, it is easy to understand why the film is so reviled. On the other, it is not really anywhere near so poor as the worst the genre has to offer, and in some respects it at least proves to be more entertaining than Argento's so-called "return to form" thriller, *Sleepless* (2001). This much is certain: It is not a feather in the cap of anybody who was associated with the production.
One of the things that jumps out at the viewer early on is how utterly ordinary it is. The film never really comes to life on a stylistic level. Argento utilizes some prowling camerawork and relies on canted angles to signify flashback scenes, but the sheer technical virtuosity that typifies his best work is nowhere to be seen. Working with cinematographer Frederic Fasano (who lensed *Do You Like Hitchcock?*, 2005, and *Mother of Tears*, 2007, in a similarly unspectacular fashion), Argento delivers a competent but completely impersonal piece of work. There is not a single memorable image in the entire film, and this is truly surprising when looking at an Argento effort. No doubt the lack of money and resources prevented Argento from really cutting loose, but one does

not want to fall into the trap of making too many excuses here. In essence, the film sees Argento coasting by as he had done on *Sleepless*, paying homage to his past works while failing to introduce anything new or fresh in the process.
The presentation of the killer is nothing short of laughable, and both Argento and Brody must share in the blame for this. It is not clear whether Agnew and Keller had any satirical aspirations in mind when they wrote the film, but this does not seem very likely. Brody's performance as Giallo (aka Flavio Volpe) is an embarrassment. Decked out in a bad make-up-and-wig job which makes him look liked a jaundiced Keith Richards (well, that may not be so far from reality, really …), he mutters his lines in a bad Italian accent and indulges in pantomime of the most amateur-hour variety. It is hard to believe that Brody or Argento intended for the character to be taken seriously, yet this is one of the film's major stumbling blocks. By transforming the character into a walking punch line, the notion of suspense and horror flies right out the window. When it gets to the scenes of Giallo huffing butane or putting a pacifier in his mouth as he masturbates to images of his crimes, it is clear that the film has gone so far off the deep end that there is no hope of recovery.
Similarly, the film seems to embrace the aesthetic of the so-called "torture porn" genre. The term deserves some elaboration. Reactionary critics who took exception to the burgeoning trend toward visceral horror films coined the term Torture porn. Following a long draught of PG-13 level fright movies in the 1990s, filmmakers cut loose with wicked aban-

don in the new millennium and sought to out-gross each other in every sense of the word. The trend is best defined by the *Saw* and *Hostel* franchises, both of which trade on images of torture and mutilation, which make even some of the harder-edged horror films of the 1970s and '80s look quaint by comparison. Yet there is no getting around the fact that the term is a pejorative one, and, like so many "clever" witticisms designed to put down entire genres, it is more than a little short-sighted. Throughout the history of the genre, the older generations have always taken exception to the excesses of newer horror titles. In the 1950s, fans of the Universal cycle decried the gore found in the films produced by Hammer Film Productions, for example, while so many children of the '80s who grew up on *Friday the 13th* bloodbaths seem to be troubled by the *Saw* franchise. And so it goes. The fact of the matter is that these excesses reflect the censorship climates of the individual periods, and to lump films together in a thoughtless fashion is simply being reactionary. No matter what one may think of the individual titles that the so-called Torture Porn movement comprises, it is difficult to argue the basic point that they should ideally be assessed on a film-by-film basis as opposed to being so summarily dismissed. Argento's foray into the field is surprisingly genteel in some respects, but the influence is mainly an aesthetic one. The presentation of the killer's lair is done in the same bleached-out, grimy and grubby fashion as one would see in the torture chambers of the *Hostel* films or the lair of psychotic serial killer Jigsaw in the *Saw* franchise. With regards to violence, much of it is actually implied rather than shown. Whether this was down to budgetary concerns or was a deliberate move on Argento's part is a mystery. Even so, two memorably vicious moments do manage to work as intended: Giallo cutting off the tip of a victim's finger (reprised from **Sleepless**, 2001, where the killer clumsily chops off a victim's finger nails to remove possible DNA traces) and a nasty scene involving a character holding on to a broken window-pane for dear life, as their hands get shredded by the fragments of glass jutting from the metal (recalling the nasty "rope burn" effect in *The Cat O' Nine Tails*, 1971).

The movie is by no means incompetent, nor is it as hopelessly inept as many reviewers would have one believe. It's just surprisingly faceless and lacking in the style and authority one expects from Argento's films. Fasano's photography is professional but it lacks atmosphere. Marco Werba's soundtrack is utterly generic, making one pine for the days of Ennio Morricone and Goblin. The shocks are generally blunt and fail to leave much of an imprint. Only the ending harkens back to the feeling of ambiguity one associates with Argento's classic output, and even this was apparently a concession. It is not clear how Argento wanted the picture to end, but apparently this was not what he had in mind.

The actors are about on the same level as the material. Brody's performance as Avolfi is effective in a mannered sort of way. He frowns and chain-smokes a lot, but his clichéd backstory—involving, you guessed it, a childhood trauma—does him no favors. Beyond that, he poses and does his best to act tough, but he lacks the sheer physical presence that an actor like Ray Liotta could have brought to the part. Brody was born in Queens in 1973 and attended acting school as a teenager. He started showing up on American TV in the late '80s and made his big-screen debut with a small role in Francis Ford Coppola's segment "Life Without Zoe" in *New York Stories* (1989). Terrence Mallick cast him in a plum role in *The Thin Red Line* (1998), but infamously cut many of his scenes in the film's tortuous editing process. He rebounded with a strong performance as the sexually confused punk kid in Spike Lee's *Summer of Sam* (1999) and won a surprising Oscar (defeating Daniel Day-Lewis, who was expected to triumph in Martin Scorsese's *Gangs of New York*) for his sensitive performance as Jewish pianist-turned-refugee Wladyslaw Szpilman in Roman Polanski's *The Pianist* (2002). He went on to appear in M. Night Shyamalan's *The Village* (2004), Peter Jackson's *King Kong* (2005) and Wes Anderson's *The Darjeeling Limited* (2005) prior to going to Turin to work with Argento. His recent credits include Woody Allen's *Midnight in Paris* (2011, playing Salvador Dalí) and Wes Anderson's *The Grand Budapest Hotel* (2014). Emanuelle Seigner, who struggles with the often awkward dialogue and seems somewhat adrift as a result, plays Linda. Seigner is a gifted actress, but the script and direction fail to make good use of her talents, and she sometimes seems rather wooden. She was born in Paris in 1966 and rose to fame as a model in the 1980s. Seigner made her film debut in 1985 and was cast by Roman Polanski in his Hitchcock homage *Frantic* (1988), in which she gives a scene-stealing performance as a hooker who holds the key to the mystery. She and Polanski fell for each other, and they were married in the summer of 1989; she would go on to appear in his films *Bitter Moon* (1992), *The Ninth Gate* (1999) and *Venus in Fur* (2013), for which she was nominated as Best Actress at Cannes. Her other credits include Olivier Dahan's *La Vie en Rose* and Julian Schnabel's *The Diving Bell and the Butterfly* (both 2007).

Argento would follow up *Giallo* with another "gun for hire" assignment, *Dracula 3D* (2012), and has hinted at returning to the *giallo* for another feature. One can only hope that if he does so, it is for a project in which he is fully immersed; at his best, this gifted filmmaker has a flair for the genre that is difficult to match, and it would be a shame to think that his final work in the field would be something as completely anonymous as this one.

Notes:
1. Jones, Alan, *Dario Argento: The Man, The Myths & The Magic* (Godalming: FAB Press, 2012), p. 375.
2. Botelho, Derek, *The Argento Syndrome* (Duncan: Bear-Manor Media, 2014), p. 226.
3. *Ibid.*
4. Jones, Alan, *Dario Argento: The Man, The Myths & The Magic* (Godalming: FAB Press, 2012), p. 375.

Negli occhi dell'assassino
(Italy)

Directed by Edoardo Margheriti; Produced by Raffaello Monteverde and Cristinia Zucchiatti; Screenplay by Alberto Ostini and Stefano Piani; Director of Photography: Franco Lecca; Editor: Fabio Loutfy; Music by Alessandro Molinari

Main Players: Antonella Troise (Commissioner Andrea Baldini); Luca Ward (Giona De Falco); Antonio Cupo (Alessandro Visconti); Eros Galbiati (Inspector Carnera)

A serial killer is terrorizing Rome. Commissario Andrea Baldini is assigned to investigate the killings and soon finds herself being threatened by the mysterious killer. She is forced to turn to famed criminologist De Falco for assistance. The problem is, De Falco is currently in jail on suspicion of murdering his wife, so strings have to be pulled to make use of his expertise in the hopes of stopping the bloodshed ...

This made-for-television *giallo* by Edoardo Margheriti suggests that the director may be poised to follow in his father's footsteps as another notable talent in Italian genre cinema.

Sadly, despite some enthusiastic reviews, the movie has yet to surface outside of Italy. Like so many Italian made-for-television films, it simply does not have the name value to prompt any DVD or Blu-ray releasing companies to take a chance on it. Perhaps if Margheriti's directing career really takes off, however, there will be an interest in gathering up his earlier works and releasing them as well, à *la* Dario Argento.

Antonella Troise, who plays the beleaguered Police Commissioner trying to catch the killer, heads the cast. Troise was born in Naples in 1977. She made her film debut in Sergio Martino's ill-fated sequel to his popular horror-fantasy *Island of the Fishmen* (1979), titled *The Fishmen and Their Queen* (1995). Her work has primarily been confined to television. Luca Ward plays the ambiguous criminologist who gets a chance to prove his innocence. Born in Rome in 1960, he is best known as a dubbing artist; among other achievements, he is renowned for being the "Italian voice" of such superstars as Russell Crowe, Pierce Brosnan and Samuel L. Jackson. In terms of his acting work, he started appearing on Italian television as a child actor in the 1970s. His career really took off in the late 1990s, and he is a popular presence in many Italian miniseries and TV films.

Margheriti was born in Rome in 1959. The son of the late cult filmmaker Antonio Margheriti (*Naked You Die*, 1968), he started off as his father's assistant on such efforts as *The Last Hunter* (1980) and *Hunters of the Golden Cobra* (1982). He would continue to work with his father until his dad retired in the early 1990s, but the younger had already begun directing on his own by the late 1980s. Like his father, Edoardo has favored dabbling in various popular genres, and he would go on to contribute to the series *6 passi nel giallo* (2012).

Italian advertising for *Negli occhi dell'assassino*; artist unknown.

2010

Symphony in Blood Red
(Italy)

Aka *Come una crisalide*

Directed by Luigi Pastore; Screenplay by Luigi Pastore and Antonio Tentori; Director of Photography: Tiziano Pancotti; Music by Claudio Simonetti

Main Players: Federica Carpico (Lisa); Tony Cimarosa (Cacciatore); Riccardo Serventi Longhi (TV Journalist); Nikol Brown (Squillo); Fabio Giovannini (Don Alfredo); Simona Oliverio (Claudia)

A young man seeks psychiatric help. The psychiatrist recommends that he go into intensive in-patient treatment, but the young man lashes out at this and kills the psychiatrist instead. This triggers a series of killings, and it soon becomes apparent that the man will go on until he has been stopped dead in his tracks ...

Like **Fatal Frames** (1996*), Symphony in Blood Red* plays like a music video version of a *giallo*. As such, the emphasis is on murder set pieces and the plot, such as it is, is entirely incidental.

The film opens with a quote from Dario Argento's 1982 classic **Tenebrae** ("The impulse had become irresistible. And so he committed his first act of murder.") and proceeds to unfold as something of a homage to the *giallo* master's catalogue of thrillers. The technical crew even includes such Argento veterans as composer Claudio Simonetti[1] and special effects artist Sergio Stivaletti. With so much emphasis on reverence, originality is pretty much thrown out the window—and this is one of the film's major stumbling blocks.

Director Luigi Pastore developed the story himself, but the final script was written in collaboration with Antonio Tentori. Born in Rome in 1960, Tentori worked as a novelist, but he became immersed in Italian horror cinema in the early 1990s when collaborating on a couple of Lucio Fulci's last projects. Most notably, he assisted the director in developing the screenplay for *Cat in the Brain* (1990), a ramshackle collage of clips from various splatter films (some directed by Fulci, some not) built around the idea that a famed horror director (played by Fulci himself) is losing his grip on reality. It was not much of a film, but it has its points of interest, especially for Fulci fans. Tentori would go on to work on such genre fare as Sergio Stivaletti's *The Three Faces of Terror* (2004) and Bruno Mattei's *Island of the Living Dead* (2006) and recently collaborated with Argento on the director's ill-fated *Dracula 3D* (2012). A quick glance at his filmography makes it clear that his credits do not encompass any of the highlights of Italian horror cinema. *Symphony in Blood Red* is therefore emblematic of so many of his scripts; it is long on shock effects and short on logic and characterization.

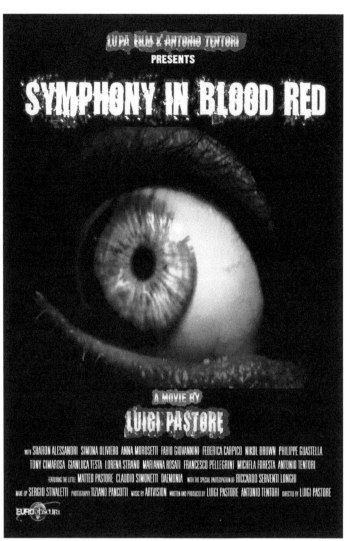

Anglo export sales promo for *Symphony in Blood Red*; artist unknown.

In essence, the film plays like a long string of murders. This is by no means unusual in the *giallo* canon. Mario Bava's **Blood and Black Lace** (1964) and **Twitch of the Death Nerve** (1971), for example, demonstrated that it was possible to build a film around artfully choreographed images of violent death. The problem is a simple one: Luigi Pastore is *not* Mario Bava. He shoots and edits the material as if it were an extended music video, and indeed the last 10 minutes are essentially a pointless recap of the vicious murders, as if they really needed recapping in the first place. Pastore tries hard to create some sleek, stylish images, but for the most part, his efforts are in vain. The film has the same harsh digitized aesthetic that marred **Darkness Surrounds Roberta** (2008), and the attempt at putting the viewer inside the killer's mind is never very successful.

The actors do the best they can under the circumstances, but they have nothing to work with. Pastore's interest is clearly geared toward generating as many shock effects as possible, so he tends to ignore everything else. The story is so loosely constructed that it vanishes into thin air; a subplot involving an obnoxious TV reporter who goads the killer is put to rest before it even has a chance to get interesting. The victims are ciphers, inspiring neither pity nor interest. And as for the killer himself, all we know is that he suffered at the hands of a cruel father (played by Tentori, possibly with an eye toward paying homage to Michael Powell's *Peeping Tom*, 1960) and that he seems to be something of a social misfit. As a final bucking of convention (read: rip-off), his identity is never even revealed. This sort of ambiguity worked well enough in Bob Clark's truly chilling *Black Christmas* (1974), but in a generally uninspired piece of filler such as this it merely comes off as lazy, as if the filmmakers simply could not be bothered to provide the picture with some real closure.

Luigi Pastore was born in Taranto in 1974. A lifelong horror buff, he started off making behind-the-scenes specials on such Dario Argento films as **The Stendhal Syndrome** (1996) and *The Phantom of the Opera* (1998). *Symphony in Blood Red* marked his directing debut; to date, he has not followed up with any other projects. He has also directed music videos for Claudio Simonetti's group Daemonia, including one for their cover version of the iconic theme for **Deep Red** (1975). In 2010, he also started up the Italian Horror Fest, serving as the program's artistic director; the festival has proved to be successful and has allowed various Italian filmmakers with ties to the genre (including Argento, Lamberto Bava, Umberto Lenzi and Pupi Avati) to be feted for their contributions.

Notes:
1. The score quotes liberally from Simonetti's previous soundtracks, including his music for **Opera** (1987).

2011

Sotto il vestito niente – L'ultima sfilata (Italy)

Directed by Carlo Vanzina; Screenplay by Carlo Vanzina, Enrico Vanzina and Franco Ferrini; Director of Photography: Carlo Tafani; Editor: Raimondo Crociani; Music by Pino Donaggio

Main Players: Francesco Montanari (Vincenzo Malerba); Vanessa Hessler (Britt); Richard E. Grant (Federico Marinoni); Giselda Volodi (Daria Marinoni); Virginie Marsan (Chris)

The fashion house of designer Federico Marinoni is dealt a serious blow when their top model is killed in a freak accident. When another model, Britt, arrives on the scene and seems poised to take her place, jealousies flare among the other models. Britt starts receiving threatening phone calls, and a mysterious killer begins eliminating various people linked with the fashion house. It is up to Inspector Malerba to get to the truth before Britt's name is listed among the casualties ...

Italian poster for *Sotto il vestito niente—L'ultima sfilata.*

Carlo Vanzina's **Nothing Underneath** (1985) was one of the few big genre hits of the 1980s. *Sotto il vestito niente—L'ultima sfilata* (Nothing Underneath—The Last Parade) was clearly undertaken in the hopes that lightning would strike twice. It did not.

The routine scenario by Vanzina, his brother Enrico and *giallo* veteran Franco Ferrini is noteworthy for its lack of inventiveness. More to the point, it seems so intent on playing to the mainstream that it avoids sensationalism almost completely. The violence is muted, there are only a handful of murders and even the promise of sex is more or less kept unfulfilled.

The film continues the fashion *milieu* of **Nothing Underneath** (and a number of other *gialli* of the 1980s), but beyond that nothing serves to connect the two pictures. Whereas Vanzina's earlier effort was stylish and included some memorably outré flourishes, this one is strictly by the numbers. The movie plays out like an episode of an Italian cop series, and only the introduction of a homosexual *ménage à trois* (hinted at rather than shown, naturally) points to the genre's propensity for the sordid. Beyond that, the film is very much a soap opera, with the murders serving as a brief respite from all the bed-hopping and surprise paternity revelations.

With its location shooting in Italy, Switzerland and Sweden, it seems that the producers had enough faith in the film to spend a bit of money on it. It is certainly a handsome looking production. Carlo Tafani's widescreen cinematography is classy and the settings and art direction display a keen eye. If only the material were not so utterly stagnant and dull.

The character of Inspector Malerba carries the narrative. Fortunately he is a sympathetic figure and is developed in such a way that he helps make the lengthy police procedural scenes bearable. Unlike so many *giallo* detectives, he has a real life outside of his work. He is a loving husband and an anxious soon-to-be father. Malerba's droll humor (in his interactions with his loyal but not-terribly-bright second-in-command) marks him as not only highly competent in his job but also blessed with a sense of humor. If only the same could be said for the rest of the characters. Truth be told, they are a generally dreary lot, though an interesting variation on the icy fashion impresario is found in the form of Federico Marinoni. He has the acidic wit one might expect of such a character, but it is also surprisingly endearing and develops him into a more interesting figure as the narrative unfolds.

Vanzina's direction is efficient if uninspired. The excessively talky screenplay is a constant hindrance, but where he is able, he manages to inject a bit of style and energy. Even so, the movie represents a major step backward from **Nothing Underneath**, and ultimately underlines just how boring and listless the genre has become in recent years. There is very little in the film that could not be shown on primetime TV and one is left with the distinct feeling that we have already seen all of this done with more conviction in other films. Even Pino Donaggio's music feels warmed over, with the main theme sounding suspiciously like the one he composed for Brian De Palma's *Body Double* (1984). That said, the picture is notable as the first *giallo* to name-check Facebook; that has got to count for something … right?

Francesco Montanari gives an excellent performance as Inspector Malerba. His engaging screen presence helps to keep the film afloat even as the material regularly lets him down. He portrays the role as a smart, slightly cynical cop and never loses sight of the character's humanity; if anybody succeeds in creating a character with a bit of depth in this (perhaps appropriately) shallow *milieu*, it is he. Montanari was born in Rome in 1984 and made his film debut in 2009. *Sotto il vestito niente—L'ultima sfilata* presented him with his first lead role, and he makes the best of it; he was rewarded with an award from the Italian National Syndicate of Film Journalists for his efforts. Richard E. Grant is his usual icy and effective self as the fashion guru. It is the type of part that an experienced actor like Grant could have played in his sleep, but like Montanari, he actually rises to the occasion and injects the role with a bit of life. Born in Swaziland in 1957, he started off as a stage actor in South Africa before making his way to England. He started appearing in films and television in 1983. He rose to prominence with his role as the permanently drunk Withnail in the cult hit *Withnail and I* (1987). He impressed in Bruce Robinson's pitch black comedy *How to Get Ahead in Advertising* and appeared in the cult horror item *Warlock* (both 1989) before going on to work for such major directors as Robert Altman (*The Player*, 1992), Francis Ford Coppola (*Bram Stoker's Dracula*, 1992), Martin Scorsese (*The Age of Innocence*, 1993) and Jane Campion (*The Portrait of a Lady*, 1996). More recently, he has guest-starred on such popular TV shows as *Doctor Who* and *Downton Abbey*. Director Francesco Barilli plays the thankless role of the Police Commissioner, whose **Pensione Paura** (1978) is one of the great unsung *gialli* of the 1970s. Barilli does what he can, but it is a nothing role and he only has a couple of scenes.

2012

TV ad for *6 passi nel giallo* miniseries.

6 passi nel giallo (Italy)

Miniseries produced by Cristiana Monteverde, Raffaello Monteverde, Cristina Pittalis and Christina Zucchiatti Monteverde; Directors of Photography: Giovanni Canevari and Stefano Paradiso; Editor: Fabio Loutfy; Music by Alessandro Molinari

Episode one: *Visions of Murder*

Aka *Presagi*

Directed by Lamberto Bava; Screenplay by Fabrizio Lucherini and Stefano Piani

Main Players: Craig Bierko (Harry Chase); Marc Cabourdin (Daniel Schembri); Eliana Miglio (Valeria Farrugia)

Episode two: *The Bodyguard*

Aka *Sotto protezione*

Directed by Edoardo Margheriti; Screenplay by Alberto Ostini and Stefano Piani

Main Players: Adriano Giannini (Marco); Katrina Law

(Eleanor); Enrico Silvestrin (Guido); Jeanene Fox (Jane)

Episode three: *Souvenir*

Directed by Edoardo Margheriti; Screenplay by Brian Hurwitz

Main Players: Demetri Goritsas (Sebastian Brody); Katinka Egres (Lucia); Riccardo Festa (Inspector Anzalone); Larissa Bonaci (Lucia's friend)

Episode four: *Gemelle*

Directed by Fabrizio Bava; Screenplay by Stefano Piani and Stefano Sudriè

Main Players: Tomas Arana (Marc Douglas); Erica Durance (Angela / Christine); Marco Leonardi (Giovanni Ravaioli); Veronica Lazar (Muriel)

Episode five: *Tailor-made Murder*

Aka *Omicidia su musura*

Directed by Lamberto Bava; Screenplay by Alberto Ostini and Stefano Piani

Main Players: Rob Estes (Randy Williams); Paolo Seganti (Cassar); Ana Caterina Morariu (Lola); Clayton Norcross (Zack)

Episode six: *Kammerspiel*

Aka *Vite in ostaggio*

Directed by Lamberto Bava; Screenplay by Alberto Ostini and Stefano Piani

Main Players: Kevin Sorbo (Dave McBain); Jane Alexander (Giovanna McBain); Antonio Cupo (Mathias); Christoph Hülsen (Kyle)

This series produced for Italian television has yet to surface outside of Italy and has not been granted a home video release anywhere in the world.

Three directors with some experience in the genre helmed the series. Lamberto Bava is, of course, an old hand at the *giallo* thanks to such films as *A Blade in the Dark* (1983) and *Midnight Killer* (1986), while his son Fabrizio has long acted as his assistant since the days of *Demons* (1985). Fabrizio was born in Rome in 1967 and caught the filmmaking bug early on thanks to the influence of his father and grandfather, Mario Bava. Fabrizio worked extensively as an assistant director throughout the 1980s, 1990s and 2000s, assisting his father on many films as well as Dario Argento on *The Card Player* (2004). He has also worked as a casting director on many productions and made his first foray into directing in 2000 with an episode of the Italian TV series *Distretto di polizia*. His segment of *6 passi nel giallo* marks only his second crack at directing. Edoardo Margheriti, the son of the late Antonio Margheriti, made his *giallo* debut with the made-for-TV thriller *Negli occhi dell'assassino* (2009).

The first segment, "Visions of Murder," tells of a medium who has a vision of a woman being murdered by a figure in black. She tries to convince the police that something terrible is going to happen, but only one of them, Harry Chase, is inclined to believe her story. This story by Fabrizio Lucherini and Stefano Piani evokes memories of Lucio Fulci's *The Psychic* (1977) and also recalls elements of Dario Argento's *Deep Red* (1975).

The second segment, "The Bodyguard," tells of the murder of a 17-year-old girl; the girl's cousin is accused of the crime and thrown in jail, but one year later a nosy journalist starts poking around and uncovers more than the police had bargained for.

In the third story, "Souvenir," an escaped lunatic attacks F.B.I. profiler Sebastian Brody and his wife, whom Brody had helped incarcerate years earlier. Brody's wife is killed and Brody avenges her by killing the lunatic. In order to forget his woes, Brody moves to a small town, but his past comes back to haunt him when he becomes mixed up in another murder scenario involving a serial killer known as The Hairdresser.

The fourth episode, "Gemelle," deals with a girl named Angela who moves to Italy, hoping to reconcile with her estranged twin sister Christine. It transpires that Christine has disappeared following a brutal rape, and Angela does everything in her power to find her. Meanwhile, the men who were responsible for the rape start turning up dead.

The fifth story, "Tailor-made Murder," tells of successful mystery novelist Randy Williams who indulges in a night of hanky-panky with a gorgeous stranger. The next morning, the stranger is nowhere to be found, but when Randy goes home, he is in for a nasty surprise. His wife Isabel has been killed. Everything points to Randy as the culprit, so he sets out to clear his name and find the real killer.

And finally, "Kammerspiel" offers up a variation on William Wyler's classic suspense thriller *The Desperate Hours* (1955). Three thugs enter Dave McBain's home and take his wife and child hostage. They are in for a nasty surprise, however, as McBain is not whom he appears to be and is prepared to go to great lengths to protect his family.

Fan reaction to the series was quite negative on the whole, with many complaining of static scripts with too much dialogue. Most of the segments also steered clear of the more outré elements of the genre, resulting in stories that were predictable and developed in a conventional manner. It would appear, based on these comments, that the atmosphere, tension and general air of weirdness one expects from a *giallo* was seldom in evidence, pointing to a trend toward neutering the genre and pigeonholing it into the American detective series model. If so, this is to be regretted, as Lamberto Bava especially has shown a real flair for this sort of material in the past. Even so, Bava's initial segment, "Visions of Murder," came in for some particularly negative notices. Some reviewers did find some value in Margheriti's two contributions, "The Bodyguard" and "Souvenir," but they appear to have been the exception rather than the rule.

The cast assembled for the series is an eclectic bunch, including American actors Craig Bierko (Terry Gilliam's

DVD release of *6 passi nel giallo*.

Fear and Loathing in Las Vegas, 1998) and Kevin Sorbo (best known as the star of TV's *Hercules: The Legendary Journeys*, which aired from 1995 to 1999) and *giallo* veterans like Tomas Arana (***Body Puzzle***, 1992) and Marco Leonardi (***The Stendhal Syndrome***, 1996). The presence of faded American actors like Bierko and Sorbo may have been intended to attract the interest of international sales, but if this was the idea it failed to come off; another odd (if decidedly novel) element is that the films were largely shot and set in the Mediterranean island of Malta. One can only regret that the talent assembled behind the camera apparently did not result in a more thrilling end result; the series drew mediocre ratings and did not lead to further *gialli* for the small screen.

L'isola dell'angelo caduto (Italy)

Directed by Carlo Lucarelli; Produced by Grazia Volpi; Screenplay by Michele Cogo, Carlo Lucarelli and Giampiero Rigosi, from the novel by Carlo Lucarelli; Director of Photography: Rocco Marra; Editor: Daniele di Maio; Music by Guido Facchini and Gianni Maroccolo

Main Players: Giampaolo Morelli (Commissioner); Giuseppe Cederna (Federal); Rolando Ravello (The Englishman); Sara Sartini (Hana)

In 1924 as Benito Mussolini rises to power, a young Police Commissioner is relocated to a small community near Sicily known as "The Isle of the Fallen Angel." The island is under the rule of the Fascist paramilitary group known as the Blackshirts. The strange atmosphere of the island begins to affect the Commissioner's wife, who becomes obsessed with a song titled "Ludovico," and wishes to return to the mainland. The unusual tranquility is disrupted by the mysterious death of a Blackshirt who is found on the cliffs. More murders take place, and the leader of the Blackshirts attempts to stop the Commissioner from investigating. Nevertheless, he continues his quest ...

Carlo Lucarelli published his novel *L'isola dell'Angelo Caduto* in 1999. It received rave reviews and seemed an ideal candidate for a film adaptation. Nevertheless, the ambitious storyline was not adapted for over a decade—by which point the multi-talented novelist was ready to take a stab at directing it.

The book offers an amalgam of fact and fantasy. Set against the rise of the Fascist party (as are a number of the author's books), it establishes a realistic framework for its fictional narrative. Lucarelli even brings in

CARLO LUCARELLI

L'ISOLA DELL'ANGELO CADUTO

though his socio-political leanings did not get in the way of telling a good thriller. Sadly, like so many of his books, it has yet to be released in the U.S. or the U.K. in a proper English translation.

When the time came to bring the book to the screen, Lucarelli took it upon himself to co-author the screenplay and leapt at the chance to direct. Given his success in other fields, there was some real buzz surrounding the film. The *giallo* had, of course, fallen into a state of decline, and if anybody stood much of a chance at reviving it, Lucarelli was more than likely the one to do it. Sadly, the build-up and anticipation worked against the picture, which premiered at a film festival in Rome in 2012 to poor reviews. Curiously, the backlash was so strong that the producers summarily abandoned all plans of a theatrical release and the film remains locked away, far from prying eyes. Lucarelli's career as a director died before it began, and the movie is impossible to see at this point in time.

Critic Marzia Gandolfi was decidedly unimpressed by the final product:

L'isola dell angelo caduto **premiere at the 7th Rome film festival: Veronica Gentili, Carlo Lucarelli, Sara Sartini, Irma Carolina Di Monte, Laura Glavan**

references to Aleister Crowley, who attempted to establish the so-called Abbey of Thelema in a small house located in the commune of Cefalù, on the coast of Sicily. Crowley (1875-1947), the famed occultist who described himself as "the most wicked man in the world," took the house over in 1920 and hoped to turn it into the spiritual center of his proposed religious and philosophical discipline of Thelema. The concepts behind Thelema are too exhaustive to get into in the context of a parenthetical aside, but Crowley's vision of rejecting conventional cultural and religious mores in favor of exploring personal pleasure in the form of mind-expanding drugs and sexual encounters made him notorious in many circles. Mussolini eventually kicked Crowley and his cult members out of the country due to the bad publicity they were receiving; local residents took it upon themselves to erase all traces of Crowley ever having been there by whitewashing the building. Clearly Lucarelli was aiming for something a little more ambitious than the usual whodunit,

Lucarelli is an excellent writer and his novels are truly a minefield for scriptwriters, as his writing style and atmosphere are very cinema-like. However, when it came to directly adapting one of his own works, the results were disheartening. All the traps that should be avoided have sprung, and the perfect balance of his book of the same name was lost. Something doesn't work in *L'isola dell'angelo caduto*, something that screeches and makes the viewer uneasy—something that must be found in the stylistic project of the film, where everything is comprehensible yet utterly improbable. The fascinating plot is smothered by a naïve cinematic discourse, which reduces such a complex novel to a story as simple as a fairytale, whose villain does exactly what he is required to in the rulebook. As the irreprehensible Commissioner, Giampaolo Morelli—who had already played Lucarelli's Inspector Coliandro in a TV series—does not convey his character's vulnerability […]. The thought-provoking point of view of his literary counterpart, who is a critical observer of a society to which he does not belong, is lost in an oneiric and surreal visual style that conveys no quality at all. Ultimately, Lucarelli's novel […] never translates into cinematic language. […] The main problem with this adaptation is its inability to find an alternative (and cinematic) way of realizing literary introspection, because in such a mystery novel everything takes place within the characters' minds, and those eventually become more important than the plot itself. The characters here—together with the very poor dialogue—are another disappointing factor.[1]

Notes:
1. http://www.mymovies.it/film/2011/lisoladellangelocaduto/

2013

Tulpa—Demon of Desire (Italy)

Aka *Tulpa—Perdizioni mortali*

Directed by Federico Zampaglione; Produced by Maria Grazia Cucinotta and Giovanna Emidi; Screenplay by Federico Zampaglione and Giacomo Gensini, from a story by Dardano Sacchetti; Director of Photography: Giuseppe Maio; Music by Andrea Moscianese, Federico Zampaglione and Francesco Zampaglione

Main Players: Claudia Gerini (Lisa Boeri); Michela Cescon (Giovanna); Ivan Franek (Stefan); Laurence Belgrave (Gerald); Michele Placido (Massimo Roccaforte)

Home Video: LFG (Region B Blu-ray)

By day, Lisa Boeri is an uptight businesswoman employed by the wealthy and powerful Massimo Roccaforte. By night, she lets her hair down and indulges her sexual whims at the exclusive club, Tulpa. Things take an unexpected turn when her various partners start meeting with brutal deaths, and Lisa must discover the culprit before her secret life is exposed ...

The *tulpa* can be traced to Tibetan and Indian Buddhism. In essence, it is a phantom or object that can be created and summoned through sheer force of thought. It is also the title of the last film in this study of 50 years of *gialli*.

The story was devised by *giallo* ace Dardano Sacchetti, though how much of his original concept remains in the finished film is debatable. In the hands of director Federico Zampaglione and his co-writer Giacomo Gensini, a potentially interesting genre-bending concept is reduced to a simple softcore thriller with some nasty deaths.

The narrative centers on the character of Lisa, a successful career woman with a dark, kinky secret. Unfortunately, like so many films of this ilk, Lisa's status as a strong, independent woman is equated with being a ball-buster who is a closet pervert. There is not a lot of depth to the character beyond this. She engages in sexual assignations with men and women alike and is more than capable of looking after herself, except when she really needs to. This allows her to degenerate into the usual shrieking damsel-in-distress when things get unpleasant, thus allowing the filmmakers to have their cake and eat it too. A truly strong, resourceful protagonist would have provided a far more interesting twist on the material, but Lisa is ultimately just another in a long line of decorous scream queens in the *giallo* canon.

The film certainly does not shy away from condemning the world of finance and big business. Pretty much everybody in Massimo Roccaforte's empire is depicted as scheming and malicious. Roccaforte is a lecher who hides behind a

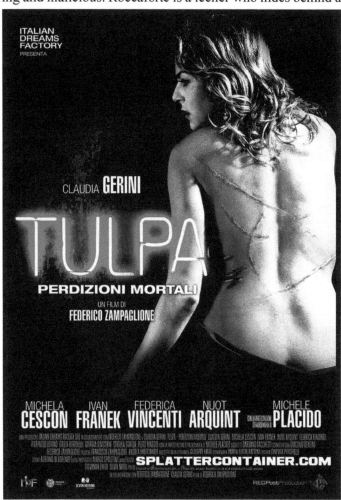

Italian poster for *Tulpa—Demon of Desire*; artist unknown.

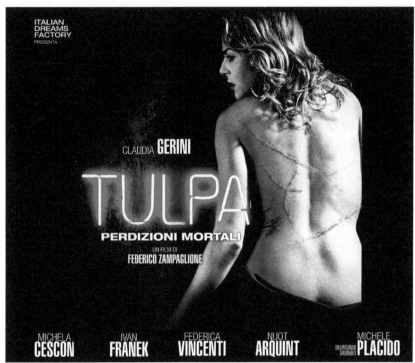

Another size of the Italian poster for *Tulpa—Demon of Desire* ; artist unknown.

kindly, genteel exterior. The people who work under him are constantly under pressure of being fired if they do not meet expectations, so they do not think twice about screwing each other over in order to maintain their livelihood.

All of this is secondary to the film's primary focus, which is to cram in as much blood and sleaze as possible. There is plenty of sex and nudity, but the film succumbs to the same problem that dogs many so-called erotic thrillers. Nothing is inherently erotic about bare breasts or people pretending to have sex. A film can be truly erotic without ever showing as much as a bare nipple. It is all in how the material is handled by the actors and the director. In the case of this movie, Zampaglione seems at a loss with how to proceed, so he simply throws as much as possible onscreen in the hopes of hitting the right notes. The end result is lots of sex scenes, which have no life or vitality as they simply take up screen time.

The film's violence level is bound to be more pleasing to the fans. The opening murder is truly vicious and unpleasant and culminates with a hinted-at castration, which goes into full-blown poor taste mode when the killer throws the man's severed member on the pillow in front of the bound and gagged female victim. It is a nasty image, to be sure, and lets the audience know right off the bat that subtlety and suggestion will not be the order of the day. The subsequent killings are quite violent as well, with one victim being very badly lacerated but left to live in a concealed spot as the killer tosses in some mean-looking rodents to finish off the job. Another victim is rigged to a makeshift merry-go-round device and is sent spinning—each time they pass by an intimidating chunk of barbed wire, they lose more and more flesh and eventually an eyeball as well. The gore effects are

well done, and Zampaglione at least does not fall into the trap that has dogged Dario Argento's recent efforts by not dwelling too long and hard on any particular set-up.

Zampaglione directs the film with a certain style and verve, though it never comes close to recapturing the special flavor of the thrillers of the 1970s. The widescreen photography by Giuseppe Maio is occasionally striking and the film does not have the same ultra-cheap digital look of some other *gialli* of the period. The pacing is generally smooth, though things inevitably grind to a halt whenever time is taken out for another sexual encounter. Fortunately this aspect is less prevalent in the second half of the picture.

Sadly, any goodwill the film builds up is more or less imploded in the last act. The decision to take the story into a mystical realm was, to put it mildly, ill advised. Perhaps if this had been developed with greater care and with some sense of irony, it may have come off. As it stands, the final *deus ex machina* is lame beyond belief and will surely send many viewers away muttering profanities under their breath.

The cast seems somewhat adrift, if not downright disinterested. Claudia Gerini gives a decent performance as Lisa, though she is only able to do so much given the inconsistent nature of the character. Gerini is able to evoke some sympathy and helps carry the film through its narrative issues. She was born in Rome in 1971 and started working in films and television as a teen actress in 1986. She rose to prominence thanks to a critically acclaimed performance in the romantic comedy *I'm Crazy About Iris Blond* (1996), in which she played the title character, and then enjoyed her greatest exposure with her role as Claudia in Mel Gibson's controversial *The Passion of the Christ* (2004). Among her upcoming credits is a Spanish/Canadian/French/American thriller titled *Twisted*, which was due in 2014 and sounds like it may be a homage of sorts to the *giallo*. Among the nondescript supporting cast, it is nice to see a gracefully aging Michele Placido in the role of Massimo Roccaforte; Placido walks through his scenes, though his presence reminds one of the better *gialli* of yesterday.

Director Federico Zampaglione was born in Rome in 1968. In addition to writing and directing, he is also a singer; he started the group Tiromancino in 1989 and to date the group, which synthesizes folk and electronica sounds, has released 12 albums. He entered films in 2007 with the dark comedy *A Dream House Nightmare*, and then attracted attention as a new voice in the floundering Italian horror film with the stylish *Shadow* (2009). **Tulpa—Demon of Desire** was hyped on the promise shown in that film, but it did little to further his career or his standing among the fans. Hopefully his future efforts in the genre will prove to be more successful, should he desire to give it another try.

Giallo:
In the Heart of the Mystery
by Luigi Cozzi

Author's Note: This piece was originally written for the Brazilian newspaper, Zero Hora, *and was published on Saturday May 11, 2013. It is included here, in a slightly abbreviated form, courtesy of Luigi Cozzi.*

Giallo is an Italian word that indicates the color "yellow," and over the past 100 years in Italy this term has also been used to label those works, either books or movies, in which the protagonists (whether they be cops or common people) investigate who committed a murder. This particular meaning attributed to the word *giallo* entered Italian popular culture in 1929, when the biggest publishing house of that time (and today as well), Mondadori, started releasing then new detective novels by such authors as Edgar Wallace and Agatha Christie using the color yellow as the background in the covers, as a characteristic sign so as to immediately identify them. Customers started asking, "Can you give me the new *giallo* book?" and then just, "Can you give me the new *giallo*?" Eventually the term *giallo* became commonly used in our language as an official synonym to indicate any work, either in cinema or in literature, in which someone investigates in order to unmask a murderer.

However, since the *gialli* published for decades (and which today are still being sold at newsstands) by Mondadori, as well as its many imitators, were almost all written by Anglo-Saxon or French novelists (such as Simenon with his *Maigret* novels), audiences gradually became convinced that these stories, in literature and in movies, could *never* be written or filmed by Italian authors. For instance, in the mid-1950s Mondadori published several very good *gialli* written by Italian novelists, but their commer-

cial failure caused the publisher to give up on Italian writers; one such writer was Sergio Donati, who would later script the most famous Spaghetti Westerns directed by Sergio Leone and starring Clint Eastwood!

(Curiously, from then on, several lesser publishers started releasing many *gialli* written by Italians, with the expedient of hiding the author's real names behind Anglicized pseudonyms; these books, on the contrary, sold quite well...)

Meanwhile, in the movies, a new director named Mario Bava, who had a hit in the United States (but not in Italy) with his feature film debut (the horror story *Black Sunday*, 1960), unleashed ***The Girl Who Knew Too Much*** (1963) and ***Blood and Black Lace*** (1964), two thrillers that were definitely extreme for their period. Bava—thanks to his visionary talent, which today is recognized all over the world—managed to codify for the first time several of those characteristics which would later be reprised, extended and perfected 10 years later by Dario Argento in his films. For example, there is the unusual metropolitan setting, which is evident mainly in ***The Girl Who Knew Too Much***, with the use of the huge monumental stairway in Piazza di Spagna (the so-called "Spanish Steps"), which becomes menacing and haunting thanks to the judicious use of lighting. Other little known Roman sites appear characterized by a disquieting architectural structure, such as Piazza Mincio, setting in the middle of Rome's only small Liberty-style district, the Quartiere Coppede ... or the extremely stylish portrayal of the ferocious murders committed by a maniac (who is always dressed in black, with a raincoat and black gloves) in Bava's other thriller, ***Blood and Black Lace***. The latter is an exemplary film, as it consists almost *exclusively*

Mario Bava's *Blood and Black Lace* (1964) set the template for years of *gialli.*

of six long sequences that are focused on the murders of just as many young and uninhibited beautiful girls.

These two films shot by Mario Bava in Rome under an explicit request on the part of the American market did not find any success in Italy, though, and nobody noticed them—except for a young film critic who would later become a screenwriter and a world-famous director in his own right. Dario Argento saw both *The Girl Who Knew Too Much* and *Blood and Black Lace* several times and was greatly impressed by this extreme and Italianized reworking of the American thriller that Bava had helped to invent.

The first film written and directed by Dario Argento, *The Bird with the Crystal Plumage* (1970), represented the birth of the modern Italian *giallo*-thriller genre; it was immediately very successful, even in the United States and all over the world, spawning at least a 100 imitations or variations until February 1975, when *Deep Red* came out. Often, such variations were artistically and commercially successful as well. That said, it would be reductive to state that only Argento inspired these films, as the many *gialli* that came in its wake also reached back to earlier thrillers by Bava and others as well.

If one wants to understand the reasons behind the almost immediate worldwide success met in 1970 by *The Bird with the Crystal Plumage*, it is necessary to acknowledge that with that film its author went far beyond the *gialli* that preceded it. Dario Argento was not even 30 when he wrote the script for *The Bird with the Crystal Plumage* in 1968 (the film was shot in the late summer of 1969), and those were the months of the great youth revolts in France and Italy. Dario Argento was pushed by the strong impulse of breaking all the habitual schemes and the most banal and repetitive clichés of commercial cinema. Those were the years in which American mainstream cinema was missing a beat, and Hollywood was not able to keep pace with young audiences and their tastes.

However, Argento was a young man, as were most of the film audiences back then, so it came naturally to him to start that filmic revolution that in very little time would turn him into a true star. He was also the master of a new kind of hyper-technological cinema that soon would see the blooming of another revolutionary young talent in Hollywood: Steven Spielberg.

We cannot really understand the origins of *The Bird with the Crystal Plumage*'s revolution in the realm of the *giallo* if we do not consider Dario Argento's collaboration with another master of cinema, Sergio Leone. For more than one year, starting in the second half of 1967, Argento and another young and promising filmmaker, Bernardo Bertolucci (who later won an Academy Award for Best Director with *The Last Emperor*), spent many hours, day after day, in Sergio Leone's huge villa in the Eur district helping to structure and collaborate the writing of the story of his new film that would emerge in 1968 as yet another masterpiece: *Once Upon a Time in the West*, starring Henry Fonda and Claudia Cardinale. The relationship with Leone was deep.

To Argento he was not only a master, but a real idol, the perfect filmmaker whom Dario absolutely wanted to imitate in all respects—so much so that when I became friends with Dario in early 1970, the young director would often talk to me about the beautiful experience he had enjoyed with Sergio Leone. It was more than a working collaboration but a lesson in life. When I asked Dario about specific particular and unusual gestures he used to make on the set of *Four Flies on Grey Velvet* in 1971 (where I debuted as his assistant director; we also wrote the film together), Argento explained, a bit uncomfortably: "Well, I do so because I saw Sergio Leone doing it on the set."

That being established, Dario Argento did not just take some gestures and ways of doing or saying things from

A suspensful moment from *The Bird with the Crystal Plumage*.

Sergio Leone. Argento and Leone had much more in common than that. During his early days in the movie business, Argento was an extraordinary sponge and was able to absorb and *personalize* everything. From Sergio Leone he learned the technique of starting work on a film without giving himself any limits. He told me that Leone always used to tell him:

> Think about the films that you liked the most, the scenes that you have seen and that you would like to have written yourself. Well, see those films again, watch those scenes again and, if you still like them, if they still move you, find a way to repeat them, even if in a different manner, and put them in the film that we are writing. If they fit well with what we are doing, great … we keep them and build the rest around them. Or else just forget them and we'll look for something else.

Dario recalls that writing the story of *Once Upon a Time in the West* took a long time and the early stages consisted of he and Bertolucci simply revising films they loved or re-reading books they appreciated, passing them between one another and looking for ideas and interesting moments to insert in the Western outline of *Once Upon a Time in the West*. Among the many books and films that Argento and Bertolucci took into consid-

eration while preparing their work on the film were numerous *gialli* … even though perhaps people have not noticed. Leone's wonderful film is actually structured as a *giallo*. The entire story of *Once Upon a Time in the West* is based on a big mystery to be solved. Why do the villains offer a great sum of money, and even commit a killing, in order to get their hands on a small and squalid farm in the middle of nowhere inherited by the insignificant character played by Claudia Cardinale?

The plot of *Once Upon a Time in the West* develops not according to the rules of that most American of genres, but by adopting the technique that is typical of the *giallo*. It is a plot riddled with puzzles, in which mysteries and surprises follow one another, while the situations and characters change continually, just as it happens in the most typical ex-

amples of detective literature and cinema. All in all, *Once Upon a Time in the West* is structured like a *giallo*, but it is actually a Western, and a beautiful one indeed.

Leone would therefore have a major impact on the *giallo*, thanks to the impression he made on his young collaborator. Dario Argento, however, never denied that, since he often declared:

> With **The Bird with the Crystal Plumage** I tried to do a *giallo*, yet one unlike the old, classic English-style examples, with somebody being murdered off-screen and whose body we only glimpse once … No, not like that, but perhaps in the way that Sergio would shoot it, if he had to make one.

Above: He may not have created the genre, but Dario Argento did more than any other director to popularize the *giallo*. Left: Argento in a posed publicity shot.

These words contain the whole essence (and the history) of the Italian *giallo*, which flourished between 1970 and 1975. That is, between the release of **The Bird with the Crystal Plumage** and **Deep Red**. Since Italian audiences rushed to see those films, there were many other similar Italian *gialli*, some of which were the work of remarkable or interesting filmmakers (Sergio Martino, Pupi Avati, Lucio Fulci). All in all, it was a golden age for Italian cinema, both artistically and commercially, since those films were very popular outside the country and were sold (and still are today, in the home video market) all over the world.

Then, since about 1976-77, violence and sex in Italian *gialli* reached a peak and got to a point of no return, just like years earlier it had been for the Spaghetti Westerns invented by Sergio Leone. To push the limits, in fact, and offer more and more blood and guts to the audience, filmmakers abandoned the *giallo* and changed the genre entirely. Then another thread started, that of out-and-out horror.

Once again, it was up to Dario Argento to lead the new path for everyone to follow, in order to go beyond the previous boundaries. He did so in early 1977, when the release of *Suspiria* spelled the birth of modern Italian horror cinema.

However, this is another story, even though many of the authors are the same …

GIALLOGRAPHY

The following is an index of some of the key names associated with the *giallo* on film. I have attempted to round up most—if not *all*—of the major "players," including directors, writers, composers and performers, and have assembled all of their *giallo* credits to date. For the most part, I have limited the selections to people who have made more than a handful of *giallo* films; I have made exceptions with a few key names who only made one or two—but whose contributions deserve to be properly celebrated. Only titles reviewed in the two volumes of *So Deadly, So Perverse* are included; borderline *gialli* which did not make the cut are not included in these filmographies. Dates (and locations) of birth and death are included where possible, but in some cases, extant biographical information is slim to non-existent. Please refer to the following key for notations next to each entry (D = Director; AD = Assistant Director; P = Producer; S = Screenplay and/or Story; E = Editor; DP = Director of Photography; OP = Camera Operator; A = Actor; M = Music; C = Conductor)

ALABISO, Eugenio (born: Rome, Lazio, Italy, 1937)
The Sweet Body of Deborah (1968) E
So Sweet ... So Perverse (1969) E
The Strange Vice of Mrs. Wardh (1971) E
The Case of the Scorpion's Tail (1971) E
The Oasis of Fear (1971) E
The Fifth Cord (1971) E
Seven Blood-Stained Orchids (1972) E
All the Colors of the Dark (1972) E
The Case of the Bloody Iris (1972) E
Torso (1973) E
Death Carries a Cane (1973) E
Spasmo (1974) E
Death Steps in the Dark (1977) E
The Scorpion with Two Tails (1982) E
Private Crimes (1993) E
Mozart is a Murderer (1999) E
ALBANI, Romano (born: Livorno, Tuscany, Italy, 1945; died: Rome, Lazio, Italy, 2014)
Snapshot of a Crime (1975) OP
The Sunday Woman (1975) OP
Phenomena (1985) DP
Obsession: A Taste for Fear (1988) DP
ANDREU, Simón (born: Sa Pobla, Balearic Islands, Spain, 1941)
Forbidden Photos of a Lady Above Suspicion (1970) A
Death Walks on High Heels (1971) A
Death Walks at Midnight (1972) A
Death Carries a Cane (1973) A

Special Killers (1973) A
Eyes of Crystal (2004) A
ARGENTO, Asia (born: Rome, Lazio, Italy, 1975)
Giallo: la tua impronta del venerdi (1987) A
Trauma (1993) A
The Stendhal Syndrome (1996) A
Sleepless (2001) (Author of the nursery rhyme used in the film)
ARGENTO, Dario (born: Rome, Lazio, Italy, 1940)
The Bird with the Crystal Plumage (1970) D, S
The Cat O'Nine Tails (1971) D, S
Four Flies on Grey Velvet (1971) D, S
Door into Darkness (1973) D, P, S, A
Deep Red (1975) D, S
Tenebrae (1982) D, S
Phenomena (1985) D, P, S
Giallo: la tua impronta del venerdi (1987) D, P, A
Opera (1987) D, P, S
Trauma (1993) D, P, S
The Stendhal Syndrome (1996) D, P, S
Sleepless (2001) D, P, S
The Card Player (2004) D, P, S
Do You Like Hitchcock? (2005) D, S
Giallo (2009) D, S
AVATI, Pupi (born: Bologna, Emilia-Romagna, Italy, 1938)
The House with Laughing Windows (1976) D, S
Tutti defunti... tranne i morti (1977) D, S
The Room Next Door (1994) S
BAKER, Carroll (born: Johnstown, Pennsylvania, USA, 1931)
The Sweet Body of Deborah (1968) A
Orgasmo (1968) A
So Sweet ... So Perverse (1969) A
A Quiet Place to Kill (1970) A
The Devil With Seven Faces (1972) A
Knife of Ice (1972) A
The Flower with the Deadly Sting (1973) A
BATTAGLIA, Gianlorenzo
Hatchet for the Honeymoon (1970) Assistant Camera
Five Dolls for an August Moon (1970) Assistant Camera
Twitch of the Death Nerve (1971) Assistant Camera
A Blade in the Dark (1983) DP, OP
Phenomena (1985) Underwater Photography
Formula for a Murder (1985) DP
Midnight Killer (1986) DP
Delirium: Photos of Gioia (1987) DP
BAVA, Lamberto (born: Rome, Lazio, Italy, 1944)
Hatchet for the Honeymoon (1970) AD
Twitch of the Death Nerve (1971) AD

Tenebrae (1982) AD, A
A Blade in the Dark (1983) D, E
Midnight Killer (1986) D, S, E
Delirium: Photos of Gioia (1987) D
Giallo: la tua impronta del venerdi (1987) D
Eyewitness (1990) D, S
Body Puzzle (1992) D, S
6 passi nel giallo (2012) D

BAVA, Mario (born: San Remo, Liguria, Italy, 1914; died: Rome, Lazio, Italy, 1980)
The Girl Who Knew Too Much (1963) D, S, DP, A (US version only)
The Three Faces of Fear (1963) D, S, DP (uncredited)
Blood and Black Lace (1964) D, S, DP (uncredited)
Naked You Die (1969) S (uncredited)
Hatchet for the Honeymoon (1970) D, DP
Five Dolls for an August Moon (1970) D, DP (uncredited), E
Twitch of the Death Nerve (1971) D, S, DP

BAZZONI, Luigi (born: Salsomaggiore Terme, Emilia-Romagna, Italy, 1929; died: Salsomaggiore Terme, Emilia-Romagna, Italy, 2012)
The Possessed (1965) D, S
The Fifth Cord (1971) D, S

BENUSSI, Femi (born: Rovigno, Istria, Italy [now Rovinj, Istria, Croatia], 1945)
Deadly Inheritance (1968) A
Hatchet for the Honeymoon (1970) A
Questa libertà di avere ... le ali bagnate (1971) A
So Sweet, So Dead (1972) A
Special Killers (1973) A
The Killer Must Kill Again (1975) A
Strip Nude for your Killer (1975), A

BLANC, Erika (born: Gargnano, Lombardy, Italy, 1942)
So Sweet ... So Perverse (1969) A
Human Cobras (1971) A
The Red Headed Corpse (1972) A
The Night Evelyn Came Out of the Grave (1972) A
Door into Darkness (1973) A
Giochi erotici di una famiglia per bene (1975) A
Body Puzzle (1992) A

BOLKAN, Florinda (born: Uruburetama, Ceará, Brazil, 1941)
A Rather Complicated Girl (1969) A
A Lizard in a Woman's Skin (1971) A
Don't Torture a Duckling (1972) A
Bad Inclination (2003) A

BOUCHET, Barbara (born: Reichenberg, Sudetenland, Germany [now Liberic, Czech Republic], 1943)
The Man with Icy Eyes (1971) A
The Black Belly of the Tarantula (1971) A
Amuck! (1972) A
The French Sex Murders (1972) A
The Red Queen Kills Seven Times (1972) A
Don't Torture a Duckling (1972) A

CAPPONI, Pier Paolo (born: Subiaco, Lazio, Italy, 1938)
Naked Violence (1969) A
Forbidden Photos of a Lady Above Suspicion (1970) A
The Cat O'Nine Tails (1971) A
Seven Blood-Stained Orchids (1972) A
Delitto d'autore (1974) A

CAVARA, Paolo (born: Bologna, Emilia-Romagna, Italy, 1926; died: Rome, Lazio, Italy, 1982)
The Black Belly of the Tarantula (1971) D
Plot of Fear (1976) D, S

CELI, Adolfo (born: Messina, Sicily, Italy, 1922; died: Siena, Tuscany, Italy, 1986)
Eye in the Labyrinth (1972) A
Who Killed the Prosecutor and Why? (1972) A
Who Saw Her Die? (1972) A
Naked Girl Killed in Park .... (1972) A
The Perfect Crime (1978) A

CIATTI, Romeo
The Night Evelyn Came Out of the Grave (1971) E
The Red Queen Kills Seven Times (1972) E
Calling All Police Cars (1975) E
Reflections in Black (1975) E

CIPRIANI, Stelvio (born: Rome, Lazio, Italy, 1937)
Twitch of the Death Nerve (1971) M
Human Cobras (1971) M
The Iguana with the Tongue of Fire (1971) M
Death Walks on High Heels (1971) M
The Devil With Seven Faces (1972) M
The Killer is on the Phone (1972) M
What Have They Done to Your Daughters? (1974) M
Death Will Have Your Eyes (1974) M
The Bloodstained Shadow (1978) M

CLERICI, Gianfranco
The Bloodstained Butterfly (1971) S
Don't Torture a Duckling (1972) S
Five Women for the Killer (1974) S
Blazing Magnum (1976) S
The New York Ripper (1982) S
Murder-Rock: Dancing Death (1984) S
Delirium: Photos of Gioia (1987) S
Phantom of Death (1988) S

COLLI, Ernesto (born: Biella, Piedmont, Italy, 1940; died: Biella, Piedmont, Italy, 1982)
Deadly Inheritance (1968) A
Kill the Poker Player (1972) A
Torso (1973) A
Autopsy (1975) A

CONTINENZA, Alessandro (born: Rome, Lazio, Italy, 1920; died: Rome, Lazio, Italy, 1996)
The Iguana with the Tongue of Fire (1971) S
The Double (1971) S
The Crimes of the Black Cat (1972) S
Il ficcanaso (1981) S

COZZI, Luigi (born: Busto Arsizio, Italy, 1947)
Four Flies on Grey Velvet (1971) S, AD, A
Door into Darkness (1973) D, S
The Killer Must Kill Again (1975) D
Giallo: la tua impronta del venerdi (1987) D

DALLAMANO, Massimo (born: Milan, Lombardy, Italy, 1917; died: Rome, Lazio, Italy, 1976)
A Black Veil for Lisa (1968) D, S
What Have You Done to Solange? (1972) D, S
What Have They Done to Your Daughters? (1974) D, S
Rings of Fear (1978) S

DE MARTINO, Alberto (born: Rome, Lazio, Italy, 1929; died: Rome, Lazio, Italy, 2015)
Carnal Circuit (1969) D, S
The Man with Icy Eyes (1971) D
The Killer is on the Phone (1972) D, S
Formula for a Murder (1985) D, S

DE MASI, Francesco (born: Rome, Lazio, Italy, 1930; died: Rome, Lazio, Italy, 2005)
The Murder Clinic (1966) M
The Weekend Murders (1970) M
The Weapon, The Hour & The Motive (1972) M
The New York Ripper (1982) M
Formula for a Murder (1985) M

DE MENDOZA, Alberto (born: Buenos Aires, Argentina, 1923; died: Madrid, Spain, 2011)
Psychout for Murder (1969) A
Perversion Story (1969) A
The Strange Vice of Mrs. Wardh (1971) A
A Lizard in a Woman's Skin (1971) A
Human Cobras (1971) A
The Case of the Scorpion's Tail (1971) A
Special Killers (1973) A

ERCOLI, Luciano (born: Rome, Lazio, Italy, 1929; died: Barcelona, Spain, 2015)
What Ever Happened to Baby Totò? (1964) P
Forbidden Photos of a Lady Above Suspicion (1970) D, P, E
Death Walks on High Heels (1971) D, P
Death Walks at Midnight (1972) D, P

FELISATTI, Massimo (born: Ferrara, Italy, 1932)
The Weekend Murders (1970) S
The Night Evelyn Came Out of the Grave (1971) S
Strip Nude for Your Killer (1975) S
Calling All Police Cars (1975) S

FELLEGHY, Tom (born: Budapest, Hungary, 1921; died: ??)
The Cat O'Nine Tails (1971) A
The Case of the Scorpion's Tail (1971) A
The Oasis of Fear (1971) A
Four Flies on Grey Velvet (1971) A
Seven Blood-Stained Orchids (1972) A
All the Colors of the Dark (1972) A
Death Falls Lightly (1972) A
Seven Deaths in the Cat's Eyes (1973) A
Door into Darkness (1973) A
Spasmo (1974) A

Puzzle (1974) A
Five Women for the Killer (1974) A
Eyeball (1975) A
Deep Red (1975) A
The Perfect Crime (1978) A

FENECH, Edwige (born: Bône, Constantine, France [now Annaba, Algeria], 1948)
Top Sensation (1969) A
Five Dolls for an August Moon (1970) A
The Strange Vice of Mrs. Wardh (1971) A
All the Colors of the Dark (1971) A
Your Vice is a Locked Room and Only I Have the Key (1972) A
The Case of the Bloody Iris (1972) A
Strip Nude for Your Killer (1975) A
Il ficcanaso (1981) A
Phantom of Death (1988) A
Private Crimes (1993) A

FERRANDO, Giancarlo
Naked You Die (1969) OP
The Case of the Scorpion's Tail (1971) OP
All the Colors of the Dark (1972) DP
Your Vice is a Locked Room and Only I Have the Key (1972) DP
Torso (1973) DP
The Suspicious Death of a Minor (1975) DP
The Scorpion with Two Tails (1982) DP
Private Crimes (1993) DP
The Girl from Cortina (1993) D, DP

FERRINI, Franco (born: La Spezia, Italy, 1944)
Rings of Fear (1978) S
Phenomena (1985) S
Nothing Underneath (1985) S
Sweets from a Stranger (1987) D, S
Opera (1987) S
Delitti e profumi (1988) S
Trauma (1993) S
The Stendhal Syndrome (1996) S
Squillo (1996) S
Sleepless (2001) S
The Card Player (2004) S
Eyes of Crystal (2004) S
Do You Like Hitchcock? (2005) S

FERRIO, Gianni (born: Vicenza, Veneto, Italy, 1924; died: Rome, Lazio, Italy, 2013)
Death Occurred Last Night (1970) M
The Bloodstained Butterfly (1971) M
Death Walks at Midnight (1972) M
The Masked Thief (1973) M
Puzzle (1974) M
Crime of Passion (1994) M

FORISCOT, Emilio
Il tuo dolce corpo da uccidere (1970) DP
The Strange Vice of Mrs. Wardh (1971) DP
Human Cobras (1971) DP
The Case of the Scorpion's Tail (1971) DP

The Masked Thief (1971) DP
FRATICELLI, Franco (born: Rome, Lazio, Italy, 1928)
Date for a Murder (1967) E
The Bird with the Crystal Plumage (1970) E
The Cat O'Nine Tails (1971) E
My Dear Killer (1972) E
Deep Red (1975) E
Il mostro (1977) E
The Perfect Crime (1978) E
Tenebrae (1982) E
Phenomena (1985) E
Sweets from a Stranger (1987) E
Opera (1987) E
FREDA, Riccardo (born: Alexandria, Egypt, 1909; died: Rome, Lazio, Italy, 1999) [aka Robert Hampton]
Double Face (1969) D, S
The Iguana with the Tongue of Fire (1971) D, S, E
Murder Obsession (1980) D, S, E
FULCI, Lucio (born: Rome, Lazio, Italy, 1927; died: Rome, Lazio, Italy, 1996)
Double Face (1969) S
Perversion Story (1969) D, S, A
A Lizard in a Woman's Skin (1971) D, S
Don't Torture a Duckling (1972) D, S
The Psychic (1977) D, S
The New York Ripper (1982) D, S, A
Murder-Rock: Dancing Death (1984) D, S, A
GALLI, Ida (born: Sestola, Italy, 1942) [aka Evelyn Stewart]
The Sweet Body of Deborah (1968) A
The Weekend Murders (1970) A
The Case of the Scorpion's Tail (1971) A
The Bloodstained Butterfly (1971) A
Knife of Ice (1972) A
Spirits of Death (1972) A
The Psychic (1977) A
Arabella, Black Angel (1989) A
GASTALDI, Ernesto (born: Graglia, Piedmont, Italy, 1934)
Libido (1965) D, S
The Murder Clinic (1966) S
A ... come assassino (1966) S
The Sweet Body of Deborah (1968) S
So Sweet ... So Perverse (1969) S
Forbidden Photos of a Lady Above Suspicion (1970) S
The Strange Vice of Mrs. Wardh (1971) S
The Case of the Scorpion's Tail (1971) S
Death Walks on High Heels (1971) S
All the Colors of the Dark (1972) S
Your Vice is a Locked Room and Only I Have the Key (1972) S
The Case of the Bloody Iris (1972) S
Death Walks at Midnight (1972) S
Torso (1973) S
Puzzle (1974) S
The Suspicious Death of a Minor (1975) S
Il ficcanaso (1981) S
The Scorpion with Two Tails (1982) S

The Killer Has Returned (1986) S
The Strange Story of Olga O (1995) S
GIORDANO, Daniela (born: Palermo, Sicily, Italy, 1947)
Your Vice is a Locked Room and Only I Have the Key (1972) A
The Girl in Room 2A (1974) A
Reflections in Black (1975) A
GRANDI, Serena (born: Bologna, Emilia-Romagna, Italy, 1958)
Delirium: Photos of Gioia (1987) A
Crime of Passion (1994) A
The Strange Story of Olga O (1995) A
HILTON, George (born: Montevideo, Uruguay, 1934)
The Sweet Body of Deborah (1968) A
The Strange Vice of Mrs. Wardh (1971) A
The Case of the Scorpion's Tail (1971) A
The Devil With Seven Faces (1972) A
My Dear Killer (1972) A
All the Colors of the Dark (1972) A
The Case of the Bloody Iris (1972) A
Il baco da seta (1974) A
The Killer Must Kill Again (1975) A
HOFFMANN, Robert (born: Salzburg, Austria, 1939)
A Black Veil for Lisa (1968) A
Carnal Circuit (1969) A
Naked Girl Killed in Park ... (1972) A
Death Carries a Cane (1973) A
Door into Darkness (1973) A
Spasmo (1974) A
INCONTRERA, Annabella (born: Milan, Lombardy, Italy, 1943)
Double Face (1969) A
The Black Belly of the Tarantula (1971) A
The Case of the Bloody Iris (1972) A
So Sweet, So Dead (1972) A
The Crimes of the Black Cat (1972) A
Clap, You're Dead (1974) A
INFASCELLI, Alex (born: Rome, Lazio, Italy, 1967)
Almost Blue (2000) D, S, A
The Vanity Serum (2004) D
KENDALL, Suzy (born: Belper, Derbyshire, England, 1944)
The Bird with the Crystal Plumage (1970) A
Torso (1973) A
Spasmo (1974) A
KINSKI, Klaus (born: Zoppot, Free City of Danzig [now Sopot, Pomorskie, Poland], 1926; died: Lagunitas, California, USA, 1991)
Double Face (1969) A
Slaughter Hotel (1971) A
KUVEILLER, Luigi (born: Rome, Lazio, Italy, 1927; died: Rome, Lazio, Italy, 2013)
A Lizard in a Woman's Skin (1971) DP
Deep Red (1975) DP
Atrocious Tales of Love and Death (1979) DP
The New York Ripper (1982) DP

Body Puzzle (1992) DP
Circle of Fear (1992) DP
Squillo (1996) DP
LASSANDER, Dagmar (born: Prague, Protectorate Bohemia and Moravia [now Czech Republic], 1943)
Hatchet for the Honeymoon (1970) A
Forbidden Photos of a Lady Above Suspicion (1970) A
The Iguana with the Tongue of Fire (1971) A
Reflections in Black (1975) A
LENZI, Umberto (born: Massa Marittima, Grosseto, Tuscany, Italy, 1931)
Orgasmo (1968) D, S
So Sweet ... So Perverse (1969) D
A Quiet Place to Kill (1970) D
The Oasis of Fear (1971) D, S
Seven Blood-Stained Orchids (1972) D, S
Knife of Ice (1972) D, S
Spasmo (1974) D, S
Eyeball (1975) D, S
LEROY, Philippe (born: Paris, France, 1930)
The Possessed (1965) A
Devil's Ransom (1970) A
Cross Current (1970) A
Naked Girl Killed in Park ... (1972) A
Circle of Fear (1992) A
LOVELOCK, Ray (born: Rome, Lazio, Italy, 1950)
The Oasis of Fear (1971) A
Autopsy (1975) A
Play Motel (1979) A
Murder-Rock: Dancing Death (1984) A
Private Crimes (1993) A
LUCARELLI, Carlo (born: Parma, Emilia-Romagna, Italy, 1960)
Almost Blue (2000) S
Lupo mannaro (2000) S
Sleepless (2001) S
L'isola dell'angelo caduto (2012) D, S
MALFATTI, Marina (born: Florence, Tuscany, Italy, 1940)
Run, Psycho, Run (1968) A
The Night Evelyn Came Out of the Grave (1971) A
Seven Blood-Stained Orchids (1972) A
All the Colors of the Dark (1972) A
The Red Queen Kills Seven Times (1972) A
MANNINO, Vincenzo
The Man with Icy Eyes (1971) S
The Killer is on the Phone (1972) S
Five Women for the Killer (1974) S
Blazing Magnum (1976) S
The New York Ripper (1982) S
Murder-Rock: Dancing Death (1984) S
Formula for a Murder (1985) S
Phantom of Death (1988) S
MARGHERITI, Antonio (born: Rome, Lazio, Italy, 1930; died: Monterosi, Lazio, Italy, 2002) [aka Anthony M. Dawson]

Naked You Die (1968) D, S
Seven Deaths in the Cat's Eyes (1973) D, S
MARTINO, Sergio (born: Rome, Lazio, Italy, 1938)
The Sweet Body of Deborah (1968) Production Manager
So Sweet ... So Perverse (1969) P
The Strange Vice of Mrs. Wardh (1971) D
The Case of the Scorpion's Tail (1971) D
All the Colors of the Dark (1972) D, A
Your Vice is a Locked Room and Only I Have the Key (1972) D
Torso (1973) D, S
The Suspicious Death of a Minor (1975) D, S
The Scorpion with Two Tails (1982) D
Private Crimes (1993) D
The Girl from Cortina (1994) P
Mozart is a Murderer (1999) D, S
MASSACCESI, Aristide (born: Rome, Lazio, Italy, 1936; died: Rome, Lazio, Italy, 1999) [aka Joe D'Amato]
No Man's Island (1969) DP
A Quiet Place to Kill (1970) OP
What Have You Done to Solange? (1972) DP, A
The Killer is on the Phone (1972) DP
Blazing Magnum (1976) DP
Stage Fright (1987) P
MATTEI, Bruno (born: Rome, Lazio, Italy, 1937; died: Rome, Lazio, Italy, 2007)
Yellow: le cugine (1969) E
The French Sex Murders (1972) E
Omicidio al telefono (1994) D, S, E
Madness (1994) D, E
MERENDA, Luc (born: Nogent-le-Roi, Eure-et-Loir, France, 1943)
Torso (1973) A
Puzzle (1974) A
Pensione Paura (1977) A
Il ficcanaso (1981) A
MINGOZZI, Fulvio (born: Lagosanto, Emilia-Romagna, Italy, 1925; died: Rome, Lazio, Italy, 2000)
The Bird with the Crystal Plumage (1970) A
The Cat O'Nine Tails (1971)
The Black Belly of the Tarantula (1971) A
The Case of the Scorpion's Tail (1971) A
Four Flies on Grey Velvet (1971) A
Seven Blood-Stained Orchids (1972) A
Door into Darkness (1973) A
Eyeball (1975) A
Deep Red (1975) A
Calling All Police Cars (1975) A
Play Motel (1979) A
The Scorpion with Two Tails (1982) A
Tenebrae (1982) A
Phenomena (1985) A
MIRAGLIA, Emilio P. (born: Casarano, Puglia, Italy, 1924)
The Night Evelyn Came Out of the Grave (1971) D, S
The Red Queen Kills Seven Times (1972) D, S

MORRICONE, Ennio (born: Rome, Lazio, Italy, 1928)
Dirty Angels (1969) M
A Rather Complicated Girl (1969) M
The Bird with the Crystal Plumage (1970) M
Forbidden Photos of a Lady Above Suspicion (1970) M
The Cat O'Nine Tails (1971) M
A Lizard in a Woman's Skin (1971) M
The Black Belly of the Tarantula (1971) M
The Fifth Cord (1971) M
Four Flies on Grey Velvet (1971) M
My Dear Killer (1972) M
What Have You Done to Solange? (1972) M
Devil in the Brain (1972) M
Who Saw Her Die? (1972) M
Spasmo (1974) M
Autopsy (1975) M
The Sunday Woman (1979) M
Il Mostro (1977) M
The Stendhal Syndrome (1996) M
NAVARRO, Nieves (born: Almería, Andalucía, Spain, 1938) [aka Susan Scott]
Naked Violence (1969) A
Forbidden Photos of a Lady Above Suspicion (1970) A
Death Walks on High Heels (1971) A
All the Colors of the Dark (1972) A
Kill the Poker Player (1972) A
So Sweet, So Dead (1972) A
Death Walks at Midnight (1972) A
Death Carries a Cane (1973) A
NERI, Rosalba (born: Forlì, Emilia-Romagna, Italy, 1939) [aka Sara Bey]
Top Sensation (1969) A
Slaughter Hotel (1971) A
Amuck! (1972) A
Smile Before Death (1972) A
The French Sex Murders (1972) A
The Girl in Room 2A (1974) A
NICOLAI, Bruno (born: Rome, Lazio, Italy, 1926; died: Rome, Lazio, Italy, 1991)
Carnal Circuit (1969) M
The Bird with the Crystal Plumage (1970) C
Forbidden Photos of a Lady Above Suspicion (1970) C
The Cat O'Nine Tails (1971) C
The Case of the Scorpion's Tail (1971) M
The Night Evelyn Came Out of the Grave (1971) M
A Lizard in a Woman's Skin (1971) C
Four Flies on Grey Velvet (1971) C
My Dear Killer (1972) C
All the Colors of the Dark (1972) M
What Have You Done to Solange? (1972) C
The French Sex Murders (1972) M
Your Vice is a Locked Room and Only I Have the Key (1972) M
The Case of the Bloody Iris (1972) M
The Red Queen Kills Seven Times (1972) M

Spirits of Death (1972) M
Eyeball (1975) M
NICOLODI, Daria (born: Florence, Tuscany, Italy, 1950)
Deep Red (1975) A
Tenebrae (1982) A
Phenomena (1985) A
Delirium: Photos of Gioia (1987) A
Opera (1987) A
Giallo: la tua impronta del venerdi (1987) A
ORLANDI, Nora (born: Voghera, Lombardy, Italy, 1933) [aka Joan Christian]
The Sweet Body of Deborah (1968) M, Vocals
Double Face (1969) M, Vocals
The Strange Vice of Mrs. Wardh (1971) M, Vocals
The Double (1971) Vocals
Death Walks on High Heels (1971) Vocals
The Devil With Seven Faces (1972) Vocals
Death Walks at Midnight (1972) Vocals
PIGOZZI, Luciano (born: Novellara, Reggio Emilia, Italy, 1922; died: Rome, Lazio, Italy, 2008) [aka Alan Collins]
Blood and Black Lace (1964) A
Libido (1965) A
Naked You Die (1968) A
Hatchet for the Honeymoon (1970) A
The Devil With Seven Faces (1972) A
All the Colors of the Dark (1972) A
The Case of the Bloody Iris (1972) A
I 2 gattoni a nove code ... e mezza, ad Amsterdam (1972) A
Seven Deaths in the Cat's Eyes (1973) A
Death Will Have Your Eyes (1974) A
The Bloodsucker Leads the Dance (1975) A
PISTILLI, Luigi (born: Grosseto, Tuscany, Italy, 1929; died: Milan, Lombardy, Italy, 1996)
The Sweet Body of Deborah (1968) A
The Case of the Scorpion's Tail (1971) A
The Iguana with the Tongue of Fire (1971) A
Twitch of the Death Nerve (1971) A
Your Vice is a Locked Room and Only I Have the Key (1972) A
Spirits of Death (1972) A
Delitto d'autore (1974) A
PITTORRU, Fabio (born: Ferrara, Italy, 1928)
The Weekend Murders (1970) S
The Night Evelyn Came Out of the Grave (1971) S
The Red Queen Kills Seven Times (1972) S
Calling All Police Cars (1975) S
Nine Guests for a Crime (1977) S
RAHO, Umberto (born: Bari, Puglia, Italy, 1922)
The Bird with the Crystal Plumage (1970) A
The Cat O'Nine Tails (1971) A
The Night Evelyn Came Out of the Grave (1971) A
The Oasis of Fear (1971) A
La stirpe di Caino (1971) A
Amuck! (1972) A
The Crimes of the Black Cat (1972) A

Tropic of Cancer (1972) A
Il terrore con gli occhi storti (1972) A
Door into Darkness (1973) A
The Flower with the Deadly Sting (1973) A
Blackmail (1974) A
Red Light Girls (1974) A
The Secret of Seagull Island (1981) A
RASSIMOV, Ivan (born: Trieste, Friulia-Venezia Giulia, Italy, 1938; died: Rome, Lazio, Italy, 2003)
The Strange Vice of Mrs. Wardh (1971) A
Cross Current (1971) A
All the Colors of the Dark (1972) A
Your Vice is a Locked Room and Only I Have the Key (1972) A
Spirits of Death (1972) A
Spasmo (1974) A
RESSEL, Franco (born: Naples, Campania, Italy, 1925; died: Rome, Lazio, Italy, 1985)
The Girl Who Knew Too Much (1963) A
Blood and Black Lace (1964) A
What Ever Happened to Baby Totò? (1964) A
The Oasis of Fear (1971) A
Cross Current (1971) A
The Devil With Seven Faces (1972) A
Eye in the Labyrinth (1972) A
Naked Girl Killed in Park ... (1972) A
A.A.A. Masseuse, Good-Looking, Offers Her Services (1972) A
Seven Deaths in the Cat's Eyes (1973) A
Calling All Police Cars (1975) A
The Perfect Crime (1978) A
RICHARDSON, John (born: Worthing, Sussex, England, 1934)
Torso (1973) A
Eyeball (1975) A
Reflections in Black (1975) A
Nine Guests for a Crime (1977) A
Murder Obsession (1980) A
RIGAUD, Jorge (born: Buenos Aires, Argentina, 1905; died: Leganés, Madrid, Spain, 1984) [aka George Rigaud]
Perversion Story (1969) A
Devil's Ransom (1970) A
A Lizard in a Woman's Skin (1971) A
Death Walks on High Heels (1971) A
All the Colors of the Dark (1972) A
The Case of the Bloody Iris (1972) A
Knife of Ice (1972) A
Eyeball (1975) A
ROMANO, Renato (born: Ischia, Italy, 1940)
Death Laid an Egg (1968) A
The Bird with the Crystal Plumage (1970) A
The Iguana with the Tongue of Fire (1971) A
The Fifth Cord (1971) A
Seven Blood-Stained Orchids (1972) A
The French Sex Murders (1972) A

ROSSI, Luciano (born: Rome, Lazio, Italy, 1934; died: Rome, Lazio, Italy, 2005)
Date for a Murder (1967) A
Death Walks on High Heels (1971) A
So Sweet, So Dead (1972) A
Death Walks at Midnight (1972) A
Il terrore con gli occhi storti (1972) A
Death Carries a Cane (1973) A
ROSSI-STUART, Giacomo (born: Todi, Umbria, Italy, 1925; died: Rome, Lazio, Italy, 1994)
The Weekend Murders **(1970)** A
The Night Evelyn Came Out of the Grave **(1971)** A
The Double **(1971)** A
The Crimes of the Black Cat **(1972)** A
Reflections in Black **(1975)** A
The Bloodsucker Leads the Dance **(1975)** A
ROSSINI, Renato (born: Rome, Lazio, Italy, 1941) [aka Howard Ross]
Five Dolls for an August Moon (1970) A
Naked Girl Killed in Park ... (1972) A
A.A.A. Masseuse, Good-Looking, Offers Her Services (1972) A
The Killer Reserved Nine Seats (1974) A
Five Women for the Killer (1974) A
The Pyjama Girl Case (1977) A
The New York Ripper (1982) A
Giallo: la tua impronta del venerdi (1987) A
SACCHETTI, Dardano (born: Rome, Lazio, Italy, 1944)
The Cat O'Nine Tails (1971) S
Twitch of the Death Nerve (1971) S
The Psychic (1977) S
The New York Ripper (1982) S
The Scorpion with Two Tails (1982) S
A Blade in the Dark (1983) S
Midnight Killer (1986) S
Giallo: la tua impronta del venerdi (1987) S
Circle of Fear (1992) S
Tulpa—Perdizioni mortali (2013) S
SAXON, John (born: Brooklyn, New York, USA, 1935)
The Girl Who Knew Too Much (1963) A
Blazing Magnum (1976) A
Tenebrae (1982) A
The Scorpion with Two Tails (1982) A
SIMONETTI, Claudio (born: São Paulo, São Paulo, Brazil, 1952)
Deep Red (1975) M (with Goblin)
Tenebrae (1982) M (with Fabio Pignatelli and Massimo Morante)
Midnight Killer (1986) M
Opera (1987) M
The Washing Machine (1993) M
Sleepless (2001) M (with Goblin)
The Card Player (2004) M
Symphony in Blood Red (2010) M

SOREL, Jean (born: Marseille, Bouches-du-Rhône, France, 1934)
The Sweet Body of Deborah (1968) A
A Rather Complicated Girl (1969) A
Perversion Story (1969) A
A Quiet Place to Kill (1970) A
A Lizard in a Woman's Skin (1971) A
The Double (1971) A
STEFFEN, Anthony (born: Rome, Lazio, Italy, 1929; died: Rio de Janeiro, Rio de Janeiro, Brazil, 2004)
The Night Evelyn Came Out of the Grave (1971) A
The Crimes of the Black Cat (1972) A
Tropic of Cancer (1972) A, S
Play Motel (1979) A
STRINDBERG, Anita (born: Sweden, 1938)
A Lizard in a Woman's Skin (1971) A
The Case of the Scorpion's Tail (1971) A
Who Saw Her Die? (1972) A
Your Vice is a Locked Room and Only I Have the Key (1972) A
Tropic of Cancer (1972) A
Puzzle (1974) A
Murder Obsession (1980) A
STROPPA, Daniele
Delirium: Photos of Gioia (1987) S
Scandal in Black (1990) S, A
Crime of Passion (1994) S, A
The Strange Story of Olga O (1995) S
TEDESCHI, Maria (born: Rome, Lazio, Italy, 1894; died: Rome, Lazio, Italy, 1992)
The Bird with the Crystal Plumage (1970) A
Seven Blood-Stained Orchids (1972) A
The Case of the Bloody Iris (1972) A
Il terrore con gli occhi storti (1972) A
Door into Darkness (1973) A
Plot of Fear (1976) A
TERZANO, Ubaldo
The Girl Who Knew Too Much (1963) OP
The Three Faces of Fear (1963) OP
Blood and Black Lace (1964) OP
A Lizard in a Woman's Skin (1971) OP
Deep Red (1975) OP
Atrocious Tales of Love and Death (1979) OP
The New York Ripper (1982) OP
TESSARI, Duccio (born: Genoa, Liguria, Italy, 1926; died: Rome, Lazio, Italy, 1994)
Death Occurred Last Night (1970) D, S (also contributed to two songs on the soundtrack)
The Bloodstained Butterfly (1971) D, S, A
TINTI, Gabriele (born: Molinella, Emilia-Romagna, Italy, 1932; died: Rome, Lazio, Italy, 1991)
Death Occurred Last Night (1970) A
Tropic of Cancer (1972) A
The Secret of Seagull Island (1980) A

Mystère (1983) A
The Monster of Florence (1986) A
TOMASSI, Vincenzo (born: Latina, Lazio, Rome, 1937; died: Rome, Lazio, Italy, 1993)
The Weekend Murders (1970) E
A Lizard in a Woman's Skin (1971) E
The Crimes of the Black Cat (1972) E
Blazing Magnum (1976) E
Play Motel (1979) E
The New York Ripper (1982) E
Formula for a Murder (1985) E
TOVOLI, Luciano (born: Massa Marittima, Grosseto, Italy, 1936)
Snapshot of a Crime (1975) DP
The Sunday Woman (1975) DP
Tenebrae (1982) DP
TRANQUILLI, Silvano (born: Rome, Lazio, Italy, 1925; died: Rome, Lazio, Italy, 1997)
The Black Belly of the Tarantula (1971) A
The Double (1971) A
The Bloodstained Butterfly (1971) A
Smile Before Death (1972) A
So Sweet, So Dead (1972) A
TRINTIGNANT, Jean-Louis (born: Piolenc, Vaucluse, France, 1930)
*Deadly Sweet (*1967) A
Death Laid an Egg (1968) A
So Sweet ... So Perverse (1969) A
TROVAJOLI, Armando (born: Rome, Lazio, Italy; 1917; died: Rome, Lazio, Italy, 2013)
Assassination in Rome (1964) M
What Ever Happened to Baby Totò? (1964) M
Deadly Sweet (1967) M
The Double (1971) M
Blazing Magnum (1976) M
Mystère (1983) M
WOLFF, Frank (born: San Francisco, California, USA, 1928; died: Rome, Lazio, Italy, 1971)
Carnal Circuit (1969) A
Death Occurred Last Night (1970) A
Death Walks on High Heels (1971) A
ZAPPONI, Bernardino (born: Rome, Lazio, Italy, 1927; died: Rome, Lazio, Italy, 2000)
Deep Red (1975) S
Plot of Fear (1976) S

KEY ENGLISH-LANGUAGE VOCAL ARTISTS

You know their voices, but chances are—you don't know their names. Here follows the vocal filmographies for some of the key dubbing artists involved in the English-language tracks of so many of these films. I have made every attempt to include all of the relevant *giallo* credits, but given that there are no dubbing credits on these films, inevitably more than a few will have escaped my notice. In any event, these abbreviated filmographies should help fans put a name to some of these talented and often ignored vocal artists.

ALEXANDER, Nick (in addition to dubbing many performances, he also directed and/or edited the English dubbing on many films)
The Iguana with the Tongue of Fire (1971) Dubbing editor
The Devil with Seven Faces (1971) Dubbing editor
Four Flies on Grey Velvet (1971) Dubbing supervisor
Who Saw Her Die? (1972) Dubbing editor
Special Killers (1973) Dubbing editor
What Have They Done to Your Daughters? (1974) Dubbing the role of the TV announcer/Dubbing editor
The Killer Must Kill Again (1975) Dubbing the role of the gas station attendant
Deep Red (1975) Dubbing editor
Strip Nude for Your Killer (1975) Dubbing some minor background roles
The Scorpion with Two Tails (1982) Dubbing the role played by Jacques Stany
Phenomena (1985) Dubbing the role of the real estate agent/Sound effects editor
Nothing Underneath (1985) Dubbing editor
Opera (1987) Sound editor
Circle of Fear (1992) ADR editor
The Stendhal Syndrome (1996) ADR editor
Sleepless (2001) Dubbing director

DE FONSECA, Carolyn
The Strange Vice of Mrs. Wardh (1971) Dubbing the role played by Conchita Airoldi
Seven Blood-Stained Orchids (1972) Dubbing the role played by Rossella Falk
Don't Torture a Duckling (1972) Dubbing the role played by Florinda Bolkan
Torso (1973) Dubbing a minor background role as a prostitute
Spasmo (1974) Dubbing the role played by Monica Monet
The Killer Must Kill Again (1975) Dubbing the role played by Tere Velázquez
Deep Red (1975) Dubbing the role played by Daria Nicolodi
Strip Nude for Your Killer (1975) Dubbing the role played by Amanda, as well as a minor role of a nurse.
Murder Obsession (1980) Dubbing the role played by Anita Strindberg
The New York Ripper (1982) Dubbing the role of Mikis' landlady
The Scorpion With Two Tails (1982) Dubbing the role played by Wandisa Guida
Phenomena (1985) Dubbing the role played by Daria Nicolodi

FOREST, Michael
Don't Torture a Duckling (1972) Dubbing the role played by Tomas Milian
What Have They Done to Your Daughters? (1974) Dubbing the role played by Mario Adorf
The Killer Must Kill Again (1975) Dubbing the role played by George Hilton
Strip Nude for Your Killer (1975) Dubbing the role played by Lucio Como

LUOTTO, Gene (in addition to doing vocal performances, he often directed the English dubs of the tracks he worked on)
Carnal Circuit (1969) Dialogue director
Naked Violence (1969) Dubbing a minor background role as a teacher
The Weekend Murders (1970) Dialogue director
Twitch of the Death Nerve (1971) Dubbing the role played by Leopoldo Trieste/Dialogue director
Four Flies on Grey Velvet (1971) Dubbing the role played by Oreste Lionello
Strip Nude for Your Killer (1975) Dubbing the role played by Franco Diogene, as well as other background characters/Dialogue director
The New York Ripper (1982) Dubbing the character of the man walking his dog in the opening scene/Dialogue director
Murder-Rock: Dancing Death (1984) Dialogue director

LUOTTO, Steven
The New York Ripper (1983) Dubbing the role played by Andrea Occhipinti
A Blade in the Dark (1983) Dubbing the role played by Andrea Occhipinti

MANNIX, Edward
Twitch of the Death Nerve (1971) Dubbing the role played by Luigi Pistilli
Four Flies on Grey Velvet (1971) Dubbing the role played by Bud Spencer

Your Vice is a Locked Room and Only I Have the Key (1972) Dubbing the role played by Luigi Pistilli

What Have They Done To Your Daughters? (1974) Dubbing the role played by Ferdinando Murolo

The Killer Must Kill Again (1975) Dubbing the role played by Eduardo Fajardo

Strip Nude for Your Killer (1975) Dubbing a minor background character

The New York Ripper (1982) Dubbing the role played by Jack Hedley

SMITH, Marc
Four Flies on Grey Velvet (1971) Dubbing the role played by Jean-Pierre Marielle

Deep Red (1975) Dubbing the role played by Glauco Mauri

SPAFFORD, Susan
The Strange Vice of Mrs. Wardh (1971) Dubbing the role played by Edwige Fenech

Your Vice is a Locked Room and Only I Have the Key (1972) Dubbing the role played by Anita Strindberg

Don't Torture a Duckling (1972) Dubbing the role played by Barbara Bouchet

Torso (1973) Dubbing the role played by Suzy Kendall

What Have They Done to Your Daughters? (1974) Dubbing the role played by Giovanna Ralli

Murder Obsession (1980) Dubbing the role played by Laura Gemser

Formula for a Murder (1985) Dubbing the role played by Christina Nagy

STARKE, Pat
What Have They Done to Your Daughters? (1974) Dubbing the role played by Micaela Pignatelli

The Killer Must Kill Again (1975) Dubbing the role played by Cristina Galbó

Murder Obsession (1980) Dubbing the role played by Silvia Dioniso

The New York Ripper (1982) Dubbing the role played by Daniela Doria

The Scorpion with Two Tails (1982) Dubbing the role played by Elvire Audray

Formula for a Murder (1985) Dubbing the role played by Carroll Blumenberg

VON KUEGELGEN, Frank
Naked Violence (1969) Dubbing a minor policeman role

Your Vice is a Locked Room and Only I Have the Key (1972) Dubbing the role played by Riccardo Salvino

Don't Torture a Duckling (1972) Dubbing the role played by Marc Porel

Spasmo (1974) Dubbing the role played by Robert Hoffmann

What Have They Done to Your Daughters? (1974) Dubbing a minor journalist role

Murder Obsession (1980) Dubbing the role played by Stefano Patrizi

The New York Ripper (1982) Dubbing the role played by Paolo Malco

The Scorpion with Two Tails (1982) Dubbing the role played by Paolo Malco

A Blade in the Dark (1983) Dubbing the role played by Michele Soavi

Murder-Rock: Dancing Death (1984) Dubbing the role played by Giuseppe Mannajuolo

Formula for a Murder (1985) Dubbing the role played by David Warbeck

Fatal Frames (1996) Dubbing the role played by Leo Daniel

Index of Titles (1974-2013)

Note: These films were inevitably granted different titles in foreign countries, but for the sake of brevity, the titles listed here are limited to the Italian originals as well as any alternate English-language ones. The purpose of this index is two-fold: first, it should facilitate finding films by listing the year under which they are filed; also, it is intended to make it easier to cross-reference for those who may know the films by a different title.

If you enjoyed this book,
write for a free catalog of
Midnight Marquee Press titles
or visit our website at
http://www.midmar.com

Midnight Marquee Press, Inc.
9721 Britinay Lane
Baltimore, MD 21234
410-665-1198
mmarquee@aol.com

Lightning Source UK Ltd.
Milton Keynes UK
UKHW050451061020
371052UK00007B/353